MW00589336

"This volume is a very worthwhile contribution to the growing body of literature being produced by evangelical scholars who are attempting to make known to a wider audience the rich resources of the history of Christian spirituality. The contributors are largely successful in avoiding the dangers, on the one hand, of theologically uncritical and eclectic readings of Roman Catholic and Orthodox texts, or on the other hand, of dismissing such texts and not allowing them to speak in their own voices. This book should prove to be a valuable resource and point of reference for pastors, seminarians, campus workers and those engaged in ministries of spiritual formation and direction."

John Jefferson Davis, Gordon-Conwell Theological Seminary

"The vistas of the Christian tradition open up wide in this volume on the Christian classics, with rich rewards for those searching for insight, reading for wisdom and aiming at the glory of God. This introduction to the writings of Christian spirituality is a gem, as it combines solid evangelical grounding with genuine generosity of spirit."

Hans Boersma, Regent College, Vancouver

"Savvy travelers rely upon guidebooks to prepare for trips to unknown destinations. The wisdom that is found among those who have 'been there, done that' is invaluable. Goggin and Strobel have assembled a team of well-traveled experts to help us make sense of the unfamiliar world of Christian spiritual classics. Of course, among Catholic and Orthodox Christians—as well as those familiar with Reformed, Wesleyan and Pietist traditions—reading spiritual classics must feel like home. But the rest of us need reliable guides to give good advice as we visit these strange worlds we've heard so much about. Sensible, balanced, hospitable and inspiring, this collection of essays not only provides the 'how-tos' of reading the classics for spiritual formation, it places the writers of this great tradition in historical context to help us appreciate the diversity of our shared faith. A mustread for those who are ready to branch out beyond the familiar environs of their favorite Christian authors."

Rodney Reeves, Southwest Baptist University

"Collections of essays around a common theme can be a grab bag and too often uneven in quality—both in terms of content and writing style. Happily, the writings found in *Reading Christian Spiritual Classics: A Guide for Evangelicals*, are uniformly excellent: informative, thorough, well-written. This will be a valued collection for evangelicals just encountering the spiritual classics for the first time and a helpful and insightful resource for those already familiar with these rich treasures of the church."

Christopher Hall, Eastern University, associate editor of
the Ancient Christian Commentary on Scripture

Reading the Christian Spiritual Classics

A GUIDE FOR

EVANGELICALS

Edited by JAMIN GOGGIN

and KYLE STROBEL

IVP Academic

An imprint of InterVarsity Press
Downers Grove, Illinois

InterVarsity Press
P.O. Box 1400, Downers Grove, IL 60515-1426
World Wide Web: www.ivpress.com
E-mail: email@ivpress.com

© 2013 by Jamin Goggin and Kyle Strobel

All rights reserved. No part of this book may be reproduced in any form without written permission from
InterVarsity Press.

InterVarsity Press® is the book-publishing division of InterVarsity Christian Fellowship/USA®, a movement of
students and faculty active on campus at hundreds of universities, colleges and schools of nursing in the United States
of America, and a member movement of the International Fellowship of Evangelical Students. For information about
local and regional activities, write Public Relations Dept., InterVarsity Christian Fellowship/USA, 6400 Schroeder
Rd., P.O. Box 7895, Madison, WI 53707-7895, or visit the IVCF website at <www.intervarsity.org>.

Scripture quotations, unless otherwise noted, are from The Holy Bible, English Standard Version, copyright ©
2001 by Crossway Bibles, a division of Good News Publishers. Used by permission. All rights reserved.

While all stories in this book are true, some names and identifying information in this book have been changed to
protect the privacy of the individuals involved.

Cover design: Cindy Kiple
Interior design: Beth Hagenberg
Images: St. Peter's Basilica ceiling: Ceiling, Interior of the Dome, St Peter´s Basilica, Rome, Lazio, Italy.
        Roy Rainford /Glowimages.com
        Dome of Kariye Museum: © yusuf anil akduygu/iStockphoto

ISBN 978-0-8308-3997-1

Printed in the United States of America ∞

 InterVarsity Press is committed to protecting the environment and to the responsible use of natural
resources. As a member of Green Press Initiative we use recycled paper whenever possible. To learn
more about the Green Press Initiative, visit <www.greenpressinitiative.org>.

Library of Congress Cataloging-in-Publication Data

Reading the Christian spiritual classics : a guide for evangelicals / edited by Jamin Goggin and Kyle Strobel.
     pages cm
  Includes bibliographical references.
  ISBN 978-0-8308-3997-1 (pbk. : alk. paper)
 1. Christian literature — History and criticism. I. Goggin, Jamin, 1982-editor of compilation.
  BR117.R35 2013
  248—dc23

                                                                                                    2013005882

P	21	20	19	18	17	16	15	14	13	12	11	10	9	8	7	6	5	4	3	2	1
Y	31	30	29	28	27	26	25	24	23	22	21	20	19	18	17	16	15	14	13			

Contents

Acknowledgments

✸

THIS VOLUME WAS A LABOR OF LOVE FOR BOTH OF US. We would like to thank the Institute for Spiritual Formation at Talbot School of Theology for instilling a twofold love: for the spiritual classics as well as for reading them evangelically. We hope that this volume will be a tool to instill that twofold value in more and more students, laypeople and pastors. We would like to thank the authors we chose to write for us. Each author brought a robust knowledge and passion to their chapters, and that passion shines through this book well. We appreciate their receptivity to our prodding and forming this book in a certain direction. They were all very generous. It was a blessing that we had the chance to work with two of our spiritual mentors. John Coe and James Houston have both served as mentors, in person and through their writing. It was great to have their wisdom included here. We would like to thank Gary Deddo and InterVarsity Press for showing interest in this project. Finally, our families have provided the space and encouragement for this project to be completed. To Kristin, Emersyn, Sawyer and Finnley, and to Kelli and Brighton, thank you for your support, care and love as your husbands and fathers poured over edits! We are deeply grateful.

Introduction

Jamin Goggin and *Kyle Strobel*

Richard Foster's *Celebration of Discipline*, first published in 1978, created a new fervor within the evangelical church for a deeply historic spirituality. Foster's attempt to thread historic spirituality through spiritual practice has, if nothing else, led to a renaissance of spirituality within the evangelical church in America.[1] What was initially implicit was made explicit when Foster edited *Devotional Classics: Selected Readings For Individuals and Groups*. This is a compilation of excerpts from spiritual classics with brief historical background, Scripture, questions, prayer exercises and reflections produced by Foster's ministry, *Renovaré*.[2]

Foster and his partner Dallas Willard are the most prominent figures in the retrieval of spiritual classics among evangelicals. But they are by no means alone. Carl Trueman, dean of Westminster Theological Seminary, states, "I think the medieval mystics should form a staple of the literary diet of all thoughtful Christians."[3] Trueman, no novice of the deep theological questions of the Christian faith, highlights the view of

[1]Richard J. Foster, *Celebration of Disciple: The Path to Spiritual Growth* (San Francisco: Harper-Collins, 1978). For example, Dallas Willard, *Hearing God: Developing a Conversational Relationship with God* (Downers Grove, IL: InterVarsity Press, 1984), and Dallas Willard, *The Spirit of the Disciplines: Understanding How God Changes Lives* (San Francisco: HarperCollins, 1988).
[2]Richard J. Foster and James Bryan Smith, eds., *Devotional Classics: Selected Readings for Individuals and Groups* (San Francisco: HarperCollins, 1990).
[3]Carl Trueman, "Why Should Thoughtful Evangelicals Read the Medieval Mystics?" *Themelios* 33, no. 1 (May 2008): 2-4.

a generous but equally cautious reader of the Christian tradition. This
stature follows in line with the great forebears to evangelicalism. For
instance, John Wesley published spiritual classics in *The Christian Library*, Luther published the *Theologia Germanica* and A. W. Tozer published spiritual classics under the title *Christian Book of Mystical Verse*.
Likewise, those like John Calvin, Jonathan Edwards and Henry Scougal
sat at the feet of the spiritual tradition reading through a distinctly Protestant lens. Foster's work, therefore, was not forging a new Protestant
interest in the spiritual tradition. Foster was recovering a well-worn
path of ancient wisdom that helped to define evangelicalism itself. Following that same line, this volume addresses the key questions regarding
spiritual classics that will lead to an informed, spiritual and distinctively
evangelical reading of these difficult texts.

Confronted with the renewed interest in spiritual classics, evangelicals
have largely followed two inclinations: concern and embrace. Those "concerned" point to the blurring of heterodoxy with orthodoxy, or, if nothing
else, the promotion of texts without equal promotion of theological discernment. These individuals range from people who see the Bible as the
only text worth reading, to those who see value in spiritual texts that are
only from within evangelicalism itself. The burgeoning interest in classic
literature within evangelical quarters has provoked this camp to ask questions of proper theological and spiritual retrieval, questions that have remained largely unanswered by the spiritual formation movement.

On the other hand, those who "embrace" spiritual classics also fall
into a wide-ranging spectrum. Two options present themselves: embracing *unwisely* and embracing *wisely*. For both groups the call to pick
up and read spiritual texts from the last two thousand years of church
history has been met with a hearty yes. However, that yes has often been
followed by a lack of wisdom in reading or appropriating. Several pitfalls are easy to identify: First, the impulse to read spiritual texts can be
wrought with spiritual temptations and deep-seated vice. Second, the
context, theological impulse and genre of these texts are often shrouded
in darkness. Last, one's own theological tradition and beliefs are rarely
developed or explicit enough to aid in a truly discerned reading. In
short, those who have embraced spiritual classics also highlight, im-

plicitly, major lacunae of how those texts should be appropriated. This volume is an attempt to take unwise readers and help them become wise readers, and take wise readers and help them read with an ever-increasing wisdom.

Many have undoubtedly picked up John of the Cross or Teresa of Ávila after reading a quote in a contemporary book and have found themselves feeling confused, unsettled or duped. *Confused* because these are texts written hundreds of years ago with theological, cultural and linguistic idiosyncrasies. *Unsettled* because they find concepts asserted that appear to run contrary to their theological heritage and are unsure how to navigate these discrepancies. *Duped* because they were led to believe these texts were guaranteed life-changing documents chalk full of quotable and brilliant material, when, instead, they seem esoteric and dry. In light of the "cloud of unknowing" that might descend on readers new to the spiritual classics, the present project seeks to acknowledge the concerned as well as those who embraced these texts without enough concern. By developing a robust hermeneutic grounded in markedly evangelical spiritual and theological commitments, this volume will seek to answer the questions that have been ignored and fill in the gaps that have remained. Indeed, the need to respectfully acknowledge the theological impulses of the concerned is unquestionably at hand. While at the same time the need for guidance and discernment for those who have embraced and are engaging the classics is no less urgent.

This volume is broken down into four major sections: *why* should spiritual classics be read, *how* should spiritual classics be read, *what* are these classics and *who* are the people behind them. The first section is titled "Approaching Spiritual Classics" and addresses the need for historic Christian literature to inform modern-day evangelicalism. This section serves as an apologetic for the reading of spiritual classics, speaks into the *spiritual* nature of reading *spiritual* literature and provides specific areas of import into present-day Christian ministry and practice.

The second section is titled "The Spiritual Classics Tradition." This section sketches the category of "Christian Spiritual Classics" and explains, broadly speaking, the schools and movements of Christian spirituality as well as, more specifically, the genre and tradition behind the spiritual classics. Building on this second section, the third is titled "Reading Evangelically," which focuses on reading *evangelically* and addresses Catholic and Orthodox traditions with guidance for reading them discerningly. In doing so, this section provides a framework for understanding a specifically *evangelical* focus on spirituality, and helps readers engage Catholic, Orthodox and even other evangelical material with specific doctrinal content in mind. The final section is titled "How to Read the Spiritual Classics," which establishes hermeneutical tools for reading the different schools of spiritual literature. Each chapter will focus on the historical context, distinctive theological issues, unique language of authors/groups, as well as any positive or negative contributions for evangelical theology and practice.

Each section represents a movement to greater discernment in reading spiritual classics. The goal of this volume is to create readers who are able to read theologically, historically, practically and spiritually for the glory of God. Philip Sheldrake's point is noteworthy: "*How* we proceed to read texts is intimately related to *why* we read them."[4] Thus, as you continue to read you will discover a hermeneutic for reading spiritual classics, born out of thoughtful theological and spiritual consideration of why we should read these texts in the first place.

---

[4]Philip Sheldrake, "Interpretation," in *New Westminster Dictionary of Spirituality*, ed. Philip Sheldrake (Louisville: Westminster John Knox, 2005), p. 14.

PART ONE

Approaching
Spiritual Classics

1

Why Should We Read
Spiritual Classics?

Steve L. Porter

W HEN IT COMES TO READING THE CLASSICS of Christian spirituality, there are often two camps: the overeager and the underwhelmed.
The overeager see reading the classics as essential to the Christian life
and often take delight in their knowledge of esoteric Christian writings.
They are aghast to find followers of Jesus who have not read John of the
Cross or Julian of Norwich. In contrast, the underwhelmed do not see
much point to the classics and often have suspicions that these writings
undermine the authority of Scripture or introduce unbiblical concepts.
They immediately bristle when someone quotes John of the Cross or
Julian of Norwich instead of the Bible. Then, of course, many lie in the
middle of these two camps, often with an appreciation of the classics but
not much actual engagement. In a manner that will hopefully chasten
the overeager, exhort the underwhelmed and motivate those who lie in
the middle, this chapter offers three biblical-theological rationales for
the practice of reading spiritual classics devotionally.[1]

THREE THEOLOGICAL RATIONALES FOR THE
PRACTICE OF SPIRITUAL READING

Before moving on to the biblical-theological grounding, it is important

---

[1]This practice is often called "spiritual reading." For guidelines on reading the classics forma-
tively, see the helpful discussion by Susan Annette Muto, *A Practical Guide to Spiritual Reading*
(Denville, NJ: Dimension, 1976), as well as relevant chapters in this book.

to be clear on what a spiritual classic is. For the purposes of this chapter, I offer the following definition:

> A spiritual classic is a writing that (1) is clearly attributable to a reborn follower of Jesus, (2) focuses on a biblical understanding of sanctification, and (3) a multitude of voices across Church history attest to its value for Christian living.[2]

Some paradigms are Augustine of Hippo's *Confessions*, John Bunyan's *The Pilgrim's Progress* and Jonathan Edwards's *The Religious Affections*. There are concerns about reading spiritual classics that this definition pushes aside. For instance, what if it is unclear whether a particular author was a regenerated Christ follower? Or what if the content of the writing is only loosely related to a biblical understanding of sanctification? Or what if the multitude of voices attesting to a particular document's worth all come from a branch of the church other than one's own? These types of questions deal with what does or does not count as a classic of Christian spirituality. While that is an important topic, that is *not* the topic of this chapter. Rather, the focus of this chapter is, given that there are a large number of documents that meet the definition provided, what sort of biblical-theological apologetic can be marshaled for reading them devotionally?[3]

And yet, given the existence of documents as defined previously, some may wonder why an apologetic for the devotional or spiritual reading of them would be necessary. The problem arises in that there are no explicit exhortations in Scripture to read spiritual classics. Of course, such an exhortation would be anachronistic since no *Christian*

---

[2]Philip Sheldrake offers a much more dynamic, but still helpful, definition: "a classic is what may be called a 'wisdom document.' Its practical value is not that it opens up the *past* (although it may indeed do this) nor that it offers detailed laws by which we may infallibly regulate our spiritual quest. The value of a classical text is not so much that it bridges the gap between the present and a normative past as that it makes the presence of divine truth accessible in our world" (Sheldrake, *Spirituality and History* [Maryknoll, NY: Orbis, 1995], p. 172).

[3]This chapter will provide *theological* reasons for reading spiritual classics, but it will not address the *practical* reasons. For a discussion of these practical motivations, C. S. Lewis's introduction to his translation of Athanasius's *The Incarnation of the Word of God* is hard to beat. See this short essay reprinted in C. S. Lewis, *God in the Dock: Essays on Theology and Ethics* (Grand Rapids: Eerdmans, 1970), pp. 200-205. See also Bruce Demarest, *Satisfy Your Soul: Restoring the Heart of Christian Spirituality* (Colorado Springs: NavPress, 1999), pp. 255-62.

spiritual classics existed by the close of the first century. However, we do have Paul's injunction not to "pay attention to myths and endless genealogies, which give rise to mere speculation rather than *furthering* the administration of God which is by faith" (1 Tim 1:4 NASB; cf. 1 Tim 4:7; 2 Tim 4:4; Tit 1:14). Many commentators believe these "myths" and "genealogies" refer to legendary tales and personal biographies on the basis of which some in Ephesus were teaching false doctrines.[4] So, on first glance it appears that the only explicit New Testament teaching regarding extrabiblical material is to stay away from it.

But to generalize from Paul's injunction against myths and genealogies in 1 Timothy 1:4 to an injunction against spiritual classics would be too hasty. Paul's objection to these extrabiblical writings was that they were being used to promote strange doctrine (1 Tim 1:3), fruitless discussion (1 Tim 1:6), and misunderstanding (1 Tim 1:7), rather than sound teaching (1 Tim 1:10). Paul is against a focused attention on these particular writings because they were clearly opposed to apostolic teaching and were being used to lead persons away from the truth of the gospel. This suggests that rather than a comprehensive ban on all extrabiblical material, the concern in 1 Timothy 1:4 is with focusing on extrabiblical material that is *un*biblical and is being used to distort biblical truth. As one commentator puts it, "While Paul does not elaborate, his reason for rejecting the false teachers' system is clear: instead of serving God's salvation plan, as proper interpretation of Scripture should, their esoteric approach causes only 'controversy.'"[5] So Paul's teaching in 1 Timothy 1:4 would not count against spiritual classics. Per the previous definition, spiritual classics are documents written by reborn Christ followers that focus on a biblical understanding of spirituality and have a longstanding reputation of building up the body of Christ.

But if spiritual classics turn out to be so tame—so attuned to the biblical text—why read them? Would it not be better to stick with the biblical text itself? Is there value added to our spiritual lives through the spiritual reading of Christian classics?

---

[4]See, for instance, Philip H. Towner, *1-2 Timothy & Titus* (Downers Grove, IL: InterVarsity Press, 1994), pp. 44-48.
[5]Ibid., p. 46.

No doubt the inspired Hebrew and Christian Scriptures are the primary and only infallible source of instruction and nourishment for Christ followers.[6] We do well to heed the Scriptures as our ultimate authority. But such a commitment to the authority of Scripture requires us to be thoroughly biblical, and the biblical text regularly points outside itself to extrabiblical resources for spiritual formation in Christ. For instance, the biblical authors repeatedly indicate that trials provide unique circumstances for being conformed to the image of Christ. An example is Paul's "thorn" that keeps him from exalting himself and teaches him much about the strengthening movement of God in and through his own embrace of weakness (2 Cor 12:5-10; cf. Jas 1:2-4; 1 Pet 1:6-7; Rom 5:3-5). The biblical text points to trials and offers a biblical-theological rationale for why trials would be beneficial in our sanctification. But the trial itself, of course, does not lie within the pages of Scripture. We must move beyond the biblical text in those cases where the biblical text points beyond itself. Again, such a view is not the abandonment of the ultimate authority of Scripture but is made in obedience to and with full acknowledgement of the authority of Scripture.[7]

So the question becomes whether the biblical text points toward the devotional reading of spiritual classics as a beneficial practice. As I have already noted, there are no explicit biblical commands to "take up and read" Bernard of Clairvaux or Hannah Whitall Smith. But this should not alarm us. There are numerous common Christian practices that are not explicitly endorsed in Scripture. For instance, the value of listening to verse-by-verse exegetical sermons, keeping a prayer diary and attending Christian summer camp does not blatantly appear in the biblical text. "But," one may protest, "those activities are appropriate contextualized applications of clear biblical teaching." That is correct. We regularly accept certain extrabiblical practices as appropriate for the Christian life because we can make sense of these practices biblically and theologically. This is what I am referring to as a biblical-theological rationale. In

---

[6]For a discussion of the formative power of the Scriptures, see Eugene Peterson, *Eat This Book* (Grand Rapids: Eerdmans, 2006).

[7]For a discussion on how to maintain fidelity to Scripture when integrating extrabiblical material, see my "Theology as Queen and Psychology as Handmaid: The Authority of Theology in Integrative Endeavors," *Journal of Psychology and Christianity* 29, no. 1 (2010): 3-14.

other words, we are attempting to determine if a Christian understanding of God, human nature, sin, salvation and sanctification make theological sense of and adequately support the value of the practice.

In what follows it will be argued that Christians do have a biblical-theological rationale for the spiritual reading of classics that takes us further than the mere claim that such reading is *permissible* for Jesus followers. Indeed, one of the main implications of the argument of this chapter is that the devotional reading of classics offers a unique opportunity or window for the Holy Spirit's sanctifying work. It is not simply that spiritual classics *can* be read, but that they *ought* to be read. There is a particular and peculiar value to their devotional use. Furthermore, it is not that they ought to be read simply for historical knowledge or intellectual stimulation. Rather, we ought to read spiritual classics looking for how the Spirit of God may choose to use these sorts of writings to bring God's transforming presence and truth to bear in our lives.

THE PNEUMATOLOGICAL RATIONALE

The first rationale for reading spiritual classics is found in a theology of the Holy Spirit's sanctifying work. A central principle of sanctification is that the Spirit of God transforms the human heart—the deepest dimension of a person's thought, will, affect—through bringing the Word of God to bear on the heart. As Jesus puts it in his high priestly prayer, "Sanctify them in the truth; your word is truth" (Jn 17:17; cf. Rom 12:2). But sanctification by the Word does not occur merely through the memorization of Scripture, daily Bible reading, listening to a steady stream of downloaded sermons or even careful meditation on select biblical passages. The sanctifying work of the Spirit through the Word of God is a Spirit-wrought application or illumination of God's truth to a receptive heart.[8]

Jesus tells his disciples, "I still have many things to say to you, but *you*

---

[8]For more on the illumination of the Holy Spirit, see Graham A. Cole, *He Who Gives Life* (Wheaton, IL: Crossway, 2004), pp. 260-66; Robert L. Saucy, *Scripture: Its Power, Authority, and Relevance* (Nashville: Word, 2001), pp. 240-42; Kevin Vanhoozer, *Is There a Meaning in This Text?* (Grand Rapids: Zondervan, 1998), pp. 407-31; Donald G. Bloesch, *Holy Scripture: Revelation, Inspiration & Interpretation* (Downers Grove, IL: InterVarsity Press, 1994), pp. 20-29; Millard Erickson, *Christian Theology*, 2nd ed. (Grand Rapids: Baker, 1998), pp. 277-83.

cannot bear them now. When the Spirit of truth comes, he will guide you into all the truth. . . . [H]e will take what is mine and declare it to you" (Jn 16:12-13, 15 emphasis added). According to Jesus, there were truths that the disciples could not yet bear, and yet the Spirit of Christ would guide them into these truths and declare these truths to them. Looking forward to this time, Jeremiah and Ezekiel prophesy that in the new covenant God will write the law within the human person (Jer 31:31-34), replacing the "heart of stone" with a heart that is inwardly moved to live in dependence on God and under his direction (Ezek 36:22-28). As Paul puts it, "God has sent the Spirit of his Son into our hearts, crying, 'Abba! Father!'" (Gal 4:6), testifying to our spirits that we are children of God (Rom 8:16; cf. 1 Thess 1:4-5). It appears, then, that the Holy Spirit is in some sense speaking the truth of who we are in Christ to the deepest recesses of the human heart. Robert Saucy writes, "Through revelation and inspiration God communicates His truth to us objectively, bringing it into the realm of human history. But He must also address that word to our hearts, for personal communication with another person is ultimately spirit with spirit, in this case God's Spirit with our spirit."[9]

The problem is that even after conversion and regeneration the human mind/will/affect (i.e., heart) remains somewhat resistant to the illuminating work of the Spirit. There is hard-heartedness (Eph 4:17-24), spiritual blindness (2 Pet 1:9), and self-deception (Gal 6:3) that ought not to remain but nevertheless does remain to some degree even after the believer's new birth in Christ.[10] This continued rebelliousness is what Paul refers to as the "flesh" (Gal 5:16-17; cf. Rom 8:1-17).[11] In 1 Corinthians 3:1-3 Paul teaches that the saints in Corinth "were not yet able

---

[9]Saucy, *Scripture*, p. 240.

[10]Notice in Ephesians 4:17-24, for instance, that Paul is exhorting the Ephesians to "lay aside the old self" (v. 22), which was darkened in understanding, ignorant and hard-hearted (v. 18). They are no longer walking like this (v. 17) in that this is their "former manner of life" (v. 22). But in Paul's familiar "already, but not yet" formulation the Ephesians are being exhorted to completely do away with the remnants of darkened understanding, ignorance, and hard-heartedness which remain. See F. F. Bruce, *The Epistles to the Colossians, to Philemon, and to the Ephesians* (Grand Rapids: Eerdmans, 1984), pp. 357-59.

[11]See R. J. Erickson, "Flesh," in *Dictionary of Paul and His Letters*, ed. Gerald F. Hawethorne, Ralph P. Martin and Daniel G. Reid (Downers Grove, IL: InterVarsity Press, 1993), pp. 303-6.

to receive" the deeper nourishment of the Spirit of God for they were "still fleshly," living like mere humans in some dimension apart from the Spirit (NASB; cf. 1 Cor 2:14). The Corinthians were unable to ingest the Spirit-illumined wisdom of God because their hearts were feeding elsewhere.[12] Richard Averbeck puts the point as follows:

> The best way of viewing illumination is to attach it to the reader's *acceptance* and *reception* of the meaning of the text rather than his or her intellectual grasp of what it says. . . . The special problem with God's word is not with the scriptures themselves, but with our acceptance of what they say as true and our willingness to welcome that truth into our lives for impact on all levels: who we are and how we live. In short, the problem is that we are sinful down to the very core of ourselves.[13]

And so the pneumatological picture we receive is that the Spirit of God brings the transformational message of God to bear on Christ followers, but in many cases (or perhaps to some degree in all cases) there is resistance. The desires of the flesh stand in opposition to the desires of the Spirit (Gal 5:17) and we are not ready to receive all of God's wisdom by the Spirit (1 Cor 3:3). Nonetheless, the Spirit works to penetrate our resistance with the sword of the Spirit (Eph 6:17). And, therefore, as Hebrews 4:12 tells us, the word of God is "living," "active" and "sharp." Thus, it penetrates and judges "thoughts and intentions of the heart."

This understanding of the Spirit's sanctifying work makes clear that the Spirit's illumination of the Word of God is a process and that this process not only involves a cognition of the meaning of Scripture (the illocutionary force) but a Spirit-communicated, heart-level reception of that meaning (the perlocutionary force). William G. T. Shedd says,

> The efficacy of the word is from the Holy Spirit applying it. The Spirit does not operate upon the truth, but upon the soul . . . and produces two

---

[12]It appears that the Corinthians continued to seek their status and value in comparison to others rather than in new identity in Christ. See Gordon D. Fee's helpful commentary on this passage: *The First Epistle to the Corinthians* (Grand Rapids: Eerdmans, 1987), pp. 121-28.

[13]Richard E. Averbeck, "God, People, and the Bible: The Relationship Between Illumination and Biblical Scholarship," in *Who's Afraid of the Holy Spirit? An Investigation into the Ministry of the Spirit of God Today*, ed. Daniel B. Wallace and M. James Sawyer (Dallas: Biblical Studies Press, 2005), p. 146.

effects: (a) the understanding is enlightened and enabled to perceive the truth spiritually and (b) the will is renewed and inclined toward it. The aversion of the heart to truth is overcome.[14]

On this basis we are in a position to understand why the Holy Spirit utilizes various means—the means of grace—to bring God's sanctifying Word to bear on human hearts. For some Protestants the means of grace are limited to the preaching of the Word, baptism and Communion.[15] In Charles Hodge's discussion of the means of grace he adds prayer to these three.[16] Shedd takes on board these four and adds confession of faith and church fellowship as additional means of grace.[17] Wayne Grudem suggests that the means of grace should include *"many varied activities within the church that God has given as special ways of receiving his 'grace' day by day and week by week."*[18] On this basis Grudem adds to the means already mentioned: worship, church discipline, giving, spiritual gifts, evangelism and personal ministry to individuals, but does not hold his list to be exhaustive.[19] Grudem's principle for including these "varied activities" seems to be that such activities are commonly experienced by Christians as sources of God's blessing.

Surely Grudem is correct in maintaining that the scope of the means of grace should be sensitive to common Christian experience. But prior to turning to Christian experience, our pneumatology provides a reasonable expectation—a biblical-theological rationale—that particular practices are peculiarly suited for use by the Spirit as means of grace. More specifically, given the earlier discussion of the illuminating work of the Holy Spirit, the following principle appears plausible: A means of grace is any practice that provides materials or fodder that is fitting or conducive to the Spirit's bringing the presence and Word of God to bear on the somewhat resistant human heart. Such a principle gives priority to practices that are obviously con-

[14]William G. T. Shedd, *Dogmatic Theology*, ed. Alan W. Gomes (Phillipsburg, NJ: P & R, 2003), p. 810.
[15]For instance, Louis Berkhof, *Systematic Theology* (Grand Rapids: Eerdmans, 1996), pp. 604-6.
[16]Charles Hodge, *Systematic Theology* (London: James Clarke, 1960), pp. 692-709.
[17]Shedd, *Dogmatic Theology*, pp. 809-10.
[18]Wayne Grudem, *Systematic Theology* (Grand Rapids: Zondervan, 1994), p. 951.
[19]Ibid.

ducive (e.g., Bible study, meditation, prayer, submission to biblical teaching). It provides an explanatory framework for the importance of other practices (e.g., solitude, embracing trials, fasting, spiritual journaling). And this principle would automatically exclude activities as means of grace that have no plausible connection to receiving the Spirit-illumined Word.

It is important to note here that while the Spirit's mediation of God's presence and Word to the receptive human heart brings about transformation, the Spirit utilizes various extrabiblical means to prepare the soil and even implant the meaning. Words that are spoken convey presence, and when understood by the receiver they also bring meaning. Personal presence and meaning, when received, influence the thoughts, affect and inclinations of the hearer. So it is no surprise that God's personal presence and meaning mediated by the Spirit brings about human transformation. "Man shall not live by bread alone, but by every word that comes from the mouth of God" (Mt 4:4). While the Word of God written contains the essential truths for a life of godliness (2 Pet 1:3-4), it is the Spirit's prerogative to bring that truth to bear on the human heart through the utilization of extrabiblical means (e.g., trials, gifts within the church, solitude, etc.). It is interesting to notice that the Spirit of God cries out in our hearts "Abba! Father!" (Gal 4:6) and yet does not quote chapter and verse in doing so. As the Spirit testifies to our spirits that we are children of God, the Spirit is applying the *meaning* and not necessarily the *letter* of God's Word to our lives. In other words, the Spirit may apply the transformational meaning of God's Word to the human heart through words that accurately convey that meaning but are not necessarily the very words of the biblical text. These words may come via a sermon, a hymn, a brother or sister in Christ, or a spiritual classic.

So all of this brings us to the first rationale—the pneumatological rationale—for the devotional reading of spiritual classics. Since the Spirit of God uses various extrabiblical means to bring his presence and Word to bear on human hearts, it is evident that one fitting mean would be the writings of other Christ followers regarding a biblical understanding of the way of holiness. Indeed, excepting the Scriptures themselves, writings that contain reflections on biblical holiness would appear to be particularly suited to the Spirit's sanctifying work.[20]

THE INCARNATIONAL RATIONALE

This understanding of the Spirit's sanctifying work—what I have called the pneumatological rationale—is foundational for the remaining two biblical-theological rationales for the spiritual reading of Christian classics. The first of these is the incarnational rationale. The point here is that spiritual classics do not only contain reflections on a biblical understanding of sanctification, but they also contain reflections on the lived experience of sanctification. Similar to the second person of the Trinity becoming incarnate in Jesus, spiritual classics offer portraits of incarnate exemplars that attempted to live out the way of Jesus in their historical-cultural context. This embodied testimony of life in the Spirit increases the potential value of spiritual classics for the Spirit's sanctifying work.

A biblical-theological case for the value of embodied or incarnate exemplars can be located in an examination of the Pauline notion of imitation (*mimētēs/mimeomai*). Paul's imitation language suggests that his embodied life as well as others' lives served as incarnate examples of following Christ that were to be observed and reflected upon by those to whom Paul wrote. Paul encourages imitation of himself as he exemplifies embracing weakness (1 Cor 4:16), seeking the good of others above himself (1 Cor 10:33), trusting in Christ's righteousness rather than his own (Phil 3:1-17), and the refusal to be a burden to those to whom he ministered (2 Thess 3:7-9).[21] When Paul calls upon his readers to "imitate" himself in these and other ways, it is not merely a technique to command obedience.

---

[20]There is, I think, more to the decision procedure for deciding what is and what is *not* a biblically grounded means of grace. For more on this see my "Sanctification in a New Key: Relieving Evangelical Anxieties Over Spiritual Formation," *Journal of Spiritual Formation and Soul Care* 1, no. 2 (2008): 129-48. See also Gerald Sittser, *Water from a Deep Well: Christian Spirituality from Early Martyrs to Modern Missionaries* (Downers Grove, IL: InterVarsity Press, 2007), pp. 18-19.

[21]For a concise analysis of these texts see S. E. Fowl, "Imitation of Paul/of Christ," in *Dictionary of Paul and His Letters*, ed. Gerald F. Hawethorne, Ralph P. Martin and Daniel G. Reid (Downers Grove, IL: InterVarsity Press, 1993), pp. 428-31. For a more lengthy discussion of scholarly opinion see Brian Dodd, *Paul's Paradigmatic "I": Personal Example as Literary Strategy* (Sheffield, UK: Sheffield Academic Press, 1999), pp. 19-29.

There is something about his embodied example that carries a meaning that the propositional imperative alone would lack. As many have argued, Paul's call to imitation has pedagogical value.[22]

We see the significance of having a concrete exemplar most clearly when Paul sends Timothy to the Corinthians as an embodied example of his own ways: "I urge you, then, be imitators of me. That this is why I sent you Timothy, . . . to remind you of my ways in Christ, as I teach them everywhere in every church" (1 Cor 4:16-17). In this passage Paul makes clear that essential to imitation is a living, concrete reminder of his ways. Timothy's teaching and his lifestyle among the Corinthians would serve as a living reminder of Paul's example.[23]

A similar move is made in Philippians 3:17, where Paul writes, "join in imitating me, and keep your eyes on those who walk according to the example you have in us". In this case an unspecified group of others on whom the Philippians' eyes can be fixed are appealed to as exhibiting an example or pattern to emulate. Paul is not physically present with the Philippians, but these others are present and therefore can be observed. Paul reinforces the importance of *seeing* the example when he writes, "What you have learned and received and heard and *seen* in me—practice these things" (Phil 4:9, emphasis added).[24] Gordon Fee writes of Paul's use of the imitation word group, "The term does not refer to one who mimics, nor even to one who follows as a disciple, but to one who actually internalizes and lives out the model that has been set before him/her."[25]

It is important to note that if Paul's embodied practices can be observed in Timothy and the unspecified others of Philippi, then it would appear that such exemplars of the Christian way could, in principle, be found throughout church history (cf. Heb 13:7). For Paul the key to having a legitimate model

---

[22]For a treatment of the pedagogical value of imitation, see Willis Peter De Boer, *The Imitation of Paul: An Exegetical Study* (Kampen, Germany: J. H. Kok, 1962), and Elizabeth A. Castelli, *Imitating Paul: A Discourse of Power* (Louisville: KY: Westminster/John Knox, 1991), and Dodd, *Paul's Paradigmatic "I."*

[23]For comments on this passage see Gordon D. Fee, *The First Epistle to the Corinthians* (Grand Rapids: Eerdmans, 1987), pp. 186-89.

[24]For comments on these passages, see Gordon D. Fee, *Paul's Letter to the Philippians* (Grand Rapids: Eerdmans, 1995), pp. 362-66, 419-20.

[25]Fee, *First Epistle to the Corinthians*, p. 186 n. 24.

is not the identity of the person but the pattern of life the person exhibits. If the person lives out the Christ life in a recognizable manner, then there is something about his or her concrete example that offers a life-sized picture of the way toward holiness. It is evident in Paul that attending to such examples adds some sort of value to propositional instruction alone.

It is difficult to say precisely what an observable, embodied life communicates that propositional teaching alone does not. Particularly when it comes to lived realities (e.g., cooking, riding a bike, playing a musical instrument, sculpting, working with electrical wiring) there is something to be gained by watching someone perform the craft that cannot be gained through step-by-step, written instructions. So while a good theology of the spiritual life is essential, there is something gained in observing that good theology lived out in concrete situations. While this happens best with persons who are physically present with us, in the absence of or in addition to physically present exemplars, written descriptions of their lifestyles can also serve as incarnational examples. As Philip Sheldrake puts the point, Christian classics "effectively translate Christian ideas into lifestyle so that the connection between theory and practice is made explicit."[26] When we read the classics attentively, we often "get to know" the author or others who are being described by the author, and the resultant picture of how they lived can bolster our spiritual imaginations, bringing conviction, encouragement and insight. For instance, consider the following story of Abba Moses from the *Sayings of the Desert Fathers*:

> A brother had committed a fault and was called before the council. The council invited the revered Abba Moses to join, but Abba Moses refused. They sent someone to get him, and he agreed to come. He took a leaking jug, filled it with water and carried it with him to the council. They saw him coming with the jug leaving a trail of water, and asked, "What's this?" Abba Moses said, "My sins run out behind me and I do not see them, and today I am coming to judge the error of another?" When the council heard these words they forgave the brother.[27]

No doubt Jesus taught the same principle that Abba Moses exem-

---

[26]Sheldrake, *Spirituality and History*, p. 173.
[27]*Sayings of the Desert Fathers*, trans. Benedicta Ward (London: Cistercian Publications, 1975), pp. 138-39.

plified: "Why do you see the speck that is in your brother's eye, but do not notice the log that is in your own eye?" (Mt 7:3). While Jesus' illustration has unequaled authority and important pedagogical value, the story of Abba Moses embodies Jesus' teaching in a particular historical-cultural context that has the potential to confront the reader afresh. The incarnational account of Abba Moses drives the teaching of the incarnate Jesus home in a manner that the Spirit of God may choose to utilize in his illuminating work.

According to this incarnational rationale, the Pauline notion of imitation points toward the unique significance of careful observation of exemplars of the Christian faith. In perhaps a fairly tacit way, attending to such models communicates a deeper understanding of the way of holiness. While it is always best to have first-person contact with these exemplars, written testimony can also serve as a witness to embodied examples. Since the spiritual classics contain such accounts, the devotional reading of them becomes an even more conducive means of grace.

yes

ECCLESIOLOGICAL RATIONALE

Thus far we have seen that the pneumatological rationale gives us reason to include the devotional reading of Christian classics as a fitting means of grace and the incarnational rationale provides a further reason to think that the classics would be conducive to the Spirit's sanctifying work. This brings us to the ecclesiological rationale. The central idea here is that a proper understanding of the role of the body of Christ in spiritual formation heightens the value of spiritual reading of the classics.

In Ephesians 4:1-16, Paul makes clear that the body of Christ is the interpersonal context in which followers of Jesus are equipped for ministry, built up and brought to maturity in Christ.

> Speaking the truth in love, we are to grow up in all aspects into Him who is the head, even Christ, from whom the whole body, being fitted and held together by what every joint supplies, according to the proper working of each individual part, causes the growth of the body for the building up of itself in love (Eph 4:15-16 NASB).[28]

---

[28]Edmund Clowney, *The Church* (Downers Grove, IL: InterVarsity Press, 1995), pp. 64-65. Clowney writes, "Holiness is the goal of the growth of the church as the body of Christ (Eph

In various ways the Spirit utilizes brothers and sisters in Christ to bring his transforming presence and Word into human lives.[29] To get some sense of the various roles of others in spiritual formation, we can think of the lists of spiritual gifts (Eph 4:11; Rom 12:6-8; 1 Cor 12:8-10; 1 Cor 12:28-30) or the "one anothers" of Scripture (e.g., "love one another" [Jn 13:34]; "encourage one another" [1 Thess 5:11]; "teaching . . . one another" [Col 3:16]).[30] While there is something irreducibly meaningful about first-person acquaintance with other members of the body of Christ who exercise some gift or express a "one another," at times a gift or a "one another" is communicated through written materials (e.g., books, sermon texts, letters, poems, etc.). The point here is not that the written materials provide an incarnational example of the way of holiness, but that the written materials mediate the ministry of the body of Christ. For instance, while C. S. Lewis died before I was even born, he has been one of my primary teachers when it comes to the doctrine of sanctification. In the same manner, while the authors of spiritual classics are deceased, their writings can be preserved and passed on, continuing as a source of teaching, exhortation, encouragement, comfort and the like.

Placing spiritual reading within ecclesiology heightens the peculiar value of the practice. Since Paul makes clear that a properly functioning church body is essential for spiritual maturation, finding and integrating oneself into such a body is indispensable for every Christian. And yet Christ followers may find themselves geographically or historically isolated from the kind of body life that is required. For instance, what if the brothers and sisters in Christ in one's local community appallingly lack

---

4:15). We are to grow together to the full maturity of Christ."

[29]For more on this, see Kent E. Brower and Andy Johnson, eds., *Holiness and Ecclesiology in the New Testament* (Grand Rapids: Eerdmans, 2007). Brower and Johnson write, "While God's call to holiness and God's sanctifying grace does not come to *isolated individuals*, it does indeed come to *communal persons*. Indeed, it characteristically comes *from* the Holy Spirit *through* the grace-enabled concrete practices of people who accompany us on our way to the eschatological new creation when our communion with the Triune God and with each other will be completely perfected" (p. xxii). See also James C. Wilhoit, *Spiritual Formation as If the Church Mattered: Growing in Christ Through Community* (Grand Rapids: Baker, 2008).

[30]In terms of the spiritual gifts, it may be best to think of these not as Spirit-empowered *abilities* but rather Spirit-empowered *callings* for the edification of the body of Christ. In support of such a view see Kenneth Berding, *What Are Spiritual Gifts? Rethinking the Conventional View* (Grand Rapids: Kregel, 2006).

the ability to encourage one another well? Healthy, spiritual encouragement requires compassion, and unfortunately there are Christian communities where compassion, and therefore encouragement, is in short supply. Or what if due to the vagaries of human history we find ourselves in a period of time where robust, Spirit-empowered, biblical teaching on holiness is rare? Indeed, we may be living in the aftermath of what Richard Lovelace has called the "sanctification gap" or what J. I. Packer termed "holiness in eclipse."[31] In these situations, moving toward our deceased brothers and sisters in Christ who encourage and teach us through their writings would be one of the only ways to embed ourselves in a properly functioning church body.

Dallas Willard writes of how the spiritual classics became for him a deep source of spiritual encouragement having come of age in a Christian community that had little to offer in that arena. After recounting his initial exposure to various spiritual writers (e.g., Madame Guyon, François Fénelon, George Fox, John Bunyan, John Wesley), Willard writes:

> That these [writers] were, by and large, quite ordinary people only impressed me all the more that the amazing life into which they were manifestly led could be mine. I had been raised in religious circles of very fine people where the emphasis had been exclusively on faithfulness to right beliefs, and upon bringing others to profess those beliefs. Now that, of course, is of central importance. But when that process alone is emphasized, the result is a dry and powerless religious life, no matter how sincere, and leaves a person constantly vulnerable to temptations of all kinds. Therefore, to see actual invasions of human life by the presence and action of God . . . greatly encouraged me to believe that the life and promises given in the person of Christ and in Scripture were meant for us today. I saw that ordinary individuals who sought the Lord would find him real—actually, that he would come to them and convey his reality.[32]

Amen!
Thank
you,
Lord

---

[31] Richard Lovelace, "The Sanctification Gap," *Theology Today* 29, no. 4 (1973): 363-69; J. I. Packer, *Keep in Step with the Spirit* (Grand Rapids: Baker, 2004), pp. 82-84.

[32] Dallas Willard, "When God Moves In," in *Indelible Ink*, ed. Scott Larsen (Colorado Springs: WaterBrook Press, 2003), p. 52. In a similar vein J. I. Packer writes, "at something of a crisis time soon after my conversion, John Owen helped me to be realistic (that is, neither myopic or despairing) about my continuing sinfulness and the discipline of self-suspicion and mortification to which, with all Christians, I am called. . . . Suffice to say that without Owen I might well have gone off my head or got bogged down in mystical fanaticism, and certainly my view of the

While it would be improper to use spiritual classics as a way to escape or avoid real-life relationships with our brothers and sisters, when we find an ongoing and widespread deficit in those relationships, we can find a place within the company of Christians across church history.

CONCLUSION

It has been argued here that a biblical understanding of pneumatology, incarnational example, and ecclesiology grounds the practice of the devotional reading of spiritual classics. But again, it is not the overly modest conclusion that spiritual reading is merely *permissible* for Christ followers. Rather, the conclusion is that there is pneumatological, incarnational and ecclesiological sense to be made of how the classics are a peculiarly fitting means of the Spirit's illumination of his transformational presence and Word. The classics of Christian spirituality offer reflections on a biblical understanding of Christian holiness as well as contextualized examples of living out such holiness, and thereby extend to us the opportunity to engage the body of Christ across the centuries.

Christian life would not be what it is today" (J. I. Packer, *A Quest for Godliness: The Puritan Vision of the Christian Life* [Wheaton, IL: Crossway, 1990], p. 12).

2

Temptations in Reading Spiritual Classics

John H. Coe

A brother questioned Abba Poemen saying, "Give me a word."

DAVID G. R. KELLER, *OASIS OF WISDOM*

T HE HISTORY OF THE CHURCH has been one continual giving and receiving of wise and spiritual words from one another in the body of Christ. These words reflect the understanding and lives of the saints, passed down from one to another, just as Paul the apostle did to Timothy who, in turn, was to do this with others (2 Tim 2:2). As time went on, these words were written down—not only as God-breathed Scripture of the New Testament documents but also as the lesser, human-inspired musings and lives of the saints gone before us.

The spiritual classics represent one major manifestation of this giving and receiving of words, not in person or "incarnate" but in written form, that have been passed down to those capable of reading from generation to generation. It was a way for the church to "fossilize" the words and lives that were a blessing to some and were meant to be a blessing to many unable to witness them first hand as well as to future generations.

I will argue that reading spiritual classics is a good thing in itself, for they provide excellent examples of spiritual advice and insight from

Scripture and real-life experience, which are examples of spiritual theology. This process of reading the spiritual theology and advice of the
ancients, in turn, is one elaborate and complex form of obeying the biblical injunctions regarding "one another." Nevertheless, I will also argue
that any particular act of reading spiritual classics may not be a good *for
me* or *you* in a particular circumstance, for it turns out that there are
several temptations that confront the believer in doing so.

READING SPIRITUAL CLASSICS AS A FORM OF "ONE ANOTHERING"

In the first place, the reading of spiritual classics is clearly one example
of how the church is to speak to one another for the sake of edification
and love. The numerous "one another" passages in the Bible imply the
reciprocal giving and receiving whereby as members one of another
(Rom 12:5) we are to build up one another (1 Thess 5:11), love one another (Rom 13:8), serve one another (Gal 5:13) and be kind to one
another (Eph 4:32). In particular, with our words we are not to lie to one
another (Col 3:9) or bite, devour and consume one another (Gal 5:15),
but rather are to speak the truth to one another in love (Eph 4:15), encourage and admonish one another (1 Thess 5:14), comfort one another
(1 Thess 4:18), and as a result of the filling of the Spirit and letting the
words of Christ dwell richly within, the body is to speak to one another
in psalms and hymns and spiritual songs (Eph 5:19; Col 3:16). These "one
another" passages become ways that we obey Paul's admonition to
follow the example of other lives: "Brethren, join in following my example, and observe those who walk according to the pattern you have in
us" (Phil 3:17 NASB).

It is clear, then, that believers are called to not only look at the Scriptures for encouragement but are commanded to look to one another, *to
others* in the body of Christ who are carrying on the apostolic pattern of
how to live the Christian life. This looking to one another involves
giving and receiving both actions and words. In particular, the writings
of the ancients provide the church an opportunity to follow the examples and insights of others through the medium of the written (or
oral) word. These written accounts become the repository of wisdom

handed down from generation to generation in the church, some as oral tradition from family to family, community to community, and then fossilized as the spiritual writings of the saints. This repository of personal, pastoral and theological musings on the Christian life became part of the written tradition called "spiritual theology," the reading of which is one way to obey Paul's admonition to observe those who are carrying on the apostolic example and faith in order to receive words of wisdom, counsel and admonition from another.

Reading Spiritual Classics as a Form of Doing Spiritual Theology

Furthermore, reading spiritual classics is a form of doing spiritual theology insofar as the latter is a particular form of using words to love, encourage, teach, help and build up one another from the wisdom and reflections of the saints on Scripture and their own experience. In its more technical sense spiritual theology is understood as a *first-order theological discipline of its own* with its own unique data for study, domain of investigation, methodology and aim (much like New Testament studies, historical theology, systematic theology).[1] In its essence and simplicity, spiritual theology is simply the task of the church seeking to understand the process of growth from the Scripture and real human experience, and to pass this on to one another.

The following, then, is a *definition* of spiritual theology.

> Spiritual theology is that part of theology which brings together
> 1. a study of the truths of Scripture with
> 2. a study of the ministry of the Holy Spirit in the experience of human beings
> 3. in dependence upon the work of the Indwelling Christ, in order to
>   A. define the *nature* of this new life in Christ by the Spirit (derived from the Bible and theology as the primary data, with some wisdom from experience),
>   B. explain the *process* of growth by which persons advance from

---

[1]For a more detailed account of spiritual theology, see John H. Coe, "Spiritual Theology: A Theological-Experiential Methodology for Bridging the Sanctification Gap," *Journal of Spiritual Formation and Soul Care* 2, no. 1 (Spring 2009): 4-43.

the beginning of the spiritual life to its full perfection in the next life (derived from the data of the Bible, theology and wisdom from experience) and

C. formulate *directives* for spiritual growth and development (derived from the data of the Bible, theology and wisdom from experience)

D. with the goal to living out this wisdom personally and in community and to passing this on for the sake of the church.[2]

In this sense, spiritual theology takes place whenever we encourage one another in the faith, whenever we use words to guide one another into a deeper understanding and practice of Christian living.

Of course, the Scriptures are certainly the central and controlling datum for the content and understanding of spiritual transformation. However, the *peculiar task* of spiritual theology is to integrate the fruit of biblical and theological studies on sanctification with *observations and reflections on real-life experience* and the manner in which the Spirit works in believers. This may also include the wisdom that can be gained from the natural disciplines such as a robust Christian philosophy and psychology. This is much like the Old Testament sage or wise man in Proverbs, who brings together wisdom gained through observation of and reflection upon both the Scriptures and real life in order to discover wisdom for living in all areas of life (e.g., Prov 24:30-34).[3] Thus, the process of understanding and living the faith is a multifaceted act of prayer, obedience, study of Scripture, observation of other spiritual examples, observation and reflection on application to personal and corporate life, and the passing of all this on to one another in word, example and writing. In that sense the Christian life itself and the ways we relate to one another in word and act are forms of doing spiritual theology involving the commonsense practice of watching, waiting and listening to the

---

[2]This definition was adapted from Jordon Aumann, *Spiritual Theology* (London: Sheed & Ward, 1980), p. 22. For more on a justification and defense for doing spiritual theology, see Coe, "Spiritual Theology," pp. 19-34.

[3]For more on the Old Testament sage as a model of gaining wisdom for living from the study of nature and written revelation, see John Coe and Todd Hall, *Psychology in the Spirit: Contours of a Transformational Psychology* (Downers Grove, IL: IVP Academic, 2010), pp. 132-65.

Spirit's work in real life on the basis of the Scriptures in response to the words and examples of one another in the body of Christ, and sharing these in turn to those in our care.

THE GOAL OF READING SPIRITUAL CLASSICS

It is clear from Scripture that the goal of all Christian learning and teaching, including the study of spiritual theology and the spiritual life from Scripture and the spiritual classics, as well as all the words that we give and receive (and all that we do) is a cluster of ultimate ends that go beyond mere reading and learning: that believers would love God and neighbor (1 Tim 1:5), would be complete or mature in Christ (Col 1:28-29), trained in righteousness (1 Tim 4:7-8) and glorify God in all things (1 Cor 10:31). Anything less than this is a deviation or distortion of the intended goal of all our speech. However, there has always been a temptation to divorce our words, reading and study from transformation and love.

THE INTELLECTUAL VICE OF CURIOSITY

Because there is a virtuous manner in which we can read spiritual classics that demands attention, practice and obedience in the Spirit, the effect of sin on the will makes it possible that there is also a vice mani-festation of this activity. Just because reading the spiritual writers is a good in itself, it is not always a good *for me* or a particular person, de-pending on the circumstances involved. The church fathers and me-dieval theologians understood this well and construed this distortion of our capacity to learn and "receive words," whether from theology or the spiritual writers, as the intellectual vice of curiosity.

According to Aquinas, *curiosity* (Lat. *curiositas*) is the intellectual vice or distortion of our capacity to know and learn.[4] It is the result of inordinate appetites, desires and loves divorced from the goal of spir-itual transformation and the love of God that distort our natural capac-ities and powers for learning and intellectual study.[5] According to Aquinas, this intellectual vice of curiosity has several forms:

---

[4]Thomas Aquinas, "On Curiosity," *Summa Theologiae* 2a2ae, qq. 166-67, ed. Thomas Gilby, Blackfriars ed. (London: Eyre & Spottiswoode), pp. 193-210.
[5]Ibid., 2a2ae, q. 166, pp. 193-99.

- The desire to know what should not be known and to learn from illicit sources (e.g., astrology from demons, pornography).

- Even more relevant to the reading of spiritual classics are the following forms of curiosity:

- The desire to know something in a manner that it should not be
  known so that it results in pride, arrogance and showing off.

- The desire to know something in a manner that it should not be
  known so that it results in a kind of "vicious sophistication" and
  idleness in the knowing and knower.

- The desire to know something in a manner that it should not be
  known insofar as the intent is to sin.

- The desire to know something with the result that one pays more attention, time and energy to the task of some particular study than
  reason and the will of God would prescribe given other responsibilities and goods to be pursued.

- The desire to know something in a manner in which it should not be
  known, that is, as an end in itself and in the "flesh" apart from the
  motive for and in the love of God by the Spirit.[6]

The vice of curiosity can be applied to many forms of intellectual and
literary pursuits, but it is particularly insidious when it involves the
study of the Bible, theology and the spiritual life. Relevant to our purposes, those who read the spiritual writers can be tempted to turn aside
to lesser goals than transformation and the love of God. Each of the
forms of curiosity has their own unique manifestation when it comes to
the temptations involved in reading spiritual classics.

One temptation of curiosity relevant to reading spiritual classics is
choosing unwise, illicit or developmentally inappropriate sources for
spiritual wisdom. In this case, a young believer may have such a vora-
cious desire to grow and learn that he or she will not have the appropriate discretion and wisdom necessary to *choose sources* and content
that are developmentally appropriate. For an advanced believer or theo-

---

[6]Ibid., 2a2ae, q. 167, pp. 200-210.

logian, it may be quite appropriate to read the church fathers or medieval Catholic, Orthodox and liberal Protestant literature in order to understand similarities and differences between various approaches to spiritual growth for the sake of gaining insight and refuting false doctrine and praxis. However, it takes a good deal of spiritual and theological sophistication to be able to discern truth from falsehood, wisdom from folly, and to pull out morsels of insight from the bones of error. Yet I can imagine a Christian so hungry to grow or so filled with guilt and shame and feelings of failure that he or she will unfortunately seek to believe and apply anything that appears helpful for growth.

Consequently, there is a need for patience to control this appetite by asking God and other saints for wisdom in how to moderate this desire and seek out wise, developmentally appropriate reading so that one seeks to grow in the Lord's way, in ways that are helpful, safe and not potentially dangerous for one's soul. The human spirit and its growth is a delicate thing that requires patient, tender care that is appropriate for what will help and not lead astray. This will vary from believer to believer. Those of us who are down the path must also beware of what we advise others to read, making sure it is age and growth appropriate to our disciples' situation and growth.

Second, curiosity may motivate the reading of spiritual classics so that it results in pride and arrogance rather than humility and increased sober, self-knowledge. In this case the believer's psychological appetites and loves have moved his or her desire to learn and understand not so much to better love and obey, serve and minister, than to show off one's learning, to be known and admired by others in it. This is often accompanied by the deception of the passions to believe that knowing something is sufficient to imagine that one is living the truth. In this case it will be helpful for the student of the spiritual classics to read this literature in prayer, opening the heart in honesty and to the truth of what is in the heart as he or she reads, to increase self-knowledge of one's failings and virtues—to have a rightful understanding of oneself before God in the reading.

A third and related manifestation of this vice of curiosity is the inordinate and distorted desire to read spiritual classics resulting in a kind of "vicious sophistication" and idleness in the knowing and knower.

This form of pride and arrogance is moved by the desire to be vogue, sophisticated, "in the know" and to consider others who are not read in these areas to be unsophisticated dullards of the ancients, simpletons about the deep things of the spiritual life. In this case reading spiritual classics is reduced to a form of self-aggrandizing, the building of an inflated ego that has developed a sophisticated spiritual palate for high and ancient ideas. And anyone who does not know these matters is beneath one's contempt and not to be given an audience. In this case the appetites have made the intellect idle and dull in its true service of the love and glory of God, of love and ministry to neighbor, of honest humble transformation. The mind has lost its compass and needs a reality check to find its way back. This "liberalizing" of the intellect may require much honest soul searching and even trials to find its way back to its true moorings.

Related to this form of curiosity is the lust to know what is considered new, "provocative" or fashionable. In this case the knower has developed an inordinate appetite for what is unusual or new, much the same way a connoisseur of fine wines or food is moved to the novel and the next delicate or subtle taste experience in order to avoid boredom by new tantalizing experiences of the appetites. As Paul Griffiths says,

> This need for novelty contributes to the obsessiveness and insatiability of curiosity's appetites: once the new thing is known, expropriated for the private enjoyment of the curious knower, it is, at once, no longer new, and therefore no longer satisfying to the curious. Something else, some new object must once be sought. The curious gaze is endlessly restless, insanely so, in fact.[7]

In that sense the knower's distorted appetite for knowledge does not arrive at its end in transformation and love, but rather for the possession of new information or knowledge, merely to be consumed and stored, and then to move on to the next interesting curiosity. In this sense the

---

[7]Paul Griffiths, *The Vice of Curiosity: An Essay on Intellectual Appetite* (Winnipeg, MB: Canadian Mennonite Press, 2006), p. 14, quoted in Teri Merrick, "Teaching Philosophy: Instilling Pious Wonder or Vicious Curiosity?" *Christian Scholar's Review* 34, no. 4 (2010): 419. For more on this vice of curiosity see Merrick's discussion of Josef Pieper, *The Four Cardinal Virtues*, trans. R. Winston, C. Winston, L. Lynch and D. Cogan (Notre Dame, IN: University of Notre Dame Press, 1966), p. 199, in Merrick, "Teaching Philosophy," p. 419.

affective satisfaction of knowing becomes a substitute for transformation, self-analysis and struggle in the knowing. The antidote is true self-knowledge in the knowledge of God, whereby the believer develops a tendency to ask God to search his or her heart regarding what is known and enjoyed in the knowing. This does not deny the joy and rest in knowing but is a reminder that what is known also has a telos to relate the heart to reality and God.

A fourth manifestation of curiosity has to do with the appetites moving one to study with the intent to sin. In this case one could study the spiritual writers as a way to rebel against one's spiritual tradition or family, to find support for one's strange and idiosyncratic ideas, doctrines and teachings, to bolster one's need to be different or daring with ideas, to gain support for one's need to be seen as a "guru" or enlightened leader, person or teacher. Of course, these attitudes may not be the conscious intentions of the heart but unfortunately result from a deep unhealthy need to stand out, be different or a deep-seated resentment toward one's parents or spiritual mentors. In this case reading spiritual classics becomes an opportunity for the flesh and the vices of the heart, whereby study is less for the love of God and more as a support to some unhealthy need and vice distortion in one's life that has not been dealt with or brought to the surface. In this case it might be good to analyze with the Lord or with a fellow believer what is truly motivating spending time in the spiritual classics.

A fifth manifestation of the intellectual vice of curiosity is when one pays more attention, time and energy to the task of some particular study than reason and the will of God would prescribe, given other responsibilities and goods to be pursued. In this case the inordinate appetites and desires move a person to study beyond what reason, love and the informed intellect would deem appropriate. The very desire to know about and participate in the spiritual life through extensive reading, though a good in itself, may actually become an opportunity of temptation by the flesh or the devil so that the well-intentioned believer begins to ignore what is one's true calling—perhaps spending time with one's family, one's spouse, the body of Christ, one's neighbor in need or one's God in prayer, other studies, or one's job. The task is to open the heart in prayer and ask God how much one should study, what other callings of God should be pursued. Again, what is a good in itself can be distorted in so many ways that what is lawful or good is no longer profitable to me.

Sixth, curiosity can take the form of knowing something but not in the love of God or for the sake of the love of God. In this case the disoriented appetites move the intellect to desire to know something but in such a way that neither (1) the knowing act is experienced as it was intended in loving God nor (2) is the knowing act done for the sake of or ultimate purpose of loving God and neighbor. In this case the knowing experience and content known fall short of their intended goals or ends in the love and glory of God. Given the fact that fallen humans become habituated in doing things in the power of the autonomous self or flesh prior to conversion, these flesh habits of the heart die hard. Thus, the believer's penchant and temptation will be to read spiritual classics in one's own power, as though the act of understanding and the thing understood are ends in themselves. This behavior is fine for the beginner who is learning the spiritual life, but over time the believer will need to be retrained—and this will take some time—to read and study dependent on the Spirit open to the love of God and loving God.

General Temptations and Unhealthy Approaches to Reading Spiritual Classics

Beyond curiosity there are other more general and typical temptations that confront the believer in approaching the spiritual writings of the church. For the ancient enthusiast, one might hold too rigidly to some particular ancients idea or to a particular tradition or to the conviction that only the ancients have wisdom on the matter. In this case the reader must beware of a slavish approach to the spiritual musings of others.

Rather, the ideas—even of the most holy of saints—are merely a piece of spiritual theology that are to be evaluated and scrutinized in the light of Scripture and the spiritual-theological reflections of others, even by contemporary spiritual theologians and the ordinary person in the pew seeking to understand the spiritual life. No one writer or tradition necessarily has all the insights. Thus, there needs to be an openness and readiness to scrutinize for truth and falsity in these matters no matter what favorite theologian or saint of old is being discussed. This scrutiny is particularly important regarding spiritual writers of the past who are not always clear about the relationship between sanctification (spiritual growth) and salvation, where there is truly a need to avoid the pitfalls of legalism and false motivations of fear, shame and guilt to grow rather than on the basis of Christ's finished work on the cross in justification. This is why each generation and in some sense each person must do spiritual theology, to test the ideas of others, including the ancients, by observation and reflection on Scripture and one's own experience of the Spirit and growth.

On the other hand, one might be tempted in the very opposite manner to not take any interest in reading the ancient Christian spiritual writers, thinking, for example, that only the Scriptures contain insight into the spiritual life. This view demonstrates ignorance of the biblical truth in Proverbs that there is wisdom available to the believer from observation and reflection on creation and life.[8]

Moreover, this Bible-only approach to understanding the Christian life ignores the importance of developing a spiritual theology in which one not only integrates the insights from Scripture regarding growth with insight and wisdom from creation, but also *applies* these truths to human experience, which requires human observation, reflection and experience. This failure to appreciate a robust spiritual theology results in a superficial understanding of growth. One might know the general prescriptions of the Bible, for example, to put aside anger and malice (Col 3:8) but may fall short in the wisdom of how to actually do this. Observation, reflection and experience will aid the believer in under-standing the dynamic processes of malice and how this vice habit of the heart might be changed over time. This is the responsibility of the church to discover in dependence on the Spirit in any particular case.

This Scripture-only approach to understanding spiritual formation also goes contrary to the Bible's own affirmations about the role of the

---

[8]For more on this biblical apologetic and understanding of insight for living from reflecting on creation in the Old Testament wisdom literature and the Old Testament sage, see Coe and Hall, *Psychology in the Spirit*, chap. 7.

body of Christ in growth. As stated earlier, Paul clearly admonishes fellow believers to follow his example and to observe and follow the example of others in their midst who followed Paul (Phil 3:17). The biblical model is to not only study the Bible but also to be related to one another in healthy ways and to be open to the examples of others that generally have followed the apostolic example of the spiritual life. In fact, we have some of the best examples of this in the writings and lives of the saints who have gone before us. Wisdom would inform us to take full advantage of this, though not at the expense of being assisted by living believers.

Along a similar vein, a believer might be tempted to think that only one's current generation has anything to say on the Christian life, so there is no reason to look to prior generations. However, wisdom of the soul and soul doctoring has been going on for centuries by insightful saints who lived a long life open to the Spirit on the basis of the Word and reality. Progress in spiritual theology is not the same as progress in physics or some technology; in fact, contemporary approaches to understanding the reality of the soul or person can miss much by ignoring the wisdom of those who have lived long lives before us.

Of course, reading spiritual classics, though a potentially wonderful way to glean wisdom from believers living before us, can become a substitute for the communal giving and receiving of words from one another in real life. In this case a believer can be tempted to use *reading* of spiritual insights as a *defense* against being with other believers and engaging in the risk and messiness of love and community. A book is safe compared to people, but the words of saints gone by are not to be a substitute for the growth that comes about only through persons in relationship in the body of Christ, loving, helping, admonishing and encouraging one another.

In general, there is the temptation of giving too charitable a reading to the ancients or to giving too little charity. One person might have a fantasy about the ancient spiritual writers, thinking that everything they say is good without proper scrutiny. Another might do the opposite, critiquing them entirely without seriously understanding their ideas in light of historical and theoretical contexts. It seems the middle ground is to try to "get in their shoes," to understand their context historically and theologically, to glean as much as possible, but to do this with a reasonably critical eye, to be able to see what is helpful and unhelpful, true and false, selecting the good from the bad. This is a reasonable way to read most writings, particularly those of the faithful who have gone before us.

Furthermore, the reading of the ancient spiritual writers is no substitute for a life of obedience. One great human malady of the intellect is its penchant in the fall to deceive the knower into construing that to know something is somehow to do or become that thing. This is especially the temptation of those who love to study and learn—even in the best of persons. The lover of knowledge experiences so intensely the thing known that this becomes a kind of *experiential substitute* for doing and character change. This is a very subtle deception, one that is not consciously pernicious but over time distances the self from what is truly going on in oneself. It is like the person in James who is a hearer (in this case, a reader) of the word and not a doer, one who sees in a mirror something good and true but walks away from it and forgets to carry into action and change (Jas 1:22-24). Rather, the temptation may be to rush off into more experiences of knowing. Again, the reader of the classics must open the heart to God and honesty regarding whether the knowing experience has become an end in itself.

A very real temptation in reading the spiritual writers is that which John of the Cross calls "spiritual gluttony."[9] In this case the spiritual glutton is one who is tempted to read spiritual classics for the spiritual feeling it produces and not for piety and the truth of a matter. The spiritual glutton rummages through pages of the ancients, "lusting" for insight that "inspires" as a way to avoid the truth of what is going on in his or her life and attending to purity and practical holiness. This vice morphs spiritual transformation into a kind of "spiritual aesthetic," an exchange of holiness for beautiful and splendorous feelings and experiences of God. This pursuit of spiritual consolation is particularly problematic for believers who feel stuck in spiritual dryness and aridity, who in their hearts cry out with the psalmist "How long, O LORD" (Ps 13:1-2)

---

[9]John of the Cross, *The Dark Night of the Soul*, trans. E. Allison Peers (New York: Image Books, 1959), pp. 53-58.

but have wearied of this and now seek for morsels of consolation and spiritual feelings as a way to not feel their deep longings and what God may reveal in the dryness. Here believers need to trust not in spiritual feelings but in the God who indwells them and calls them to open their heart to what the Spirit is searching (Ps 139:23-24).

Finally, there is the temptation to use reading spiritual classics as a substitute for personally opening to God in prayer. In this case the believer can be tempted to substitute opening to the living God for a spirituality of intellectualism or experientialism. So rather than honestly opening to what is really going on in one's prayer life with its potential dryness and loneliness, the person avoids this confusion by searching the pages of some ancient for an insight, idea or experience that might console the heart or illumine the mind in order for a moment to forget the internal chaos. It is a fine and legitimate thing to employ others in the body of Christ and their ideas to find solace, comfort and insight when we are feeling distant from God or confused. Nevertheless, reading and insight should never become a defense such that we over time altogether avoid the crucible of prayer. There are seasons where prayer will decrease and the need for a brother or sister (or reading) will increase as we attempt to understand and discern the ways of God. But these times are not meant to be forever but as means and graces to once again open the heart to God in prayer.

EPISTEMOLOGICAL-SPIRITUAL DISCIPLINES AS HEALTHY CORRECTIVES IN READING SPIRITUAL CLASSICS

In light of human sin and the temptations that beset believers in their intellectual life, various spiritual-epistemological disciplines will be important for those who intently study Scripture and the writings of the saints in order to intentionally aim in all their studies at love and transformation. Spiritual disciplines that assist the person in staying rightly focused in the knowing process are as follows: *honesty* before God in study, *truthfulness* in study, *prayer* in study, openness to the Spirit to *search the heart* while in study, *meditation* on Scriptures and truths in study, *contemplation* on the love of God and loving God in study. These disciplines help open the heart to the truth of what God intends, in the manner in which God intends (being filled with the Spirit), to the reality of what one is studying and in honesty regarding the motivations by which one studies.[10]

The spiritual-epistemological disciplines also protect the person in the process of study from unhealthy influences. They guard the learner from unwillingness to see the truth of what is being studied, from being driven by vices that hinder one from being open to reality, from false agendas, fantasy, grandiosity, overconfidence, timidity, arrogance and pride—curiosity in all its forms.

THE FUTURE OF READING SPIRITUAL CLASSICS

Interest in spirituality and reading the spiritual classics in these last decades continues to increase in the church, in both Roman Catholicism and Protestantism, particularly evangelicalism. This movement has encouraged a renaissance in studying the history of spirituality and in bringing back some rigor to the study of the spiritual life. This is a good direction that needs to be sustained if the church is to provide an understanding of the spiritual life that is not only biblically grounded but historically informed and intellectually and experientially vital. The church has always been a stronghold for the giving and receiving of words one to another. Whether it is from the educated or the unschooled, the scholar or the ordinary believer in the pew, the church must be open to the spiritual theology passed from one generation to the next for the love of God and in the Spirit of truth.

---

[10]For more on these epistemological-spiritual disciplines, see Coe and Hall, *Psychology in the Spirit*, pp. 105-20.

3

The Value of Spiritual Classics in Soul Care

Betsy Barber

Whoever walks with the wise becomes wise,
but the companion of fools will suffer harm.

PROVERBS 13:20

B ROTHER LAWRENCE WAS MY FIRST FRIEND among the writers of the spiritual classics. I met him when I was in middle school because the impact of his words changed my mother's hatred of cooking.

My mother grew up in a broken home with a partying mother who helped to put the "roar" in the Roaring Twenties. Though she learned to work hard growing up during the Great Depression, my mom was never instructed in cooking. When she eventually rebelled against her hard-living family by not only becoming a Christian but going even further and marrying a young preacher boy, she found herself stuck with the job of cooking three meals a day from scratch, due to a tight, ministry-provided budget. And my mother hated to cook.

My extroverted mother let us know about that fact repeatedly until the day there was a special speaker for the women's meeting at our Evangelical Free Church who spoke on a little book called *Practicing the Presence of God* by Brother Lawrence of the Resurrection (sometimes retitled *Closer Than a Brother*).[1]

Brother Lawrence was a monk in the 1600s; he was not particularly skilled at anything beside prayer, so his monastery assignment was to kitchen duty. The routine was relentless: garden produce to be gathered, water to be carried, massive piles of potatoes to be peeled, pots and pans to be scrubbed. Day after day Brother Lawrence worked and prayed, worked and prayed. And he practiced the presence of God with him. His message was simple and clear: Jesus is here in the kitchen; I am in the presence of God as I peel these spuds and he is pleased with my obedience and spiritual service to him. Known for his great peace and contentment, Brother Lawrence told of the joy of doing little things for God: "And it is not necessary to have great things to do," he continues. "I turn over my little omelet in the frying pan for the love of God. When it is finished, if I have nothing to do, I prostrate myself on the ground and adore my God from whom the grace came to make it. After that, I get back up, more content than a king."[2]

Brother Lawrence's example caught fire in my mother's heart and transformed her daily life in the kitchen. Mom pored over *Practicing the Presence of God*, a book that she re-reads still, and she found in this little praying Carmelite monk a brother in faith and in experience. Brother Lawrence's words gave her hope and instructed her concerning the sanctity of her vocation as a homemaker. I remember clearly hearing her singing and praying aloud as she cooked, worshiping God in her kitchen. Brother Lawrence's small booklet, written over three hundred years previous to her 1960s life in the American Midwest, heartened her and blessed me significantly in turn. As a result of this blessing I too learned to talk to the Lord Jesus as I did my Saturday chores, knowing he was present with me as I did mundane work. I learned to fight sloth and the despair of acedia (the temptation to not persevere) in my own vocational work as a child and I learned to talk to the Lord Jesus as I worked. Brother Lawrence's prayer became one of my favorites: "But so that my work may be better, Lord, work with me; receive my work and possess all my affections."[3]

---

[1]Brother Lawrence, *Practicing the Presence of God* (Brewster, MA: Paraclete Press, 2007).
[2]Ibid., p. 126.
[3]Ibid., p. 21.

This is the legacy of the spiritual classics in the care of souls: in the life and in the writing voiced by an older follower of the Lord Jesus, across time and space and culture, we hear the testimony of one who is imitating Christ, and we are instructed.

In my mother's experience with Brother Lawrence's work, there was a mating of orthodoxy and orthopraxy, the cultural considerations were minimal, and his psychological growth process fit her own. These are four of the areas for consideration when we explore the usefulness of the spiritual classics to a living believer: orthodoxy, orthopraxy, culture and growth. Concerns and advice regarding orthodoxy and the classics are addressed elsewhere in this volume (chapter 9), but here we will look at some of the orthopraxic considerations.

The spiritual classics are of value to us today because they meet us at our developmental level of spiritual growth (sanctification), they challenge our cultural assumptions and provide reality testing for our beliefs, they build scaffolds for our process of maturation. We use them as guides and mentors, and these brothers and sisters in the gospel whose words and lives have stood the test of time act as spiritual trainers to our current sanctification process. Their words and examples attend to and tend our spiritual formation. They point to the narrow way, the way of the cross. They tell of the way home, the way to the Father's house.

THE DEVELOPMENTAL NATURE OF READING
THE SPIRITUAL CLASSICS

Spiritual classics are not generally known as easy reading; they are not primers. Typically we do not start baby Christians on a diet of Augustine, the desert fathers and mothers, John of the Cross, Jonathan Edwards and Teresa of Ávila, rather we disciple them with the Word and with more contemporary writers. But why is this so? Why don't we feed these new believers the classics? Why is it that these nutrient rich spiritual resources often confound, bore and even discourage many of us when we first read them? The very characteristics that make the spiritual classics so valuable in soul care are also the very circumstances that render them so dense and seemingly unattainable.

Many of these works are ancient, and all of them are old. The spiritual classics by definition are works that have endured over time; they have been scrutinized and tested by generations of Christians and have been found to be faithful and truthful statements of spiritual essence. These works are vital in the best sense of the word: they support true life—the life of the church, the life in the Spirit. God has been transforming the church into the image of the Lord Jesus through the power of the Holy Spirit for centuries since Pentecost, and these writers have witnessed and experienced that transformation. We read the classics to find how the Bridegroom has had his way with his bride, how the Father has nourished his children, how the Chief Shepherd has cared for his flock, how the Creator has kept his creation, how the Vinedresser has husbanded his vineyard, how our Big Brother Jesus-the-firstborn has befriended his siblings, how the Holy Spirit has enlivened and enlightened the body of Christ. This is *our* family narrative; our story continues and completes the spiritual story of these witnesses.

That we need the help of older, wiser believers in order to grow in Christ is not unusual: "Be imitators of me, as I am of Christ," says the apostle Paul in 1 Corinthians 11:1. The ministry of the care of souls, soul care, has always been one of mediated grace given the progressive as well as the punctiliar nature of sanctification. Through faith in the Lord Jesus and his work on the cross, we are transferred in a moment from the "domain of darkness" into the kingdom of God's beloved Son; we are forgiven and redeemed (Col 1:13-14). And then progressively we are being saved, we are working out our salvation, for it is God who works in us, as Paul says in Philippians 2:12-13. And the ministry of soul care assists in this progressive growth, this working out of our salvation, this "childbirth" of Christ being formed in us (Gal 4:19). So the ministry of soul care then is developmentally keyed to the disciple's process of spiritual formation; it is progressively graded.

It makes sense then that some of the classic writers would sound like *non*-sense to someone in a different stage of spiritual growth. Developmentally keyed classics will fit believers differently along the various stages of growth in sanctification.

In Scripture, for example, the writer of Hebrews refers to this notion of a developmentally sensitive gradation of teaching in Hebrews 5:12–6:3

by making a clear distinction between the elementary doctrines of Christ and the milk-y foundational teachings for new believers versus the solid food for the "mature, for those who have their powers of discernment trained by constant practice to distinguish good from evil" (Heb 5:14). Therefore for those working with the very young Christians, one of the earliest of the spiritual classics, Hippolytus writing in the *Apostolic Tradition*[4] might be useful for outlining a program of soul care for those needing the teaching and enfolding work of the "basic principles of the oracles of God" (Heb 5:12). This "milk" includes such elementary doctrines as "repentance from dead works and of faith toward God, and of instruction about washings, the laying on of hands, the resurrection of the dead, and eternal judgment" (Heb 6:1-2). Clint Arnold's article "Early Church Catechesis and New Christians' Classes in Contemporary Evangelicalism" on this early discipleship process in the church is a helpful entry into the wisdom of the *Apostolic Tradition*.[5] The *Apostolic Tradition* gives a picture of how the early church instructed and enfolded the new believers, discipling them in the faith; this programmatic approach has vitality across time for the church today.

Another entry-level classic would be *The Way of the Pilgrim*, a very accessible little classic, not so far removed from us in time and space.[6] This anonymous Russian work from the 1800s tells of the quest of the Pilgrim, already a serious Christian, who, having been struck to the heart by Paul's instruction to the Thessalonians to "Pray without ceasing" (1 Thess 5:17) goes on a journey to find a spiritual father who can tell him how to pray in this manner. The Pilgrim finds a wise old father (a *starets*) who points him to a classic (*The Philokalia*) for answers, and who also instructs him in the use and reading of the classics, explaining that the classics are not more holy than the Bible, but that they assist our understanding of the Bible much as a small piece of darkened glass allows us to examine the splendor of the sun.[7] The *starets* then teaches him to

---

[4]Paul F. Bradshaw, *The Apostolic Tradition: Hermeneia, A Critical and Historical Commentary on the Bible* (Minneapolis: Augsburg Press, 2002).

[5]Clinton E. Arnold, "Early Church Catechesis and New Christians' Classes in Contemporary Evangelicalism," *Journal of the Evangelical Theological Society* 47, no. 1 (March 2004): 39-54.

[6]Anonymous, *The Way of the Pilgrim*, trans. R. M. French (San Francisco: HarperCollins, 1965).

[7]Ibid., p. 10.

practice the "Jesus Prayer," taken from the combined cries of two of the men in Luke 18, the tax collector and the blind beggar: "Lord Jesus have mercy on me, a sinner!" (Lk 18:13, 38) and then sends the Pilgrim on his way praying this prayer all day long. As the Jesus Prayer permeates the Pilgrim's life, he finds that it moves from his head to his heart, and this formative process also assists in other spiritual activities such as fighting addictions, evangelism, repentance, service, almsgiving and so on.

When my husband was fighting cancer, there were many days when praying this prayer was as high as I could reach. "Lord Jesus Christ, have mercy on us sinners," I would pray, and "Lord Jesus, have mercy," and then "Jesus, have mercy," and sometimes merely "Jesus." This "out of the depths" experience of prayer allowed me to call on the Lord continually. It became a foundation for me prompted by the Holy Spirit that gave me a means to practice the reassurance: "He is here with us, I am his, nothing can remove me from the Father's hand."

Going beyond the beginnings, for those beloved mature believers who the writer of Hebrews cites as already demonstrating things that "belong to salvation," such as vigorously serving the saints with faith and patience (Heb 6:9-12), a more fitting classic to suggest might be the rigorous nine-month training program and discernment process based on meditating on the life of Christ as presented in the Gospels that is laid out in the *Spiritual Exercises of St. Ignatius.*[8]

Reading Ignatius' *Spiritual Exercises* hand-in-hand with a trustworthy evangelical guide such as Larry Warner's *Journey with Jesus* or even Andre Ravier's more Catholic guidebook will indeed assist the mature believer in finding God in all things, as the Ignatian way promises.[9] Working through this dense material is most beneficial with a spiritual director for guidance along the way, as Warner asserts.[10]

Ignatius of Loyola wrote his *Spiritual Exercises* to train men already in the ministry. He later adapted the *Exercises* with a series of annotations

---

[8]Ignatius of Loyola, *The Spiritual Exercises*, trans. L. J. Puhl (New York: Random House, 2000).

[9]Larry Warner, *Journey with Jesus: Discovering the Spiritual Exercises of Saint Ignatius* (Downers Grove, IL: InterVarsity Press, 2010); Andre Ravier, *A Do-It-At-Home Retreat: The Spiritual Exercises of St. Ignatius of Loyal According to the "Nineteenth Annotation,"* trans. M. Buckley (San Francisco: Ignatius Press, 1991).

[10]Warner, *Journey with Jesus*, pp. 41-43.

to fit ardent laypeople as well. The *Exercises* are to be a guide for discernment of one's own calling by the Lord Jesus into deeper discipleship and service within the kingdom of God. Not for the faint of heart, the *Exercises* require either a thirty-day commitment within a guided retreat or a nine-month commitment to two hours of daily meditation on the Gospels and a regular meeting with a spiritual director. The reward of this devotional pursuit for the mature believer is a deeper discernment of the work of God and of his deep continual presence with his followers.

One of the classical understandings that the church has had for hundreds of years concerning spiritual formation and progressive sanctification is often referred to as the "threefold way."[11] This descriptor used primarily in Catholic theology refers to a developmental progression through stages of awakening, purgation, illumination and union. The transition between each of these ways is via an uncomfortable experience of a "Dark Night" period.

We Protestants understand the sanctification process differently, trusting that at initial sanctification our spirits have been joined to the Holy Spirit (1 Cor 6:17), and we work out our salvation *from* this reality of union rather than working *toward* this reality. However we do experience seasons of desolation as we grow in grace, seasons when the psalms of lament (e.g., Ps 13; 25; 88) become our truest prayer: "How long, O LORD? Will you forget me forever?" (Ps 13:1). And when our Christian journey progresses into this puzzling "dark night" phenomenon as we mature in the Lord, then the spiritual classics written by John of the Cross and Teresa of Ávila provide a welcome guide through the dark.[12] A modern guide such as Dubay's *Fire Within* aide us in using these writers fully, assisting in the discernment between a "dark night" and a bout of psychological depression (for instance) or instructing the reader in the ultimate blessings of detachment and freedom from sin which result from these times of trial.[13]

---

[11]See Benedict J. Groeschel, *Spiritual Passages: The Psychology of Spiritual Development* (New York: Crossroads, 2002), pp. 103-93.

[12]John of the Cross, *The Collected Works of St. John of the Cross*, trans. O. Rodriguez and K. Kavanaugh (Washington, DC: Institute of Carmelite Studies, 1991); Teresa of Ávila, *The Collected Works of Teresa of Ávila*, 3 vols., trans. O. Rodriguez and K. Kavanaugh (Washington, DC: Institute of Carmelite Studies, 1976, 1980, 1985).

[13]Thomas Dubay, *Fire Within: St. Teresa of Ávila, St. John of the Cross, and the Gospel—On Prayer* (San Francisco: Ignatian Press, 1989).

THE CULTURAL NATURE OF READING THE SPIRITUAL CLASSICS

One of the great benefits of reading the spiritual classics comes from the differing cultural contexts of the writings. Our cultural blindness is exposed by the voice of the classics over the years, and our cultural corporate sin is challenged. Like the overlapping circles of a Venn diagram, the unified voices of Christian testimonies from other centuries and from other cultures give us the essence of the experience of the church and allow us to reality test and judge our own experience in Christ. This is crucial in order for us to discern the blindness of our own culture in a measured manner.

We are no more commonly aware of our cultural assumptions than we are of our eyewear or of the air that we breathe. We only become conscious of these things when they are challenged. We move through our own culture like we move through air and air moves through us. We are embedded within our cultures, and our cultural view defines our perception of reality: our culture tells us what is "there." Just as eyeglasses bring things into focus, so our own culture elucidates our spiritual reality. On the other hand, the varying cultures of the spiritual classics bump up against us and out of our hearts comes a reaction, a culturally tinged reaction. Examining this is so valuable for our sanctification; being challenged by earlier believers is helpful, perhaps at times essential, in finding our cultural blind spots.

True followers of Jesus Christ must always move against their culture since we are literally "not of this world" (Jn 15:19; Rom 12:2; Jas 4:4; 1 Jn 2:15), but these standards of life are very difficult to perceive because they are part of our assumptive worldview. The classical writers unite to instruct us in countercultural living. Rather than seeking the soft rich life of Western materialism, for example, we are instructed in the joyful way of simplicity. Consider your own heart's cultural response to the story of the desert father who sold the only copy of the Gospels he owned, explaining, "I have but sold that word which ever said to me, 'Sell that thou hast and give to the poor.'"[14]

Or consider the life and teaching of Francis of Assisi, known for the richness of the gifting that the Holy Spirit poured out on him, who

---

[14]*The Desert Fathers*, trans. H. Waddell (New York: Vintage Books, 1998), p. 25.

forcefully walked away (some say, danced away) with joy from a life of inherited wealth into the life of a poor traveling missionary priest.[15] Francis's Rule instructs,

> 1. The rule and life of these brothers is this: to live in obedience, in chastity, and without anything of their own, and to follow the teaching and the footprints of our Lord Jesus Christ, Who says: 2. If you wish to be perfect, go (Mt 19:21) and sell everything (cf. Lk 18:22) you have and give it to the poor, and you will have treasure in heaven; and come, follow me.[16]

As if this suggested off-loading of possessions weren't enough to expose our cultural holdings, humility is also required to listen to these "old" voices of the spiritual classics. Scripture supports seeking the old ways of wisdom, for although our modern Western culture holds "new" as a value, and equates *new* with *worthwhile*, we know that it is a stance of wisdom to admit that we have nothing new to say: the wise preacher of Ecclesiastes assures us of this.

> What has been is what will be,
> and what has been done is what will be done,
> and *there is nothing new under the sun.*
> Is there a thing of which it is said,
> "See, this is new"?
> It has been already
> in the ages before us. (Eccles 1:9-10, emphasis added)

And so we read the classics humbly to find old, commonly shared wisdom.

Beyond the cultural challenges, though, the old classics also encourage us, sweetly telling us the things that we *all* already know. As we read more broadly in the spiritual classics, focused themes of the lived human experience of sanctification begin to emerge that *transcend culture.* Not surprisingly, the love of God is such a theme. For example, from Dame Julian of Norwich in fourteenth-century England we hear of the homely courteous manner of the love of God: "I saw that for us

---

[15]Gerald L. Sittser, *Water from a Deep Well: Christian Spirituality from Early Martyrs to Modern Missionaries* (Downers Grove, IL: InterVarsity Press, 2007), pp. 194-97.
[16]Francis of Assisi, *Francis and Claire: The Complete Works* (New York: Paulist Press, 1982), p. 109.

He is everything that is good, comforting and helpful; He is our clothing, who, for love, wraps us up, holds us close; He entirely encloses us for tender love."[17] Then we are assured by Julian that all manner of things shall be well.

Spiritual warfare is a theme. Rather than explaining away with natural means all spiritual warfare, voices as distinct as Susanna Wesley, Francis of Assisi and Teresa of Ávila tell us how to fight. Holy living and fighting temptation resounds throughout the classics. Ignatius in his instructions to the spiritual directors who lead others through the *Exercises* gives fulsome consideration to discerning the source of various movements within one's heart by attending to the times of consolation versus the times of desolation. He notes that the devil or evil spirit approaches the person differently depending on their particular state and stage of sanctification. To the morally weak, the devil tempts with the delights of sin; to the morally strong, he tempts with anxiety and scrupulosity.[18] He is alternatively a bully, a masquerader of light and always a liar. Ignatius blows the enemy's cover by exposing his schemes: "In the same way, the enemy becomes weak, loses courage, and turns to flight with his seductions as soon as one leading the spiritual life faces his temptations boldly, and does exactly the opposite of what he suggests."[19]

Suffering well is a theme. Both our humanity and our industrialized culture see suffering as an interruption to life, an intrusion to be medicated away as soon as possible. But the writers of the classics see it differently. Brother Lawrence at seventy-nine writing to a sixty-three-year-old nun counsels, "Sometimes we should ask for His grace, and sometimes we should offer Him our sufferings. . . . Let us live and die with God!"[20] And Dame Julian, having lived through the Black Plague only to endure much physical pain and suffering sounds a similar note: "All this life and this languishing that we have here is only a point, and when we are suddenly taken out of our pain into bliss, then the pain shall be nothing. . . . It is God's will that we accept His arrangements and His comforting as greatly

[17]Julian of Norwich, *The Revelation of Divine Love*, trans. M. L. del Mastro (Liguori, MO: Triumph Books, 1994), p. 67.
[18]Ignatius, *Spiritual Exercises*, p. 48.
[19]Ibid., p. 118.
[20]Brother Lawrence, *Practicing the Presence of God*, p. 72.

and strongly as we can take them."²¹ The echo of the apostle Peter's words is strong here: "Therefore let those who suffer according to God's will entrust their souls to a faithful Creator while doing good" (1 Pet 4:19).

This theme of enduring physical suffering patiently is echoed by the already-discussed theme of waiting faithfully through the spiritual suffering of the dark night of the soul. Spiritual suffering is most fully explored by John of the Cross, who views it as valuable and necessary:

> The soul must needs be in all its parts reduced to a state of emptiness, poverty and abandonment. . . . For the sensual part is purified in aridity, the faculties are purified in the emptiness of their perceptions and the spirit is purified in thick darkness. All this God brings to pass. . . . Here God greatly humbles the soul in order that He may afterwards greatly exalt it.²²

Rest and quiet are expected and valued spiritual friends in this process. Again we notice a different cultural experience and expectation: many of these classics were written before electricity cut our night hours by half and the human norm was to have time each day for prayer and meditation versus our continually available distractions of media and work and mobility. To a book, the spiritual classics assume daily time for meditation on the Scriptures and regular prayers. This is the standard of practice within the family of God through the ages.

One of the means of understanding and acquiring this cultural discernment is to use helpful auxiliary books to guide us through the cultural and theological pathways of these classics. Due to historical and theological differences, some of these classics are more nourishing if they are premetabolized for us. Indeed sometimes a first reading does knock us off our foundation internally, and when this happens it is indicative of a developmentally inappropriate book for solitary reading. At this point we need a guide. For example, Grace Jantzen's book on Julian of Norwich illuminates the sometimes puzzling life of this powerful woman who followed God powerfully; Thomas Dubay provides invaluable coherence to John of the Cross and Teresa of Ávila for twenty-first-century Westerners; Olivier Clement's *The Roots of Christian Mysticism* opens the door to the

---

²¹Julian of Norwich, *Revelation of Divine Love*, pp. 176-77.
²²John of the Cross, *Dark Night of the Soul*, trans. A. Peers (New York: Doubleday, 1989), pp. 105-7, 152-56.

potentially cryptic writings of the Cappadocian Fathers and the *Philokalia* within the first few hundred years of the church.[23] Current voices can help us read with more care and with discernment.

USING THE SPIRITUAL CLASSICS TODAY

For those of us who minister as pastors, counselors, spiritual directors or disciplers, the spiritual classics are a rich resource.

When discipling a young believer in this turbulent world, Benedict's notion of a rule of life gives a profound template for godly living. Esther de Waal tells us in her excellent book on St. Benedict that Benedict wrote his Rule for his brother monks in the early 500s when the civilized world was falling apart around him, when the fall of Rome and the barbarian invasions were the order of the day.[24] De Waal characterizes Benedict's Rule as a sturdy ark of safety, which was "to contain a family" and which set up the standards for community life in the church.[25] Discerning and setting up a personal rule clarifies priorities and assists in practicing the disciplines. For centuries the standard of Benedict's Rule has provided a model for Christians to live humble, obedient, productive lives together, continually seeking a deeper conversion of life in Christ.

When ministering in spiritual direction with a more mature follower of Jesus who is growing steadily into the deeper life in Christ, Teresa of Ávila might be a better resource and companion. When I first approached Teresa's writings I was in my late teens. Like a child eavesdropping on the late-night conversation of the company of adults in the other room, I was enticed by her words, yet I only half-understood her concepts on spiritual growth. I was frustrated in my reading even as I leaned in closer to try and comprehend her thoughts. It took me four attempts over years to read the *Interior Castle* with a fuller degree of comprehension, but now even her letters and other writings on prayer are treasured companions.[26] Teresa's writings are for her beloved spir-

---

[23]Grace M. Jantzen, *Julian of Norwich: Mystic and Theologian* (New York: Paulist Press, 1988); Dubay, *Fire Within*; Oliver Clement, *The Roots of Christian Mysticism* (New York: New City Press, 1995); *The Philokalia*, vols.1-4, trans. K. Ware and P. Sherrard (London: Faber & Faber, 1979, 1982, 1986, 1999).
[24]Esther de Waal, *Seeking God: The Way of St. Benedict* (Collegeville, MN: Liturgical Press, 1984).
[25]Ibid., p. 19.
[26]Teresa of Ávila, *Interior Castle*, trans. A. Peers (Radford, VA: Wilder Publications, 2008).

itual daughters and sisters, and her focus is on the deeper stages of prayer and intimacy in their devotional life with the indwelling Trinity.

For those in pastoral ministry, one of the richest resources is found in the Wesleys. The writings of the Wesley family can be used similarly to those of Benedict, and as fellow Protestants they are more immediately palatable. Beginning with Susanna Wesley (one of my personal heroines of the faith) and continuing through the multitudinous writings of John and the sung theology of Charles, this family casts a brilliant light on the spiritual formation and soul care process.

Wondering how to teach Christian parenting? Read pastor's wife Susanna's letters and journals on how to disciple nineteen (!) children and grieve the deaths of nine of them, how to remain faithful in a difficult marriage, to pray and preach from the kitchen, to obey the lordship of Christ even as a strong-willed woman.[27] Working with lay leaders who need to learn how to grow in grace and faith in the work of Christ on the cross even when their internal performance judge is accusing them nonstop? When they never quite reach their idealized goals, and when they fail miserably and publically in ministry? Read the writings and histories of John and Charles and get together a small covenant group and employ the "method" of the Methodists to grow in Christlikeness![28] The writings of these saints are a rich vein of wealth which we may mine quite easily today. Their Protestant life and culture is not so far removed from our own, and their writings translate easily into our praxis.

CONCLUDING THOUGHTS

In the end it is not so much that we read the spiritual classics, but that they read us; it is our life and our formative process that is descriptively illuminated by these ancient voices. They train us in discernment, teaching us to hear and recognize the voice of the Holy Spirit to the church over time, the voice that is still speaking to us today. Reading the ancients fights arrogance—it cries "Help me, instruct me." This reading

---

[27]Susanna Wesley, *The Complete Writings*, ed. C. Wallace Jr. (Oxford: Oxford University Press, 1997).

[28]John Wesley and Charles Wesley, *John and Charles Wesley: Selected Prayers, Hymns, Journal Notes, Sermons, Letters, and Treatises*, ed. F. Whaling (New York: Paulist Press, 1981). On Christlikeness, see ibid., pp. 134-45.

rests upon the nonarrogant assumption that our experience is not sin-
gularly unique or strange or alien, but that it reflects normal family re-
semblance and growth patterns. We are part of the body of Christ. We
find as we study, that there is a normal developmental trajectory of
growth within Christ; and that the Holy Spirit has been working in this
way and revealing this process to the church for centuries. Over many
years and in strange languages, we hear the Father's voice, we recognize
the family dialect, and we recognize the same formative sanctification
process through different cultural screens.

Due to the historical and cultural strangeness of many of these
writings, it is beneficial to practice hospitality as we read: to entertain
these ideas as guests. As with guests, you may not appreciate or benefit
from all they say, but give them prayerful space and consideration for a
time. Listen for the common family-of-God dialect in their words. In all
of our interactions with the classics, our purpose in reading is not just to
"know" them or even to "know about" them, but also to "do" them. *We
read for the purpose of formation and transformation.*

We turn to the spiritual classics to give us insights into the way that
God works in his people and the way in which he calls his people to
work.[29] We investigate the praxis of ministry: preaching, counseling,
praying, almsgiving, evangelizing and discipling. We come with questions to those ahead of us on the journey, we bring queries to the texts
concerning what believers do to grow in Christ, and how the church has
viewed the Christian life. We compare their lifestyle to our own and
prayerfully ponder the differences. We look for the main and plain path
of the narrow way in order to walk in it, following the footsteps of our
sisters and brothers that overlay the footsteps of our Lord as we walk
into the increasing light of the dawn of the day of the Lord.

The path of the righteous is like the light of dawn,
    which shines brighter and brighter until full day. (Prov 4:18)

---

[29]Obviously in this chapter I have referred to only a very few of the spiritual classics. The other
chapters in this book will give you a wider view, and two published series of spiritual classics
that will give you an excellent range of this material are The Vintage Spiritual Classics published
by Random House, and the immense Classics of Western Spirituality published by Paulist
Press. I commend them both to you as good sources for the original autographs.

PART TWO

The Spiritual Classics
Tradition

4

The Schools of
Christian Spirituality

Evan B. Howard

CLASSICS AND SCHOOLS

Christian spiritual classics are written by people located in space and time. They arise from a particular region or era, and their sense of relationship with God reflects something of that region or era. For example, we can describe Angela of Foligno's spirituality as "Italian," as "Medieval," as "Roman Catholic," as "Franciscan" and as "visionary." Insofar as a spiritual classic reflects identifiable patterns of thought or experience (whether regional, doctrinal, experiential, etc.) we can think of these classics as expressions of distinct forms of Christian spirituality. These forms can be divided into basic types: *lay* spirituality, *schools* of spirituality and *countermovements*.[1] Lay forms of spirituality express the life of primary dwelling communities. Countermovements exist outside recognized structures of spiritual life. A school of spirituality describes a certain approach to or community of faith which brings together features of the spiritual life into an organic whole and communicates them to future generations of recognized followers.[2] Some of the Christian

---

[1] See Kees Waaijman, *Spirituality: Forms, Foundations, Methods*, trans. John Vriend (Leuven: Peeters, 2002), pp. 9-212.

[2] See Adolphe Tanquerey, *The Spiritual Life: A Treatise on Ascetical and Mystical Theology*, 2nd rev. ed. (Tournai, Belgium: Desclée, 1938); Pierre Pourrat, *Christian Spirituality*, 4 vols., trans. William Henry Mitchell and S. P. Jacques (London: Burns, Oates and Washbourne, 1922);

spiritual classics were written while an expression was a counter-movement and only later were recognized as expressions of a recognized school of spirituality, while others were summaries of well-respected schools of spirituality. Some people speak about "schools" in terms of basic divisions of spirituality (Protestant, Catholic, Orthodox), while others focus on smaller subdivisions (such as Alexandrian, Vincentian or Keswick). The remainder of this chapter will take a middle ground, introducing a few schools of Christian spirituality recognized by one or another of the larger divisions of the Christian church.[3]

SURVEY OF SELECT SCHOOLS

Desert spirituality. The movement of men and women who relocated to the deserts of Egypt, Syria and Palestine in the fourth century might better be regarded as a countermovement than a school. Nonetheless, by the end of the fifth century no one could deny the existence of a distinct approach to relationship with God associated with the deserts of the Near East, which brought together features of the spiritual life into an organic whole and communicated them to future generations of recognized followers.

It is best to identify the birth of the desert tradition as a *school* of spirituality with the publication and popularity of Athanasius's *Life of Antony* (written somewhere between 356 and 362).[4] This account of the life of one of the primary figures of the desert movement stimulated a wave of interest in this expression. Many withdrew to the desert in an effort to imitate Antony's solitary pursuit of God, and other believers sought to express a similar form of life through alternative desert communities. The vision of desert life rapidly spread throughout the Christian world. Collections of the lives and sayings of the desert elders

---

Lucian Marie de Saint Joseph, "École de Spiritualité," in *Dictionnaire De Spiritualité: Ascétique Et Mystique, Doctrine Et Histoire*, ed. Marcel Viller, Charles Baumgartner and André Rayez, vol. 4 (Paris: G. Beauchesne et ses fils, 1960), cols. 116-28; and Waaijman, *Spirituality*, pp. 117-211.
[3]Space does not permit treatment of the Teutonic schools, the Radical Reformation, American Transcendentalism and other movements.
[4]See Athanasius, *The Life of Antony and the Letter to Marcellinus*, trans. Robert C. Gregg, Classics of Western Spirituality (New York: Paulist Press, 1980). This chapter will only be providing select resources for each tradition. For fuller lists of resources, see the chapter(s) associated with each school.

became spiritual classics in their own time, inspiring the foundation of many "desert" expressions of spiritual life.[5]

Though there were a variety of influences present in the development of desert spirituality, one common element was a worldview which saw human life as the nexus of a transformative work of God. The desert tradition looked toward both the participation in and the embodiment of the life of Christ. It modeled—for a crumbling society—an alternative way of life rooted in the values of simplicity, purity and humility. It confronted demonic opposition through prayer, watchful self-examination and accountable relationships. While profound experience of God was acknowledged, the desert tradition was careful to avoid privileging one particular type of spiritual encounter. These features are present not only in the early expressions of desert spirituality but have also characterized later representatives of the desert school such as Martin of Tours (d. c. 397), Romuald (c. 950-1027), Sergius of Radonez (c. 1314-1392), Thomas Merton (1915-1968), and Eve Baker, who founded the Fellowship of Solitaries in 1990.[6]

A number of classics have emerged from the influence of desert spirituality. In addition to the examples already mentioned, a few others are worthy of note. John Cassian's fourth-century *Monastic Institutes* transmits desert life to the Latin world. The hymns and discourses of Symeon the New Theologian (949-1022) express similar themes in the context of the Byzantine world. The *Philokalia*, a collection of the "best of" spiritual literature in the Orthodox church, is steeped in the desert tradition. The life of solitude is being explored anew today and is worth considering as representative of the school of desert spirituality.[7]

---

[5]For example, Norman Russell, trans., *The Lives of the Desert Fathers: The Historia Monachorum in Aegypto*, Cistercian Studies Series (Kalamazoo, MI: Cistercian Publications, 1980); Palladius, *The Lausaic History of Palladius* (Willits, CA: Eastern Orthodox Books, n.d.); and John Cassian, *John Cassian: The Conferences*, trans. Boniface Ramsey, Ancient Christian Writers (New York: Paulist Press, 1997).

[6]For an introduction to the early desert tradition see William Harmless, *Desert Christians: An Introduction to the Literature of Early Monasticism* (New York: Oxford University Press, 2004).

[7]John Cassian, *The Monastic Institutes* (London: Saint Austin Press, 1999); Symeon the New Theologian, *The Discourses*, Classics of Western Spirituality (New York: Paulist Press, 1980); Symeon the New Theologian, *Hymns of Divine Love* (Denville, NJ: Dimension Books, 1976); Nicodemus the Hagiorite and Makarios, Metropolitan of Corinth, compilers, *The Philokalia: The Complete Text*, trans. and ed. G. E. H. Palmer, Philip Sherrard and Kallistos Diokleia (London: Faber

The Augustinian/Dominican School. While desert spirituality cannot be identified with a single founder, Augustinian spirituality is rooted in the life and works of a single man. If we were to date the origin of the Augustinian School, it would be perhaps best be identified with Augustine's ordination as bishop in 395, the time at which the wider world came to recognize his authority and influence. Augustine was the founder of a monastic community and author of a vast corpus of theological and devotional writings, some of which are considered among the most significant classics of Christian spirituality.[8] Augustinian spirituality is influenced by desert spirituality—Augustine's conversion was stimulated by a reading of the *Life of Antony*—yet bears the distinct stamp of Augustine's own personal and theological development: an inward turn, a practical realism, an emphasis on love, a musing on trinitarian themes, a story of conversion.

Augustinian ideas were pervasive in Western Christianity throughout the early Middle Ages. The Augustinian vision of community life and service was taken up by what became identified in the eleventh century as "canons": clergy who lived in community according to a quasi-monastic Rule, yet devoted themselves to the service of local congregations. In 1139 a council declared that regular canons would follow the Rule of Augustine. The canons' pastoral vision, sense of common life, moderate intentionality, flexibility and balance of prayer and action all carry the Augustinian spirituality of late antiquity into the church life of the Middle Ages.

Dominic de Guzman, at the start of the thirteenth century, served as canon regular in his native diocese of Osma, and it was from these Augustinian roots that he founded the Order of Preachers, also known as the Dominicans. Like Augustine, Dominic found himself involved in theological controversy and the defense of the faith. Like Augustine, Dominican ministry was primarily urban. As with Augustinian spirituality, a balance of prayer, study and action characterize Dominican life. Dominicans, following the lead of the canons and of Augustine's early community

---

and Faber, 1979–1995); Paul A. Fredette and Karen Karper Fredette, *Consider the Ravens: On Contemporary Hermit Life* (New York: iUniverse, 2008).
[8]See Augustine, *Augustine of Hippo, Selected Writings*, Classics of Western Spirituality (New York: Paulist Press, 1984).

of priests, has been centered around apostolic preaching: Dominicans are the Order of *Preachers*. A wide variety of classics have flowered from Dominican sources, such as Catherine of Siena's *Dialogues* (1347-1380), Meister Eckhart's essays and sermons (c. 1260-1327), and Bartolomé de Las Casas's defense of the rights of native populations (c. 1484-1566).[9]

The Benedictine School. Like the Augustinian School, the Benedictine School points to a single founder at its origin. Benedict of Nursia (c. 480-c. 550) was, after a season of solitude, sought out by disciples and founded a network of monasteries. After being sent out from these monasteries, he moved on to Monte Cassino, where for the last years of his life he founded another monastery, converted and cared for his surrounding region, and wrote his Rule for monks. It is this Rule, and the communities established in relationship to this Rule, which are the center of the Benedictine School of spirituality. Whereas the Augustinian School of spirituality associates itself with a large corpus of Augustine's thought and writings, the Benedictine School is essentially a school of one classic. Yet this classic has proved to be one of the most influential documents in Christian spiritual history.[10]

Benedictine spirituality expresses a way of living together, a way of ordering a community around the virtues and worship of Christ. Upon entrance, Benedictines commit to a few key values: stability (persevering with the community), conversion (an intention to change one's habits such that they fit an authentic expression of an individual's relationship with God in the context of community life), and obedience (ultimately, a surrender of one's will to the community and more particularly to the abbot). These values are characteristic not only of Benedictine monks but of the wider school of Benedictine spirituality nourished by the Rule of Benedict. Benedictine spirituality is also characterized by a sense of rhythm, the division of the day between prayer, study, manual labor and,

---

[9]On Dominican spirituality see Simon Tugwell, *Early Dominicans: Selected Writings*, Classics of Western Spirituality (New York: Paulist Press, 1982); and Phyllis Zagano and Thomas C. McGonigle, *The Dominican Tradition*, Spirituality in History Series (Collegeville, MN: Liturgical Press, 2006).

[10]Benedict of Nursia, *RB 1980: The Rule of St. Benedict in Latin and English with Notes*, ed. Timothy Fry (Collegeville, MN: Liturgical Press, 1981). See also Lowrie J. Daly, *Benedictine Monasticism: Its Formation and Development Through the 12th Century* (New York: Sheed & Ward, 1965).

at times, service to others. The regular pattern of prayer throughout the day (the Divine Office) is central to Benedictine life. Benedictine-shaped communities have frequently been self-supporting, nurturing the values of creative work and relationship with the land. Finally, hospitality to guests is another feature of Benedictine life which has enriched travelers in the past and spiritual seekers in the present.

A few classics have emerged from the communities associated with the Rule of Benedict. First of all is the *Rule of Benedict* itself. The Rule of Benedict is, along with the Rules of Basil, Augustine, Columba and Francis, one of the primary documents of Christian monastic life. Gregory's (c. 540-604) *Life of Benedict* is also something of a classic. Hildegard of Bingen (1098-1179) was a Benedictine abbess, and her works reflect the Benedictine milieu. A number of Cistercians have written classics, such as Bernard of Clairvaux's (1090-1153) *On the Love of God* and Aelred of Rievaulx's (1109-1167) treatise *On Friendship*.[11]

Spiritualities of the British Isles. Under this heading are grouped three separate expressions—Celtic spirituality, the English mystics, and Anglican spirituality—all of which emerged in the British Isles. Of these, the first may be the only one to which a founder can be identified. Patrick, apostle to the Irish, evangelized Ireland in the fifth century, planting monasteries and pioneering an approach to relationship with God that would be further developed by succeeding generations of disciples. Missionaries like Columba (c. 521-597) and Columbanus (d. 615), movements such as the eighth-century Culdee reform, and texts such as the Stowe Missal helped to voice a spirituality that was uniquely Celtic even after the Irish church submitted to Roman leadership in the twelfth century.

Celtic spirituality carries forward, in a Christian expression, elements of Celtic culture more generally: an interest in incantation, a value for the education of children and a sense of identification with nature. Celtic Christianity was centered in the monastery, unlike the European diocesan structure, and it often emphasized a rigorous asceticism. Whereas desert spirituality emphasized withdrawal, Celtic spirituality emphasized missionary advance. It is thoroughly trinitarian, frequently

---

[11]For an overview of the spirituality of the Benedictine school, see Laura Swan, *The Benedictine Tradition*, Spirituality in History Series (Collegeville, MN: Liturgical Press, 2007).

calling upon Father, Son and Spirit in turn to accompany those who offer prayer. Finally, Celtic spirituality honors the ordinary, blessing the most mundane of daily tasks. Celtic classics include biographies such as Patrick's *Confessions*, liturgical texts such as the *Stowe Missal*, monastic texts such as the *Rule of Columba* and a delightful collections of prayers, incantations and poetry.[12]

The term *English mystics* identifies the works of four independent writers in fourteenth-century England: Richard Rolle (1300-1349), the unknown author of the *Cloud of Unknowing*, Walter Hilton (c. 1343-1396), and Julian of Norwich (c. 1342-c. 1416). While independent writers, they write with some common elements: they all write in English, pioneering the use of vernacular for devotional works; they write as individuals for individuals, often writing either as a hermit or for one living a solitary form of life; and they write with a simple directness—basic and experiential spirituality for nontheologians. Richard Rolle's *Fire of Love*, the *Cloud of Unknowing*, Walter Hilton's *The Scale of Perfection* and Julian of Norwich's *Revelations of Divine Love* are all considered classics.[13]

Anglican spirituality, like English mystics, does not identify a group of followers around a single leader or origin. Nonetheless the term does refer to a generations-long way of understanding relationship with God. In one sense Anglican spirituality is a spirituality of one classic. The *Book of Common Prayer*, in its various editions, is perhaps the most influential liturgical document of the past five centuries. The essential characteristics of Anglican spirituality emerge from an acquaintance with this document. Anglican spirituality is "common" spirituality, a spirituality for common people, and for the people gathered together in common. The aim is to make Christian worship accessible to all and expressed by all within a common life. Though Protestant in its reduction of the sacraments to two, the prayer book is Catholic in its celebration of each stage and situation of life (birth, baptism, confirmation, marriage, ordination, reconciliation, Eucharist, sickness, death). An-

---

[12]For an overview of Celtic spirituality see Oliver Davies and Thomas O'Loughlin, *Celtic Spirituality*, Classics of Western Spirituality (New York: Paulist Press, 1999).

[13]See Clifton Wolters, "The English Mystics," in *The Study of Spirituality*, ed. Cheslyn Jones, Geoffrey Wainwright and Edward Yarnold (New York: Oxford University Press, 1986), pp. 328-37.

glican spirituality also tends to be a spirituality of intention. Through morning and evening prayer, the confessions, the collects, and the prayers for various occasions, Anglicans repeatedly voice their intention to live a Christ-worthy life. Other classics associated with Anglican spirituality are the poetry of George Herbert (1593-1633), William Law's (1686-1761) *Serious Call to a Devout and Holy Life*, Jeremy Taylor's (1613-1667) *Rule and Exercise of Holy Living (and Holy Dying)*, and William Temple's (1881-1944) *Christianity and Social Order*.[14]

Franciscan spirituality. Perhaps more than any other, the Franciscan School reflects the spirituality of its founder, Francis of Assisi (1181/2-1226). Furthermore, whereas the Augustinian and Benedictine schools developed out of an appropriation for the writings of their founders, Franciscan spirituality looks particularly to the *life* of their founder to shape their form of relationship with God. Indeed, the most characteristic classics of Franciscan spirituality, from Thomas of Celano's first *Life of Blessed Francis* (1229) to Franco Zeffirelli's movie *Brother Sun, Sister Moon* (1973), are biographies of Francis. Francis's life is a profound inspiration to wholehearted gospel living. The Franciscan Orders grew quickly from a collection of twelve men governed by a simple rule of faith to one of the largest and most influential forces of the thirteenth century.[15]

Franciscan spirituality is distinguished foremost by its emphasis on simple gospel obedience. Francis wanted most of all just to live like Jesus, a community of brothers without possessions or positions, wandering or working as needed, always eager to proclaim the good news in word and deed. Francis also had a particular love for Lady Poverty, and those who followed him were obliged to honor that love, however differently they understood their practice. Franciscans, like Dominicans, were traveling mendicants, not cloistered monks. And like Dominicans, the Franciscans joined radical living with an equally radical com-

[14]For Anglican spirituality see *The Book of Common Prayer and Administration of the Sacraments and Other Rites and Ceremonies of the Church: Together with the Psalter or Psalms of David* (New York: Church Hymnal Corporation, 1979); and Paul V. Marshall, "Anglican Spirituality," in *Protestant Spiritual Traditions*, ed. Frank C. Senn (New York: Paulist Press, 1986), pp. 125-64.
[15]For the life of Francis see Julien Green, *God's Fool: The Life and Times of Francis of Assisi* (San Francisco: Harper & Row, 1985). On the development of the Franciscan Order see John R. H. Moorman, *A History of the Franciscan Order from Its Origins to the Year 1517* (Oxford: Clarendon Press, 1968).

mitment to the church. Yet whereas the Dominican School emphasized the life of *mission*, Franciscans pursued a missionary *life*. The Franciscan School of spirituality has reflected these values throughout its history. Franciscan liberation theologian Leonardo Boff, for example, blends a missionary vision for the restoration of Latin American people with a respect for the radical life of Francis and a personal commitment of identification with the poor.

A number of classics have their origins within the Franciscan School. In addition to the early *Lives* written by Thomas of Celano and Bonaventure, one must mention the popular fourteenth-century *Fioretti or Little Flowers of St. Francis*, which narrates a number of stories of Francis's life. Many of the works of Bonaventure (c. 1217-1274), Minister General of the Franciscan Order from 1257-1273, are considered classics, in particular his essays on *The Soul's Journey into God, The Tree of Life* and *The Triple Way*. Mystics (for example, Angela of Foligno, 1248-1309), missionaries (such as Junípero Serra, 1713-1784) and martyrs (like Maximillian Kolbe, 1894-1941) have all claimed association with Francis.[16]

Lutheran/Pietist spirituality. The Lutheran/Pietist School of spirituality originated with the thought and actions of its founder Martin Luther. Yet it was much more the seed and fruit of the near-spontaneous emergence of a general reformation of the church. Whereas Augustinian, Benedictine, Franciscan and Dominican spiritualities are lived, for the most part, within exclusive communities of believers, the group of Luther's followers at Wittenberg and elsewhere sought to transform the way *all* Christians understood and practiced their relationship with God. The Protestant Reformation was not only about theology but also spirituality. Reformation spirituality was an intentional break from the mechanics of late medieval popular spirituality, from the corruption (as well as some of the fundamental distinctives) of late medieval monastic spirituality, from the speculations of late medieval scholastic spirituality and from the institutions of late medieval ecclesial spirituality.[17]

---

[16]See Regis J. Armstrong and Ingrid J. Peterson, *The Franciscan Tradition*, Spirituality in History (Collegeville, MN: Liturgical Press, 2010).

[17]See Evan B. Howard, "What Did the Protestants Protest? Reflections on the Context of Reformation Spirituality as a 'Break' with Roman Catholicism," Evangelical Scholars in Christian Spirituality, 1993, www.evangelicalspirituality.org/papers/otherpapers/protprot.

Three distinct schools of spirituality (Lutheran/Pietist, Reformed/Puritan, Ignatian/Jesuit) and a fourth less distinctly identifiable school (Radical Reformation expressions) emerged in this milieu, each transmitting their original character into slightly altered forms as the centuries brought new challenges. Martin Luther, in his 1517 "Ninety-five Theses," condemned the sale of indulgences, contrasting the treasures of the church with the wealth of the gospel. Through his translation of the Bible into German and through the reformation of the mass, he made that gospel available to the ordinary Christian, a spirituality of hearing the Word through faith, enriched by the singing of hymns. Through his own marriage and his catechism, he made family life a center of spiritual growth. These are primary characteristics of Lutheran spirituality. Luther was a reformer, a theologian and a student of Scripture. A few of his writings, like his treatise on *The Freedom of a Christian* and his little *A Simple Way to Pray*, written to his barber, can be considered spiritual classics.

Nonetheless, while his interest was in the spiritual life of believers, Luther's writing was caught up in the doctrinal controversies of the time. In the seventeenth and eighteenth centuries, however, the significance of Lutheran thought for spiritual life was taken up more directly and Pietism emerged as a fresh expression of Lutheran spirituality. Pietism applied Lutheran interests to the lives of believers. They fostered the hearing of the Word in faith through small group Bible studies. They clarified the nature of faith—a faith which is not merely intellectual assent but also a trust of the heart—through a renewed emphasis on repentance and rebirth. They encouraged the expression of faith in love through a variety of compassionate ministries. A number of classics, such as Johann Arndt's *True Christianity* (1606) and Philip Spener's *Pia Desideria* (1675) were written during this period.[18]

The Reformed/Puritan School. Whereas the Lutheran/Pietist School emerged from the reforming impulse in a primarily German setting, the Reformed/Puritan School emerged from the reforming impulse in

---

[18]For Martin Luther see Martin Luther, *Luther's Spirituality*, ed. Philip D. Krey and Peter D. S. Krey, Classics of Western Spirituality (Mahwah, NJ: Paulist Press, 2007). For Pietism see *Pietists, Selected Writings*, trans. and ed. Peter C. Erb, Classics of Western Spirituality (New York: Paulist Press, 1983).

Switzerland, France and the British Isles. And while the influence of
John Calvin (1509-1564) looms large, the school developed through the
interaction of a number of figures and forces. Like the Lutheran School,
the Reformed School arose in reaction to the state of the Roman church
of the time. And like the Lutheran School, it was nurtured (to some
extent) within the protection of the state. The emphases on Scripture,
faith and a simplified worship are common to both. Yet where Lutheran
spirituality is hesitant about the role of the law for Christians, the Reformed School finds in the law a valuable guide for the life of faith.
Where the Reformed School might be cautious about the role of externals (buildings, icons, sacramental elements and such), Lutherans
see such externals as the manifestation of God's presence. The Reformed School tends to be more explicit about the Holy Spirit's ministry among believers, and about the importance of knowledge.[19]

As with Germany, the early generations of Reformation in Switzerland
and France were caught up in doctrinal issues. Yet as the genre of sermon
collections developed, and as the Calvinist stream of thought made its way
into the Netherlands and the British Isles, new expressions of the Reformed
School blossomed. Puritans began to encourage intentional spiritual practices inspired by the principles of Calvinist teaching. Devotional manuals
such as Bayly's *The Practice of Piety* (3rd ed., 1613) followed Calvin's
structure of knowledge of God and of ourselves to guide the believer into
maturity. Reworked sermon/essays such as American Puritan Thomas
Shepard's *The Parable of the Ten Virgins Unfolded* (1659) brought biblical
exposition and Reformed theological explication together in one spiritual
text. John Bunyan's *Pilgrim's Progress* (1678) shared spiritual wisdom
through the vehicle of a pilgrimage story. Puritan spirituality took Calvinist theology regarding the transforming work of the Spirit of God and
taught the believer how to facilitate, notice and respond to this work.[20]

The Ignatian/Jesuit School. With Ignatian/Jesuit spirituality we return

---

[19]For Calvin's spirituality see John Calvin, *The Soul of Life: The Piety of John Calvin*, ed. Joel R.
Beeke, Profiles in Reformed Spirituality (Grand Rapids: Reformation Heritage Books, 2009).
For Reformed spirituality more generally see Howard G. Hageman, "Reformed Spirituality," in
Protestant Spiritual Traditions, ed. Frank C Senn (New York: Paulist Press, 1986), pp. 55-79.
[20]For Puritan spirituality see E. Glenn Hinson, "Puritan Spirituality," in *Protestant Spiritual Tradi-
tions* (New York: Paulist Press, 1986), pp. 165-82.

once again to a spirituality of a particular religious community inspired by the leadership and writings of a single founder, Ignatius of Loyola (c. 1491-1556). Ignatius's own story bears some similarity to that of Francis of Assisi: an eager and self-seeking youth powerfully confronted by God. Ignatius saw his early followers as a *Compañía de Jesús*, a military "company" for Jesus (translated "Society of Jesus"). Their aim was to labor for the propagation of the faith and the help of souls, especially through the use of Ignatius's *Spiritual Exercises*, a guide to personal retreat and formation. Often using education as a base of operation, the Jesuits evangelized, offered mercy to those in need, heard confessions and gave retreats through the *Exercises*. Although suppressed by the Roman Catholic Church in the later seventeenth century and the persecuted in the eighteenth century by Enlightenment European leadership, the Jesuits today are one of the largest religious orders in the Roman Catholic Church.[21]

The Ignatian/Jesuit School of spirituality reflects the chivalric character of Ignatius himself, the unique perspective of the *Spiritual Exercises* and the bold missionary vision of the order. Ignatian spirituality is characterized by a sensitivity to the nuances of Christian discernment. Ignatian spirituality is rooted in engagement with the mystery of God, which the *Exercises* are structured to provide. The combination of regular meditation on Scripture and regular self-examination is critical and characteristic of Jesuit life and spirituality. Finally, there is the rhythm of retreat and service. Jesuit life is a life of active service, and nourishing one's vision for that service is an important part of Ignatian spirituality. Yet at the same time there is the need for retreat: daily self-examination, frequent communion and more extended retreats at least once a year. Jesuit classics include the *Spiritual Exercises*, Ignatius's *Autobiography*, Jean Pierre de Caussade's (1675-1751) *Abandonment to Divine Providence* (also called *The Sacrament of the Present Moment*, a work which bears as much affinity with the French School as with the Ignatian School), and the poetry of Gerard Manley Hopkins (1844-1889).[22]

---

[21]For Ignatius and the early development of the Society of Jesus, see Ignatius of Loyola, *Ignatius of Loyola: The Spiritual Exercises and Selected Works*, ed. George E. Ganss, Classics of Western Spirituality (New York: Paulist Press, 1991); and John W. O'Malley, *The First Jesuits* (Cambridge, MA: Harvard University Press, 1993).

[22]See Kevin F. Burke and Eileen Burke-Sullivan, *The Ignatian Tradition*, Spirituality in History (Collegeville, MN: Liturgical Press, 2009).

The Carmelite School. The Carmelite School is unique among the schools of spirituality in that its character today owes more to later developments in the community than its origins. While the Carmelites began as a community of contemplative hermits in the Holy Land, they eventually moved to Europe in the thirteenth century, dwelling in small communities, traveling for pastoral missions and gaining positions in the universities. In time, some of the Carmelites longed for the contemplative solitude of their origins.[23]

The most influential single figures in Carmelite history appeared in the sixteenth and still later in the nineteenth centuries. Doña Teresa de Ahumada, a nun at Ávila founded in 1562 the first community of discalced (barefoot) Carmelites. Teresa of Ávila (1515-1582), and John of the Cross (1542-1591), her partner in the reform of the order, contributed significantly to a Carmelite return to their contemplative roots. Thérèse of Lisieux (1873-1897) modeled in her life, and in her posthumously published *Story of a Soul,* a simplicity of faith, which has had an enduring affect on the Carmelite Order and beyond.

It is this tension between the contemplative and the active, love for God and for others, that most characterizes Carmelite life. The contemplative impulse, either in its early monastic format, or later in Teresa of Avila's or John of the Cross's more modern sense of individual perceptual experience of God, or even in Thérèse of Lisieux's "little way" of devotion, is given high regard in the Carmelite School. And yet this emphasis on contemplation is often accompanied by pastoral concern. Our marriage with Christ is expressed in love for others. As Thérèse of Lisieux put it, "it is love alone that counts." Along with the brief Carmelite *Rule* and the *Institutions of the First Monks,* the works of Teresa of Avila, John of the Cross, and Thérèse of Lisieux are to be regarded as the classics of the Carmelite tradition.[24]

The French School, "Quietism" and other related expressions. The

---

[23]For the origins and development of the Carmelite order see Frances Andrews, *The Other Friars: The Carmelite, Augustinian, Sack and Pied Friars in the Middle Ages* (Woodbridge, UK: Boydell Press, 2006), pp. 7-68.

[24]See John Welch, *The Carmelite Way: An Ancient Path for Today's Pilgrim* (New York: Paulist Press, 1996) and Keith J. Egan, "Carmelite Spirituality," in *The New Dictionary of Catholic Spirituality*, ed. Michael Downey (Collegeville, MN: Liturgical Press, 1993), pp. 117-24.

term *French School*, or the *Berullian School*, properly refers to a circle of figures in seventeenth-century France who revitalized both the priesthood and the popular spirituality of the day. Pierre de Bérulle (1575-1629) founded the French Oratory in 1611, dedicated to the improvement of clergy life and image. Through her leadership and letters, Madeline St. Joseph (1578-1637) worked in concert with Bérulle to clarify and promote their understanding of the ways of the soul. Others like Jean-Jacques Olier (1608-1657) and John Eudes (1601-1680) were also part of this circle: writing, pastoring and working for the renewal of the spiritual life more generally. Christ, Mary and individual interiority are common themes in the French School. Their works offer, at times, an almost scientific analysis to the life of the soul.[25]

Others, like Francis de Sales (1567-1622), Jane Frances de Chantal (1572-1641) and Vincent de Paul (c. 1580-1660) had association with this group, adapting the French School approach to relationship with God both for the laity and in the context of active service. Classics that arose from this circle include Francis de Sales' *Introduction to the Devout Life*, and the letters of spiritual direction between de Sales and Jane de Chantal. The Sisters of Charity, founded by Vincent de Paul, was the first congregation of women who were not enclosed. They were entirely dedicated to the care of the sick and poor, and their foundational documents are classics of religious life. Brother Lawrence's *The Practice of the Presence of God*, communicating an approach to simple prayer, which is at least indirectly connected with the French School, was also collected during this period.

Some took the emphasis on individual interiority to extremes. Spanish spiritual director Miguel de Molinos (c. 1640-1696) stressed the significance of Teresa of Ávila's "prayer of quiet" to the degree that exterior matters such as almsgiving, confession, ascetical practices, temptations and such had little importance. Portions of the works of Madame Guyon (1648-1717) and François Fénelon (1651-1715) came under condemnation by the Catholic authorities as "Quietist" literature. Later Jean Pierre de Caussade (1675-1751), Jean Nicholas Grou (1731-1803) and others rekindled

---

[25]On the French School proper see *Bérulle and the French School: Selected Writings*, ed. William M. Thompson-Uberuaga, trans. Lowell M. Glendon, Classics of Western Spirituality (Mahwah, NJ: Paulist Press, 1989).

an appreciation for interior prayer in the midst of post-Quietist Catholicism. These writers all minimized the role of the particular techniques of prayer in an effort to highlight the significance of one's simple surrender of will in prayer and in life. From these French writers we find such classics as Madame Guyon's *Life* and her *Short and Easy Method of Prayer*, Fénelon's *Christian Perfection*, and Grou's simple outline *How to Pray*.[26]

Wesleyan/Holiness spirituality. The Wesleyan school of spirituality, following the lead of its founder John Wesley (1703-1791), is a case study of the tension between Quietism and Methodism, merging elements of strict Anglicanism with a Moravian sense of inner transformation.[27] The inner witness of the Spirit is placed together with the outer witness of a changed life. The work of the grace of God is understood to be effected through the means of grace: fasting, prayer, Scripture reading, attendance at worship, fellowship. Where the Anglican tradition emphasized the three-legged stool of Scripture, tradition and reason, Methodists would speak of a "quadrilateral" of Scripture, tradition, reason and *experience*.

As early as 1744 John Wesley appended a "b" to the ticket of those who would attend certain classes (the origins of the "bands"). The designation identified those who were "firmly committed to the quest for Christian perfection."[28] The Wesleyan school believed in—and pursued—perfection nearly from its inception. John Wesley's *A Plain Account of Christian Perfection* was a classic in its own time. Other Wesleyan followers, such as John William Fletcher (1729-1785) and Adam Clarke (c. 1760-1832) perpetuated Wesley's doctrine of perfection or "entire sanctification." In the American colonies, under the influence of the First and especially the Second Great Awakenings, this doctrine/experience received particular emphasis. By the mid-nineteenth century, in the context of the relaxation of Methodist revival fervor, some sought to

---

[26]For an overview of the varieties of French spirituality, see Liz Carmichael, "Catholic Saints and Reformers," in *The Story of Christian Spirituality: Two Thousand Years, from East to West*, ed. Gordon Mursell (Oxford: Lion, 2001), pp. 224-44.

[27]On John Wesley and the early development of the Methodist movement see Stephen Tomkins, *John Wesley: A Biography* (Grand Rapids: Eerdmans, 2003), and *The Cambridge Companion to John Wesley*, ed. Randy L. Maddox and Jason E. Vickers, Cambridge Companions to Religion (Cambridge: Cambridge University Press, 2010).

[28]David Lowes Watson, "Methodist Spirituality," in *Protestant Spiritual Traditions*, ed. Frank Senn (New York: Paulist Press, 1986), p. 236.

rekindle the interest in perfection and "holiness." In 1835 Methodist
Phoebe Palmer (1807-1874) and her sister sponsored a small gathering
of women (later enlarged to receive men) specifically devoted to
promote entire sanctification. In time Palmer proclaimed the gospel of
holiness throughout the world in speaking tours and through her
writings. The Holiness movement was to influence not only the formation of later Wesleyan expressions but also the origins of the Pentecostal movement of the twentieth century.[29]

Evangelicalism as a school? If we consider a school as a certain approach to or community of faith which brings together features of the
spiritual life into an organic whole and communicates them to future
generations of recognized followers, it is reasonable to consider "evangelicalism" as a broad school. The trans-Atlantic dialogue between Pietists, Methodists and American revivalists of the First Great Awakening (c. 1730-1750) created a single community which, to some extent,
was more significant than the Wesleyan, Calvinist, Baptist divisions that
identified various denominations. Characteristic of their approach were
an emphasis on the experience of conversion, a commitment to the
Scriptures and to the basic doctrines of the faith, an interest in missions
of various sorts, a desire to appropriate the work of God's Spirit, and a
tension with regard to worldly occupations. These kinds of characteristics would shape a spirituality—a *school* of spirituality—that formed
figures like Jonathan Edwards (1703-1758), George Whitefield (1714-
1770), Hannah More (1745-1833), William Wilberforce (1759-1833),
Charles G. Finney (1792-1875), Dwight L. Moody (1837-1899) and A. W.
Tozer (1897-1963). Indeed, these figures were not only formed by the
school, but they helped to form and create the school itself, a school of
spirituality that is shaping evangelicals to this day.[30]

---

[29]See David Lowes Watson, "Methodist Spirituality," in *Protestant Spiritual Traditions* (New York:
Paulist Press, 1986), pp. 217-73.

[30]On evangelical spirituality see Richard F. Lovelace, "Evangelical Spirituality: A Church
Historian's Perspective," *Journal of the Evangelical Theological Society* 31, no. 1 (1988): 25-35; D.
Bruce Hindmarsh, "Contours of Evangelical Spirituality," in *The Zondervan Dictionary of
Christian Spirituality*, ed. Glen G. Scorgie (Grand Rapids: Zondervan, 2011), pp. 146-52; and
Evan B. Howard, "Evangelical Spirituality" in *Four Views of Christian Spirituality*, ed. Bruce
Demarest (Grand Rapids: Zondervan, 2012).

5

Spiritual Theology

A HISTORICAL OVERVIEW

Greg Peters

THE PURPOSE OF THIS CHAPTER is to address spirituality as it has evolved and adapted through church history. Along the way note will be made of historical circumstances, cultural issues and theological developments that affected the living tradition of the church's spirituality. To that end, spirituality (or "spiritual theology") is understood as the living out of the gospel of Jesus Christ, arising from an intense spiritual experience, resulting in a "reordering of the great axes of the Christian life in terms of this contemporary experience."[1] Spirituality is the lived reality of the Christian tradition, a reality that changes according to historical and theological variation and fluctuation. This trajectory of spirituality is best evidenced through several themes, evidenced clearly in the spiritual classics: (1) through two overarching motifs that merged into one by the seventeenth century: the tripartite divisions of beginner, advanced and perfected, coupled with the tripartite division of purification, illumination and union; (2) the concept of spiritual ascent; and (3) a spiritual theology of love.

---

[1]Gustavo Gutiérrez, *A Theology of Liberation: History, Politics, and Salvation* (Maryknoll, NY: Orbis, 1988), p. 117.

THE TRIPLE WAY

Treatises on spirituality date to at least the third century and were written to assist Christian believers in the promotion of their personal spiritual life. This became more important after the conversion of the Roman emperor Constantine in 313, when the Christian church began emerging from an extended period of persecution. No longer were there the numerous opportunities of martyrdom that had existed for over two centuries. Along with this change in society came a transformation in how Christians viewed their role as members of the kingdom of God. The eschatological expectation of the parousia enunciated by Paul and other apostolic writers began to diminish with the end of the persecutions by Emperor Diocletian in 305. Christians no longer anticipated the immediate and imminent return of Jesus Christ. Instead, after two centuries of suffering, the faithful had to determine how to live daily without the threat of either martyrdom or being "caught up together . . . in the clouds to meet the Lord in the air" (1 Thess 4:17). Thus, distinct Christian spiritualities began to emerge in the fourth century and have continued to develop until the present. Yet, sometime around the year 1200 "the practice of theology emancipated itself from a system of Scripture readings and opted for a conceptual framework derived from philosophy. Parallel to these processes, spirituality too began to systematize itself and to develop its own conceptual patterns around such basic modern categories as affectivity and experience."[2]

This was most often accomplished by the use of a tripartite division of the spiritual life into beginner, advanced and perfected. The earliest proponents of this tripartite scheme were Clement of Alexandria (d. c. 215) and Origen (d. c. 254). For Clement, the goal of the spiritual life is the vision of God, gained by attaining knowledge and practicing love by way of ethical activity. Origen, in his *Commentary on the Song of Songs*, states that the biblical books of Proverbs, Ecclesiastes and the Song of Songs correspond to the three stages of the spiritual life: Proverbs to ethical activity, Ecclesiastes to the contemplation of God's creation and the Song of Songs to the contemplation of the divine being.[3] Origen's disciple and

---

[2]Kees Waaijman, *Spirituality: Forms, Foundations, Methods* (Leuven: Peeters, 2002), p. 369.
[3]Peter Tyler, "Triple Way," in *The New Westminster Dictionary of Christian Spirituality*, ed. Philip Sheldrake (Louisville: Westminster John Knox Press, 2005), p. 626.

the greatest popularizer of the tripartite division was the Egyptian monk Evagrius of Pontus (d. 399). Though Evagrius's influence has only been recovered during the past century, it is now clear that he is one of the greatest systematizers and architects of early Christian spiritual theology. The threefold division is summarized most clearly in his three works: *Praktikos, Gnostikos* and *Kephalaia Gnostica*. In the first stage, one eradicates evil through the acquisition of virtues by way of grace and discipline. In the second stage of his schema, the contemplation of the physical world, one starts by contemplating the physical creation and then moves up to a contemplation of the spiritual creation of heaven. From here one can transition to the third stage, contemplation of the Holy Trinity.[4]

This tripartite division found its way to the Western church via Evagrius's disciple John Cassian (d. 435), especially influencing those living as monks since the *Rule* of Benedict of Nursia legislated that the monks are to read the works of Cassian.[5] For example, the Benedictine monk Gregory the Great (d. 604), in his *Moralia on Job*, says that there are various "steps of merit" to ascend before one is perfected: "For every elect person sets out from the tenderness of his embryo in the first instance, and afterwards comes to firmness for strong and vigorous achievements."[6] A similar sentiment is found in the Cistercian monk Bernard of Clairvaux (d. 1153), who employed the threefold schema in his *The Steps of Humility and Pride*:

> Beginners are not able to enjoy the sweetness of milk until they have been purged by the bitter draught of fear. It must cleanse them of the infection of carnal pleasures. The perfect now turn from milk since they have had a glorious foretaste of the feast of glory. Only those in the middle, those who are growing, who are still delicate, are content with the sweet milk-foods of charity.[7]

---

[4]See Greg Peters, "Evagrius of Pontus (c. 346-399)," in *Dictionary of Christian Spirituality*, ed. Glen G. Scorgie (Grand Rapids: Zondervan Academic, 2010).

[5]See the *Rule of Benedict*, chap. 73.

[6]Gregory the Great, *Moralia on Job* 22.20, English translation in *Morals on the Book of Job, by S. Gregory the Great*, vol. 2 (Oxford: John Henry Parker, 1845), p. 586.

[7]Bernard of Clairvaux, *The Steps of Humility and Pride* 2.4; English translation in *Bernard of Clairvaux, Treatises II: The Steps of Humility and Pride and On Loving God* (Kalamazoo, MI: Cistercian Publications, 1980), p. 33. The Cistercians were a monastic reform movement beginning in 1098 in France. They are a reform of the Benedictines and, therefore, also live according to the *Rule* of Benedict.

For most authors that follow this schema, baptism serves as the moment of initiation as a beginner; therefore all believers are beginners, whereas those who progress to the stage of advanced and perfected require further training and discipline.

Having reached the high Middle Ages, this threefold way of beginners, advanced and perfected took a definitive turn in the theology of the Franciscan friar Bonaventure (d. 1274) who wrote a work titled *The Triple Way*. This "triple way," wrote Bonaventure, was the way laid out by the popular sixth-century Syrian mystical theologian Pseudo-Dionysius to describe the spiritual life's progress, consisting of purgation, illumination and perfection (or union). In Bonaventure's thought, this triple way orders the human soul to its proper actions and to its distinctive and proper end: union with God. Purgation leads to peace through the purification from sin, leading to an upright life. Illumination attends to truth and the imitation of Christ. Perfection, through love, makes the believer ready to receive Jesus Christ as Spouse. The purgative way consists in one's active cleansing and is aided by spiritual exercises and ascetic practices, through the cultivation of humility and by practicing the virtues. Further advancement is made with the assistance of meditation, prayer and contemplation. The illuminative way is characterized by further meditation, prayer and contemplation, combined with the reception of the gifts of the Holy Spirit, additional spiritual exercises and a devotion to the Virgin Mary. The unitive way involves the exercising of proper Christian love until one experiences or achieves mystical union with God as Trinity. Though the purgative and illuminative ways involved the activity of the soul, the unitive way is characterized by passivity, awaiting God's imputation of grace.

Like the Origenistic tripartite division discussed previously, this tripartite way also became influential and pervasive, proving "to be so powerful that it absorbed the other triad (beginners, advanced, perfect). This produces a remarkable duplication: the way of purification for beginners, the way of illumination for the advanced, and the way of union for the perfect."[8] In fact, the presence of the triple way of purgation, il-

---

[8]Waaijman, *Spirituality*, pp. 375-76.

lumination and perfection is a *sine qua non* of spiritual theologies. This schema retained its place in the writings of the greatest Catholic Reformation spiritual authors of the sixteenth century, such as Ignatius of Loyola (d. 1556), John of the Cross (d. 1591) and Teresa of Ávila (d. 1582).

Taking John of the Cross as representative of this era, *The Ascent of Mount Carmel* views the Christian life along the tripartite classical structure, though John devotes much of *The Ascent* to a discussion of the way of purgation. There are two major movements along the way to purgation, both of which are described as "dark nights." The first concerns the purgation of the sensory part of human nature, whereas the second concerns the purgation of the spiritual part of the human soul. The first purgation is active and passive, stilling the fire of love's urgent longings. The second purgation is also active and passive, involving a journey through darkness and concealment, leading to stillness of the soul. Sensory purgation involves a mortification of the senses and appetites, whereas spiritual purgation is when a person, by faith, ascends a ladder that moves them beyond the light of the senses and intellect. This is an ascent into the deep things of God, resulting in a supernatural vision that leads the way to union with God.[9]

This schema was not limited, however, to only Roman Catholic authors but also found its way into important post-Reformation Protestant spiritual texts, if not in name then at least in details. For example, Johann Arndt (d. 1621) uses the tripartite division in his *True Christianity*, published from 1605 onward. Drawing a parallel between the steps of the "natural life" (childhood, manhood and old age), Arndt says that the spiritual life also has three steps. He writes that the Christian life has "its beginnings in repentance, by which man daily betters himself. Thereafter follows middle age, more illumination, through the contemplation of divine things, through prayer, and through suffering. . . . Finally, the perfection of old age comes. It consists in the full union through love."[10] Arndt's book was hugely influential in the Pietist movement, which in turn exercised a considerable influence on later evangelical Protestantism,

[9]*The Collected Works of St. John of the Cross*, trans. Kieran Kavanaugh and Otilio Rodriguez (Washington, DC: Institute of Carmelite Studies, 1973), pp. 73, 102-16.
[10]*Johann Arndt: True Christianity*, trans. Peter C. Erb (New York: Paulist Press, 1979), p. 221.

including Philipp Jakob Spener (d. 1705). In his essay "On Hindrances to Theological Studies," Spener maintains that there is not much of a difference between "scholastic dogmatics" and the mystics. Dogmatics designates what is true and correct in "single articles," convincing others of the truthfulness of these articles through written forms and logic. Mysticism moves beyond "mere knowledge," taking the mind and all the powers of the soul into its realm in order to restore the divine image in each human. Furthermore, it "stresses practical purification, illumination, and union with God." Thus, every teacher of theology, says Spener, needs to show his students how the truth contained in theological articles "is to be understood as practical."[11] In this way each student will know how to grow spiritually and will be encouraged to do so in a zealous manner. For Spener, every theologian is a mystical theologian.

Not only did the Pietists employ the tripartite schema but so did Anglican authors, including William Law (d. 1761), who alludes to it in his *An Humble, Earnest, and Affectionate Address, to the Clergy*. In this work Law speaks at length on the need for union with God, and only those who partake of God's goodness can have such union. God's love, which brought all things into existence, is not diminished by the fall; therefore, God is always at work to restore humankind to their original "state of goodness." Though fallen humanity is under a curse and is punished by God, the complete purpose of the Christian life, "from the beginning to the end," is nothing other than God's work of restoring humankind to himself. These "works of purifying love . . . burn away all that dark evil, which separates the creature from its first created union with God." For Law, there is no discontinuity between God's works before the fall and those that he engages in after the fall: "God creating, God illuminating, God sanctifying, God threatening and punishing, God forgiving and redeeming, is but one and the same essential, immutable, never ceasing, working of the divine nature." God has always been in the business of casting illumination among the "saints and angels."[12]

---

[11]All quotations taken from Peter C. Erb, ed., *The Pietists: Selected Writings* (New York: Paulist Press, 1983), p. 68.

[12]All quotations taken from William Law, *An Humble, Earnest, and Affectionate Address, to the Clergy* (Edinburgh: Guthrie & Tait, 1817), p. 159.

Though Law does not lay out the tripartite division in a linear fashion, the influence is there when he speaks of fallen humankind's union with God by way of "works of purifying love" and illumination.

SPIRITUAL ASCENT

Another common theme in the history of spirituality is that of spiritual ascent. Making use of images such as Jacob's Ladder and Moses' ascent of Mt. Sinai, Christian spiritual theologians regularly structured their spiritual texts around the ideas of progression and ascent. These images were also complimented by biblical passages like Psalm 63, where the psalmist speaks of yearning and thirsting for the Lord:

> O God, you are my God; earnestly I seek you;
>> my soul thirsts for you;
> my flesh faints for you,
>> as in a dry and weary land where there is no water. (Ps 63:1)

Well-known examples of this motif in the history of spirituality are John Climacus's (d. c. 649) *Ladder of Divine Ascent*, Bonaventure's *The Soul's Journey into God*, George Herbert's (d. 1633) *The Temple*, John Bunyan's *Pilgrim's Progress* and, most importantly, Dante Alighieri's (d. 1321) *Divine Comedy*. In all of these texts the figurative, literary ascents are indicative of a real interior journey where the Christian's soul seeks to return, in the present life, to God. This scheme is based on spiritual theology's borrowing of the so-called *exitus-reditus* interplay of Christian Platonism. In this philosophical theology all things come forth (or exit) from God and, therefore, all things, especially human beings, return to him. In biblical language one might say that all the creation comes forth or exits from God in his unique creative act (Gen 1–3) and redemptively, after the fall into sin of the whole creation, all things return to him (Rom 8:19-23). Though the immortal soul's full and final return is only accomplished after death, the concept of spiritual ascent enacts a journey undertaken while living, since the soul longs for communion and union with its Creator and Spouse.

In his work *Understanding the Medieval Meditative Ascent: Augustine, Anselm, Boethius and Dante*, Robert McMahon offers an excellent commentary on this spiritual motif. Though the final consummation of the soul's journey to God is only accomplished after death, the spiritual ascent (or, in McMahon's words, the "meditative ascent") enacts an interior journey in this life due to the soul's longing to be united to God, its divine source. Importantly, this spiritual ascent is not to be equated with a mystical rapture or an ineffable moment of beatitude, but is centered in the soul's progression "by stages of philosophical and theological discourse," until it finally arrives "at a discursive vision of divine things."[13] This ascent is possible due to God's grace, which he bestows freely on the believer. Therefore, the ascent begins with God (by way of his impartation of grace) and ends with God (in union). It is important to note that the ascent progresses in stages, latter stages are dependent on earlier stages. Of course, God may grant the pilgrim an immediate vision of himself through an abundant gifting of grace, but the "normal" pattern found in spiritual literature is that of progression in stages, culminating finally in union with God. Dante Alighieri's *Divine Comedy* illustrates this theme well.

The *Divine Comedy* was written between 1308 and 1321, and comprises three parts: Inferno, Purgatory and Paradise. In the poem, Dante the pilgrim journeys through the physical places of hell, purgatory and heaven, but his journey is also that of the soul's interior journey. Dante's journey begins when he finds himself in a dark wilderness midway upon the journey of his life, having "wandered from the straight and true" (1.3).[14] Now lost, the pilgrim Dante (traditionally understood to be the personification of all Christians) is sent a guide from God—the virtuous pagan poet Virgil. Virgil tells Dante that he will guide him through hell "where you will hear the groans of hopeless men . . . crying in torment for the second death" (1.115-117). Next they will enter Purgatory where Dante "will look upon those souls content to wait in fire" before they finally enter heaven (1.118-119). Virgil also tells Dante that he will journey through heaven but "another soul" (1.122) will come to lead him since

---

[13]Robert McMahon, *Understanding the Medieval Meditative Ascent: Augustine, Anselm, Boethius and Dante* (Washington, DC: Catholic University of America Press, 2006), p. 1.

[14]All quotations are from Dante Alighieri, *The Inferno*, trans. Anthony Esolen (New York: Modern Library, 2002). Canto and line numbers will be given in parentheses after each quotation.

Virgil, as a righteous pagan, is unable to enter heaven. The work culminates in Dante's beatific vision of the triune God, but before that moment Dante the author divides the work into distinct stages as is expected from a work on the spiritual ascent.

Dante the pilgrim's journey through hell, the first stage, is for the purpose of teaching Dante and his readers the need to recognize that one is lost, that is, alienated from God, and to recognize the extent and negative effects of sin. Such a sense of alienation and being lost were certainly acute in the early fourteenth century as outbreaks of plague and famine were devastating Europe. Further, the Crusades against the Muslims had failed and intense warfare was becoming more common throughout Europe and the Middle East. Thus, as already mentioned, Dante finds himself at the beginning of the work lost in a dark forest. It is this state of being lost that initiates Dante's journey, and it is not necessarily a stage within his ascent. Rather, the believer needs to acknowledge his state of disorientation and alienation from God in order to begin the spiritual ascent. Once the ascent has begun, however, one must immediately begin to understand the nature and depth of sin.

The nature of sin in Dante's *Inferno* emerges throughout. Dante holds that one's level in hell is based on one's sins since Minos, God's chosen instrument for judging the severity of individual sins, "weighs all the sins and sends the wicked down according to how far he winds his tail" (5.5-7). As well, Dante states that the damned are fully aware of their sins yet "they hurl curses at the power of God" (5.36). Dante comes the closest to offering a definition of sin when he writes that "their reason [is] subject to desire" (5.39) and they are "cross-eyed in . . . mind" (7.41).[15] Dante believes that sin is against human nature; that is, to sin is not to be fully human: "you were made before I was unmade" (6.42; cf. 6.107-108: "when a thing at last is whole it feels more pleasure," implying that sinners are not whole persons). Dante's theology of sin follows the biblical trichotomy established by the apostle John in 1 John 2:16 ("the desires of the flesh and the desires of the eyes and pride of life"). Dante writes that "avarice, pride, and envy are the three principal flames that

---

[15] In *Paradise* Dante defines sin as "trespassing the mark" (26.117).

set their hearts afire" (6.74-75) and anyone who gives in to these is not of
the Father but of the world, is not spiritual but sinful.

It appears that Dante espouses a concept of original sin when he
writes that there is "a sluggish smoke within our hearts" (7.123). The
object of sin is Fortune, which is Dante's way of talking about God's
sovereignty/providence. That is, sinners act against and contrary to
God's good plan for the world: "She [Fortune] is the one so cursed and
crucified by the same people who should give her praise" (7.91-92; cf.
9.94-97: "Why do you kick your heels against the will of Him whose
ends can never be cut short, who many a time has made your torments
grow? What good is it to butt your heads at fate?"). The result of sin is
the judgment of God, where each sinner shall "hear his sentence thun-
dering through eternity" (6.98-99). Over and above Dante's theology
of sin is his understanding of sin according to traditional categories.
For example, he uses the traditional list of the seven deadly sins to
organize upper hell.

Once Dante emerges from hell he now begins his ascent through purgatory, pictured in the *Divine Comedy* as an ascent up a mountain called
Mt. Purgatory. In purgatory Dante travels through two more stages.
First he travels through the stage of the forgiveness of sins. At the bottom
of Mt. Purgatory Dante the pilgrim's forehead is marked with the letter
P seven times.[16] Throughout his ascent Dante learns from Purgatory's
inhabitants the true nature of virtue and how the cultivation of virtue
eradicates the corresponding vice. For example, as Dante travels through
the ring of the proud, he learns that pride is the "twisted way" that makes
the crooked (i.e., sin) seem straight (10.3).[17] Pride is unnatural and can
be viewed as a turning in on oneself, pictured in Dante by the prideful
being hunched over, bearing a great weight on their backs, so much so
that their "knees crushed against [their] chest" (10.132). Once Dante understands the nature of pride and realizes his own pride, the first of the
seven Ps is erased from his forehead. This pattern continues throughout
Dante's ascent through purgatory.

---

[16]In Latin *peccata* means sin and the seven Ps stand for the seven deadly sins.
[17]All quotations are from Dante Alighieri, *Purgatory*, trans. Anthony Esolen (New York: Modern
Library, 2003). Canto and line numbers will be given in parentheses after each quotation.

The second stage that Dante passes through in purgatory is a stage of final purification. Having reached earthly paradise atop Mt. Purgatory, Dante meets St. Matelda, who leads the pilgrim through the waters of the river Lethe. It is tempting to see this as an image of baptism, but it is not Dante's baptism since only those baptized, according to Dante the author, can even make the journey through purgatory and paradise.[18] It would seem that moment of cleansing is to purge Dante the pilgrim of any remaining vestiges of sin, indicating that though purgation has happened progressively throughout his ascent of purgatory, this is the complete and definitive erasure of all memory of sin and its effects. These waters of Lethe can assail Dante's heart (cf. 31.12) so much so that he will be "washed clean" (31.103).

Dante's *Paradise* provides the fourth and final stage of spiritual ascent—the vision of God. Having passed through the first stage of seeing the depth of sin, the second stage of receiving forgiveness of his sins, and the third stage of being purified and made forgetful of sin, Dante the pilgrim now enters the final stage of seeing God "face to face" (1 Cor 13:12). For Dante the pilgrim this encounter with God happens when he reaches the highest levels of the heavenly empyrean:

> Buy in my vision winning valor so,
> > that sole appearance as I changed by seeing
> > appeared to change and from itself anew.
> Within that brilliant and profoundest Being
> > of the deep light three rings appeared to me,
> > three colors and one measure in their gleaming:
> As rainbow begets rainbow in the sky,
> > so were the first two, and the third, a flame
> > that from both rainbows breathed forth equally . . .
> O Light that dwell within Thyself alone,
> > who alone know Thyself, are known, and smile
> > with Love upon the Knowing and the Known! (33.112-127)[19]

Though there are many views of how the Christian attains this union

---

[18]Just before entering hell proper, Dante places righteous pagans (such as the philosopher Plato) in limbo, saying that they came close to the Christian faith but still lacked baptism.

[19]Dante Alighieri, *Paradise*, trans. Anthony Esolen (New York: Modern Library, 2004), p. 357.

and when it happens, works of spiritual ascent tend to culminate in a person's direct encounter with God. For example, Christian's journey in Bunyan's *Pilgrim's Progress* culminates with his death, at which point he is then able to continue into the Celestial City of the King. Bunyan writes that Christian entered into the gate of the city and immediately he was "transfigured" and had "Raiment put on that shone like God."[20] He was on the way to meet the King of the city—God himself. Thus, the characteristics of the spiritual ascent involve some number of discreet stages, leading to a vision of God.

A SPIRITUAL THEOLOGY OF LOVE

The aim of the Christian life is to love God with all of our heart, soul and mind, and to love our neighbor as we love ourselves. Thus, "love is the central reference point of Christian spirituality."[21] Placing love as both the source and summit of the Christian life goes back to the Scriptures themselves. In the Old Testament the Israelites were admonished to love Yahweh with all their heart, soul and might (Deut 6:5), and the Psalms are replete with references to Yahweh's "steadfast love" that endures forever (cf. Ps 107). In the New Testament Jesus himself repeats the *Shema* of Israel from Deuteronomy (e.g., Lk 10:27), and Paul claims that without love everything the believer does will simply sound like a bad song played on loud instruments (cf. 1 Cor 13). Both biblical Testaments acknowledge the link between loving God and loving neighbor; you simply cannot have one without the other.

This biblical focus on love was elaborated on by postapostolic Christian theologians, and famously so in commentaries on the Song of Songs. Throughout much of Christian history the Song of Songs has been interpreted as an allegory of God's love for the church and the church's love for God. Thus, when Solomon opens the book by saying, "Let him kiss me with the kisses of his mouth," commentators interpreted it to mean that God desires, out of love, to enter into an intimate

---

[20]John Bunyan, *The Pilgrim's Progress*, ed. N. H. Keeble (Oxford: Oxford University Press, 1966), p. 132.
[21]Werner Jeanrond, "Love," in *The New Westminster Dictionary of Christian Spirituality*, ed. Philip Sheldrake (Louisville: Westminster John Knox Press, 2005), p. 415.

relationship with the bride (i.e., the church) by way of contemplation. As Theodoret of Cyrus (d. c. 466) writes, "by 'kiss' we understand not the joining of mouths but the communion of pious soul and divine Word."[22] This focus on love as the guiding motif of the Christian life found full exposition in the early Christian church in the homilies of Augustine of Hippo on 1 John. To love any created thing, for Augustine, is to love God, and by extension to fail to love something that should be loved is to fail to love God as he is supposed to be loved: "to act against love is to act against God."[23]

The greatest treatise on love, however, to come from the pre-Reformation church is Bernard of Clairvaux's (d. 1153) *On Loving God*.[24] In this treatise Bernard says that there are four degrees of love: (1) man loves himself for his own sake; (2) man loves God for his own benefit; (3) man loves God for God's sake; and (4) man loves himself for the sake of God. The believer moves through these stages during the Christian life, hoping to reach, at least in passing, the fourth and highest degree. These are not sequential steps for Bernard but degrees of love that merge into one another and between which a Christian will vacillate throughout life. It is necessary to reach the highest degree, writes Bernard, because this is when the believer has an ineffable experience of God: "to lose yourself, as if you no longer existed, to cease completely to experience yourself, to reduce yourself to nothing is not a human sentiment but a divine experience."[25]

At this point the Christian sees him- or herself for who he or she is, created by and loved by God, realizing that the Christian exists for God's will alone and for his pleasure, not his or her own. This degree is not attained, says Bernard, by human efforts but is the gift of God. During this moment of rapture one sees God as love, that is, by loving rightly one is brought into God's very self, for "charity is the divine substance."[26]

---

[22]Theodoret of Cyrus, *Commentary on the Song of Songs* 1. See Robert C. Hill, trans., *Theodoret of Cyrus: Commentary on the Song of Songs* (Strathfield, Australia: St. Paul's Publications, 2001).

[23]Augustine, *Homilies on 1 John* 7.5, Homily 7 on the First Epistle of John, *New Advent*, www.newadvent.org/fathers/170207.htm.

[24]Bernard of Clairvaux, *Bernard of Clairvaux: On Loving God*, trans. Robert Walton (Kalamazoo, MI: Cistercian Publications, 1995).

[25]Ibid., p. 29.

[26]Ibid., p. 37.

Bernard believes that love is the intratrinitarian bond between the Father and the Son.[27] Thus, their affection for one another is a relationship of love, who is the Holy Spirit. Therefore, to attain to the fourth degree of love is to attain to the very love of the Trinity and to partake in a "deifying" manner in the Godhead.

Though with different emphasis, a focus on love as the height of Christian perfection and spirituality continued into the modern period. Perhaps the greatest exponent of a spiritual theology of love whose works continue to exercise influence is Henri Nouwen (d. 1996). On May 17, 1991, Nouwen gave a radio talk titled "The Life of the Beloved," in which he says that the spiritual life is the life of the beloved.[28] The core of Nouwen's teaching on this matter is that each person, regardless of gender, ability or "usefulness" to society, is God's beloved and is favored by God. This was an important message for Nouwen, who spent the last ten years of his life working with developmentally disabled persons at L'Arche Daybreak near Toronto, Canada. Moreover, in the abortion- and euthanasia-driven late-twentieth and early-twenty-first century this message runs counter to the dominant culture of death.

For Nouwen, God's beloved have been chosen by him, blessed by him, broken by him and given by him. Because we are chosen by God we are unique in his eyes and precious in his sight. By virtue of being God's beloved we are then blessed by God, that is, God says good things about us. He values us. As broken people we need to embrace our brokenness. We should not run from it, says Nouwen, but instead we must give our broken selves back to God. Only by living as people who are taken, blessed and broken, can we then give ourselves fully to God and to others in loving service. God loves us and we in turn must love others. Such a focus makes Nouwen's message profoundly simple and biblically centered by bringing the spiritual life back to its biblical core of love of God and love of neighbor.

---

[27]This view is also held by Peter Lombard (d. c. 1161) in his *Sentences* and, later, by Thomas Aquinas (d. 1274).

[28]Nouwen published a book with the same title the following year, and in it he elaborates on the themes mentioned in the radio address. See Henri Nouwen, *The Life of the Beloved: Spiritual Living in a Secular World* (New York: Crossroad, 1992).

CONCLUSION

From this overview it can be seen that the history of the Christian spiritual tradition is rich with schemas and motifs for the individual believer's spiritual journey. From the early Christian era the tradition developed around a tripartite schema that captured the imagination of subsequent writers and continued to influence the tradition down to the modern era. Though this tripartite schema is not the only historical way of thinking about and organizing spiritual theology, it gained a level of acceptance unparalleled in the tradition when compared with other organizational patterns.[29] The beginner/purgative, advanced/illuminative and perfected/unitive schema is still widely used to organize the spiritual tradition, so modern students of spirituality will be well served by knowing its details and history.

As stated earlier, spiritual texts that adopt an image of ascent are frequent and transcend any one particular Christian tradition, being employed by Roman Catholic, Eastern Orthodox and Protestant spiritual writers. The benefits of this motif lie in its biblical-centered imagery (e.g., Jacob's ladder) and its hierarchical, heavenly oriented presentation. Though Dante is considered by many the master of this motif in spiritual literature, its influence can also be seen in other mediums meant to communicate spiritual truths. For example, many churches constructed in the Renaissance era, especially those in Rome, are organized along the lines of a spiritual ascent. On the floor level are the currently living Christians who enter these churches to worship God in Word and sacraments. Above the living, painted on walls and memorialized in statuary are the "saints," those who have died and whose lifestyles are meant to serve as an example. In many churches the images are of the saints engaging in works of mercy and deeds of holiness, models for the living. Above these saints, painted high on altar pieces and domes are the

---

[29]The triple way only fell out of favor in the latter half of the twentieth century after being seriously questioned by the Roman Catholic theologian Karl Rahner (d. 1984) and in light of the developments in Roman Catholic theology initiated by the Second Vatican Council that met in Rome from 1962-1965. See Karl Rahner, "Reflections on the Problem of the Gradual Ascent to Christian Perfection," *Revue d'Ascétique et de Mystique* 19 (1944): 65-78. This work is reprinted in Karl Rahner, *Theological Investigations*, vol. 3, *The Theology of the Spiritual Life*, trans. Karl-H. and Boniface Kruger (Baltimore: Darton, Longman & Todd, 1967), pp. 3-23.

Trinity and the angels, representing the highest heaven—the place of beatific vision and union. These images remind the Christians walking and worshiping below of their spiritual destination, the goal of their spiritual ascent. It is Dante, Bunyan and John Climacus in paint, bronze and marble. It is the texts of spiritual ascent given concrete reality for thousands to see.

Spiritual theologies of love continue to be written and continue to exercise the imagination of students of the Christian spiritual tradition. If Nouwen is one of the most well-known of the modern exponents, he is not the only one. Within evangelicalism there is the so-called New Monasticism or New Friars movement. Texts written by practitioners of these lifestyles emphasize the need to love the "other" to such an extent that one is willing to even adopt the lifestyle of the other. Thus, middle-class Westerners, for example, find themselves serving slum-dwellers in Manila and Mexico City by living in the slums alongside those whom they are called to love. It is love incarnated in the twenty-first century much as Love himself became incarnate in the first century. In short, the Christian spiritual tradition is too rich to be ignored by evangelicals as it has been in the past. It is time for evangelicals not only to know the historical tradition but to begin reading the very texts that constitute the tradition.

6

Engaging Classic Literature

Genre, Use, Value

James M. Houston

Perhaps no modern Christian apologist has been so varied in his use of literary genres as C. S. Lewis. Poetry, romance, fable, narrative, children's stories, lectures, letters, essays, science fiction, literary criticism, historical reflections—Lewis has exemplified them all. Although he was too modest to point this out, he clearly believed that the fullness of Christian truth requires us to use all forms of literary expression to communicate the fullness and mystery of the gospel.

"The Classic" as Defense Against Reductionism

Lewis saw the value of "old books" to remind us of our cultural "blind spots," when we become biased in favor of the present. He faults too many theologians as being in bondage to their contemporary frame of mind.[1] Lewis wrote to his brother that while his range of books had grown expansively as he became more educated, there was also a steady decline in the books he later assessed more critically as being "worth reading."[2] Most of all, Lewis saw the great danger of secularism embracing such forms of reductionism as logical positivism and literary scientism. Its denial of the human being created in the image and

---

[1] C. S. Lewis, *God in the Dock* (Grand Rapids: Eerdmans, 1970), pp. 200-207.
[2] C. S. Lewis, *Letters of C. S. Lewis*, ed. W. H. Lewis (London: Geoffrey Bles, 1966), p. 148.

likeness of God (*imago dei*) was deeply disturbing. Lewis told me personally that his indictment of scientism in his lectures on "the abolition of man" was the most important message of all his writings.[3]

Since then, even our secular culture has been in reaction to the rationalism of modernism in its replacement by the pluralism of post-modernism. Biblical scholarship has opened up the diversity of literary genres within the text much more than previously appreciated. So we are all more aware that the communication of Christian life and faith requires all the varied possible means of literary communication.

For all serious study, the universal dictum now is: "the innate logic of an object studied, determines how it should be studied." By their long survival, "Christian classics" have illustrated this dictum in being truthful to what it is to be inspired and nurtured to be more fully human before God.

WHAT IS A CLASSIC?

Classical is a wide-ranging term, beginning with its primary sense of Greek literature that ended about 325 B.C., to Greco-Roman literature that ended with the reign of Augustus, to be superseded by Christian literature.[4] The term *classicus* meant "of the highest class," having a broadly superlative quality. The term owes its origin to Tullius Servius, who divided the Romans into five classes; the first or most eminent he called the *classici*.[5] The term was revised in the Enlightenment, and more loosely the French *classique* became associated with school and college education. In American education such works as The Harvard Classics and The Great Books of the Western World have been basic.[6] Now more comprehensive of religious classics are the popular Catholic series of Classics of Western Spirituality.[7]

---

[3]He told me this in 1955; later he wrote in a letter to an American lady "[*Abolition of Man*] . . . is almost my favourite among books, but in general has been almost totally ignored by the public," *Letters to an American Lady* (Grand Rapids: Eerdmans, 1967), p. 39.
[4]Paul Harvey, *The Oxford Companion to Classical Literature* (Oxford: Oxford University Press, 1989), p. 106.
[5]*Encyclopaedia Britannica* (Edinburgh: A. Bell & C. Macfarquhar, 1771), 2:207.
[6]The Great Books of the Western World, ed. Robert Hutchins and Mortimer J. Adler (Chicago: University of Chicago Press, 1952).
[7]Classics of Western Spirituality are published by Paulist Press.

Previously, recovery of classic literature was often associated with educational or spiritual renewal movements. Discontented as I was in the 1970s with the rationalistic presentation of much systematic theology, I edited in the next decade ten works of Christian classics.[8] These were for me personally a new beginning in the exploration of what "spiritual theology" might be. Their engagement was selective of distinctive forms and periods of spiritual renewal, past and present.

Little did I realize at the time that this was much more than a personal journey. For "spirituality" has become a universal cultural change, fed by three differing types of classics. First, in the Greek sense a classic may inspire a hero or shape a friendship. Second, on the "religious classic" David Tracy observes:

> Here we find something valuable, something "important"; some disclosure of reality in a moment that must be called one of "recognition" which surprises, provokes, challenges, shocks and eventually transforms us; an experience that upsets conventional opinions, and expands the sense of the possible; indeed a realized experience of that which is essential, that which endures.[9]

Yet such a classic conforms culturally to the unity and continuity of that religious society. Third, the uniqueness of the Christian classic is that its focus is on the advent and continual presence of Jesus Christ; such classics contribute to our becoming ever more Christlike.[10]

THE CONTEMPORARY ABUSE OF SPIRITUAL CLASSICS

However, in the ambiguity of human motives, we can both use and abuse these varied types of classics. It is a feature of contemporary pluralism to make syncretism fashionable, being careless of the truth or even denying its existence, valuing instead the cleverness of what is

---

[8]These ranged from Bernard of Clairvaux, to Walter Hilton, Juan de Valdes, Teresa of Ávila, Richard Baxter, John Owen, Pascal, Jonathan Edwards, William Wilberforce and Charles Simeon. First published from 1980 onward by Multnomah Press in Portland, Oregon, most of them are still available through Regent Publishing in Vancouver.

[9]David Tracy, *The Analogical Imagination: Christian Theology and the Culture of Pluralism* (New York: Crossroad, 1981), p. 108. I am indebted to my colleague Bruce Hindmarsh for reference to this text.

[10]Ibid., pp. 248-304.

novel or imaginative. The contemporary culture values the eclectic and the collage effect of incongruities brought together. So using the classics, whether Greco-Roman (including Buddhist, Islamic or other more esoteric texts) or Christian sources, is now part of courses in religious studies in college education. The strangeness of the theme studied now becomes its own power, so that curiosity, once a vice for medieval Christians, today becomes a virtue. The breakdown of what is true makes inclusiveness its esteemed substitute.

There is also the abuse of the publishing industry itself, now that classics have become so popularized. The money made out of them prompts publishers to revamp them in new format.[11] Like the popular BBC program "Desert Island Discs," which asked each celebrity interviewed, "What one/three books would you take with you to your island?" we shall be persuaded soon, "Choose your favorite classics for your preferred lifestyle."

Third, there is the abuse of professionalism itself. Never was there a more professionalized generation than ours today. We are endlessly creating new professions. Christian spirituality itself has become a new profession, perhaps succeeding religious studies as another related discipline. Arthur Holder not only fears popular use of Christian classics as a disservice to the academy but also as being too restrictive in its dogma for the new culture of pluralism and contemporary eclecticism.[12]

The church's long use of the Christian classic to deepen and to transform the life of the believer in the life of Christ himself is vanishing in this eclectic professionalism, which would reduce the Christian classic to a stylistic concept instead of being the personal witnesses of God's presence.

The Christian Faith Is Logocentric

As the apostle Paul confronted the Stoics and the Epicureans on Mars Hill, he made a classic biblical statement that in contrast to "the unknown god" (*agnōstos theos*) whom they worshiped, the biblical faith is

---

[11]See complaint of Arthur Holder, "The Problem with 'Spiritual Classics,'" *Spiritus* 10, no. 1 (2010): 32-33.
[12]Ibid., p. 24.

grounded upon the revealing and speaking God. The one truly blessed, as Psalm 1 depicts, meditates on the word of the Lord, day and night. Later Origen, Ambrose and other of the church fathers speak of Psalm 119 as the *beati*, expressive of a truly blessed logocentric life. *Per Verbum*, God has spoken in creation, which has culminated in "the Word became flesh and dwelt among us" (Jn 1:14). This greatly challenged the pagan world whose gods were mute and deaf, with a silence reigning in an ineffable absence of language. In contrast, the Old Testament uses the diverse genres of the mythic, narrative, prescription, oracular, apocalyptic, hymnic and sapiential, to which the New Testament adds the parabolic, epistolary and exhortative.

THE GREAT TRADITIONS OF CLASSICAL LITERATURE

Until the twelfth century, Christian writers integrated scholarship with personal sanctity. By this means they produced Christian classics. Their varied genres reflected their personal lives in handling the Word of God. Their efficacy as teachers depended on the moral quality of their lives as well as of their writings. The allegories of Origen, Gregory of Nyssa and Augustine; the rhetoric of John Chrysostom; the poetry of Gregory Nazianzus; the liturgical chants of Ambrose; the scholastic rigors of Anselm and Thomas Aquinas; the heart's recollection of Bernard of Clairvaux and Francis de Sales; the "plain meaning" of John Calvin and John Owen; even the hymnody of Isaac Watts and Charles Wesley; all reflected on both the truthfulness of their lives as well as their literary standards already established within the Bible itself.

As the apostle Paul himself affirmed, "you are a letter from Christ delivered by us" (2 Cor 3:3), so these literary achievements were expressive of God's loving presence within individuals, whose ministry of the word (*ministerium verbi*) is the ministry of loving service. The author was not concerned about his own reputation, only the glory of God.[13] The spiritual literature produced reflected then upon the spiritual experiences of the writers themselves, who composed not just to produce a literary affect but to communicate the truth of their own personal experiences of

---

[13]Jean Leclerc, *The Love of Learning and the Desire for God* (New York: Fordham University Press, 1974), p. 320.

God's presence and love. They wrote with freedom, in unconscious self-forgetfulness and in purity of heart. Their writings remain devotional classics, for they wrote as saints, not as rhetoricians. They were most themselves when they were most "in Christ," so that their freedom lay in their self-detachment.

Their literary talent is not the focus but rather the fruit of their indescribable delight in deeply personal experiences of God's love. They all shared the same intrinsic character—personal encounters with God, as Abraham was called of God to journey with him or as Moses met God at the burning bush or as an unknown lover (possibly a woman) experienced the love of God in the Song of Songs.

THE CLASSICS OF THE EARLY FATHERS

Patristic interpretation of Christian faith begins about A.D. 150. It develops in differing polemical needs, with Justin Martyr demonstrating how Christ is the fulfilment of Old Testament prophecy, Origen penetrating the inner meaning of the Old Testament and Basil distinguishing the person of God the Father from that of the Son and of the Holy Spirit. Tyconius establishes principles for the typological exegesis of Scripture, while Theodore and Theodoret anchor the text in historical statements. Jerome explores comparatively the translations and texts available. Hilary of Poitiers experiences the mystery of the Trinity, presenting insights followed by later theologians such as Augustine. But all this begins with the original genres of the New Testament itself, of which the epistolary genre is the most common—nineteen of its twenty-seven books.[14] For embedded in "the letter" is a holistic genre that communicates so much of domestic, personal life.[15]

1. *The genre of the letter*. The apostle Paul contributes most significantly in this genre, to be imitated by many of the church fathers. Ever since, letters have been of central importance in the teaching of the church. As expressions of friendship, itself a moral source of shaping the

---

[14]James M. Houston, *Letters of Faith Through the Seasons* (Colorado Springs: Honor Books, 2007), 2:175-230.
[15]See Ryan S. Olson, *Tragedy, Authority, and Trickery: The Poetics of Embedded Letters in Josephus* (Cambridge, MA: Harvard University Press, 2010), pp. 11-30.

ethical life, Paul uses letters as second best to the face-to-face conversation with friends (Rom 15:14-33; 1 Cor 4:14-21; 1 Thess 2:17-3:13; Gal 4:12-20). But while Roman letters were quite terse and to the point, Paul's are much longer, using a scribe and dictated with a strongly pastoral intent. They are dialogical in answering many pastoral issues among Christian communities. Typically there are seven components to the letter, as is well illustrated in Paul's letter to the Philippians:

1. epistolary prescript—introducing the writer

2. thanksgiving and *exordium*

3. body of the letter—"I wish you to know . . ."

4. *propositio*—providing the basic thrust of the letter

5. *probatio*—as well as refutation, if there was disputation

6. *peroratio*—the final appeal and exhortation

7. final greetings and closure

The early Christians also inherited from the Greco-Roman culture the virtue of friendship, since friendship was basic to cultivating the virtuous life. Plato attributed to Socrates the statement "I have a passion for friends."[16] Aristotle is claimed to have appreciated friendship more than justice, since with friendship one would not need justice. A strong component was having fidelity in a relationship because the honorable qualities of the one admired are themselves lasting qualities. While Cicero's classic on friendship, *de amicitia*, has had the greatest influence culturally on the ideals of friendship, Seneca as a Stoic theorist on friendship practiced it extensively in his *letters*. As a contemporary of Paul, Seneca has fascinated scholars regarding their distinctive in being Christian and Stoic. Seneca believed men are bonded by nature to help each other, highly esteeming friendship, while for Paul, friendship was secondary to the love of God and to his command "as friends" to obey his commands.[17] His epistle to the Philippians may be considered a classic regarding how the imitation of Christ, and of his servant, is expressed in humility,

---

[16]Preston King and Heather Devere, eds., *The Challenge to Friendship in Modernity* (Portland, OR: Frank Cass, 2000), p. 12.

[17]Jan N. Seventer, *Paul and Seneca* (Leiden: E. J. Brill, 1961).

in works of charity, in concern for others and in the unity of the faith.[18]

The letters (*Epistulae*) of Augustine of Hippo are among the most numerous extant of the early fathers (249 written by him and 49 written to him). Some are long enough to be considered treatises. The letters are a vast treasure trove of the bishop's pastoral concerns and friendships. Some are with his prickly scholarly superior Jerome, with whom he had "a distant relation," both in place and mutual understanding. Augustine's many doctrinal controversies are also mirrored in his letters, as well as clerical scandals, pastoral edification and direct responses to requests, such as that to the wealthy widow Paulina on how to pray.[19]

One of the most illuminating letters is that of Athanasius to his friend Marcellinus. It uniquely summarises the bishop's use and appreciation of the Psalter as the lay Christian's "miniature Bible," much of which he doubtless learned from the desert fathers themselves, in their desert hermitages. It is a classic on the appreciation of the psalms as the Christian's prayer book.[20]

2. Patristic allegory as the quest for spiritual meaning. As Moses both learned and made use of the wisdom of the Egyptians, so too cultured Christians like Origen, Gregory Nazianzen, Gregory of Nyssa, John Chrysostom and Augustine deployed their rhetorical skills in letter writing, biography/autobiography and poetry—but particularly in sermons. They all quote the example of Moses. They all value Greek *paideia* education as the cultivation of friendship for character formation, as blending virtue with intellect.[21] But now, argue the Fathers, it is the Holy Spirit, not the spirits of the gods, who provides divine inspiration for this spiritual transformation. With the guidance of the Holy Spirit the Fathers now seek for the spiritual meaning of the text.[22]

---

[18]Ben Witherington III, *Friendship and Finances in Philippi* (Valley Forge, PA: Trinity Press International, 1994).

[19]James M. Houston, *Letters of Faith Through the Seasons* (Colorado Springs: Honor Books, 2006), 1:272-79.

[20]Athanasius of Alexandria, *The Life of Antony and the Letter to Masrcellinus*, trans. Robert C. Gregg (New York: Paulist Press, 1980).

[21]Werner Jaeger, *Early Christianity and Greek Paideia* (Cambridge, MA: Belknap Press, 1961).

[22]See the important work on the return to sacramental mystery by my colleague Hans Boersma, *Nouvelle Theologie and Sacramental Ontology: A Return to Mystery* (Oxford: Oxford University Press, 2010).

The anthropomorphic language used in Scripture Origen now relates to the shallow levels of meaning that need to be further deepened into spiritual understanding, by the guidance of the Holy Spirit, to assist us in exploring their meaning most deeply. While typology has long been abused by preachers for popular communication, patristic allegory is the opposite—a highly sophisticated, creative and innovative application to biblical texts in a new situation, from the Jewish synagogues into the new Christian communities. Christ and his church are the new parameters—especially for the Psalms—where Augustine identifies the differing voices of the original psalmist, of David, of Christ, of the church or indeed of the contemporary Christian.

Allegorical or, more accurately, intertextual interpretation provides this openness to further fulfilling meaning than the literal text. The senses of Scripture can move beyond the literal to the spiritual or indeed to their moral application. While today we focus on the production of the text, patristic exegetes emphasize the differing receptions of diverse readers. Instead of viewing texts through a clear glass as we do, the fathers like Ambrose, Hilary and Augustine see through a crystal, scattering its multiple rays of diverse colors.[23] Accepting this will help us to reappreciate the sacramental or liturgical dimensions of Origen's original "spiritual" approach. Origen saw the literal interpretation of Scripture as "the body of the text," while the figurative could penetrate to reveal "the soul of the text."[24] Pastorally, he interpreted the primary purpose of the Bible as making us wise unto salvation.

In his sermons on the Psalms, *Enarrationes in Psalmos,* Augustine of Hippo sees God's unique discourse as giving profound unity to all the Scriptures (*unus sermo Dei*). It is Christ now who speaks through the Psalter, while David still serves as his voice.[25] Augustine searches strenuously for the mind and will of God throughout the Psalms, seeing divine love as the heart of their message. The *totus Christus* is their hermeneutical center, not just as an objective focus about Christ and his church

---

[23]Christoph Jacob, "The Reception of the Origenist Tradition in Latin Exegesis," in *Hebrew Bible/ Old Testament*, ed. Magne Saebo, vol. 1/1 (Gottingen: Vandenhoeck & Ruprecht, 1996), p. 699.
[24]Joseph W. Trigg, *Origen*, Early Church Fathers (New York: Routledge, 1998).
[25]Pamela Bright, ed., *Augustine and the Bible* (Notre Dame, IN: University of Notre Dame Press, 1999).

but as individual Christians crying out as the living subjects of psalm after psalm. Insights are conveyed, often in a brief sentence or two, to affirm or confirm what has already been revealed and received of wisdom.[26] Augustine himself is revealed developmentally in the course of the *Enarrationes*.[27]

A further classic of patristic allegory is the adoption of the Song of Songs by Origen, further developed by Gregory of Nyssa in sermons, which he sent to a friend, the widow Olympias, before c. 405. He follows on Origen's interpretation that the Song of Songs in its mystery refers to three developments: (1) the progressive growth of the Christian by grace and teaching, into purification and light, in the soul's struggles against sensual passions and worldly ways; (2) the awareness of how basic grace in the life of the believer opens up deeper insights of the spiritual nature of the life of the Christian; and (3) there follows the mystical ascent to God through the cloud of darkness or "unknowing" as *epectasis* or the indefinite progression of soul, as Paul describes it to be "straining forward to what lies ahead" (Phil 3:13-14). Gregory the Great again makes use of the Song of Songs in the late sixth century, which Bernard and his successors then wholeheartedly dwell on in the "Bridal Mysticism" of the twelfth century onward.

Gregory's *Life of Moses*, written at the end of his life, concludes that while we may contemplate the mystery of God's ineffability all our life, our progression lies in the darkness of the unknowable, or apophatic. This makes absolute our dissatisfaction with infinite desiring. But where we can "know" God lies in his humility in the incarnation, and this is what makes us like himself, in being humble.[28] John of the Cross is later to dwell upon Gregory's mysticism, making it his own.

Basic to all such allegorical/spiritual usage is the Christian's sense of transcendence. This is stretched between self-knowledge and the knowledge of God. In his *Confessions*, Augustine cries out, "let me know

[26]Bruce Waltke and James M. Houston, *The Psalms as the Church's Worship* (Grand Rapids: Eerdmans, 2010).
[27]Michael Cameron, "Inerrationes in Psalmos," in *Augustine Through The Ages*, ed. Allan D. Fitzgerald (Grand Rapids: Eerdmans, 1999), pp. 290-96.
[28]Robert Louis Wilken, *The Spirit of Early Christian Thought* (New Haven, CT: Yale University Press, 2003), pp. 276-77.

Thee, O Lord, let me know myself!" So too Origen uses the verse of Song of Songs 1:8 as the key to this mysticism: "If you do not know [yourself] follow the tracks of the flock," implying that if you do not have God's knowledge of yourself, you will merely follow the ways of sinners, which custom and habit create, but in which we will perish. Instead, if you follow the transcendent ways of God in seeking to know yourself in the light of his ineffability, allegory will help you to not take the material reality of this world so idolatrously. Gregory then quotes Matthew 25:34: "Come ye, blessed of my Father, possess you the kingdom prepared for you from the foundation of the world."[29]

There are those who would distinguish typology as biblical, and allegory as merely literary.[30] But this does not explain that for the Fathers the quest was to go beyond the knowledge of the literal text to transform the reader by his or her "participatory reading," to live in and to expand existentially from the "spiritual" meaning being found intertextually.

We may then summarize this patristic use of allegory as following Paul's own way of interpreting the Old Testament. As he states himself: "the letter kills, but the Spirit gives life" (2 Cor 3:6). Paul uses Psalm 19 in Romans 10 figuratively. In 1 Corinthians 10:11, Paul states that what happened to the Israelites was "as an example," while in Galatians 4 he calls Abraham's two wives an allegory. Christ now becomes the subject and the key to Old Testament exegesis. Intertextual links become the clothing of Christian reinterpretation.[31] We may further call biblical allegory *evangelical*, since it applies the Christian gospel to all the Old Testament Scriptures. Instead of being locked against a non-Jewish readership, the figural opens the door for the Old Testament to become the Christian Scriptures.

---

[29]Gregory of Nyssa, *From Glory to Glory: Texts from Gregory of Nyssa's Mystical Writings*, sel. Jean Danielou, trans. and ed. Herbert Musurillo (Crestwood, NY: St. Vladimir's Press, 1979), pp. 159-63.

[30]That typology is rooted in the historical particularities of salvation history is the argument of scholars such as Jean Danielou, *From Shadows to Realities: Studies in the Biblical Typology of the Fathers*, trans. W. Hibberd (London: Burns & Oats, 1960); and R. P. C. Hanson, *Allegory and Event: A Study in the Sources and Significance of Origen's Interpretation of Scripture* (Richmond: Westminster John Knox, 2002).

[31]Robert Louis Wilken, *The Spirit of Early Christian Thought* (New Haven, CT: Yale University Press, 2003), pp. 70-77.

Prudentius, a Christian poet contemporary of Ambrose, used allegory in this way. His *Psychomachia* (Spiritual Warfare), like Bunyan's later *Pilgrim's Progress*, is about the inner life of the Christian, as Everyman, in his struggle to set his affections on Christ and not on the world.[32] It echoes the call of Abraham. Such allegory invites us to enter into the lives and stories of biblical characters like Abraham to become our story too. As being iconic, and not idolatrous—as even critical biblical scholarship can also become idolatrous—Scriptural allegory provides an openness to allow God's Spirit to apply God's Word to our own lives, to free us from self-preoccupation and to become translatable into the community of his church. For it is applicable to all God's pilgrims, who have as yet not already attained but seek after the deepening mysteries of God.

MEDIEVAL MONASTIC GENRES

What was germinal in the early church flourished institutionally in the later liturgical monastic practices. Basic was the fourfold interpretation of the text as literal, allegorical, tropological and anagogical. As the phrase went, "the letter teaches what took place; the allegory what to believe; the moral what to do; and the anagogy what goal to strive."[33] Set within the monastic practices of reading, prayer, meditation and contemplation, or *lectio divina*, a rich community life was promoted, with friendship and personal prayer life as Anselm pioneered, or with letter writing and pastoral care, as Bernard of Clairvaux later exemplified. Monasticism, arising from the incipient culture of the desert fathers, now became the religious, dominant force of the Middle Ages, which incorporated all these features.

Itier of Vassy's poem makes clear that while the monks were versed in the classics both Christian and pagan, their role was not just to be literate; each had a spiritual calling to glorify God in worship:

Monks chant the psalms: let others make rhymes.
The monk's heart is reserved for the praise of his God.

---

[32]Ibid., pp. 228-36.
[33]Henri Lubac, *Medieval Exegesis*, trans. Mark Selbanc (Grand Rapids: Eerdmans, 1998), 1:79.

He abandons poetry to think of God's glory;
In his words and deeds let him honour the Lord. . . .
To weep is fitting for a monk, the writing of poetry is not.[34]

Jean Leclercq has outlined so clearly that as monastic culture matured in the twelfth century—particularly under the Cistercians—it intensified its longing and devotion for heaven. It promoted rumination on Scripture, not for its knowledge but for its thirst-quenching living water, and its intensifying of desire for the love of God. Bridal mysticism based on the Song of Songs, originating with Origen, developed by Gregory the Great, now reaches its climax in Bernard of Clairvaux. Indeed, this paramount genre moves from the allegorical to the tropological, from beliefs to behavior. The Victorines of Paris then introduced it into the vernacular piety of the later Middle Ages. Bridal mysticism was later applied ecclesiastically, to be not just the love of the soul with Christ but the love of the Virgin Mary with God.[35]

Yet major changes occurred in the twelfth century: the rise of the individual, the new teaching in secular schools and the rise of scholasticism, with its increasing abstraction, precision of concepts, priority of objective knowledge and rationalism. Peter Abelard (1079-1142) was the first to treat *theologia* as an abstract idea for analysis and not as the living presence of God.[36] With him was the first split between Christian sanctity and scholarship, and between the monastic and the scholastic approaches to truth.[37]

Another distinctive of the twelfth century was the renewed focus on friendship fostered in the monastic culture. Since God is love and God is our most intimate friend, friendship and letter writing went together. Bernard of Clairvaux (1090-1153) exemplified all these features. Prompted by deep experience of the intimacy of faith in loving God,

---

[34]Itier of Vassy, quoted by Jean Leclerc, *The Love of Learning and the Desire for God* (New York: Fordham University Press, 1974), p. 172.

[35]E. Ann Matter, *The Voice of my Beloved: The Song of Songs in Western Medieval Christianity* (Philadelphia: University of Pennsylvania Press, 1990), pp. 14-15.

[36]M. T. Clanchy, *Abelard: A Medieval Life* (Oxford: Blackwell, 1999), p. 7.

[37]Jean Leclercq, "Monastic and Scholastic Theology in the Reformers of the Fourteenth to Sixteenth Centuries," in *From Cloister to Classroom, Monastic and Scholastic Approaches to Truth,* ed. E. Rozanne Elder (Kalamazoo, MI: Cistercian Publications, 1986), pp. 178-201.

Bernard demonstrated how spiritual experience could so transform monastic literature. It explains the unique influence Bernard had within his time, while it also permitted other writers to compose their classics, such as William of Thierry, Aelred of Rievaulx and John of Ford. Aelred of Rievaulx's *Spiritual Friendship* was itself modeled on Cicero's *de Amicitia*, the unique Latin classic. But his purpose is to show how the universal love of God can be exercised in preferential friendship within a monastic community.[38] The fact that some monastic orders banned the book until Vatican II in the 1960s suggests how this tension remained for over nine hundred years.

LATE MEDIEVAL MYSTICAL THEOLOGY

While the term *mystical/mysticism* is traceable to the early church, referring to an intense personal experience(s) of God, it suggests also a further literary cultural expansion beyond both monastic and patristic theology. Common to both is the role of the Latin Vulgate, whose monopoly was expressive of the ruling class, ecclesial and secular, until after the late Middle Ages. This only began to be reformed in the thirteenth century by the rise of vernacular languages. Previously considered vulgar, they began to have their own dignity, elevated as expressive of personal experiences of God now being communicated in people's own languages and dialects.[39] The Council of Toulouse in 1219 reaffirmed the use of the Psalms in the vernacular.[40] As Michel de Certau describes it, "the art of speaking" as being only Latin was overcome when "mystics" arose like "the Trojan horse of rhetoric within the city of theological science."[41] The mobility of Dominican and Franciscan preachers contributed to this popular, vernacular upsurge of piety among the common people. Commerce and a newly independent mercantile class further fostered new regional movements of popular devotion.

---

[38]Aelred of Rievaulx, *Spiritual Friendship* (Kalamazoo, MI: Cistercian Publications, 2005).

[39]Christine Mohrmann, *Etudes sur le latin des Chretiens*, vol. 136 (Rome: Storiae Letteratura, 1958).

[40]Waltke and Houston, *Psalms as the Church's Worship*.

[41]Michel de Certau, *The Mystic Fable*, trans. Michael B. Smith (Chicago: University of Chicago Press, 1995), 1:114.

Hildegard of Bingen (d. 1179), in poetic use of Medieval Latin, composed her *Scivias* (*Know the Ways of the Lord*). Poems and narratives were written by Beguines in Antwerp (mid-thirteenth century) in Middle Dutch. Autobiography was used by Beatrice of Nazareth (d. 1268) in the Thiois dialect. Personal reflections were given in *The Mirror of Simple Souls* by Marguerite Porete (d. 1310) in French. Richard Rolle (d. 1349) wrote his commentaries on the Psalms in Middle English, as also Julian of Norwich (d. c. 1416) wrote her *Showings*, which she experienced through intense suffering. Catherine of Siena (d. 1380) collated messages of her letters and meditations into her five-day ecstasy, *The Dialogue*, in her own Sienese dialect. Much of this material was a fusion of memorized Scripture with intimate feelings, mystical experiences and prayer.

Like commerce, these mystic languages crossed national boundaries to become translational, into further diverse vernaculars. Venice became a key city of both commerce and of the printing of books, which were then circulated as spiritual classics into many lands.[42] Thomas à Kempis's *Imitation of Christ* became the most widely translated classic in Western Europe, while Lorenzo Scupoli's *The Spiritual Combat* (1589) circulated widely in the east. It was translated into the Balkan languages and eventually into Armenian and Russian. The fluidity of translatability lay in preference to vernacular word usage over received ecclesial definitions.[43] Mostly the translators remained anonymous, often for political reasons of prudence.

Only later did poets like George Herbert and his friends in Little Gidding in the seventeenth century and George Stanhope in the eighteenth century begin publicly to translate and to circulate Spanish mystics like Luis de Leon, Luis de Granada, Teresa of Ávila, John of the Cross and Ignatius of Loyola into Protestant England. François Fénelon and Madame Guyon were later translated widely. Later still, John Wesley issued abbreviations of "modern classics," beginning with William Law, for the use of his Methodist preachers.

---

[42]James M. Houston, ed., *Juan de Valdes: The Benefit of Christ* (Portland, OR: Multnomah Press, 1984).
[43]de Certaeau, *Mystic Fable*, p. 118.

As long as Christian literature after the Reformation was still life-changing in its devotion, there have remained Christian classics. So we can include the *Institutes of the Christian Religion* of John Calvin, the hymns of Isaac Watts and of Charles Wesley, Jonathan Edwards's *Treatise Concerning the Religious Affections* or the political manifesto of William Wilberforce on true Christianity. But Hans-Georg Gadamer concluded that "it requires hermeneutical reflection of some sophistication to discover how it is possible for a normative concept such as the classical to acquire or regain its scholarly legitimacy."[44] For it is still raised above the vicissitudes of changing times and literary tastes.

But today the theological distinctive of a Christian classic is not always clear. Ellen T. Charry uses the Greek norm of *aretē* or "excellence as a person" as the motive for the use of classics today. "Becoming an excellent person is predicated on enjoying God. For these theologians, beauty, truth, and goodness—the foundations of human happiness—come from knowing God and nowhere else."[45] Is this not part of Methodist heritage—the pursuit of perfection—as John Wesley himself rediscovered the classics?

This has not been their use in the Reformed Christian mainstream of orthodoxy. Rather, with the biblical awareness of our sinful condition, for John Calvin and the Puritan writers later, Christian perfection is an oxymoron, even though later Catholic writers such as François Fénelon advocated its pursuit. Biblical growth and maturity are not to be confused with Greek perfection.

Meanwhile, since the eighteenth century the progress of the historical-critical method has intruded into the appreciation of the classics with three faces: the history of sources, the history of composition and the history of redaction. For example, in attacking the Song of Songs as a unique allegorical genre of medieval devotion, historical criticism now reduces the Song to an erotic love song, possibly composed by a

---

[44]Hans-Georg Gadamer, *Truth and Method*, trans. Weinsheimer and Marshall, rev. ed. (New York: Continuum, 1989), pp. 285-90.
[45]Ellen T. Charry, *By the Renewing of Your Minds* (New York: Oxford University Press, 1997), p. vii.

woman who seeks love with no moral constraints. As such it is cut off from its roots in Jewish devotion for Yahweh, as well as in Christian devotion to Christ.[46]

CONCLUSION: READING CHRISTIAN CLASSICS APPROPRIATELY

Since Christian classics center on the advent and person of Jesus Christ, they are tested by the reader's doctrinal and devotional adherence to the Scriptures themselves.[47] Christian mysticism is not just about unknown knowledge but rather concerns the ineffable yet personal human experience of God's presence and love.[48]

Christian classics are intrinsically personal reading, to be read more by heart than as an academic exercise. They require seasons of openness and acceptance, since at one phase of life the book may mean nothing to us, yet at another it may have lasting consequences. Likewise, selective choice is needed pastorally, so that the classic recommended personally needs to fit the spiritual needs of a particular reader.

---

[46] Andre La Cocque and Paul Ricoeur, *Thinking Biblically: Exegetical and Hermeneutical Studies*, trans. David Pellauer (Chicago: University of Chicago Press, 1998), pp. 235-306.

[47] James M. Houston, "A Guide to Devotional Reading," *Classics of Faith and Devotion* (Vancouver, BC: Regent Publishing, 1983-2003).

[48] James M. Houston, "Reflections on Mysticism: How Valid Is Evangelical Anti-Mysticism?" in *Loving God and Keeping His Commandments*, ed. Markus Bockmuehl and Helmut Burkhardt (Basel: BrunnenVerlag, 1991).

PART THREE

Reading

Evangelically

7

Reading Catholic Spirituality

Bruce Demarest

GIVEN THE HISTORY OF SUSPICION between Protestant evangelicals and Catholics, I write this chapter with some unease. Insights from my personal spiritual journey hopefully will provide a context to this chapter.

PERSONAL ENGAGEMENT WITH CATHOLIC SPIRITUALITY

After graduating from a leading evangelical college and seminary and completing doctoral work with Professor F. F. Bruce at Manchester University, I served for a decade with two leading evangelical mission boards in Africa and Europe. Subsequently I have taught theology and spiritual formation at Denver Seminary. Teaching a course on Catholic theology at my seminary reinforced concerns about aspects of its theology.

In the late 1980s a renewal team from the Catholic Archdiocese of Denver presented a six-week course on spiritual formation at our evangelical church. Attending the course after initial resistance, I experienced an immediate resonance with their teaching on protocols for nurturing Christian spiritual life. At the conclusion of the course I journeyed with the team leader in a spiritual direction relationship for several years that proved highly formative for my life in Christ.

My spiritual director encouraged attendance at workshops and retreats at a Benedictine renewal community in New Mexico. In 1995—again with some trepidation—I enrolled in the community's six-week, residential School of Spiritual Direction, attended equally by charismatic Catholics, renewal Anglicans and Protestant evangelicals. The liturgies, teachings, formation groups and spiritual direction significantly influenced my spiritual and emotional worlds.

Returning from the monastery to my seminary, I developed graduate courses in Christian formation and soul care, and wrote about my experience with God in *Satisfy Your Soul: Restoring the Heart of Christian Spirituality*, which won a national award. Dr. Ralph Martin, the Catholic president of Renewal Ministries, wrote on the book's flyleaf, "What an amazing journey Bruce Demarest has been on. While remaining solidly rooted in his own evangelical tradition, he has, with great honesty and courage, opened himself to the deep and vital life in Christian history that has much to offer us today."[1] Introduced by providence to the world of spiritual formation, my pathway has become more classically Christian, missional and compassionate.

WISDOM OF SELECTED CATHOLIC SPIRITUALITY

Many Christians read the spiritual classics, including Catholic sources. Can these works be safely and fruitfully read by Bible-believing people? This section highlights spiritual wisdom imbedded in selected Catholic classical writings—often overlooked by evangelicals—that can enrich our spiritual lives and ministries. The following observations characterize the period between the Great Schism (1054) and the Second Vatican Council (1962-1965). Limitations of space require that citations be selective and brief.

Love for God. Many Catholic spiritual writers of the period fervently sought to know and love God. In his treatise *On Loving God*, Bernard of Clairvaux (1090-1153)—abbot of the famous Clairvaux monastery—passionately expressed development of love in four stages: love of self for self, love of God for self, love of God for God, and love of self for God. He wrote, "God himself is the reason we love him, and the measure of that love is to love him without measure."[2] Bernard also expressed love

---

[1]Bruce Demarest, *Satisfy Your Soul* (Colorado Springs: NavPress, 1999).
[2]Bernard, *On Loving God* 1.1, in *Bernard of Clairvaux: Selected Works*, trans. G. R. Evans, Classics of Western Spirituality (New York: Paulist Press, 1987), p. 174.

for God in hymns such as "Jesus the Very Thought of Thee," "O Sacred Head Now Wounded" and "Jesus, Thou Joy of Loving Hearts." Bernard's writings were thoroughly Christ-centered: "To know Jesus and Jesus crucified."[3] The Cistercian influenced Luther, Calvin and the Puritans, who quoted him approvingly. Wrote Luther, "I regard Bernard as the most pious of all the monks and prefer him to all the others."[4]

Intimacy with God. Julian of Norwich (c. 1342-c. 1416), an anchoress who lived in a cell attached to St. Julian's church in Norwich where she prayed and offered spiritual counsel, made three requests of God in order to deepen intimacy with him. "The first was to have recollection of Christ's passion; the second was a bodily sickness; and the third was to have, of God's gift, three wounds."[5] The last involved "the wound of contrition, the wound of compassion and the wound of longing with my will for God."[6] In her thirtieth year Julian suffered a nearly fatal illness from which she allegedly experienced miraculous healing.

Shortly thereafter Julian reported receiving sixteen visions of Jesus' passion. *Showings* contains her intimate dialogue with God in the context of her visionary experiences. Of her first vision she wrote, "For until I am substantially united to him, I can never have perfect rest or true happiness, until, that is, I am so attached to Him that there can be no created thing between my God and me."[7] According to Archbishop Rowan Williams, Julian's *Showings* "may well be the most important work of Christian reflection in the English language."[8]

University of Paris professor and head of the Franciscan order, Bonaventure (1221-1274) wrote *The Soul's Journey into God*, describing six stages of contemplation by which the soul achieves union with God. Concerning the soul's rising to intimate union, Bonaventure stated the necessity of divine grace.

[3]Richard J. Foster and Gayle D. Beebe, *Longing for God* (Downers Grove, IL: IVP Books, 2009), p. 40.
[4]Martin Luther, cited in John Michael Talbot, *The Way of the Mystics* (San Francisco: Jossey-Bass, 2005), p. 33.
[5]Julian of Norwich, *Showings*, trans. Edmund Colledge and James Walsh, Classics of Western Spirituality (New York: Paulist Press, 1977), short text 1, p. 125.
[6]Ibid., p. 127.
[7]Ibid., long text 5, p. 183.
[8]Rowan Williams, cited in Jonathan Wilson-Hartgrove's review of *Julian of Norwich: A Contemplative Biography* by Amy Frykholm, in *Christianity Today*, August 2010, p. 51.

But we cannot rise above ourselves
Unless a higher power life us up.
No matter how much our interior progress is ordered,
Nothing will come of it
Unless accompanied by divine aid.[9]

A life of deepening prayer. In *The Interior Castle* Teresa of Ávila (1515-1582) described the life of deepening prayer imaged by seven rooms of a medieval castle, the innermost room signifying the deepest recess of the soul where Christ dwells. In the castle's first rooms the soul is preoccupied with temporal concerns, and prayers are verbal, brief and lukewarm. In the middle rooms the journeyer engages God more sweetly through the prayer of quiet recollection. "The soul, instead of striving to engage in discourse, strives to remain attentive and aware of what the Lord is working in it."[10] In the castle's final rooms the soul is so united with its heavenly Spouse through prayerful communion that profound transformation in Christ occurs. Here the sojourner's reposed life becomes one ceaseless prayer, empowered to suffer and serve as a slave of God.

Imitating Jesus Christ. One of the most widely read spiritual books, *The Imitation of Christ*, emerged from the fourteenth- and fifteenth-century renewal movement known as the Brethren of the Common Life, whose members nurtured godliness and sought to live as Jesus' faithful disciples. Collection and editing of *The Imitation* is attributed to Thomas à Kempis (c. 1380-1471), a member of the Brethren who was a gifted preacher, teacher and spiritual counselor.

Augustinian in orientation. *The Imitation* reflects New Testament injunctions to pattern life after Jesus by radically imitating him (1 Pet 2:21). The summons to self-denial and suffering for Christ is reflected in the following. "Jesus has always many who desire consolations, but few who care for trial. He finds many to share His table, but few to take part in His fasting. All desire to be happy with Him; few wish to suffer anything

---

[9]Bonaventure, *Bonaventure: The Soul's Journey into God* 1.1, trans. Ewert Cousins, Classics of Western Spirituality (New York: Paulist Press, 1978), p. 59.
[10]Teresa of Ávila, *The Interior Castle*, trans. Kiernan Kavanaugh and Otilio Rodriguez, Classics of Western Spirituality (New York: Paulist Press, 1979), p. 79.

for Him."[11] Anabaptists, Pietists, Dietrich Bonhoeffer and many evangelicals have embraced this Kempian theme of radically following Christ and imitating his virtues and actions.

Soul care and spiritual direction. Catholic spirituality emphasizes the ministry of spiritual direction, whose value is being recognized in evangelical circles today. Ignatius of Loyola (c. 1491-1556), founder of the Jesuits, made fruitful contributions to soul care through his famous *Spiritual Exercises*. Designed as a manual by which spiritual directors lead others on guided retreats, the *Exercises* contains guidelines for discerning between good and evil spirits, deepening the life of prayer and discovering God's will. Ignatius insisted that a person without a soul companion is like a body without a head.

John of the Cross (1542-1591) noted that many who set out on the spiritual journey make little progress because they "misunderstand themselves and are without suitable and alert directors who will show them the way to the summit."[12] Although God is the principal guide of souls, the direction of every sojourner should be undertaken by a spiritual companion. Through this direction relationship the Spirit detaches the disciple from worldly attractions and infuses godly virtues, thus transforming professing Christians into Christlikeness. The spiritual director must be skilled at engaging three great enemies of the soul: the world, the flesh, and the devil—the latter being the most formidable. Effective spiritual directors are people of knowledge, discretion, prayer and experience.[13]

Catholic spiritual authorities such as Bernard of Clairvaux, François Fénelon and Friedrich Von Hügel exercised fruitful soul care ministries by letter writing that helpfully instruct us today.

Researcher Bruce Hindmarsh concludes that the evangelical movement drew heavily on "a common core of classical Christian spirituality" represented largely by Roman Catholic writings.[14] He adds,

---

[11]Thomas à Kempis, *The Imitation of Christ*, Hendrickson Christian Classics (Peabody, MA: Hendrickson, 2004), p. 47.

[12]John of the Cross, "The Ascent of Mount Carmel," *The Collected Works of St. John of the Cross*, trans. Kiernan Kavanaugh and Otilio Rodriguez (Washington, DC: Institute of Carmelite Studies, 1991), p. 115.

[13]John of the Cross, "The Living Flame of Love," *Collected Works* 3:29, p. 685.

[14]Bruce Hindmarsh, "Seeking True Religion," in *Life in the Spirit: Spiritual Formation in Theological Perspective*, ed. Jeffrey P. Greenman and George Kalantzis (Downers Grove, IL: IVP Academic, 2010), p. 15.

"Early evangelicalism is best interpreted therefore as a devotional movement in continuity with classical Christian spirituality, expressed under modern conditions."[15]

CAUTIONS READING CATHOLIC SPIRITUALITY

This section highlights areas of theological concern that biblically grounded evangelicals must carefully evaluate while reading Catholic spiritual writings.

Biblical interpretation and authority. Catholic spiritual writers placed church tradition on a par with Scripture following the Roman church's claim to be the definitive interpreter of the Bible. Moreover, medieval spiritual writers often employed a fourfold, rather than a literal, interpretation of Scripture.

Bernard of Clairvaux judged that the Song of Songs is not primarily about the love between a man and a woman, but about Christ and his church. Consider the saying of the woman in Song of Solomon 1:16-17:

> Behold, you are beautiful, my beloved, truly delightful.
> Our couch is green;
> > the beams of our house are cedar;
> > our rafters are pine.

Bernard interpreted the text as follows: "The 'bed' is the church's monasteries and cloisters, where there is no distraction by the cares of the world. 'Our house' is the community of Christians. The 'beams' are the supporting structure of doctrine and regulations that prevent weakening of the structure by individuals. The 'rafters' are educated, dedicated clergy."[16]

Like many spiritual authorities of the period, Bonaventure subscribed to a fourfold exegesis: the literal and "the tropological, that purifies one for an upright life; the allegorical, that illumines one for clarity of understanding; and the anagogical, that perfects through spiritual ecstasies and sweet perceptions of wisdom."[17] Fourfold exegesis was judged fruitful for expounding the "richer" treasures of the Christian mystery.

---

[15]Ibid., p. 116.
[16]Bernard of Clairvaux, *Talks on the Song of Songs*, ed. Bernard Bangley (Brewster, MA: Paraclete Press, 1980), p. 83.
[17]Bonaventure, *Bonaventure* 4.6, p. 91.

Evangelicals hold that while instructive for faith and life (cf. Lk 1:1-4), tradition—the transmission of "truth" from one generation to the next— must always be verified against the final authority of Scripture. The Bible must be interpreted in its literal, historical sense (allowing for legitimate figures of speech), reflecting the intention of the Sprit-directed writer.

Supremacy and infallibility of the pope. Based on Matthew 16:18 and the belief that Peter founded the church at Rome and was martyred there, Catholicism holds that the popes as successors of Peter assume supremacy over all other bishops. In the medieval era the infallibility of the pope while teaching on matters of faith and morals (*ex cathedra*) was established.

Spiritual writer Julian of Norwich upheld the God-given teaching authority of the papacy. Regarding her sixteen *Showings*, she wrote, "I was not drawn by it away from any article of the faith which the Holy Church teaches me to believe," adding, it is an entirely good thing "to be fastened and united to our mother Holy Church, who is Christ Jesus."[18] The favorite name for the pope proposed by Catherine of Siena (1347-1380) was "Christ on earth."[19] She insisted that Christ gave the keys of the kingdom of heaven to "the chief pontiff Peter," the prince of apostles, and "to all the others who have come or will come from now until the final judgment day with the very same authority that Peter had."[20] The pope allegedly holds the key to the door to eternal life sealed by Adam's sin.

The claim that the Roman popes throughout history represent divinely chosen successors of Peter and infallible purveyors of doctrine lacks biblical support. Fallible Peter's role in the early church was ordained to be one of service, not of centuries-long dominance. Papal infallibility became established church dogma only in 1870 and was later modified by Vatican II where the bishop of Rome assumes a collegial relationship with the college of bishops as their spokesman.

A low view of the fall and human sinfulness. Catholicism asserts that due to the fall the faculties that constitute the *imago Dei* were merely

---

[18]Julian of Norwich, *Showings*, long text 33, p. 234; 61, p. 302.

[19]Catherine of Siena, *The Dialogue*, trans. Suzanne Noffke, Classics of Western Spirituality (New York: Paulist Press, 1980), p. 215 n. 18.

[20]Ibid., p. 214.

weakened, not seriously corrupted. Thus pre-Christians possess the natural ability to choose and know God salvifically.

Julian of Norwich envisioned sin as the outcome of human naiveté, ignorance and weakness. Emphasizing God's mercy, Julian portrayed God judging humanity as blameless victim rather than perpetrator of wrong. Of sin Julian boldly wrote, "You are nothing."[21] Julian claimed that since God is love, wrath does not exist in God. "God is that goodness which cannot be angry, for God is nothing but goodness."[22]

Petitioning God for a vision of hell, Julian saw only the devil, since humanity has been caught up into the life of God. "For all mankind . . . will be saved by the sweet Incarnation and the Passion of Christ."[23] Julian's famous saying—"All will be well, and all will be well, and every kind of thing will be well"—concerns what the loving God will accomplish for all persons on the last day.[24]

Scripture teaches that one of God's attributes is righteous wrath against sin (Jude 14-15). Moreover, as a consequence of Adam's fall in Eden the entire human race became morally corrupted, inclined to evil and subjected to eternal punishment (Mt 25:46). Not only was righteousness and right standing with God lost due to original sin, but the human faculties of intellect, will, emotions, conscience and so on are corrupted and hostile to God (Jer 17:9).

A clear call to conversion often lacking. Catholicism believes that the sacrament of baptism remits the guilt of sin, regenerates through the infusion of sanctifying grace and delivers from eternal punishment. Baptism is alleged to work *opere ex operato*—simply by performance of the rite. (The adult baptized must possess faith or the desire to receive the sacrament.)

Typical of Catholic writers, Bernard of Clairvaux affirmed that baptism heals the wound of original sin.[25] Moreover, Catherine of Siena wrote, "You receive this innocence and grace in holy baptism by the

---

[21]Julian of Norwich, *Showings*, short text 23, p. 166.
[22]Ibid., long text 46, p. 259.
[23]Ibid., 51, p. 256.
[24]Ibid., 27, p. 225; cf. ibid., 34, p. 236: "But when God did show me about sin, then he said: All will be well."
[25]Bernard of Clairvaux, *Talks on the Song of Songs*, p. 38.

power of the blood that washes away the stain of original sin in which you were conceived, which you contracted from your father and your mother."[26] Believing that baptism regenerates, the invitation to repentance and faith often was muted.

Repentance and faith as a requisite for salvation is abundantly attested in Scripture by John the Baptist (Mt 3:2), Jesus (Mk 1:15), the apostle Peter (Acts 2:38) and the apostle Paul (Acts 20:21). In the New Testament baptism follows a person's explicit confession of sins and trust in Jesus (Mk 1:5; Acts 2:41), where baptism serves as the public sign of repentance and forgiveness of sins.

Justification by faith alone? In Catholic thought justification occurs in two stages. At baptism a new nature is infused into the soul and past sins are remitted. Persons then strive for eternal life by love-inspired, virtuous works. Justification thus amounts to the lifelong process of making righteous. Since justification can be lost by mortal sin, assurance of final salvation normally is not possible.

Catherine of Siena records God stating that a person can make satisfaction for sin for him- or herself and others by works of charity. Catherine petitioned God for suffering in order to atone for offenses committed against him,[27] whereupon God allegedly replied, "But such suffering can atone [for sin] if it is united with the soul's desire and heartfelt contrition."[28] The Lord reportedly added, "The sufferings you endure will, through the power of charity, suffice to win both atonement and reward for you and others. For you they will win the fruit of life. . . . As for others, because of your loving charity I will pardon them."[29]

The doctrine of justification by faith alone is largely absent in the Catholic spiritual classics—its absence is reaffirmed in the Council of Trent's "Decree Concerning Justification" (1547) recorded in session six, canon 9. Canon 14 states, "If anyone says that the sinner is justified by faith alone, meaning that nothing else is required to co-operate in order to obtain the grace of justification, . . . let him be anathema."[30] In

---

[26]Catherine of Siena, *The Dialogue*, p. 279.
[27]Ibid., p. 29.
[28]Ibid., p. 361.
[29]Ibid., p. 30.
[30]"The Canon and Decrees of the Council of Trent," *Creeds of the Churches*, ed. John H. Leith, 3rd

the 1999 Joint Declaration on Justification Catholic and Lutherans declared an end to the Tridentine anathema directed against the doctrine of justification by faith. Scripture, we affirm, teaches that justification is based not on our good works, but is God's pronouncement of righteousness on the basis of faith in Christ's atoning sacrifice (Gal 2:16). Only God, not humans, are able to forgive sin and grant right standing with himself.

Redemptive role ascribed to Mary. Believing that sexual relations, even within marriage, are defiling, early church fathers claimed that Jesus' mother remained perpetually a virgin. In medieval times Mary was envisioned as a channel for saving grace and thus was given the title "Mediatrix" or comediator with Christ.

Deeply devoted to the virgin Mary, Bernard of Clairvaux hailed her as the dispenser of grace, intercessor for sinners and spiritual refuge. Thus, sinners need "a mediator with the Mediator, and there is no one more efficacious than Mary."[31] Catherine of Siena depicted God as saying, "For my Goodness, in deference to the Word, has decreed that anyone at all, just or sinner, who holds her [Mary] in due reverence will never be snatched or devoured by the infernal demon."[32]

In *Showing* eleven Julian of Norwich reported that Jesus enabled her to see the virgin Mary three times in visions. Julian averred that contemplation of Mary yields "the virtues of her blessed soul, her truth, her wisdom, her love through which I am taught to know myself and reverently to fear my God."[33] Since Mary is more worthy than all earthly persons, she is to be venerated. The Marian cult developed further with the dogmas of her immaculate conception (1854) and heavenly assumption (1950).

Protestants readily acknowledge that Mary, the mother of our Lord as to his humanity, is worthy of honor, but reject praying to her and seeking her intercession from heaven. Scripture depicts the mother of our Lord as the recipient of God's grace (Lk 1:28, 42-43), not the bestower of

---

ed. (Louisville, KY: John Knox Press, 1982), p. 421.

[31]Bernard of Clairvaux, cited by Richard P. McBrien, *Catholicism* (Minneapolis: Winston Press, 1980), p. 875.

[32]Catherine of Siena, *The Dialogue*, 139, p. 286.

[33]Julian of Norwich, *Showings*, long text 25, p. 222.

saving grace. In parts of the world such as Central and South America the cult of Mary, in which elements of animism and Christianity are synergistically wedded, flourishes.

Invocation of saints and Mary. Catholic spirituality believes that because of their virtue and proximity to Christ, saints serve as intercessors for earthly wayfarers. (Catholicism defines a saint as a person canonized by the church for outstanding piety and accomplishments.) Rome believes that through the so-called intercessions of saints miracles have occurred at their tombs or through their relics.

Thomas à Kempis implored the saints for their intercessions as well as venerating them. "It is better to invoke the saints with devout prayers and tears, and with a humble mind to beg their glorious aid, than to search with vain inquisitiveness into their secrets."[34] Bonaventure (c. 1217-1274) believed that Christians have access to the Father "through the intercession of the most holy Virgin Mary, the mother of the same God and Lord Jesus Christ, and through the intercession of blessed Francis [of Assisi], our leader and father."[35] Julian of Norwich enumerated the practical helps afforded by Mary and the saints, noting they "are a part of our redemption and of our endless salvation."[36]

As interpreted by evangelicals, the Old Testament identifies saints as all God's redeemed people (1 Sam 2:9; Ps 30:4). The New Testament refers *hagioi* to all believers in Christ who have been set apart for God (Rom 1:7; 1 Cor 1:2). Protestants regard leading Christians in history as positive models of spirituality and ministry, but, given Christ's unique mediatorship, deny that those canonized by the church function as intercessors and benefactors for earthly pilgrims.

Practice of severe asceticism. Not a few Catholic spiritual authorities practiced harsh asceticism in the form of self-flagellation, denial of sleep and excessive fasts that often ruined health. Punishing the body reflected the Greek belief that the flesh is inherently sinful, that merit could thereby be accrued and that the ascetic would participate in Christ's sufferings. Thomas à Kempis averred, "The more violence you

[34]Thomas à Kempis, *Imitation of Christ*, pp. 63, 128.
[35]Bonaventure, *Bonaventure*, p. 53.
[36]Julian of Norwich, *Showings,* long text 25, p. 222.

do to yourself, the more progress you will make [in the spiritual life]."[37]

Identifying physical pleasure with sin, Catherine of Siena pursued a fanatically ascetic lifestyle. Self-flagellation inflicted gaping wounds on her body, which she referred to as her "flowers." Catherine "fasted; she denied herself sleep; she wrapped a chain with crosses around her body so tightly that it caused her to bleed, and she scourged her body three times a day with a chain that was tipped with sharp hooks."[38] Anorexic, she died of starvation at age thirty-three. The second of Julian of Norwich's petitions, noted earlier, sought illness that would bring her near death. *Showing* 15 idealizes self-inflicted suffering in typical medieval fashion.

Christians will not engage in practices of severe asceticism. The gracious God is not rendered propitious to sinners by acts of self-inflicted punishment. Paul inveighed against "promoting self-made religion and asceticism and severity to the body" that "are of no value in stopping the indulgence of the flesh" (Col 2:23). Spiritual disciplines exercised in love facilitate Christlikeness, but the harshest regimens neither excise sin nor render us acceptable to God.

Promoting an unbiblical mysticism. The church has long been involved with mystical theology (e.g., Pseudo-Dionysius, *The Cloud of Unknowing*, John of the Cross). Julian of Norwich, as noted earlier, claimed mystical revelations and experiences that contradict Scripture, particularly her low estimate of sin and the alleged universal redemption of humankind.

The Cloud of Unknowing (c. 1375), an anonymous, mystical guide to contemplative prayer written by an English monk, claims that since God is unknowable, humans must suppress all mental processes. "Resist intense mental activity when seeking this dark contemplation. Intellectual activity will hinder you."[39] Moreover, "Let us abandon everything within the scope of our thoughts and determine to love what is beyond comprehension."[40] Code words such as *God* and *love* enable the contemplative to pierce the Cloud of Unknowing and gaze on the pure being

---

[37]Thomas à Kempis, *Imitation of Christ*, p. 32.
[38]Talbot, *Way of the Mystics*, p. 91.
[39]*The Cloud of Unknowing*, ed. Bernard Bangley, Christian Classics (Brewster, MA: Paulist Press, 2006), p. 20.
[40]Ibid., p. 14.

of God. God then may "send a ray of spiritual light to illumine *the cloud of unknowing*" and "reveal some of his unspeakable secrets," even the "fire of devotion."[41]

Helpfully, we may distinguish between hard and soft forms of mysticism. The latter consists of the believer's direct experience in the heart of the living God that cannot be fully expressed in words. The three disciples on the Mount of Transfiguration (Mt 17:1-8) and Paul caught up into the third heaven (2 Cor 12:2-4) are notable examples of soft mysticism. Hard mysticism, on the other hand, denies the reception of intelligible concepts and typically involves the absorption of the self into the World Soul or the Absolute. The latter form of mysticism tends toward pantheism.

Eastern religions as a pathway to God. Thomas Merton (1915-1968), a prominent Catholic spiritual writer who became attracted to Eastern religions, lived within the time frame of this essay. Moreover, Merton was a highly prolific writer, having penned some sixty books and six hundred articles.[42] One spiritual authority states that Merton "likely is the most widely read monk in all of Christian church history."[43] Contemporary readers can hardly ignore the writings of this influential figure.

Toward the end of his life Merton became attracted to the spirituality of Buddhism. In *Mystics and Zen Masters* Merton concluded that no essential conflict exists experientially between Buddhism and Christianity. Buddhism represents a legitimate pathway to the perennial human quest—the birthing of pure awareness leading to enlightenment. "Zen is perfectly compatible with Christian belief and indeed with Christian mysticism (if we understand Zen in its pure state, as metaphysical intuition)."[44] Merton spoke comfortably of Christian Zen or Zen Catholicism. To the rejoinder that Christianity and Buddhism offer very different belief systems, Merton responded, "One needs to focus on the experience more than on the explanation."[45]

---

[41]Ibid., p. 38.
[42]"I do not think any Catholic author has ever reached a larger audience" (M. Basil Pennington, *Engaging the World with Merton* [Brewster, MA: Paraclete Press, 2005], p. 57).
[43]Barry L. Callen, *Authentic Spirituality* (Grand Rapids: Baker Academic, 2001), p. 98.
[44]Thomas Merton, *Zen and the Birds of Appetite* (New York: New Directions, 1968), p. 47.
[45]Ibid., p. 38.

Merton also became attracted to Chinese Daoism, judging that Daoism's call for complete transformation is analogous to what "Christianity would call *metanoia*."[46] He alleged that leading Daoist virtues are replicated in Jesus' teachings. Merton, in sum, argued for a religious pluralism that welcomes all who seek Absolute Reality and Absolute Love. Spiritual writer Merton was a universalist who believed that the human family is one in God.

Given God's universal, general revelation (Rom 1:19-21), all persons know aspects of truth about the Creator and his relation to the world of humans. Elements of moral truth, therefore, are found in the world's leading religions. But eternal salvation comes only though Christ who stated, "I am the way, and the truth, and the life" (Jn 14:6).

SUMMARY

It has been said that the history of Christian spirituality—including Catholic spirituality—is essentially (albeit not infallibly) correct in its desire to love and honor God. Having read many spiritual classics, I agree with this statement. Let us note that we evangelicals may err in two ways when reading the classics. First, we may dismiss Catholic spirituality altogether and thereby miss the nuggets of edifying spiritual wisdom embedded therein. In the context of research on Teresa of Ávila's *Interior Castle*, R. Thomas Ashbrook testifies that reading Catholic authors as sources for spiritual growth was initially problematic for him. Then

> I was reminded that God has revealed His truth to His followers throughout history, quite apart from their particular denominational affiliation. We are free to learn from others without accepting everything about their theology or the church practice of their time. The Holy Spirit has been at work throughout human history . . . teaching us how to know and love God. . . . It sometimes takes a person from another perspective or tradition to challenge our blind spots and presuppositions.[47]

My own experience has been similar to his.

---

[46]Thomas Merton, *Mystics and Zen Masters* (New York: Farrar, Straus & Giroux, 1967), p. 50.
[47]R. Thomas Ashbrook, *Mansions of the Heart: Exploring the Seven Stages of Spiritual Growth* (San Francisco: Jossey-Bass, 2009), pp. 40-41.

Second, we may uncritically accept Catholic spiritual writings in their entirety and thus embrace unbiblical assertions such as those cited previously. Medieval writings, for example, that elevate the system of indulgences, Mary as comediator with Christ, salvation by works and universal salvation must be rejected as less than orthodox. The presence of suborthodox elements such as these explains why John Wesley, for example, carefully edited the Catholic classics he included in his fifty-quarto-volume series, The Christian Library—that substantial collection of books intended for the nurture of new converts. Lawrence S. Cunningham, Catholic professor of theology at Notre Dame University, concedes that "not everything in the Catholic spiritual tradition is above reproach. Indeed, some elements that run like a thread in the tradition need correction or better, benign neglect. . . . Some devotional works and practices barely escape the charge of magic, while others seem rather undernourished in their theology of grace."[48]

Our responsible approach as evangelicals then is to welcome all that is true and edifying in the Catholic spiritual tradition and to dismiss what is contrary to Scripture and evangelical doctrine. We do well, in other words, to separate the wheat from the chaff, or welcome the gold while rejecting any dross we encounter. Richard Foster correctly stated, "We need a vision that welcomes the rich diversity of the body of Christ while being absolutely clear on the essentials of Christian life and faith."[49]

As we read Catholic spirituality we are likely to find greater agreement spiritually than theologically. At my first serious encounter with Catholic spirituality a quarter of a century ago, I concluded that Protestant evangelicalism possesses a better theology (think "head") and a better mission praxis (think "hands"). But faithful Catholic (and Orthodox) spirituality can be invaluable for nurturing spiritual life (think "issues of the heart"). As Philip Sheldrake notes, "The great classical texts are not concerned primarily with ideas about doctrine but about practice of the Christian life."[50]

[48]Lawrence S. Cunningham, "The Way and the Ways: Reflections on Catholic Spirituality," in *Life in the Spirit*, ed. Jeffrey P. Greenman and George Kalantzis (Downers Grove, IL: IVP Academic, 2010), p. 96.

[49]Richard Foster, "Pastoral Letters," *Renovaré* 9, no. 2 (2002), which can be accessed at www.renovare.us/ViewNewsLetter/tabid/2404/Default.aspx?ID=68.

[50]Philip Sheldrake, *Spirituality and Theology* (Maryknoll, NY: Orbis, 1998), p. 99.

The reality is that the gracious and sovereign God has been at work in the lives of his people through all the periods of church history. As we read the spiritual classics we do well to keep an open mind and heart to new and fruitful insights the Spirit of God may teach us. The most faithful and nurturing of Catholic spiritual writings likely will send us back to Scripture with clearer vision and renewed appetite for deeper relationship with God and the transformed life that comes through Jesus Christ.

Reading Orthodox Spirituality

James R. Payton Jr.

You can't get there from here." While that common old declaration may seem out of place in a day when a global positioning system can give precise directions to almost anywhere, it is not far off the mark to talk about getting from an evangelical stance to Orthodox spirituality. The journey is possible, but it is a challenging trek through foreign territory, unmapped in the typical evangelical atlas.

To change the metaphor, there is no "instant rice" or "two minutes in a microwave" access to Orthodox spirituality. Getting familiar enough with Orthodoxy to appreciate and benefit from it requires a slow-cooker approach willing to let the ingredients steep in their own juices. It takes some diligent reading and patient reflection on the part of an evangelical to imbibe enough of an Orthodox mindset to be able to process Orthodox teaching on its own terms. Orthodox spirituality offers rich Christian sustenance, indeed, so the meal is worth the effort, but there is no way to rush it and get the flavors right. Why is that?

Readers should recognize by this point in the volume that they cannot simply assume their own prized doctrinal or devotional attitudes as the starting points for works of Christian spirituality written by siblings in Christ from other backgrounds. A Baptist will have to make some adjustments if he or she is reading a work by a Lutheran; a Pentecostal must do the same with something from an Anglican; and a Methodist will find it necessary to make some accommodations in these regards to benefit from a Puritan. The adjustment any of them would have to make in reading a work of spirituality from the Roman Catholic tradition would be even more significant. But the degree of adjustment in all these instances is far less than what it would be for any of these evangelicals to make in order to read and benefit from a work of Orthodox spirituality. The reason for this is easy to state but challenging to assimilate.

THE HISTORICAL PATHS OF WESTERN AND EASTERN CHRISTIANITY

More than we often realize, our approach to the Christian faith has been shaped by the milieu in which we grew up—not just our Baptist or Methodist or Pentecostal (or whatever) background, but our situation in Western Christianity. Lutherans, Anglicans, evangelicals of all stripes and Roman Catholics all share a common historical background in Western Christianity. By contrast, Orthodoxy's background is in Eastern Christianity. This has deep roots in the historical development of Christianity.

The Roman Empire into which Christianity spread in the first centuries of the Christian era knew two divergent cultural mindsets. The Latin-speaking western half had been shaped by the overwhelming influence of Rome, with its focus on law and good rule. The Greek-speaking eastern half had long since assimilated the Hellenistic culture spread by the conquests of Alexander the Great centuries earlier. In the West, questions about legal standing and about how to make things work well for good government dominated cultural attitudes. In the East, though, the tensions of life and death, of freedom and fate, of light and darkness—profoundly reflected on by generations of Greek philosophers but made accessible to multitudes through the works of Greek playwrights—predominated.

Winsome Christian witness spoke in a contextually sensitive fashion to the concerns and questions of the two dissimilar segments of the single empire. In so doing, the common Christian message emerged with divergent emphases—all still rooted in and drawing on dominical and apostolic teaching, but stressing the various elements in it which spoke more directly to the questions people in the respective halves of the empire were already concerned with. The point to note here is that when you ask different questions, you get different answers: from early in the history of the ancient church, Western and Eastern Christianity dealt with different questions and so gave different answers.

This continued in the turbulent subsequent centuries down to the present day and has affected the ways Western and Eastern Christians respectively appropriate and practice the Christian faith. With the Germanic invasions and the collapse of the western half of the Roman Empire, but the continued flourishing of the eastern Roman Empire (Byzantium) for another thousand years (to 1453), with the virtually independent developments of a Western Christendom under the leadership of the medieval church headquartered in Rome and of the Byzantine culture in which Eastern Christianity played so significant a role (but one so different from that of the church in the West), with the further development of Western Christianity in the Reformation era and the subsequent division into multitudes of competing church allegiances (including evangelicalism), but the suppression of Eastern Christianity under Muslim conquest or Russian tsarist domination—with all this, the two sides of Christianity developed in significant independence of each other. Along the way the spirituality that arose in the two Christendoms took on distinctive emphases as it embodied the faith embraced in the two cultural contexts.

The divergent centuries-long historical trajectories of Western and Eastern Christianity, respectively, have led to quite different, even contrasting views on several questions that both see as essential to Christian faith. Because of this, any evangelical reader who intends to read works of Orthodox spirituality needs to count on expending considerable intellectual effort at assimilation and reflection in order to get the lay of the land in Orthodoxy: that reader will need to read this brief treatment assiduously, carefully work through a couple of book-length introductions to Orthodoxy, and assimilate these well. Unless the reader does, he or she will be primed to misunderstand, misrepresent and possibly misappropriate Orthodox spirituality. The endeavor is worth the effort, but the process takes time: there is no way to rush it.[1]

---

[1]Those interested in pursuing this journey should, after reading this treatment, start with a good introduction to Orthodoxy; the best one available is Kallistos Ware, *The Orthodox Church*, 2nd

HEAD VERSUS HEART?

Another striking divergence between evangelicalism and Orthodoxy highlights the significantly different paths the two movements have traversed.[2] Within evangelicalism, we are familiar with what we call the head-heart contrast. By this we refer to a problem that repeatedly surfaces in our circles—namely, that someone can intellectually process the doctrines mastered by diligent study but may well not yet give evidence that these doctrines have taken root in the deepest core of his or her being and so transformed him or her. We recognize this as an anomaly, a situation that ought not to be; the frequency with which we encounter it, though, shows that it is a common malady.

Within Orthodoxy, such a head-heart contrast is inconceivable. One reason for this is that Orthodoxy has never allowed (as we will later see) that one could master doctrine, no matter how well versed the student might become; the other is that the Orthodox have always stressed that the Christian faith changes the person who is learning it. In the long history of Orthodoxy, those counted the teachers of Christian faith were not graduates of some special academic institute specializing in Christian instruction, but were the monks—people who devoted themselves not to intellectual explorations but to embodying the Christian faith in the whole of their existence. For the Orthodox down through the centuries those marked by an unmistakable devotion to God, manifest not only in monastic commitment to him but also by undeniable attainments in becoming more "like God," were the theologians who could be trusted.

The seed of a head-heart dichotomy cannot take root in such soil. In a profound sense Orthodox doctrine and spirituality are inseparable.

---

ed. (New York: Penguin, 1993). Building on this, one could move on to a volume by an evangelical conversant with Orthodoxy that offers elaboration of Orthodox teaching and practice and relates it to evangelical perspectives, such as my *Light from the Christian East: An Introduction to the Orthodox Tradition* (Downers Grove, IL: IVP Academic, 2007), or Donald Fairbairn, *Eastern Orthodoxy Through Western Eyes* (Louisville, KY: Westminster John Knox Press, 2002). Doing so would offer, if thoughtfully assimilated, a basic foundation for appropriately reading and processing works by Orthodox writers.

[2]From this point we will focus specifically on evangelicalism as the segment of Western Christianity for which this volume is intended; much of what is noted later applies, mutatis mutandis, for the rest of Western Christian teaching and practice.

Any solid work of Orthodox theological scholarship will and must be a work of spirituality as well.

As we turn now to consider some of the divergences in teaching between the two Christian traditions, an evangelical reader should be aware that each of the Orthodox doctrinal perspectives to be discussed carries significant implications for spirituality, even if the person cannot immediately intuit what they might be. We will touch on some of them specifically. As this treatment comes to an end, I will offer some suggestions for those who desire to explore Orthodox spirituality.

SALVATION

Christianity declares that the salvation promised by God to our first parents was accomplished in Jesus Christ. The understanding of how salvation is achieved in evangelicalism and Orthodoxy, though, is shaped by what each sees as the human predicament before God. Divergent assessments of that problem—both rooted in Scripture but nonetheless dissimilar—result in divergent perspectives on salvation.

In evangelicalism, the human problem is that we have broken God's law and stand justly condemned for our sin. Our first parents disobeyed God's commandment and became guilty before the divine Judge. In them we are also adjudged guilty: we share original sin as their descendants, with our sinful human nature their tainted inheritance to us. We all manifest solidarity with Adam and Eve, though, by our own violations of divine commands. With whatever nuances, qualifications and adjustments various strands of evangelicalism offer on the further details, this summary describes how evangelicals see the human situation: the primary focus is on our legal standing before God. This perspective is biblical, to be sure; however, it is also unquestionably, from a historical vantage point, a reflection of our Latin-speaking Roman cultural background.

Orthodoxy views our human predicament in a different way. Created in God's image, human beings were to attain the divine likeness.[3] By living in communion with God, humankind was to become ever more

---

[3]Following the common Greek patristic understanding of Genesis 1:26, Orthodoxy distinguishes "image" as a creational *gift* from "likeness" as the divinely intended *goal* for humanity to attain by divine grace and faithful living before God.

like God—loving, righteous and holy. If they did, God would bless them with everlasting life, the life that belongs only to God.[4]

But our first parents yielded to the serpent's beguiling suggestion that there was an easier way to become "like God" (Gen 3:5). Eating the fruit, they relied on the creation rather than the Creator—but the creation has no life in itself. In so doing they turned from life and fell into death, placing themselves and their progeny in bondage to death.[5] According to Orthodoxy, God does not account subsequent humanity guilty of the transgression of Adam and Eve: the Orthodox do not espouse original sin or original guilt. But that bondage to death leads humankind to look to the fleeting pleasures found in the creation rather than finding its delight in the everlasting God. Occasional choices in the other direction only demonstrate the overall pattern—which each of us follows by our own volition. Human history is a tragic story of life and death played out on a cosmic scale but acted out by each individual. This too is a biblical theme, but it unquestionably reflects, from a historical vantage point, the ancient Hellenistic cultural mindset which Eastern Christianity first spoke to.

The respective stresses in evangelicalism's and Orthodoxy's understandings of how salvation is accomplished and received respond to these divergent assessments of the human predicament. Evangelicals focus virtually exclusively on Christ's substitutionary death on the cross: in it he endured the judgment we deserved and paid the debt we owed. He satisfied divine justice for us, so that we could be forgiven and justified—accounted right with God. All this is weighted heavily with the legal themes that reflect our heritage in the Latin-speaking half of the Roman Empire.

While from an evangelical perspective, on the cross Christ is victim, for Orthodoxy on the cross Christ is victor.[6] The Orthodox stress that

---

[4]According to the Greek church fathers, creation as it issued from God's hand was not and could not be eternal: created out of nothing, it had no lasting life in itself. Only God necessarily lives. By divine blessing, though, everlasting life would have been bestowed as a gift on his image bearers who would become *like* him.

[5]This is a strikingly different understanding than evangelicals commonly bring to the early chapters of Scripture, but it is worth pondering that God's declaration about the result of eating the forbidden fruit (Gen 2:17) identified death as the consequence, not becoming guilty or sinners.

[6]While this will strike many evangelicals as a strange notion, it comports with what the apostle Paul urges about Christ "triumphing over" those enemies in the cross (Col 2:14-15).

on the cross Christ triumphed over humankind's enemies—sin, death and the devil—by taking into himself, as God incarnate, the death that had no claim on him. In Orthodoxy the cross is always viewed in the dazzling light of Christ's resurrection: he destroyed death by swallowing it up into himself and returning to life in the resurrection—thus ensuring eternal life for all those who are united to him.

This contrast entails different understandings of the goal of salvation. Both evangelicals and Orthodox recognize that in salvation God rescues us from sin and its consequences. For evangelicals, peace with God—having our sins forgiven and being made right with God—is the goal. For Orthodoxy, likeness to God—intended for humanity in the first Adam, secured for humanity in the last Adam (cf. 1 Cor 15:45)—is that goal.

Initial justification is not the final step for evangelicals, to be sure: God intends us to serve him by a life of devotion to him and love for others. Among the various strands of evangelicalism, the precise emphasis and balance vary on such matters, with some stressing almost exclusively living up to such expectations by evangelistic witness bearing, others focused on involvement in questions of culture and social justice, and yet others espousing a wide variety of nuanced interrelationships between these two poles.

Orthodoxy is undivided on this point: the rescue involved in salvation is but a necessary step to the ultimate divine goal—namely, return to our divinely intended objective of becoming "like God." As we slowly grow in that regard, we engage in bearing witness and get involved in the problems of culture and social justice. Salvation in Christ opens the door to humankind to resume its divinely appointed purpose—to attain the divine likeness: as the fourth-century church father Athanasius memorably put it, "He became human so that humans might become divine."[7] As we yield to divine grace and follow the leading of the Holy Spirit, as Orthodox commonly put it, "we become by grace what he is by nature." Increasingly conformed to the image of Christ (Rom 8:29), human beings grow in likeness to God in what the Orthodox call "theosis" or "deification."

---

[7]Athanasius, *On the Incarnation of the Word* 54.

However strange this term sounds to evangelicals, it captures the Orthodox view of the original goal for humanity in creation, a purpose now held forth as the ultimate result of divine salvation. Theosis does not point to any obliteration of the distinction between Creator and creature: in the fullness of salvation, the redeemed will be distinct from and other than God. But on a creaturely level, the redeemed will be as much "like God" as a creature could possibly become. Through deification humans become what God intended them to be—"like God."

With all this, one finds a striking difference in the ways siblings in Christ in the two Christendoms speak about their own salvation. Evangelicals are usually expected to be able to give a hearty positive answer to the question whether they are saved: if they believe in Christ and thus accept what he has done to make them right with God, then they are justified in God's sight. From an evangelical perspective such a person can *know* that he or she "is saved." In the evangelical approach, "being saved" is focused on the inception of Christian life. But with the creational intent of likeness to God as the goal of divine salvation, an Orthodox would necessarily speak more cautiously—not out of doubt of divine faithfulness or promise, but because of the Orthodox understanding of what salvation is. If asked whether he is saved, an Orthodox might well respond, "I trust that by the grace of God I have been saved [in what Christ has accomplished], I am being saved [through deification], and I will be saved [brought to full likeness to God in the final day]." In the Orthodox approach, "being saved" is focused on the culmination of Christian life.

Scripture and Tradition

For a variety of historical reasons, evangelicals have commonly distinguished Scripture and tradition, viewing the latter with considerable suspicion. It is consequently startling for an evangelical to discover that the Orthodox discern no such tension between the two. Indeed, the Orthodox insist that tradition—in its oral form, as proclaimed by the apostles and passed on (the literal meaning of "tradition") by their followers—historically preceded New Testament Scripture, which subsequently became the written form of the apostolic tradition. For the Orthodox, tradition is the living presence of the Holy Spirit in the church, guiding it through the centuries, leading it into all truth (Jn 16:13)—a truth that does not contradict the written form of that tradition found in Scripture.

HISTORICAL CONTINUITY

Between evangelicalism and Orthodoxy there is a great historical gulf fixed. If evangelicalism were charged with being historically aware, there might not be enough evidence for a conviction. To be sure, many evangelicals can say something about the worthies of their particular denomination or movement and relate a few incidents from its past, but apart from some degree of familiarity with the Reformation movement in the sixteenth century, most evangelicals—whether laypeople or leaders—are not particularly attuned to the history of Christianity.[8]

In striking contrast, Orthodoxy glories in its continuity with the church through the ages, back to the apostles. For the Orthodox the great doctrinal teachers were the church fathers of Christian antiquity, whose works still shape Orthodox thought and practice. Similarly, the pattern of Orthodox worship in the present day, while elaborated through the centuries, is recognizably the pattern followed back through the centuries into Christian antiquity.

This is not, for the Orthodox, a negotiable option. The risen Christ promised to be with his church to the end of time (Mt 28:20), so to stand with him means to stand deliberately and conscientiously in the line of the faithful down through the ages. From such a perspective, historical continuity is to be cherished and protected.

A striking manifestation of this is the elaborate liturgy used for forty Sundays of the church year in every Orthodox congregation in every locale throughout the entire world—the Liturgy of St. John Chrysostom, who died in 407. (The liturgy used on the other twelve Sundays offers a more elaborate but somewhat older version.)[9] Recognizing that some

---

[8]In many ways even much of what is "known" in this regard is suspect; see my *Getting the Reformation Wrong: Correcting Some Misunderstandings* (Downers Grove, IL: IVP Academic, 2010).

[9]On those twelve Sundays the rubric used is the Liturgy of St. Basil (d. 379), which is somewhat lengthier and in certain regards more detailed than the other. (When an Orthodox priest who is a friend spoke to one of my classes, he referred with a smile to the Liturgy of St. John Chrysostom as Orthodoxy's "new" liturgy.)

modifications have been made to this liturgy along the way, it is never-theless the case that, by 2007, it had been used for at least 83,200 weeks in a row—in every Orthodox church in the world. Historical continuity is not just a fine ideal for the Orthodox: as they claim, it is their reality, a reality they prize and protect.

Orthodoxy has no interest in the latest doctrinal fads or novelties; the fact that the Orthodox church is often called "the church of the seven ecumenical councils" is in this regard striking and noteworthy. The seventh ecumenical council was held in 787; it put the seal on the historic church's defense of the apostolic teaching about God (as triune) and Christ (as both divine and human). The resolute defense of that seventh council in 843, after some renewal of the controversy which led to it, is celebrated every year as "The Triumph of Orthodoxy"—by which the Orthodox focus not on Eastern Christianity as over against Western Christianity but on the faith passed down from the apostles through the generations and defended against all the heresies that would have under-mined the apostles' and the church's subsequent proclamation of who God is and what God has done for our salvation. For the Orthodox there is no "going beyond" or "advancing" or "improving on" that: it is the Christian faith, the apostolic message defended, that must be faithfully proclaimed and transmitted down through history to the return of Christ.

This accounts, in part, for why Orthodoxy looks to the church fathers of Christian antiquity as the ultimate teachers of Christianity (after the apostles). For the Orthodox one can do no better than listen to those who had learned the Christian faith in a historical line from the apostles or those taught by the apostles, leaders who defended it against all comers and thus held fast to the apostolic tradition. The church is not called to spawn new ideas but to pass on the oldest ones—those that came through the apostles themselves.

Suspicion of Human Thought

Along with this goes an attitude toward human reason when it speaks about God and addresses religious questions that will likely surprise most evangelicals. To be sure, many of them will have their reservations about *unbelieving* human reason dealing with these issues. But the plethora of books on various doctrines, end-times themes and ethical questions produced by Christian authors to meet the interests of an evangelical readership indicates that we have a pretty positive view of what *believing* human reason can accomplish (assuming some proper training or experience, with some organization to the thoughts [and perhaps some ghost-writing]). Down through the centuries to the present, Orthodoxy has been marked by quite a different attitude.

Orthodoxy is suspicious not only of *unbelieving* human thought but also of *believing* human thought that takes upon itself the challenge of expounding God and his ways toward us. Back to its earliest days Eastern Christianity has emphasized that our human thoughts, even when saturated in Scripture and devoted to God in profound faith, are incommensurate with what such endeavors seek to expound. In the first century the apostle Paul had described God's ways as unfathomable (Rom 11:33); in the second century, Irenaeus of Lyons commented, "God cannot be measured by the heart, and he is incomprehensible by the mind"; in the early fourth century, Cyril of Jerusalem asked rhetorically, "If the smallest of his works cannot be comprehended, can the Creator of all things be comprehended?" Later in that century Gregory of Nyssa declared, "He who transcends the universe certainly transcends speech."[10] Further citations to this general effect are plentiful throughout the whole patristic period, down to the seventh ecumenical council; they find echoes in the teaching within Orthodoxy in all subsequent centuries—*without a single contrary voice.*

What doctrine assays to deal with is and remains beyond human comprehension and utterance: it would speak of God and his ways. That it must be done is unquestionable, of course; sermons must be preached and catechetical teaching needs to be given. But in all such endeavors the faithful Orthodox teacher walks the well-worn paths traversed by the church through the centuries. It is not the mark of an Orthodox theologian to produce some new systematic (or other) theology; it is the task to pass on the wisdom God has imparted to the church as it has taught and faithfully transmitted what it has received. That leaves no

---

[10]Irenaeus, *Against Heresies* 4:19,2; Cyril of Jerusalem, *The Catechetical Lectures* 6:9; Gregory of Nyssa, *Commentary on Ecclesiastes*, sermon 7. (All translations are my own.)

room for creativity: doctrinal or exegetical novelty is not a virtue in Orthodox theology. One must hold firmly to the original, pristine message, which has been faithfully handed down through the ages.

The contrast in this regard between evangelicalism and Orthodoxy can be noted easily. Down through the centuries, within evangelicalism (and more broadly, throughout Western Christianity) studies of doctrine that purport to present the materials from fresh perspectives or with special insights have appeared regularly; their titles are legion. By contrast, within Orthodoxy the standard treatment of doctrine used through the centuries has been *The Orthodox Faith* by John of Damascus—*who died in the mid-eighth century!* Orthodoxy saw no need for an updated or new treatment down through the intervening twelve centuries: the Damascene collated what the church fathers had taught, on the basis of the apostolic tradition, and communicated it winsomely. For the Orthodox there was no need to try to progress beyond that.[11]

The Orthodox caution vis-à-vis even Christian human thought is deeply rooted. It is the mark of godly wisdom to refrain from trying to puzzle out the ways of God with humankind, but to open oneself to God in wonder, silence and humility. Indeed, this leads to a noteworthy approach to theology—"negative" (or "apophatic") theology. This theology accepts what we can appropriately state regarding what God has revealed about himself and what he has done and continues to do for humankind (which is styled "positive" [or "cataphatic"] theology). But negative theology recognizes that all our understandings, our thoughts and insights, and the words in which we utter them, are only ours—not God's: even in his revelation to us in Scripture, God had to use human words to communicate what must remain beyond our comprehension or expression. So, according to Orthodoxy, the most faithful and humble theological stance builds on this positive theology but goes beyond it— not to deny it but to recognize that the God who loves us and has revealed himself to us in word and deed is far beyond our comprehension

---

[11]In this regard, though, it is striking that the notable Romanian Orthodox theologian Dumitru Staniloae (1903-1993) published *Dogmatic Orthodox Theology* (in Romanian, 1978 [in process of English translation]), a dense exploration and exposition of Orthodoxy that wrestles profoundly with the intellectual currents of the twentieth century. Significantly, Staniloae also devoted his scholarly attention to studies in Orthodox spirituality through the ages.

and expression. This calls us to "negative" theology—a way of teaching about God that rejects all limitations on him.

Some of this will be recognizable to evangelicals: we confess with all other Christians that God is invisible, infinite, unchangeable, incomprehensible and so forth. Such affirmations serve mostly as a cautionary reminder of God's greatness without particularly shaping the rest of our teaching. In Orthodoxy, though, apophatic theology is prized as the purest theology: it believes but does not define; it stays silent in awe rather than fumbling to find inadequate words; it opens itself to the wonder of God who is far beyond all we can imagine rather than contenting itself with a tamed deity that stays within the caged confines of our systems of thought. Orthodoxy prizes silence and awe as a way to approach God; as most of us recognize, in evangelicalism silence is awkward.

MYSTERY

With this, it should be scarcely surprising that Orthodoxy welcomes mystery. To be sure, all Christian teaching recognizes at least formally that we come face to face with mystery as we encounter God and his ways. But Orthodoxy sees mystery not as what is left after we have explained as much as we can or dare, but as the substratum of all God's dealings with us. Mystery is not a threat: it points to who God is and how he deals with us, remembering always that he is "the lover of humankind,"[12] who is always faithful to his people. Embracing mystery is one way to acknowledge that God's ways are not our ways, nor his thoughts our thoughts (Is 55:8). Mystery entails allowing God to be God, without our attempting to figure out everything we might like to know.

For the Orthodox mystery is to be celebrated, not solved. Orthodoxy views all God's works with and toward us as beyond our ken—as mysteries in which God deals in love with and for us. Indeed, within Orthodoxy the common term for what evangelicals (and other Western Christians) call "sacraments" (or in the free church traditions, "ordinances") is "the mysteries." Western Christianity has argued and split over conflicting understandings of baptism and the Lord's Supper, and

---

[12]This declaration is uttered twelve times in the Liturgy of St. John Chrysostom, fifteen times in the Liturgy of St. Basil.

within evangelicalism is found a wide array of perspectives on what the Orthodox thus style "the mysteries." In stark contrast Orthodoxy has never attempted to explain how baptism and the Eucharist work: what God promises to do in the sacraments he achieves in ways beyond human comprehension. For the Orthodox, consequently, the response is not explanation and argument but believing and grateful praise for divine beneficence lavished upon his people.[13]

SUGGESTIONS FOR EXPLORING ORTHODOX SPIRITUALITY

By now, an evangelical reader should have discerned that Orthodoxy "comes at" the faith in a way significantly other than he or she does. There is enough commonality to recognize a familial relationship, but enough dissimilarity to drive home the awareness of a dramatically different heritage within the family. Evangelicalism and Orthodoxy live out the faith in distinct ways.

From all we have considered, it should be obvious that an evangelical who wants to explore Orthodox spirituality needs first to develop a sound acquaintance with Orthodox doctrine—which flows into and out of Orthodox spirituality. Without that acquaintance, an evangelical will almost certainly misunderstand, misconstrue and misrepresent what is read. There is no shortcut to such acquaintance: it takes time, patience and thoughtful openness to Christian perspectives quite other than one's own.

Another caution should be noted. The Orthodox recommend—indeed, virtually insist—that one needs a spiritual father to serve as guide. Such a guide might be one's parish priest, a monk or someone else respected as an "elder." The point to note here is that Orthodox do not view spirituality as an individualistic enterprise in which an enthusiast finds his or her own way. Spirituality is inherently a complicated, challenging and even dangerous venture; for it, the Orthodox urge, one needs a guide. This may give evangelicals pause; at the least they should recognize the cautions raised by Orthodoxy on the score.

---

[13]This makes it possible for the Orthodox to embrace in straightforward faith the New Testament declarations that baptism is a "washing of regeneration" (Tit 3:5), in which we "put on Christ" (as a garment [Gal 3:27]) and are adopted as God's children and so become his heirs (Gal 4:7), on the one hand, and of our partaking of the body and blood of Christ in the Lord's Supper (1 Cor 10:16), on the other.

A good way for those who want to proceed toward reading Orthodox spirituality would be to take up a doctrinal treatment by a respected Orthodox author; any such work will in significant part reflect Orthodox spirituality. One could select a work by—to name only a few—Vladimir Lossky, John Meyendorff, Elisabeth Behr-Sigel, Anastasios Yannoulatos or Alexander Schmemann. Each of these has a number of publications, any of which would serve the purpose well. Especially valuable in this regard is Kallistos Ware's *The Orthodox Way*, which offers an overview of Orthodox doctrine focused on God as the center of each topic, with every chapter concluding with quotations from church fathers, notable Orthodox authors or liturgical rubrics on the theme.[14]

Fundamental to these treatments are the works of the Greek church fathers. Works by Athanasius of Alexandria, Cyril of Jerusalem, Gregory of Nazianzus, Basil of Caesarea, Gregory of Nyssa, Cyril of Alexandria, John Chrysostom, Maximus Confessor and John of Damascus offer rich possibilities for exploring the faith and spirituality that have taken root and borne fruit in Orthodoxy.

An inviting way into Orthodox spirituality is found in journals kept by travelers who sought out Orthodox regions in order to experience Orthodox spirituality at first hand.[15] Additional help is found in two recent introductions written by respected Orthodox scholars in the Traditions of Christian Spirituality series; they offer contemporary treatments of Orthodox spirituality in ways accessible to those who possess a basic acquaintance with Orthodox teaching.[16]

It is often said that Orthodoxy is "half taught, half caught." Reading about Orthodoxy opens up an avenue into Orthodox spirituality, but unless one also imbibes the liturgical richness Orthodoxy proffers, that person will have at best an attenuated sense of Orthodox spirituality.

---

[14]Kallistos Ware, *The Orthodox Way*, rev. ed. (Crestwood, NY: St. Vladimir's Seminary Press, 1995).

[15]Three excellent ones are William Dalrymple, *From the Holy Mountain: A Journey in the Shadow of Byzantium* (New York: Harper Perennial, 2005); Kyriacos C. Marakides, *The Mountain of Silence: A Search for Orthodox Spirituality* (Colorado Springs: Image Books, 2001); and Scott Cairns, *Short Trip to the Edge: Where Earth Meets Heaven—A Pilgrimage* (San Francisco: HarperSanFrancisco, 2007).

[16]John Anthony McGuckin, *Standing in God's Holy Fire: The Byzantine Tradition* (Maryknoll, NY: Orbis, 2001); John Chryssavgis, *Light Through Darkness: The Orthodox Tradition* (Maryknoll, NY: Orbis, 2004).

An evangelical interested in experiencing Orthodox spirituality would do well to visit an Orthodox congregation to drink in the ethos of its worship. Reading through and reflecting on the liturgies commonly used within Orthodoxy mentioned previously, plus the liturgical rubrics used when Orthodoxy celebrates Lent, Advent and the other annual feasts would expose one to the spiritual abundance found in Orthodox worship.[17]

We come, finally, to some classics from the Orthodox spiritual tradition. The *Philokalia* has been revised and refined over several centuries. It offers excerpts from revered Orthodox leaders from the fourth through the fifteenth centuries, organized by topic. The *Philokalia* has played a significant role in shaping Orthodox monastic spirituality, which in turn has profoundly influenced spirituality among the Orthodox faithful.

One of the gems of Orthodox spirituality is the "Jesus Prayer," developed in ancient Eastern Christian monasticism as a way of capturing everything one could pray for and allowing the practitioner to engage in ceaseless prayer: "Lord Jesus Christ, Son of God, have mercy on me, a sinner." The Jesus Prayer has commended itself subsequently to Orthodox faithful through the centuries as a way to stay centered on God in all thought and activity. Several books by respected Orthodox authors offer introductions to the prayer and how to use it.[18] One way it has been used is found in a winsomely written Russian novel *The Way of the Pilgrim*. Set in Orthodox Russia, it recounts the story of a simple layman who seeks communion with God and openness to others by intense practice of the Jesus Prayer.

All these find support in apophatic mysticism, which entails an openness to God that builds on but goes beyond the limits of written revelation in Scripture to seek communion with God beyond words and

---

[17]These materials have been translated into English and edited by Mother Mary and Kallistos Ware in, respectively, *The Lenten Triodion* (1978; reprint, South Canaan, PA: St. Tikhon's Seminary, 2002), and *The Festal Menaion* (1969; reprint, South Canaan, PA: St Tikhon's Seminary, 1998]).

[18]Two fine books are Lev Gillet, *The Jesus Prayer*, rev. ed. (Crestwood, NY: St. Vladimir's Seminary Press, 1997); and Frederica Mathews-Green, *The Jesus Prayer: The Ancient Desert Prayer that Tunes the Heart to God* (Brewster, MA: Paraclete Press, 2009).

thoughts. First adumbrated in Gregory of Nyssa's *The Life of Moses* during the late fourth century, apophatic mysticism becomes the default mode of Orthodox spirituality in subsequent centuries. It came to be associated with the practice of *hesychasm*—"spiritual silence." During the hesychastic controversy of the fourteenth century, Gregory Palamas emerged as the chief defender of and most articulate spokesman for this form of monastic spirituality. His teachings have been deeply imbibed not only in the monastic tradition but also in general Orthodox spirituality to this day throughout the Orthodox world.[19]

Hesychasm has come to dominate Orthodox spirituality. However, one cannot begin to understand hesychasm unless one has thoroughly opened to it, imbibed and learned to appreciate Orthodoxy teaching on its own terms. That cannot be done without intense reading and reflection. If one is willing to put in the effort, the rewards are rich—but there is no "Palamas for Protestants" shortcut.

If you want to read Orthodox spirituality, you have a lot of preliminary homework to do, just to get ready. The effort will be challenging, even arduous. But the benefits can be rich.

---

[19]See the masterful treatment by John Meyendorff, *St. Gregory Palamas and Orthodox Spirituality* (Crestwood, NY: St. Vladimir's Seminary Press, 1974).

9

Reading Spiritual Classics as Evangelical Protestants

Fred Sanders

THE GREAT TRADITION OF SPIRITUAL CLASSICS is a mighty force to be reckoned with in the life of the evangelical Protestant churches. It is ancient and it still exists; it has shaped us and it still exerts power on us; it calls to us and it demands a response. Even if we attempted to ignore or silence the manifold witness of the spiritual classics, we would be responding (in the negative) to its call and thereby confessing that some response is necessary. But the negative response would be a bad one. The evangelical Protestant comportment toward the great tradition should not be closed; it should be open but cautious.

FIRST OPEN, THEN CAUTIOUS

"Open but cautious" is a characteristically evangelical motto. It originated among noncharismatic Christians describing their attitude toward charismatics and Pentecostals: While affirming that God could move in mysterious ways among his people, they reserved the right to make individual judgments about whether any particular manifestation was in fact the work of the Holy Spirit. The Spirit can move someone to speak in tongues or prophecy, but not every instance of glossolalia or prophecy should be automatically endorsed. Of course, charismatics could see for themselves that noncharismatics were abundantly cautious, but have often wanted to press the question of whether people so meticulously cautious could be described as authentically open. Writing as a noncharismatic, I can testify that "theoretically possible, but practically quite unlikely" is often a more accurate account of the attitude toward putative miraculous gifts. Still, the expressed ideal is to be open but cautious, and the expressed ideal is wise.

Evangelical Protestants confronting two thousand years of Christian spiritual classics can apply the same terms. But echoing the concerns of the worried charismatic, we might need to spend a little time insisting that evangelical Protestants should prove their openness before going on to describe their cautiousness. In other words, the evangelical attitude toward the spiritual classics ought to be first open and then cautious. To be more precise: If evangelical Protestants know what they are about as people of the biblical gospel, first of all they will read widely in the spiritual classics, and second they will read evangelically. To read spiritual classics widely is to begin with almost any old book that has a reputation for spiritual helpfulness; the book you are holding is full of recommended texts. Take up and read! To read spiritual classics evangelically is to read for the gospel: seeking out the gospel, presupposing the gospel, guided by the gospel and jealous for the gospel. Of these four elements of the evangelical attitude (seeking out, presupposing, guided by and jealous for), the first two are positive, while the second two imply norms and canons of judgment.

RECOMMENDING BOOKS

It is certainly part of the culture of evangelical Protestantism to read spiritual classics. The movement is of course characterized by its focus on the Bible, but along with that focus it has always worked with a steady stream of other writings. Alongside Bible reading there has always been a recognition of the value of spiritual reading more broadly, of engaging in the reading of extrabiblical devotional writings as a spiritual practice. We could go further and say that evangelicals not only recognize the reading of books as a spiritual practice but actually make recommending books into a spiritual practice with serious pastoral implications. To know the right books to recommend to inquirers is a sign of pastoral insight.

Take an example from the evangelical Protestants on the cusp of fun-
damentalism. A hundred years ago, in a 1911 issue of *The King's Business*,
the founders of the Bible Institute of Los Angeles made this proclamation: "Buying and selling books with some, is like buying and selling
potatoes—a mere perfunctory business. With us, buying and selling
books is a matter of as much spiritual import as teaching the Bible."[1]
Could these doughty, radical evangelicals, these proto-fundamentalists,
whose glory was their confession that the Bible and the Bible alone is the
very word of God, really have meant to call book selling "a matter of as
much spiritual import as teaching the Bible"? Indeed, they meant it, because evangelicals have long understood that the power of life and death
is often in the recommendation of a book. They were not, of course, sug-
gesting that other books were on a level with Scripture. They said no
such thing. What they said was that they considered their ministry of
handling books (stocking them in their downtown bookstore, endorsing
and recommending "Best Books," distributing them free of charge when
possible) to be a ministry as serious as their ministry of teaching
Scripture. Evangelicals handle and distribute books differently than any
other items, because they are not just merchandise ("like buying and
selling potatoes") but written words that form souls, move hearts,
change minds. These are books! The editors went on to say:

> We handle books for the glory of God and cannot buy or sell those that
> we do not believe will accord with the teaching of God's Word. The
> reading of one book might undermine the faith of a person or destroy his
> soul. The reading of another book might lead a soul into the eternal light
> or arouse to a life of devotion.[2]

It is almost a hallmark of evangelicalism to take book recommendations so seriously. Evangelical Protestants have no *nihil obstats* or impri-
maturs from a central magisterium, but in place of them they have a
network of endorsements and recommendations. Seen from this perspective, maybe one of J. I. Packer's most important ministries has been
his ubiquitous endorsing of good books for decades. The evangelical

---

[1]"About the Book Business," *The King's Business* 3, no 5 (1912), p. 131, www2.biola.edu/
kingsbusiness/view/3/5/36.
[2]Ibid.

book-recommending network is as old as evangelicalism itself; the evangelical movement seems to have been born in a flurry of literary recommendations. The Reformation in England started as a network of book recommendations among the scholars at Cambridge: not just a covert circulating library for forbidden books by Luther or for the Greek New Testament, but a regular Erasmus Book Club meeting at the White Horse Inn. In the Great Awakening of the mid-eighteenth century, the circulation and recommendation of best books was a driving force. Susannah Wesley recommended the "excellent good book," Henry Scougal's 1677 book *The Life of God in the Soul of Man*, to her son Charles, who recommended it to George Whitefield in 1733. Whitefield later testified that he never knew what true religion was until he was enlightened by that book: "O what a ray of divine life did then break in upon my soul!"[3] The same circle of evangelicals circulated among themselves August Francke's book *Nicodemus, Or, Against the Fear of Man*, which they credited as being directly responsible for encouraging them to take their gospel preaching out of the churches and into the public spaces. Not only the content of their evangelical preaching (the life of God in the soul) but the style and some of the methods (exhortations to countercultural boldness) were derived from the careful recommending and circulating of spiritual classics.

SEEKING THE GOSPEL

To read spiritual classics evangelically is to read in a way that seeks out the gospel. In broadest terms this is the same thing as reading devotionally. The good that is in spiritual classics has to be dug out, and only a reader who comes to the book with a determination to hear from God through it will be rightly prepared.

For an example of this kind of reading, we can turn to John Wesley. In 1735 he published an abridgment of Thomas à Kempis's classic 1441 book *The Imitation of Christ*. Wesley's edition was called *The Christian's Pattern*. By way of introduction to the classic, Wesley gave his readers a short set of directions "concerning the manner of reading this (or any other) reli-

---

[3]George Whitefield, cited in F. F. Bruce, *Paul: Apostle of the Heart Set Free* (Grand Rapids, Eerdmans, 2000), p. 472.

gious treatise." He published the instructions for readers "who, knowing they have not yet attained, neither are already perfect, mind this one thing, and, pressing toward the mark, despise no assistance which is offered them."[4] The instructions were not quite of Wesley's own devising; he translated and modified them from the Latin introduction of a seventeenth-century edition of the *Imitation*. If John Wesley had written these notes from scratch, they would be worth attending to because of Wesley's stature and credentials as an evangelical leader. But the notes in fact give us much more, with multiple layers of agreement. They are tips on devotional reading, inspired by one of the bestselling spiritual classics of all time, a fifteenth-century work. They were composed by an anonymous seventeenth-century commentator and then edited by John Wesley in the eighteenth century. The result is classic advice on exactly how to do it: Schedule time for spiritual reading, read for a changed heart and ask God to make it happen, read "leisurely, seriously, and with great attention," get into the attitude of the work you're reading, finish books, look for action points and pray for God to do what only God can do.

Wesley's first tip is to "assign some stated time every day for this employment; and observe it, so far as you possibly can, inviolably." One thing to note is that spiritual reading is important enough to be done this often. But Wesley's main point is that the time should be definitely scheduled, and that schedule should be kept: "But if necessary business, which you could not foresee or defer, should sometimes rob you of your hour of retirement, take the next to it; or, if you cannot have that, at least the nearest you can."[5]

As for the reading itself, it must be done prayerfully and earnestly, with spiritual formation as the goal. "Prepare yourself for reading, by purity of intention, singly aiming at the good of your soul, and by fervent prayer to God, that he would enable you to see his will, and give you a firm resolution to perform it."[6] Wesley went on to recommend the sort of prayer that ought to be offered before spiritual reading: "An excellent

---

[4]The best available edition of these remarks is "Advice on Spiritual Reading," in the *John and Charles Wesley*, ed. Frank Whaling, Classics of Western Spirituality (Mahwah, NJ: Paulist Press, 1981), pp. 88-89. Whaling explains the complex publishing history on p. 66 of his introduction.
[5]Ibid., p. 88.
[6]Ibid.

form of prayer for this very purpose you have in the second or third book of this Treatise."[7] In pointing to prayers from *The Imitation of Christ*, Wesley may have in mind any of a dozen passages from books 2 and 3. Perhaps the prayer "thou art my wisdom" is most appropriate.

Such reading takes time and attention, and Wesley is quite warm on this subject:

> Be sure to read, not cursorily or hastily, but leisurely, seriously, and with great attention; with proper pauses and intervals, that you may allow time for the enlightenings of the divine grace. To this end, recollect, every now and then, what you have read, and consider how to reduce it to practice. Farther, let your reading be continued and regular, not rambling and desultory. To taste of many things, without fixing upon any, shows a vitiated palate, and feeds the disease which makes it pleasing.

Wesley considered that time and attention would also lead readers to read a book through all the way to the end, though they could then go back and re-read the isolated passages that were more pertinent to their own situation or inclinations. After grasping the whole of the book, these individual passages could be "pressed home to the soul" if the reader would add "a particular examination" of their own conscience under each of them.

Most important, Wesley exhorted evangelical readers of spiritual classics to bring themselves into spiritual alignment with the book they were reading. Each classic demanded to be read in the spirit in which it was written. At the time of actual reading, this meant that a certain kind of intense prayer was required:

> work yourself up into a temper correspondent with what you read; for that reading is useless which only enlightens the understanding, without warming the affections. And therefore intersperse, here and there, earnest aspirations to God, for his heat as well as his light.[8]

Again turning from more holistic advice to more fragmentary, Wesley recommended special treatment for a few "remarkable sayings or advices," advising readers:

---

[7]Ibid.
[8]Ibid.

treasure them up in your memory; and these you may either draw forth in time of need, as arrows from a quiver against temptation (more especially against the solicitations to that sin which most easily besets you) or make use of as incitements to any virtue, to humility, patience, or the love of God.[9]

Wesley's final advice was to conclude any time of spiritual reading with a brief prayer of consecration, placing yourself in the hands of God that he "would so bless the good seed sown in your heart, that it may bring forth fruit unto life eternal."[10] Wesley's advice for readers of spiritual classics, in other words, is to read as if life depended on it. In his presentation we have an example of an evangelical reading of spiritual classics which is demonstrably wide open to instruction.

READING WITH A STANDARD

Evangelical Protestants who read spiritual classics drawn from other sectors of the church, and especially from the long traditions of Roman Catholic and Eastern Orthodox spirituality, face a special challenge. They have a unique need to be open but cautious. When reading across confessional lines in this manner, the evangelical reader should extend generosity and charity for several reasons. For one thing, when it comes to recognized classics of spiritual writing, the evangelical Protestant will usually find more areas of agreement with the Catholic and Orthodox writers than areas of disagreement. Some sense of measure and perspective is necessary. The Roman Catholic and Eastern Orthodox churches have preserved and confessed the doctrine of the Trinity, the incarnation and the atonement. Turning from these high, central doctrinal matters to more practical matters, spiritual classics from these traditions will focus on prayer, Scripture and service. Just naming these two triads of concerns ought to be enough to demonstrate that the area of common ground is extensive, at both the practical and the doctrinal ends of the spectrum. Most of Christian spirituality is located in the areas that we have in common with the other Christian confessions.

---

[9]Ibid.
[10]Ibid., p. 89.

Even if we turn our attention to the standard points of contention, such as *sola scriptura* and *sola fide*, the supreme authority of Scripture alone and salvation by faith alone, a generous evangelical will admit that writers from other traditions come close to getting it right. At least they do not say the opposite. For example, if evangelical Protestants say that Scripture has authority, Roman Catholics don't say that it doesn't. Catholics confess that Scripture is authoritative in the church. Though at its worst the Roman Catholic tradition has flirted with formulations about Scripture and tradition as two sources of revelation, at its best the Roman Catholic Church has even given Scripture a position of primacy over its magisterial interpreters. Evangelicals who come to Roman Catholic spiritual writings looking for a clear and compelling confession of the supremacy of Scripture will be disappointed. They will find an unclear and less than compelling confession of Scripture's authority. They will find what they were looking for, but they will find it compromised and cluttered, set in the wrong context and juxtaposed with distractions. Similarly, evangelicals reading Eastern Orthodox spiritual classics will be encouraged by the evident reverence for the Word of God, but in the next moment will find Scripture being juggled away into the larger dialectic of Holy Tradition, as one element within it. To take the other crucial area of disagreement, soteriology, an evangelical looking for a perfectly clear statement about salvation by grace will find instead, by his lights, a host of imperfect and unclear statements. It is not so much that these other churches deny the crucial doctrines about Scriptural authority and salvation by faith. They do not deny them. They teach them, but they teach them badly. That judgment is harsh enough, but note that it is considerably less harsh and functions less as a pretext for dismissiveness than the judgment that these churches deny the doctrines. Even in the areas of Scriptural authority and salvation by faith, in other words, there are significant areas of overlap before the decisive disagreement is reached.

Still, if the areas of disagreement are important enough, they can spoil the entire mixture. Rat poison is 95 percent corn meal, and no pleading about percentages or a sense of proportion will suffice to make it healthy. Generosity and charity only go so far toward sustaining a relationship in the face of serious disagreement. These nonevangelical traditions may hold the gospel itself in stewardship, but they are messing it up, and a messed-up gospel is not the gospel; its result is dysangel, not evangel; bad news, not good.

THE GOSPEL IS EASILY SPOILED

Anglican bishop J. C. Ryle (1816-1900) provided the most helpful warning about how to distinguish evangelical religion from nonevangelical, and his guidelines are useful for discerning how to read spiritual classics evangelically. "There are many ways in which the faith of Christ may be marred and spoiled, without being positively denied," Ryle wrote.[11] Much religion that goes by the name of Christian is not consistently evangelical. There are five characteristics of truly evangelical religion. Evangelical religion emphasizes:

Scripture as the only rule of faith and practice, the only test of truth, the only judge of controversy

the doctrine of human sinfulness and corruption

the work and office of Jesus for salvation

the inward work of the Holy Sprit

the outward work of the Holy Spirit in the life[12]

Ryle admits that these five elements are all to be found widely scattered in nonevangelical Christian theology. They can each be found, if considered one by one. "Propound them separately, as points to be believed, and they would admit them every one."[13] But evangelicals are concerned not only that these doctrines be taught but that they be emphasized, that they stand out, that they are the first things to arrest the attention of hearers and the main focus of disciples. From the evangelical perspective, the other systems teach them, but badly.

---

[11]J. C. Ryle, "Evangelical Religion," in *Knots Untied: Being Plain Statements on Disputed Points in Religion from the Standpoint of an Evangelical Churchman* (London: National Protestant Church Union, 1898), p. 19.
[12]Ibid., pp. 4-9.
[13]Ibid., p. 9.

They do not give them the prominence, position, rank, degree, priority, dignity, and precedence which we do. And this I hold to be a most important difference between us and them. It is the position which we assign to these points, which is one of the grand characteristics of Evangelical theology. We say boldly that they are first, foremost, chief, and principal things in Christianity, and that want of attention to their position mars and spoils the teaching of many well-meaning Churchmen.[14]

Ryle says this failure to emphasize evangelical truths "mars and spoils" the statement of Christian truth in much religion. The main idea seems to be that the presentation of the gospel is actually spoiled, as Ryle goes on to develop the metaphor. "The Gospel in fact," he warns, "is a most curiously and delicately compounded medicine, and a medicine that is very easily spoiled."[15] He lists four ways it can be spoiled: By substitution, addition, interposition, disproportion or confused and contradictory directions.[16]

The gospel is spoiled "by substitution" when the Christian message is presented in such a way that any object besides Christ crucified is presented as the object of saving faith. Substitution implies both a negative and a positive moment: Christ is set aside out of the line of vision (the negative moment), and something else is put in the place he should occupy (the positive moment, where another object is posited). The substitute will of course be something good, usually something biblical. It could be (as Ryle's conflict with unevangelical Anglo-Catholicism suggested to him) "the Church, the Ministry, the Confessional, Baptism, or the Lord's Supper," all good and some necessary elements of the Christian religion. But as soon as they are put in the place of Christ, "the mischief is done. Substitute anything for Christ, and the Gospel is totally spoiled! Do this, either directly or indirectly, and your religion ceases to be Evangelical."[17] For our purposes, we can say "the spiritual classic you are reading ceases to be evangelical."

Another way to spoil the gospel is "by addition." Ryle uses very similar language to describe this error:

---

[14]Ibid.
[15]Ibid., p. 19.
[16]Ibid., pp. 19-20.
[17]Ibid., p. 19.

> You have only to add to Christ, the grand object of faith, some other objects as equally worthy of honour, and the mischief is done. Add anything to Christ, and the Gospel ceases to be a pure Gospel! Do this, either directly or indirectly, and your religion ceases to be Evangelical.[18]

He does not say anything more specific under this heading, but the obvious idea is that more is less; anything added to Christ as an object of faith subtracts from his unique honor. Closely related is spoiling the gospel "by interposition." Spatially, this metaphor involves not setting something alongside Christ, but pushing "something between Christ and the eye of the soul, to draw away the sinner's attention from the Saviour." As with the previous errors, "the mischief is done. Interpose anything between man and Christ, and man will neglect Christ for the thing interposed!"[19]

More subtle, perhaps, is spoiling the gospel "by disproportion." "You have only to attach an exaggerated importance to the secondary things of Christianity, and a diminished importance to the first things, and the mischief is done. Once alter the proportion of the parts of truth, and truth soon becomes downright error!"[20]

Note that this critique is one that Ryle would be just as likely to level at other evangelical Protestants. Anybody with a temptation to adopt a favorite doctrine, or to emphasize denominational or party distinctives out of proportion to the main things, is liable to spoil the gospel by disproportion. R. A. Torrey once complained of a disproportional emphasis on eschatology among evangelicals who were committed to premillennialism. He believed the doctrine was true, but he insisted "it is not enough to teach the truth; it should be taught in Scripture proportions."

> Doubtless another thing that causes very determined opposition to Pre-millenarian teaching and Pre-millenarian teachers, is that so many Pre-millenarians make a hobby of their doctrine. The truth of the Pre-millenarian position is precious to the writer of this editorial, but there are many other things taught in the Bible beside the Pre-millenial Coming of our Lord, and it is not enough to teach the truth; it should be taught in

---

[18]Ibid.
[19]Ibid., p. 20.
[20]Ibid.

Scripture proportions; and to be everlastingly harping on just one truth, no matter how true it is, and no matter how precious it is, does harm and not good and even serves to bring that truth into reproach and disrepute.[21]

Ryle's final warning is that the gospel can be spoiled "by confused and contradictory directions." He describes this problem at more length:

Complicated and obscure statements about faith, baptism, Church privileges, and the benefits of the Lord's Supper, all jumbled together, and thrown down without order before hearers, make the Gospel no Gospel at all! Confused and disorderly statements of Christianity are almost as bad as no statement at all! Religion of this sort is not Evangelical.[22]

PRINCIPLED ECLECTICISM

How do Ryle's strictures apply to an evangelical reading of spiritual classics? How do we evaluate books with these gospel-spoiling dangers in mind? We read widely in the classics, presupposing the gospel in the sense that we know what it is before we start reading, and we will recognize it when we come across it in a spiritual classic. We are guided by the gospel, so that we will immediately know when it is missing from what we are reading. We seek out the gospel, meaning that we read in such a way that can find the good news even when it is present in a fragmentary, disguised or distorted way. And we are jealous for the gospel, meaning that we cannot be satisfied by any disguised, distorted or otherwise deficient presentation of the gospel. If we are to go shopping in the spiritual classics with this kind of attitude of freedom and potential criticism, we had better be appropriately humble about how much we have to learn, but also appropriately bold about confessing that we know what an evangelical reading of the classics would look like. Ryle's own five-point list of things to be emphasized included the authority of Scripture as "the only rule of faith and practice, the only test of truth, the only judge of controversy," the doctrine of human corruption, the work and office of Jesus for salvation, and the work of the Holy Spirit both inwardly and outwardly. There are other ways of verbalizing the core

---

[21]R. A. Torrey, "Light on Puzzling Passages and Problems," *The King's Business* 7, no. 1 (1916): 24.
[22]Ryle, "Evangelical Religion," p. 20.

commitments of evangelical theology and spirituality; the solas that summarize the Reformation's teaching might also serve: sola scriptura, sola Christus, sola gratia, sola fide and soli Dei Gloria.

Such a clear statement of principles will equip evangelicals to read widely and critically in the spiritual classics. Evangelicals will still need generosity, teachableness and charity at every step, especially when handling ancient works that have proven themselves useful and edifying to multiple generations. But if our principles are sound, we should not be cowed by mere antiquity, popularity or consensus. Even in the church's earliest postbiblical literature, there is an evident mixture of the good and the bad, such that categories of judgment must be made clearer. In the collection known as the Apostolic Fathers, texts like the *Epistle to Diognetus* are charming and thrilling, falling easily into line with the codified doctrine of later ages. On the other hand, in the same ancient collection is the *Shepherd of Hermas*, whose edifying value is less obvious (though Athanasius praised it highly) and whose false trails and dangers are immediately evident.

We also encounter ancient books with minor points of provocation in them. In feasting on the writings of Athanasius, we may be caught short to find him calling Mary not just the virgin but the "ever-virgin," that is, testifying to his belief in the perpetual virginity of Mary. Often these minor points should be considered irritations, not obstacles. It would of course be wonderful if all authors of spiritual classics lined up exactly with our own beliefs and commitments. But ancient authors follow their own rules, and wise readers will rapidly adjust their expectations. The teaching about the perpetual virginity of Mary is a relatively minor issue; in fact many Protestants, including Turretin, have taught it as likely and as biblically defensible. Anyone who runs across such a reference in a classic author like Athanasius is not so much critically judging Athanasius as being judged by the book itself: if you cannot come to see the perpetual virginity of Mary as a minor issue, you are suffering from a weak sense of proportion.

But there is no universal guarantee, censoring service or "safe list" that might determine for all times who is trustworthy and who is not. Most authors are mixed bags, with something to teach us and some-

thing to avoid. When an expression, passage or line of thought seems
to run afoul of evangelical guidelines, the alert reader must quickly
decide whether the deviation is simply annoyance-level deviation or a
sign of a serious problem. John Henry Newman's beautiful and profound poem *The Dream of Gerontius* is a classic poetic meditation on
the death of a Christian. It includes stanzas as good as anything ever
written in English spirituality:

> Praise to the Holiest in the height,
> And in the depth be praise;
> In all His words most wonderful;
> Most sure in all His ways![23]

And there is nothing else quite like it by any other author. Yet the opening
lines are immediately annoying to readers with Protestant commitments:

> Jesu, Maria—I am near to death,
> And Thou art calling me; I know it now.[24]

Hardly a promising note for ecumenical appreciation, especially for
evangelical Protestants reading this spiritual classic by a Roman Catholic.
Should this invocation of Mary (a few lines later the speaker cries, "Mary,
pray for me!") be shrugged off as merely annoyance? Or is it symp-
tomatic of something deeper, not just an error in Mariology but a
symptom of a disorderly doctrine of grace itself? Just how unevangelical
is *The Dream of Gerontius*? Is it an evangelical message with a little too
much Mary slipped in? Or is it profoundly anti-evangelical? Either
could be the case with John Henry Newman as author. But when it
comes to a proven, time-tested classic like *Gerontius*, the judgment must
come in the actual reading.

When making judgments about spiritual reading, the safest course is
to have a well-developed set of theological categories, a solid and sharp
set of tools for discriminating between the helpful and the harmful. But
not everybody has the kind of biblical knowledge or theological

---

[23]John Henry Newman, *The Dream of Gerontius* (London: Longmans, Green, 1888), pp. 39-40.
[24]Ibid., p. 5.

training to make these decisions incisively. Often a spiritually sensitive but theologically untrained believer will have an uneasy feeling when reading some spiritual classic. Without being able to articulate the reasons for the discomfort, the reader will nevertheless register a definite disturbance, feeling that something is amiss. What is to be done with these inarticulate feelings? Unless they can be drawn out, analyzed and stated in biblical or theological terms, they may be false alarms, prejudices or obstinate resistance to new ideas. On the other hand, they may just as easily be very real danger signs which the reader should heed. There are two good ways to proceed in such a case. First, seek the advice of somebody with greater understanding, training and exposure. A more mature believer may be able to clear away obstacles, explain confusions and redescribe the dynamics of a text. A more mature believer may also be able to recognize that some texts contain more harm than good, and ought in fact to be avoided. In recent years, for example, there has been an increased mingling of non-Christian spiritualities with Christian ideas, and some books that are eagerly circulated and recommended are in fact confusing mixtures of biblical and nonbiblical elements. Books like that should not be approached with the same openness as a genuine spiritual classic. They can be read, but with a more pronounced critical mindset rather than with a desire to hear from God and be transformed by the text. Remember that the old evangelical network of book recommendations is a kind of pastoral practice, and a good literary spiritual adviser would know you well enough to know what you need. The second way to proceed, if a trusted adviser is not at hand, is simply to play it safe and set the book aside. You can admit that you don't have enough theological training to render a final verdict on the book, while still doing justice to your sense of unease by acknowledging that this book is at least not likely to be good for you at this time.

Thomas Chalmers once said about Thomas à Kempis's *The Imitation of Christ* that it was "a very impressive performance." In a letter to a friend, he mused about whether this book passed evangelical muster. After all, it talks about being like Christ in our conduct, without putting its emphasis on the finished work of Christ for us. Chalmers recognizes the charge and knows its seriousness. But he defends à Kempis's *Imitation*:

> Some would say of it that it is not enough evangelical. He certainly does not often affirm, in a direct and ostensible manner, the righteousness that is by faith. But he proceeds on this doctrine, and many an incidental recognition does he bestow upon it; and I am not sure but that this implies a stronger and more habitual settlement of mind respecting it than when it is thrust forward and repeated, and repeated with a kind of ultra-orthodoxy, as if to vindicate one's soundness, and acquit oneself of a kind of exacted homage to the form of sound words.[25]

Chalmers knew what he was about when it came to the gospel and to reading evangelically. But he also knew that an exaggerated insistence on the right formulas was counterproductive. He found in *The Imitation of Christ* all he needed from a spiritual classic, and what was lacking (an insistence on imputed righteousness) he presupposed a doctrine that the author "proceeds on" or presupposes with only "an incidental recognition" here and there.

Life or Death

Evangelicals need to be open but cautious in their reading of the spiritual classics. We began with John Wesley advising how to approach the classics in such a way that we are wide open to being transformed by God as we interact with these books. We end with John Wesley from just a few years later in his career, in an instance where he used very sharp language in a letter to the actual author of a devotional book. "Books from time to time bowled Wesley over," says one historian, and a born influencer like John Wesley was bound to pass along these books which had become events in his life.[26] Contrarily, when he read a bad book (especially by an author he had reason to expect better of), he warned people away from it as if it were poison. Though he had learned so much from William Law's early works, when Law's later works took a turn toward the mystical, Wesley denounced them in public and scolded Law

---

[25]Thomas Chalmers, cited in James Stalker, *Imago Christi: The Example of Jesus Christ* (New York: A. C. Armstrong, 1889), p. 10.
[26]Gordon Rupp, *Religion in England 1688-1791* (Oxford: Clarendon Press, 1986), p. 353.

in a personal letter. In fact, after his evangelical awakening at Aldersgate, Wesley wrote to Law in the strongest terms, demanding to know why Law had never written more clearly about justification by faith. For all the good that Wesley had drawn from Law's books, when he looked back on them he noticed that the most important thing was missing. He wrote to Law:

> How will you answer it to our common Lord that you never gave me this advice? Did you never read the Acts of the Apostles, or the answer of Paul to him who said, "What must I do to be saved"? Or are you wiser than he? Why did I scarce ever hear you name the name of Christ; never, so as to ground anything upon "faith in His blood"? . . . If you say you advised other things as preparatory to this, what is this but laying a foundation below the foundation? Is not Christ, then, the first as well as the last? If you say you advised them because you knew that I had faith already, verily you knew nothing of me; you discerned not my spirit at all. I know that I had not faith, unless the faith of a devil, the faith of Judas, that speculative, notional, airy shadow, which lives in the head, not in the heart.[27]

Wesley presses Law even further, asking him to "consider deeply and impartially, whether the true reason of your never pressing this upon me was not this—that you had it not yourself."[28]

These are harsh words, but Wesley strikes the true evangelical note when he talks of books as having the power of life and death in them. Once he came to experience saving faith in Christ, he looked back with shame and horror on some of the books he had recommended before. They were good books, but some of them talked up obedience to the exclusion of faith, highlighted personal righteousness and obscured the righteousness of Christ. Little wonder that Wesley spent so much energy in later life in circulating "Best Books," books he selected more carefully with an eye on the main things of the gospel: his Christian Library that he distributed through his network of preachers.[29]

---

[27]John Wesley, cited in Luke Tyerman, *The Life and Times of the Rev. John Wesley, Founder of the Methodists* (London: Hodder & Stoughton, 1876), 1:186.
[28]Ibid.
[29]See Thomas Walter Herbert, *John Wesley as Editor and Author* (Princeton, NJ: Princeton University Press, 1940), pp. 25-31.

"Buying and selling books with some, is like buying and selling potatoes." But evangelicals are in earnest about the books they recommend
and pass around to each other. The simple question, "What's a good
book to read on subject X?" is not just a bibliographic query. It can
provoke considerable soul-searching. On that book recommendation
hangs serious responsibility, and the possibility of great blessing.

PART FOUR

How to Read the Spiritual Classics

10

The Church Fathers and Mothers

Michael Glerup

THE PERIOD OF THE CHURCH FATHERS AND MOTHERS, some-
times referred to as the patristic period, after the Greek *pater* (father),
extends from the end of the apostolic age (A.D. 100) to the beginning of
the Middle Ages. Some consider the fifth century, specifically the First
Council of Chalcedon (451), as the end of the patristic period; others
extend the period for the Latin Church to Gregory the Great and for the
Greek Church to John of Damascus (c. 675-c. 749). For the purposes of
this present study, we will begin with the *Didache* (before 100) and conclude with Maximus the Confessor (c. 580-662).

In this chapter we will focus on works that were influential on later
spiritual writers but today are not widely known outside of certain academic circles. The first to be considered is Origen's *Commentary on the
Song of Songs*, an immensely influential work of Christian spirituality by
the preeminent theologian of the early church. Next is Gregory of
Nyssa's *Life of Moses*, which picks up on many of the spiritual themes of
Origen and recasts them in light of Nicene orthodoxy. These two well-
known figures are followed by the spiritual classics of Pseudo-Dionysius,
Syrian theo-poet Ephrem and the great theologian of the east Maximus
the Confessor.[1]

---

[1]Patristic scholar Frances Young once said that there are two types of patristic scholars—those
that study Augustine and those that study the rest. This study will focus on the rest and will omit
any significant discussion of Augustine's works. The reader should not conclude that I do not

Learning to read the classics of early Christianity is like learning a foreign language or living in a foreign culture. Their favorite Bible passages are different than ours. Their philosophical presuppositions differ from philosophical assumptions that hold sway today. Consequently, to receive the maximum benefit from these works a short primer on the historical circumstances and theological context of early Christian spirituality would be useful before discussing the actual works. Five areas to be considered: (1) Christianity as a way of life, (2) reading Paul, the apostle of transformation, (3) the witness of the martyrs, (4) human beings created in the image of God and (5) priority of the spiritual over material.

Historical Circumstances

1. A way of life. In 1873 Archbishop Philotheos Bryennios, sifting through the manuscripts at the Holy Sepulchre in Istanbul, happened upon a collection of early church writings that included the *Didache*. Preoccupied with other tasks, Bryennios delayed publication of the manuscript for another ten years. Soon after its publication and subsequent translation into English, scholars recognized its importance for understanding the development of the early church. The *Didache* most likely originated in Syria during the latter half of the first century. An unknown author compiled the *Didache* from a variety of sources in order to develop an instruction manual used for the formation of Christian converts from paganism.

The *Didache* begins, "There are two ways: one of life and one of death! (And) [there is] a great difference between these two ways. . . . [T]he way of life is this: first: you will love the God who made you; second: [you will love] your neighbor as yourself."[2] The author follows the *Shema*

believe Augustine made a significant contribution to the history of Christian spirituality. Quite the contrary. I would argue that he made such a substantial contribution to Christian spirituality that it would take a whole chapter to adequately discuss his works. In addition to his masterpiece, *Confessions*, one would need to survey his *Tractates on the Gospel of John, Homilies on the Psalms, Homilies on the First Epistle of John* and *On the Trinity*. Fortunately, excellent studies on each of these works are available in the secondary literature. And for a truly groundbreaking study of Augustine I would recommend Phillip Cary's *Inner Grace* and companion volume *Outward Signs* both available through Oxford University Press.
[2] Aaron Milavec, *The Didache: Text, Analysis, and Commentary* (Collegeville, MN: Liturgical Press, 2003), p. 3.

(love God) and the Great Commandment (love your neighbor as yourself) with a negative form of the Golden Rule ("as you might wish not to happen to you do not do to another"). This teaching is followed by a second rule, which consists of the Ten Commandments and prohibitions against speaking falsely, acting hypocritically and scheming or plotting evil against your neighbor. In chapter 5 the author describes the "way of death" in terms of vices, which are to be avoided, and concludes with an exhortation not to wander from this way of training.

In the second part of the document the author outlines regulations concerning baptism, fasting, prayer, eucharistic practice (Communion) and prayer of thanksgiving. After initiation into the Christian community through baptism, Christian converts were expected to fast on Wednesdays and Fridays, pray the Lord's Prayer three times a day and participate in the eucharistic meal. Typically, the Eucharist was served on Sundays after the completion of the work day. As a result, we can see that from the very beginning of the Christian church its spirituality was rooted in a "way of life" comprising a distinct morality and a spiritual culture that commenced with baptism and promulgated through regular practices of fasting, prayer and Communion. This way of life took on a variety of permutations, but its core affirmations were evident in the common teaching of the churches and the lives of its most faithful witnesses.

2. Reading Paul. As the composition of the church changed with the addition of Gentile converts, the church had to firmly establish its relationship to Hebrew Scriptures. Were the Hebrew Scriptures to be considered Law? Prophecy? What was their historical or spiritual relevance to the Christian church? The debate that grew out of this issue of biblical interpretation reached a critical stage in the mid-second century. The debate centered on Paul's reading and use of the Old Testament in his letters to the various Christian churches. For later interpreters Paul served as a model on how to read the Old Testament in light of the fact that the *Word of God became human and dwelt among us.*

Early Christian interpreters viewed Paul as both an *author* of Scripture and an *interpreter* of Scripture.[3] As a result, Paul's writings provided

---

[3]See James L. Kugel, *The Bible as It Was* (Cambridge, MA: Belknap Press, 1997), pp. 17-23.

both inspired instruction in the spiritual life and examples of how to read the Hebrew Scriptures. Pauline passages such as 1 Corinthians 10:1-11 (warning from Israel's history), 2 Corinthians 3:7-17 (removing the veil of Moses), Galatians 4:21-24 (allegory of Sarah and Hagar), and Romans 7:14 (understanding the law spiritually) offered the early interpreters examples to imitate as they interpreted the Old Testament. Furthermore these passages illustrate a few basic premises that New Testament authors shared with early Christian interpreters. First, the Bible is a book of instruction, a reliable guide to salvation and spiritual transformation. It was written as an example for the Christian community (1 Cor 10:6) and therefore was relevant to readers of subsequent generations. It was assumed that the *hermeneutical gap* between the written world and early church interpreters could be easily bridged. Second, early Christians viewed the Bible as a library of books composed by a variety of writers and yet maintained its true author was the Holy Spirit. As a result, the Bible received as two testaments—Old and New—is one testimony because it is inspired by the same Spirit and teaches the same salvation. Consequently, early Christian interpreters assumed that the Scriptures were inerrant, spoke in a single voice and maintained that it was methodologically appropriate to interpret one Bible passage by means of other Bible passages—the hermeneutical principle, "explaining Scripture by Scripture." Finally, though the Bible is inspired, inerrant and reliable, in many instances it is difficult to understand. Ancient interpreters assumed the Bible was cryptic and that it would not easily yield its spiritual treasures. This is why many of the great spiritual writers looked to Paul—a model of transformation and reading the Bible transformatively—as a dependable guide, particularly in the case of difficult biblical passages, to access these spiritual treasures.

3. Martyrs and spirituality. The most popular form of Christian literature in the early church, aside from the Bible, were the accounts of early Christian martyrs. These widely read texts produced some of the most celebrated men and women of the early church: Perpetua, Felicitas, Blandina, Ignatius, Justin and Cyprian. The spirituality of the earliest of Christians would have been quite different if it were not for these sporadic yet intense persecutions.

These martyrs were remembered, not only textually but throughout the church year with special celebrations associated with their "birth(days)" into the kingdom of God (martyrdom.) As in the case of Cyprian, once a year crowds gathered at his burial site to remember his death and commemorate his faithful witness by participating in a Eucharist service. Closely connected to the martyrs were recurrent Christian themes: imitation of Christ as sacrifice, the cosmic battle between forces of light and darkness for the salvation of the world, and the in-breaking of the kingdom of God. Similar to the Corinthian faithful, who served as Paul's letter of recommendation, the martyrs were Christ's letter of recommendation to be read by the world; letters written not by ink but by the Spirit of the living God, who dwelled in them (cf. 2 Cor 3:2). These spiritual "letters" of Christ provided the Christian community models for imitation, training documents for martyrdom, if you will, and opportunities for personal self-examination, and for later generations a benchmark for faithfulness.

Though these martyr accounts were composed in a variety of cultural settings over three centuries, they share two important convictions: first, in the cosmic battle for the salvation of the world, the sacrifice of the martyrs will eventually overcome the imperial sacrifice and the ruler of the world, and second "that male and female combatants needed intensive training for the battle, a training dependent on words and visible human examples."[4] Later, as persecution subsided and Christianity gained legitimacy, these convictions adapted to this new reality. The cosmic battle extended to the deserts, where the ruler of the world still ruled with little opposition and the training became codified, not only the texts of the desert fathers and mothers, but in exegetical works such as Gregory of Nyssa's *Life of Moses*.

THEOLOGICAL CONTEXT AND ASSUMPTIONS

4. Image of God. References to human beings as made in the *image of God* rarely occur in Scripture, but when they do they come at significant moments—the high point of creation, the beginning of the genealogies and

---

[4]Robin Darling Young, *In Procession Before the World: Martyrdom as Public Liturgy in Early Christianity* (Milwaukee: Marquette University Press, 2001), p. 71.

the prohibition against murder. After Genesis, we find only hints of the theme in the remainder of the Hebrew Scriptures. It then reappears in the New Testament, after having been the object of considerable conjecture in the philosophical works of Philo and the Deuterocanonical texts.

The theme of humanity made in the image of God, though lacking prominence in both the New and Old Testaments, became central to the theology of the early church. The theme of the *image* enabled the early Christian theologians to interpret the Scriptures in light of the philosophical tradition they inherited and it provided a theological basis for human transformation.

Christian writers from the early second century made a distinction between *image* and *likeness* in Genesis 1:26. For these commentators *image* referred to an inborn capacity of human beings for relationship and identification with God, and *likeness* referred to the fulfillment of that design acquired through the dynamic union of humanity with God. The ancient reading of the text was as follows: "let us make man in our image, after our likeness." The Greek word used to translate the Hebrew suggests a process rather than a state. As a result, human beings originally created in the image of God will be transformed through the glory of God and in the end will image God's likeness.

Epiphanius of Salamis, a significant figure in ancient monasticism, argued that this distinction was confirmed in the New Testament by Paul's use of the terms *eikon* and *doxa*. He writes, "[Paul] speaks of the image simply, but explains the nature of the likeness by the word glory (*doxa*)."[5] Paul uses the combination of image and glory on four occasions (Rom 1:23; 1 Cor 11:7; 2 Cor 4:4; 2 Cor 3:18) with his reference in 2 Corinthians 3:18, "transformed from glory to glory," summing up this dynamic quality of human spiritual growth.

Doxa (glory) in the Greek usage referred to reputation or public esteem, a quality or status highly regarded in the Greek world. Yet its customary usage in the Old Testament was much different. Contemporary scholars agree with early Christian writers such as Origen that *doxa* was utilized in the Septuagint to translate the Hebrew word *kābôd*,

---

[5]Epiphanius of Salamis, "Letter 51.6," in *Ante-Nicene Fathers*, ed. Philip Schaff (Peabody, MA: Hendrickson, 1995), 4:272.

which refers to the presence of God (see Ex 40:34-35; 1 Kings 8:10-11; Ex 34:29-30). In rabbinical literature, God's *kābôd* was given at creation but was lost at the fall and expected to be restored with return of the Messiah. The *kābôd* was perceived in the receiving of the law (Moses' glorified face) and continued to be present to the Israelites in the law of Moses. As Paul argued (2 Cor 3:7-15), the *kābôd* of the law ended at the advent of Christ and now is available through the gospel of the glory of Christ. The story of humanity may then be read as follows: Humanity, created in the *kābôd* of God, rebelled against it but was later renewed in the *kābôd* of Christ and transformed in the *kābôd* of the Spirit.

This conceptualization of God's plan of salvation as the sharing of the divine glory with humanity animated the theological reflection of the early Christian spiritual writers, especially in the East, and stands in contrast to later developments in the West, which emphasized God's salvation primarily in terms of "justification by faith."

5. Cosmology: spiritual transformation as a reality of the universe. Early Christian theologians, like their non-Christian counterparts, assumed the priority of the "unseen" over the "seen." Christian theologians, like Origen, reinterpreted the leading philosophical and scientific theories of their day in light of the revealed truth of Scripture.[6] Origen argued that the cosmos did not always exist but was freely created by God. Consequently, not only was creation "out of nothing" (*ex nihilo*) but also "out of love." Creation for Origen and subsequent Christian theologians was an act of grace. This was a radical reorientation of ancient philosophy.

Origen argued that all rational beings created by God existed initially in spiritual bodies.[7] These rational beings, dependent on God, united with a spiritual body, were created equal and endowed with free choice. As contingent beings these rational beings had the propensity to lapse in their contemplation of God through negligence. As such, they were not culpable for their lapse but for how far they fell away from their original contemplation. The extent of their fall depended on their negligence.

---

[6]His success at developing a truly Christian view of the cosmos is still debated. Did he Christianize Hellenism (Greek culture and thought)? Or did he Hellenize Christianity?
[7]Unlike modern usage, rationality does not refer only to the intellect. Rationality refers to the totality of the person—moral, intellectual and spiritual.

Beings that returned to their contemplation soon after their lapse became angels and were allowed to remain close to God.[8] Other beings stopped themselves later on and were assigned material bodies. Stars, planets and the moon are rational beings, and their higher position in the universe represents their earlier return to contemplation of God. Some rational beings stopped themselves even later and received human bodies. In this instance these rational beings acquired a certain *heaviness* and "fell" to the center of the universe, earth.[9] As a result, it is not unusual for Origen to describe spiritual formation as a process of "freeing" or "lightening" the soul[10] from the weight of its earthiness.[11]

Origen's belief that spiritual beings "fell" into physical bodies provided a fitting explanation for two important concerns: the problem of theodicy and the diversity of the human circumstances in light of their original unity. For Origen, when each rational being stopped their negligence they received a material reality that matched their choice and provided the perfect learning environment for each being to choose freely to love God and ascend back to God through contemplation. Each rational being's situation reflects their moral history—defending God's justice—and each being is provided a situation perfectly suited for their spiritual ascent to God—defending God's mercy. The final destination of each rational being is to return to God and obtain a body appropriate to "seeing" God as he really is.[12]

Though this view of the cosmos is no longer supported by Christian theologians and spiritual writers, some of its implications are still affirmed. First, the spiritual life is viewed as an ascent, as a movement upward. Second, our conversion is a returning to our original creation or,

---

[8]Christ was the only being that remained inseparably joined to God. Only one being, out of all the rational beings, chose not to stop itself—Satan.

[9]Note: Origen's system correlated the leading scientific theories of his day, the geocentric cosmos of the Ptolemaic system, with Christian notions of redemption.

[10]Peter Brown notes that what we now refer to as the soul, the subjective self, resulted from a subtle cooling off of the original ardor of the primal, deepest self: the "spirit." See his *The Body and Society: Men, Women, and Sexual Renunciation in Early Christianity* (New York: Columbia University Press, 1988).

[11]Gregory of Nyssa employs similar terminology and recommends practices that "lighten" the soul. He also uses imagery that describes growth in spiritual maturity is an upward movement toward God.

[12]Origen's doctrines of the primordial fall of the soul and *apokatastasis*—the restoration of all rational beings to their original condition—were condemned by later theologians.

in today's popular vernacular, "true self." Third, created freely by God as an act of will, it is only by freely choosing to obey God that human beings return to God and their true self. Finally, the world was lovingly created for a dramatic encounter between God and his creatures. Life is meaningful. The difficult circumstances and struggles we encounter in this life are not pointless. They are the context in which we encounter God, the God who loves his creation and was willing to send his Son to save it.

HERMENEUTICAL FRAMEWORK

Exegetical works. The earliest spiritual classics of the church fathers and mothers were works of exegesis (interpretation of Scripture). Beginning with Origen, there were three common forms of exegesis: scholia, homilies and books.[13] The latter two were the dominant forms that comprised the spiritual classics of the early church. Homilies were "spoken treatises" or "sermons of the people." Usually delivered in worship settings to the faithful, these works were characterized by their powerful and persuasive form of speech. Sometimes they interpret the spiritual implications of an important biblical figure or interpret an entire book of the Bible. Origen, John Chrysostom and Gregory of Nazianzus provide some of the most important examples of this form of spiritual classic.

Commentaries, also known as "dictated treatises," were longer and more systematic interpretations of a book of the Bible, an important passage or a biblical figure. Origen was a particularly important figure in the development of this form of exegesis. Drawing from the customary literary practices of his day, his commentaries became the model for later generations of Christians reflecting on the Scriptures. His *Commentary on the Song of Songs* became the first major Christian work sketching out a theory of mystical union with the bridegroom. As Louis Bouyer, the great scholar of Christian spirituality wrote, "Almost all Christian spiritual and ascetic literature, ever since, has been indebted to Origen's foundational architecture of Christian mysticism."[14]

---

[13]Scholia were short margin notes or explanations of Scripture. They might serve as a basis for a longer work but were not significant in regards to spiritual classics.

[14]Louis Bouyer, *The Christian Mystery: From Pagan Myth to Christian Mysticism* (Petersham, MA: Saint Bede's, 1990), p. 210.

Origen's **Commentary on the Song of Songs.** Origen was born in Alexandria in around 185. He was thoroughly educated in the Christian Scriptures from an early age and received a standard classical education. Origen's father, Leonides, most likely a convert to Christianity, was imprisoned and beheaded during Emperor Septimius Severus's persecution of the church. Origen himself was not pursued by the authorities, which suggests that he took on the lower Egyptian status of his mother. Origen spent his early career studying and teaching in Alexandria and his mature years in Palestinian Caesarea. It was during a long visit to Athens from 238 to 242 that Origen composed the first five books of his *Commentary on the Song of Songs.* He finished the last five books when he returned to Caesarea. Origen's original in Greek did not survive.[15] What remains is Rufinius's Latin translation of the first four books he made in A.D. 410 and Jerome's Latin translation of Origen's two homilies on the Song of Songs. Jerome said of Origen's *Commentary on the Song of Songs:* "while Origen surpassed all writers in his other books, in his Song of Songs he surpassed himself." This is high praise considering that it comes from what many believe to be the most significant Bible scholar of the early church.

Origen understood the Christian life as a three-stage journey of contemplation: the moral, natural and *theological* (contemplative). These stages correspond to the three-act movement in the three books of Solomon: Proverbs, Ecclesiastes and Song of Songs.[16] The *moral* represents practical knowledge: the beginning of moral purification, keeping the law and the gaining of virtue. The *natural* includes intellectual for-

---

[15]In 553, almost three hundred years after his death, Origen, along with Didymus the Blind and Evagrius, was formally condemned (anathematized) by the Council of Constantinople II. Many of his works were subsequently destroyed. Though many orthodox theologians—Basil of Caesarea, Gregory of Nazianzus, Ambrose, Augustine—were indebted to the Origen's writing, this was largely unacknowledged. Though his positive contributions to Christian exegesis and Christian spirituality were considerable, for the last fourteen centuries he was primarily known as a intellectual precursor to arch-heretic Arius and as a theologian who corrupted the truth of Christianity with pagan ideas. It wasn't until the twentieth century that an unexpected reclamation of his writings and reassessment of his significance for the history of Christian spirituality began. Now most contemporary scholars marvel at the breath of his biblical scholarship, his immense intellectual capabilities and yet acknowledged the failings in some of his key theological teachings.
[16]See Origen's prologue to *Commentary on the Song of Songs.*

mation and the discernment of the deeper purposes of creation, and the perfection of Christian love. The *theological*, a special gift of God, signifies divine illumination and the gaining of spiritual knowledge of God. As with subsequent writers, Origen considers that only at the gaining of interior freedom, the aim of ascetical practices, does the life of contemplation begin. The contemplation stage includes two movements: contemplation of nature and contemplation of God, that is, direct communion with God.

The Song of Songs, coming at the end of the three-stage movement, occupies a special place in the quest for the spiritual life. This book was not for the untrained. Only those schooled in the moral life and trained to distinguish between "good and evil" would remain unharmed by the love imagery of the bride for her heavenly bridegroom and worthily receive its teaching that fellowship with God is attained by the paths of charity and love. Biblically, the spiritually mature are the perfect who are nourished in Christ by "solid food" (cf. 1 Cor 3:1-3). Origen follows Jewish precedent on keeping the Song of Songs, along with the beginning of Genesis and the beginning and end of Ezekiel, out of the hands of the spiritually immature.

At the literal level Song is a dramatic retelling of the longing and love between a bride and her bridegroom. Interpreted spiritually, it may be understood as God speaking to Israel, or the Word of God (*Logos*) addressing his bride. For Origen there was no doubt that the groom was the Word of God. On the other hand, the bride represented both the church of Christ and the soul of the disciple. In Jerome's translation the bride is clearly portrayed as the church of Christ. Here Origen follows the tradition of the church passed on to him. In Rufinus's translation the bride is the individual soul. Here Origen does not seem to be following church tradition but is making his own original contribution. It is important not to overstate this distinction between the bride as church or soul, for as Origen showed, what may be appropriately applied to the church is also accomplished in the soul of all faithful persons.

As mentioned previously, arriving at a fitting spiritual interpretation required discernment, which may be acquired through the practice of the contemplative life and thorough knowledge of the divine economy revealed in the redemption of Christ. In addition, the application of proper reading methods gained from the classroom and divinely inspired interpreters such as Paul were required. A critical aspect of determining a proper spiritual interpretation was to establish the spiritual meaning of key words by comparing the word's meaning in its various uses in both Testaments. The Greek version of the Hebrew Scriptures, the Septuagint, the version used by the early church, lent itself to these type of word associations with the New Testament. The typical meaning of the word, through comparison and contrast with its various meanings throughout Scripture, is determined through this intensive reading of Scripture. Though there are numerous examples of Origen's use of this reading strategy, an early example appears in his reading of verse Song 1.2b (LXX) and his effort to establish the spiritual meaning of *breast*. Origen begins "now let us enquire what the inner meaning holds. We find the *principle cordis* (highest part of the soul) described in the divine scriptures by different words according to the cases and circumstances that are being discussed."[17] He then traverses through various Scripture passages linking the various uses of *breast* to *heart*. He concludes, "So in this present passage, where the behavior and the conversation of lovers is described, I think that this same *principle cordis* (highest part of the soul) is very happily called 'breasts.'"[18] Many modern readers find this exercise overly repetitive and a distraction from the actual interpretative process, but if the meaning of the word is to be discerned it must be read in light of its other uses by the Spirit in the various books of Scripture.

Gregory of Nyssa's **The Life of Moses.** Gregory of Nyssa, the much younger brother of Basil of Caesarea, was the last of the great Cappadocians. He was born in about A.D. 335 in Cappadocia, a rather desolate region to the northeast of modern Turkey.[19] As far as it is known, he did not receive his education at any of the major intellectual centers, but from his brother, Basil, and his sister Macrina. It is clear from his lit-

---

[17]*Origen: The Song of Songs, Commentary and Homilies,* Ancient Christian Writers 26, trans. R. P. Lawson (Mahwah, NJ: Paulist Press, 1957), p. 63

[18]Ibid.

[19]Anthony Meredith, *Gregory of Nyssa* (New York: Routledge, 1999), p. 1.

erary works he read widely in Hellenistic literature, philosophy and science. He inherited much of his thought from Origen and Philo, and he developed in his writings many of the themes of Basil and Macrina. In 372 Basil appointed him bishop of Nyssa, a small Cappadocian town in what is now south central Turkey. His lack of administrative skills and nimbleness in church politics made his tenure as bishop unsuccessful and short-lived. Arian opposition forced Gregory into exile in 376, in which he stayed until the pro-Nicene emperor Theodosius I replaced Emperor Valens at his death in 378.

After the death of Basil in January 379, Gregory entered into a period of intense activity. It was during this period that Gregory played a substantial role in the councils of Constantinople, where Theodosius described him as a key spokesperson for orthodoxy. Gregory's most important spiritual work, *On the Life of Moses*, was composed late in his career.

The *Life of Moses*, presented in two books, depicts Moses as a model of Christian perfection. In the opening section Gregory offers a short description of the pertinent episodes of the life of Moses. In the second section he provides a considerably longer interpretation of these episodes, offering a spiritual interpretation of various stages that Christians must journey in order to reach spiritual perfection.

The Jewish philosopher Philo of Alexandria and Origen influenced Gregory's reading of the life of Moses. Gregory's exegesis operated under a few assumptions; first the passage, particularly in the case of texts of a spiritual nature, has a specific aim of guiding the reader on the journey of acquiring Christian virtue and ascending through successive levels to spiritual maturity. And second, he applied the allegorical method to bridge the distance between biblical events and his contemporary audience. Gregory "read" the life of Moses to discern the pattern of the spiritual life, "tracing in outline like a pattern of beauty," so that each one of us "might copy the image of the beauty which has been shown to us by imitating his way of life." By imitating the pattern of the spiritual life discerned by Gregory, the historical distance between his audience and the historical setting was bridged. Gregory concludes his exposition encouraging his friend "to look at that example and, by transferring to your own life what is contemplated through spiritual interpretation of the things spoken literally, to be known by God and become his friend."[20]

Why Moses? First, because the divine voice said of him "I have known you more than all others," and similarly Moses was called "a friend of God" by God himself. Second, Moses offers an example worthy of imitation in that he would rather suffer death with his fellow Israelites if God was unwilling to forgive their errors. And, pragmatically, his intercession worked, which offered divine confirmation that Moses was a model of perfection worthy of emulation.

Gregory divides Moses' progress into three stages, in which God manifests Godself to Moses in *light* (the burning bush), next in the *clouds* (on top of the mountain), and finally in *darkness*. Gregory is particularly interested in Moses' entry into *darkness* because it is here Moses understands that God's infinity transcends all that can be known of him. It is in the dark cloud that Moses discovers that finding God means *we seek him without ceasing*. Coming nearer to God is to enter darkness. As the soul seeks God in itself,

> It goes always towards the more inward, until the activity of the intellect arrives at the invisible and the incomprehensible and there it sees God. For the true knowledge and seeing of what we seek consists in this, *in not seeing*, because that which we seek transcends all knowledge, cut off, as it were, on every side by incomprehensibility, as by a thick cloud.[21]

Following this discussion Gregory observes that Moses, who speaks with God face to face as one speaks with a friend (Ex 33:11) asks to see God's glory. Yet to see God is not possible, so God hides Moses in a cleft of rock, allowing him to see only his back parts (Ex 33:22-23). Gregory's investigation into this episode suggests that this reveals that "this is the vision of God: never to be satisfied in the desire to see him." Moses learned how to see God—"to follow God wherever he might lead." Contemplation of God, then, is to follow God as a guide similar to a hiker on a narrow mountain pass neither turning to one side nor the other.

This episode confirms and illustrates two themes central to Greg-

[20]Gregory of Nyssa, *The Life of Moses*, trans. Abraham J. Malherbe and Everett Ferguson (Mahwah, NJ: Paulist Press, 1978), p. 132.
[21]Ibid., 2.163

ory's spirituality: first, his principle of eternal progress in God, and, second, the *skopos* (end or goal) assigned to texts of a spiritual nature. First, for Gregory, perfection is progress itself. The perfect person is the one who continually grows in his or her knowledge of God. No limit may be set on growth or progress toward God because the object of faith's desire, the Trinity, is limitless. Knowledge of God is such that when the faithful experience God in his infinity, they experience the paradox of deep satisfaction in God's presence, and yet, at the same time, they experience God's absence because God remains constantly beyond human understanding. Second, the specific end or goal of every biblical book of a spiritual nature assigned by Gregory is that of ascent. In his spiritual works Gregory guides the reader in the difficult journey of the practice of virtue from the lowest level of the purification from sins to the dizzying heights of "seeing by not seeing." Each episode is then interpreted as a journey higher in the spiritual life. In others works, the spiritual life is conceived as a ladder on which one climbs toward perfection.

Finally, Gregory follows up Moses' vision of God with Aaron's and Miriam's jealous outburst against Moses narrated in Numbers 12. Gregory uses this episode to illustrate the progress Moses had made in his journey with God. Not only did Moses refuse to defend himself against their painful accusations, he sought out God's mercy on their behalf. Gregory claims Moses "would not have done this if he had not been behind God, who had shown him his back as a safe guide to virtue." Moses' virtuous actions confirmed his knowledge of God.

For Gregory virtue and vision are intimately related. The God that passed in front of Moses was the Lord who is compassionate and gracious, slow to anger and abounding in love and faithfulness, maintaining love to thousands and forgiving wickedness, rebellion and sin (Ex 34:6-7). The attributes that describe God—compassionate, gracious, faithful, love—are also virtues. Consequently, to share in these virtues is to know or to participate in God. When Moses came near to God he experienced God as merciful, compassionate and patient. Consequently, he knew the path of virtue and acted accordingly which confirmed his vision and provided another opportunity to know God.

Theological poetry and hymns. The ancient Syrian church has a long
storied history in the development of Christianity and Christian spirituality. Beginning from its most Hellenized city of Antioch, the birthplace
of the church's mission to the Gentiles and where the Jesus movement
became known as "Christians," to its unique spirituality expressed in the
brilliant theo-poet Ephrem. Pre-fifth-century Syriac Christianity east of
Antioch, marginally influenced by Hellenizing forces, exhibited a highly
ascetic form of church life. Early on the Syriac church only admitted
into full church membership those who embraced the ideal of *ihidaya*.
The term *ihidaya* applied to baptized Christians who had become followers of Christ, the *ihida*, that is, "the only Son of God." *Ihidaya* meant
single, celibate or single-minded, and later was closely identified with
the Greek term *monachos,* meaning solitary or monk. This ideal was
closely connected to the theme of the marriage between Christ and the
church, as well as the spiritual marriage between the soul and Christ
which occurred at baptism.

It was not unusual for Syrian Christians to embrace celibate lifestyles
while waiting for the return of Christ, the heavenly bridegroom. As a
result, textual images of the bridal chamber and marriage banquet are
found frequently throughout the various Syrian writers. Other themes
such as baptism as the reentry into paradise, baptism as putting "on
Christ" and its coterminous theme of the recovery of the "robe of glory"
lost by humanity at the fall are frequently found in these writings.

Ephrem (c. 306-373), a contemporary of Athanasius and the Cappadocians, serves as one of the finest representatives of early Syrian spirituality. Like many of his Syrian contemporaries (pre-fifth century),
Ephrem was ascetically oriented but never formally became a monk. He
lived in Nisibis, where he served as a catechetical teacher and deacon. In
363, as a result of the Roman Emperor Jovian's forced surrender of
Nisibis to the Sassanids (pre-Islamic Persian Empire), Ephrem was
forced to move west in order to remain in the boundaries of the Roman
Empire. He settled in Odessa, where he continued his literary output
and established a school for theological studies.

Ephrem detested literal theological definitions. He much preferred to
express himself theologically in types and images employing symbolic

and paradoxical language. He composed biblical commentaries, poetry and hymns. The latter were immensely influential in all aspects of church life and, along with his biblical commentaries, became the standard for ensuing Syriac literature and spirituality.

His hymns or "teaching songs" were incorporated into the church's worship and typically recited after the readings of the Scriptures.[22] Eventually these hymns were arranged into collections according to themes by his followers and later editors. How much Ephrem was involved in this compilation process is not known, but we do know that by the sixth century the collections were, for all practical purposes, in the same form we have them today.

Similar to worship songs performed by choirs, these songs required practice in order to be performed properly. Women were integral to their performance. Later writers described Ephrem as "a second Moses for women." As Jacob of Sarug said of Ephrem:

> In you, even our sisters were encouraged to sing [God's] praises, although it was not permissible for women to speak in church. Your teaching opened the closed mouth of the daughters of Eve, and now the congregations of the glorious [church] resound with their voices. It is a new sight that women would proclaim the Gospel, and now be called teachers in the churches. The aim of your teaching is the wholly new world, where, in the kingdom, men and women are equal. Your work put the two sexes together as two lyres, and you made men and women at once equal to sing [God's] praises.[23]

For Ephrem theological insight required humility, devotion and prayerful cultivation of spiritual discernment—an inner, "luminous eye." God, who is hidden, manifests Godself to the eye of faith through signs and symbols rooted in creation, Scripture and most fully in the incarnation of the Word. Christ in the incarnation, clothed in a human body and human language, reveals God yet retains God's hiddenness. Ephrem writes, "Who will not give thanks to the Hidden one, most hidden of all, who came to open revelation, most open of all for He put on a body, and

---

[22]"Teaching songs" are known as *Madrashâ* in Syrian.
[23]Jacob of Sarug, cited in *A Metrical Homily on Holy Mar Ephrem*, ed. Joseph P. Amar, Patrologia Orientalis t. 47, fasc. 1 (Washington, DC: Brepols, 1995), pp. 34-37.

other bodies felt him—though minds never grasped him."[24] In the incarnation God remains utterly transcendent yet reveals his intimate love for humanity.

To benefit from reading Ephrem's *Hymns of Paradise* or *Hymns of the Nativity*, two of his most important works in Christian spirituality, it is important to know some of his key assumptions. First, Ephrem is adamant that the breach between God and creature is unbridgeable. The divide between God and humanity can only be crossed over by God and not by humanity. For the love of his creation, God did cross this divide in order to reveal himself to humanity. God descended to the level of humanity, revealing himself within the limits of human language and understanding. God reveals himself primarily in three ways. First, God reveals his divinity through signs in nature. As Creator, God has infused his creation with signs and symbols that point both to his existence and creative activity. Second, Scripture is filled with types and symbols that reveal God's nature. Ephrem says of these two witnesses: "In his book Moses described the creation of the natural world, so that both Nature and Scripture might bear witness to the Creator: Nature through man's use of it, Scripture through his reading of it."[25] In addition, God employs names and titles such as Father, Creator, Living One, Giver, Healer and Lord, which by God's grace provide real revelation of God to humanity. Analogous to the incarnation in which the Word of God "put on a body," so God "puts on names and titles" in order to reveal himself within the limitations of human comprehension. Ephrem says, "He clothed Himself in language so that He might clothe us in His mode of life."[26] Therefore it is important, just as the disciples saw beyond the humanity of Christ and perceived his divinity, that students of the Bible penetrate beyond the literal meaning of the biblical text and perceive the hidden reality or truth disclosed in the symbol. Finally, the high point of God's revelation of Godself occurs in the Word of God "taking on flesh," the incarna-

---

[24]Ephrem the Syrian, *Homilies on Faith* 19:7, trans. Sebastian Brock, in Brock, *The Luminous Eye: The Spiritual World Vision of Satin Ephren the Syrian,* Cistercian Studies 124 (Kalamazoo, MI: Cistercian, 1992), p. 28.

[25]Ephrem the Syrian, *Hymns on Paradise,* trans. Sebastian Brock (Crestwood, NY: St. Vladimir's Seminary Press, 1990), p. 102.

[26]Ephrem the Syrian, *Homilies on Faith* 31.2, in Brock, *Luminous Eye,* p. 60.

tion.[27] Here the incarnate Son puts on not only flesh but titles (Prophet, King, etc.) and symbols (the Lamb of God) for the purpose of guiding humanity to himself.

In works like his *Hymns of the Nativity*, Ephrem explores the wondrous paradox of God becoming human. He writes, "A wonder is thy mother. The Lord entered her and became a servant; the Word entered her and became silent. . . . [T]he Rich One went in and came out poor; the High One went in and came out lowly." Ephrem knits this tension between the divine and the human, the hidden and the revealed in order to invoke in the reader the attitude necessary for faithful theological engagement—awe and wonder. Ephrem's hymns bursting with theological content should be read meditatively like one would read the Psalms. This allows the mind to make the trek through the scriptural images, like a bridge, and so by, entering into the presence of God.

In addition to Ephrem's sway, later Syriac spiritual writers were shaped by spiritual themes found in the Macarian homilies, Evagrius and works of Dionysius the Areopagite. Spiritual writers in this tradition included John the Solitary, Philoxenus of Mabbug (c. 440-523), Martyrius (or Sahdona, fl. 635-640) and Isaac of Nineveh (d. c. 700). The latter, also known as Isaac the Syrian, after Ephrem, is the most recognized of the ancient Syriac spiritual writers. Isaac, a native of Qatar, served a short term as the bishop of Nineveh before retiring to live the life of a solitary. The best known of his few surviving works is known today as *The Ascetical Homilies*, which consists of eighty-two chapters. Central to his theological and ascetical program was his insistence that God is above all immeasurable and boundless love. Influenced by John the Solitary's threefold outline he suggests progress in the spiritual life includes renunciation of the world, silence, ministry of prayer, struggle against passions and temptations, and the development of a deep humility characterized by compassion. After this initial stage the mystic transitions to a life of prayer and then, rarely, to a life beyond "pure prayer," which is characterized by silence and complete rest.

---

[27]For early Christian writers the incarnation referred to the whole life of Christ—conception, birth, growth, ministry, death and resurrection.

DIONYSIUS THE AREOPAGITE: PHILOSOPHICAL THEOLOGY

Dionysius the Areopagite, an unknown author, lived in the late fifth century, possibly in Syria, and wrote in Greek.[28] He adopted the persona of the Areopagite, the Athenian convert mentioned in Acts 17:22-34, to lend apostolic authority to his work. In the Eastern tradition he was regarded as the first bishop of Athens, and in the West as a martyr bishop of Paris. His work had profound influence on spiritual writers of both the East and the West. In the East his work was transmitted through the work of Maximus the Confessor. In the West his works profoundly influenced Gregory the Great, John Scotus Eriugena and Albert the Great.

Due to the pseudonymous nature of these writings it is difficult to say much about the historical context of these works or their intended audience. Consequently the interpretation of his *Mystical Theology*, a short but influential book, should be read in the context of his other major works *Celestial Hierarchy*, *Ecclesiastical Hierarchy* and *The Divine Names*.

For Dionysius all reality springs forth from the eternal self-giving love of the Trinity and produces two additional levels of reality—the celestial hierarchy and the ecclesiastical hierarchy. Each of these levels is triadic and descends orderly from God. At the first level the angelic hierarchy is divided into three orders of three—seraphim, cherubim and "thrones," then dominations, powers and authorities, and finally the principalities, archangels and angels. The ecclesiastical hierarchy follows a similar pattern. The first order is the mysteries of the church: baptism, Eucharist and chrismation. The next level is the realm of those that administer these mysteries: bishops, priests and deacons. And finally the lowest level is those who receive the mysteries: monks, laity and the uninitiated.

At the center of Dionysius's system is the process of procession and ascent, whereby the soul returns to the divine presence, which is manifested through the created hierarchies. This process of ascent described as an "assimilation to likeness with God" (*theosis*) or union is achieved through the threefold way of purgation, illumination and union. Pur-

---

[28]He is referred to in modern literature as Pseudo-Dionysius.

gation, achieved through rigorous application of spiritual disciplines and ascetical practice, cuts off all that hinders the journey toward God. Illumination, the gift from God, enables mystical insight into essential Christian truths and spiritual sensitivity to the symbolic reality of a world bathed in the love of God. And union is the way of participative knowledge of God, in which knowing is beyond knowing or "unknowing knowing."

This latter stage is required because figures, symbols, concepts and words ultimately fall short in the presence of the One who is beyond our intellectual grasp. In the treatise *The Divine Names*, Dionysius offers positive statements on God, yet he continually reminds the reader that none of these thoughts can reach him who is unknowable. What we can say about God is genuine, that God is really known, because God reveals himself in the world. But God remains unknowable because he is not an object of knowledge. Therefore the one seeking God must, at the same time, offer positive statements about God and deny those statements, not as false, but as inadequate to the nature of God. For Dionysius the *unknowing* of denial is more fundamental; it is the path to a deeper awareness of God. Throughout much of the Dionysian corpus we witness this creative interplay between cataphatic and apophatic theology.

For Dionysius,

> [God] is made manifest only to those . . . who pass beyond the summit of every holy ascent, who leave behind them every divine light, every voice, every word from heaven, and who plunge into the darkness where, as scripture proclaims, there dwells the One who is beyond all things. . . . Here, being neither oneself nor someone else, one is supremely united to the completely unknown by an inactivity of all knowledge, and knows beyond the mind by knowing nothing.[29]

In this last sentence Dionysius speaks of *ecstasy*, the soul "going out" of itself and uniting to God. This is an ecstasy of love, a passive forgetfulness of self in the presence of God. In the end, beyond negation and

---

[29]*The Mystical Theology* 1.3, from *Pseudo-Dionysius: The Complete Works*, trans. Colm Luibheid (Mahwah, NJ: Paulist Press, 1987), pp. 136-37.

affirmation, the soul experiences God as God gives himself in the communication of the divine love.

Maximus the Confessor: Chapters or Centuries

Maximus the Confessor (c. 580-662) is one of the few great theologians and spiritual writers recognized equally in the Eastern and in the Western Christian tradition. Maximus most likely was born into a family of Byzantine nobility. Later in life he embarked on the ascetic life, living in a monastery across the Bosporus from Constantinople. In 626, under the threat of a Persian invasion, Maximus left the monastery and eventually made his way to Carthage in North Africa. Here he became embroiled in the christological controversy of monothelitism and monoenergism. Viewed by those in power as a threat to the unity of the Byzantine Empire, Maximus was subsequently arrested, tried and sent into exile. But Maximus refused to be silent, continuing to argue his position, and as a result he was ordered to return to Constantinople. Again he was condemned, but this time his punishment included disfigurement: his tongue was cut out and his right hand cut off. He later died in exile in Caucasus. Not long after his death he received the title Confessor.

Maximus's work *The Four Hundred Chapters on Love* was written to cultivate in the reader a love and desire for God. Maximus revised and rewrote sayings of earlier church fathers on Christian love in the form of chapters or brief statements. These statements were then organized into four centuries or groupings of one hundred in order to improve memorization. Each chapter is connected logically to chapters proceeding and following, though each chapter can stand alone on its own merits. These chapters were not intended to be skimmed or to be read through in a hurry. Rather they were to be read carefully and meditatively with the hope that through God's grace these perceptive observations would reveal spiritual insight to the soul.

Maximus's spirituality is grounded in the redemptive work of God in Christ. For Maximus, *theosis*, which is the result and the intention of the incarnation, was the goal of the spiritual life. The *kenosis* (self-emptying) of the Son revealed the nature of God as love and as such is the model of personal formation. Human formation is then a grace-enabled participation in the Son's self-emptying by the self-emptying of the passions.[30] The passions—greed, lust, envy, resentment, vanity, anger and the like— grow out of an inordinate concern for self and hinder the faithful from loving God and neighbor as well as they should. Consequently, it is important for the faithful to learn to live like Christ by gaining freedom from the passions and acquiring virtue. Passionless (*apatheia*) is a word that appears frequently in *Four Hundred Chapters on Love*. Passionless does not refer to a "lack of passion" in the modern sense of "lacking emotion" or "disconnected." Nor does it mean apathy. Rather it refers to, in the positive sense, "inner freedom" or "inner serenity," or in the negative sense "detachment."[31]

Yet for Maximus this is not enough; the faithful must also cultivate a love for God that is much stronger than their love for the things of the world.[32] A deep love and desire for God produces in the soul a disinterest in sinful indulgence. As a result, the internal change acquired in the exchange of vice for virtue as the believer takes on the characteristics of Christ becomes sustainable only if it is undergirded with a deep love (*agapē*) for God.

Maximus's spirituality affords an important role for both knowledge and practice. God's redemptive action in Christ was not merely a restoration to an Edenic innocence; it was also the bestowal of a new status as adopted children of God. The dignity of this new status accomplished by Christ is the basis for any meaningful Christian formation. Yet this new status must be persistently cultivated by the practice of the commandments. Commandments refer not only to the Decalogue but more fully to the Beatitudes in the Sermon of the Mount. For it is in the Beatitudes that Christ himself, that is, his beauty, is most strikingly described. As a result, as one practices the commandments, one conforms to Christ, and the beauty given by grace is cultivated from God's image into Christlikeness.

---

[30]Maximus, working within the philosophical traditions of ancient world, views the soul as divided into three parts: the mind (*nous*), which is above the concupiscible (*epithymia*) and irascible *(thymos)* elements. The concupiscible is associated with lust, and the irascible is associated with anger.

[31]*Maximus Confessor: Selected Writings*, trans. George C. Berthold (Mahwah, NJ: Paulist Press, 1985), p. 88.

[32]See Maximus, *Four Hundred Chapters on Love* 3.67

POSSIBLE USE FOR THE CHURCH TODAY

The church fathers and mothers present to us a holistic faith—right thinking, right living, right worship—which is big enough to fully engage us as human beings. For the church fathers and mothers there was a connection between thinking and doing. As a result, early saints were prepared to alter their way of life as the result of a chain of reasoning. Christian faith was not merely a question of feeling or will or power or tradition. It was a matter of knowledge. And since Christian faith was about reality, it served as a reliable guide to individual and communal formation. This leads to the first way that this literature is useful today: it provides us a model of biblical spirituality that challenges contemporary spiritualities that undercut the connection between right thinking and right living. What we think influences what we do, and what we do influences what we think. For a spirituality to be biblical its practices, morality and core beliefs must be grounded in the revelation of Jesus Christ.

Second, guided by Scripture, early Christian writers were convinced that if a person set his or her heart to inquire, discuss, investigate, pray, meditate on the Word of God and put into practice its instruction, he or she would experience the blessing of the Lord—"Christ in you the hope of glory." They were convinced that the entire Bible, even in obscure Old Testament books such as the Song of Songs, was a treasure trove of spiritual wisdom, which now could be accessed through Christ, the "internal logic" of the Bible. Many of the most spiritually and intellectually accomplished interpreters wrote down their meditations; some, as Augustine said, "for fear that my mediations escape from me through forgetfulness"; others, because they believed their deliberations might benefit their communities. In any case, eventually these meditations made their way into sermons, commentaries and theological writings that inspire us today. This leads to the second application for today: these spiritual classics are a "history of the Holy Spirit." As these church fathers and mothers interpreted the Bible with the same Spirit that inspired the biblical writings they left a record of the Spirit's work in the life of the church, which can today be a continued source of inspiration and insight into the work of the Holy Spirit.

OTHER IMPORTANT TEXTS FROM THE CHURCH FATHERS AND MOTHERS

Augustine's (354-430) *Confessions* is a long meditation on his life and conversion. The first section (bks. 1-9) focuses on his interior life from his birth until the time he is writing. The last four books focuses on religious and philosophical issues of memory (bk. 10), time and eternity (bk. 11), and exegesis of Genesis (bks. 12-13). *Expositions of the Psalms*, never envisioned by Augustine as a single work, was compiled from his treatise and sermons on the Psalms by later editors. Guided by a Christ-centered interpretation, this work became the most influential work on the Psalms in Western Christianity for the next millennium.

Egeria's (4th cent.) *The Travels* was one of the first formal writings by a woman in Western Europe. In her travel diary Egeria, a Spanish nun, describes the monks and pilgrimage sites of the Holy Land and Egypt in the fourth century. She provides valuable details concerning the worship practices at the church in Jerusalem, along with information on the development of the Christian calendar of holy days and seasons.

Origen's *On Prayer* was one of the earliest and most influential discourses on prayer. In this work Origen discusses the age-old problem of why one should pray even though God already knows what we need.

SUGGESTED READINGS

Secondary Sources for Augustine

Byassee, Jason. *Praise Seeking Understanding: Reading the Psalms with Augustine.* Grand Rapids: Eerdmans, 2007.

Kenney, John Peter. *The Mysticism of Saint Augustine: Rereading the Confessions.* New York: Routledge, 2005.

Ayres, Lewis. "Augustine, Christology, and God as Love: An Introduction to the Homilies on 1 John." In *Nothing Greater, Nothing Better: Theological Essays on the Love of God.* Edited by Kevin Vanhoozer. Grand Rapids: Eerdmans, 2001.

Secondary Sources on the Church Fathers and Mothers

Brakke, David. *Athanasius and Asceticism.* Baltimore: Johns Hopkins University Press, 1998

Demacopoulos, George E. *Five Models of Spiritual Direction in the Early Church.*
     Notre Dame, IN: University of Notre Dame Press, 2007.
Brock, Sebastian. *The Luminous Eye: The Spiritual Vision of Ephrem the Syrian.* Cis-
     tercian Studies 124. Kalamazoo, MI: Cistercian Publications, 1992.
Clément, Olivier. *The Roots of Christian Mysticism: Text and Commentary.* Trans-
     lated by Theodore Berkeley. New York: New City Press, 1995.
Louth, Andrew. *The Origins of the Christian Mystical Tradition: From Plato to Denys.*
     2nd ed. New York: Oxford University Press, 2007.

11

The Desert Fathers

Gerald L. Sittser

IN THE LATE FOURTH CENTURY two adventurous travelers, John Cassian and his good friend Germanus, made their way through Asia Minor, Syria and Palestine in search of the desert fathers, a group of spiritual masters whose reputation for rigorous self-discipline was making them famous around the Mediterranean world. During the course of their travels they kept hearing reports about one group of monks in particular who seemed to rise above all the others—the desert fathers of Egypt. After a brief sojourn in Bethlehem they journeyed to Egypt and spent several years there with the most illustrious of these Egyptian masters.

What they discovered in Egypt astonished them. There they met men and women who were devoted—tenaciously, even fanatically so—to a highly rigorous expression of Christian discipleship. Inspired by these "spiritual athletes" and "bloodless martyrs," as they were called, Cassian and Germanus decided to submit to their teaching and follow their example. They wanted to become spiritual athletes. As one master stated,

> Whatever man, my children, is desirous to attain skill in any art, unless he gives himself up with the utmost pains and carefulness to the study of that system which he is anxious to learn, and observes the rules and orders of the best masters of that work or science, is indulging in a vain hope to reach idle wishes any similarity to those whose pains and diligence he avoids copying.[1]

---

[1]Cited in *John Cassian: The Conferences* (Bloomington, IN: Xlibris, 2000), p. 440.

This idea of the "spiritual athlete" introduces us to the strange world of the desert fathers.[2] The literature of these masters of self-discipline poses a special problem to modern Christians who wish to expand the repertoire of their spiritual reading. The reason is simple enough: the literature seems—and, in truth, is—exotic, so much so that it can and often does offend modern sensibilities. That is partly the result of the movement itself, for it is—and, for that matter, *was*, even to contemporaries—exceedingly strange, almost cartoonish. But it is partly the result of the spirit of our own age too, which recoils from anything that demands too much from us, at least spiritually.

I hope in this essay to make a case for why modern readers should take this literature seriously. It will not be easy. It is apparent, even at a first glance, that a huge gap exists between their world and ours, which probably explains why most Christians have not even heard of the desert fathers, to say nothing of reading their literature. There are obvious reasons why their literature seems so alien to us. That it is ancient in origin provides one reason. Protestants in particular tend to ignore and dismiss a great deal of Christian literature that was written in late antiquity and in the early medieval period, tainted, as it is, with the reputation of originating in the "Dark Ages." That the literature seems strange and bizarre is another reason. Even admirers will admit that it is quite peculiar, for it is full of wild stories and extreme asceticism and esoteric teaching. That the literature is difficult to read is a third reason why we know so little about this fascinating group of people. Not that it is difficult in the same way that, say, Aquinas's or Barth's writings are. In the case of the desert fathers the literature is not difficult to understand (as in the case of Aquinas and Barth) but to accept and put into practice. It offends modern tastes, for what it demands seems unreachable and unreasonable.

But there is inestimable value in this literature, all the same, if we are willing to read it on its own terms. At its heart resounds a calling, clear and bold, to become *spiritual athletes*, doing whatever it takes to follow

[2]The movement did include some women, as Laura Swan shows so successfully (see note 8). But they played a much less prominent role, especially in the formation of the literature. I will therefore use "desert fathers" to describe the movement.

Jesus. Such a commitment requires the courage to become cultural outsiders, as we shall see in the case of Antony, to struggle to die to ourselves and live to God, as the great Abbas taught in their *Sayings*, to
submit to a regimen of training, as the *Rule of St. Benedict* outlines, and
to practice serious, almost ruthless self-examination and purgation, as
Cassian urges. If read slowly, if read in humility (as well as with a critical
eye), if read with transformation in mind, then surely this literature will
come alive to you. It certainly has to me.

HISTORICAL CIRCUMSTANCES

The movement of the desert fathers and mothers emerged in the third
century and reached its pinnacle in the fourth and fifth centuries. Apologists of the movement cited the Bible itself as source and inspiration,
and they used the example of Moses, Elijah, Elisha, John the Baptist and
Jesus' temptation in the wilderness and frequent retreats there as justification to withdraw into the desert to search for God, to fight the devil
and to practice a highly rigorous form of discipleship. They also drew
from pagan sources, among them peripatetic philosophers, who taught
their disciples how to live wisely and well (not simply how to think and
speak cleverly), and Stoic teachers who challenged followers to become
masters of the self.

Thus inspired, Christians seeking for a deeper spiritual life began to
practice the ascetic disciplines, both in isolation and in community.
Groups of women, for example, organized small communities of virgins
in urban centers, as if to create a new kind of ascetic family, and older
sages, practicing a severe form of asceticism, served as spiritual masters
and mentors for those who, living in cities and villages, hoped to make
progress in the spiritual life.[3] Persecution played a role too. Wishing to
escape possible martyrdom, some Christians sought refuge in the desert,
where they formed small communities to keep faith alive under hostile

---

[3]See Philip Rousseau, *Ascetics, Authority and the Church in the Age of Jerome and Cassian* (New
York: Oxford University Press, 1978); Susanna Elm, *"Virgins of God": The Making of Asceticism in
Late Antiquity* (Oxford: Clarendon Press, 1994); James E. Goehring, *Ascetics, Society, and the
Desert: Studies in Early Egyptian Monasticism* (Harrisburg, PA: Trinity Press International, 1999);
and Derwas J. Chitty, *The Desert A City: An Introduction to the Study of Egyptian and Palestinian
Monasticism Under the Christian Empire* (Crestwood, NY: St. Vladimir's Seminary Press, 1999).

circumstances. These various experiments of ascetic Christianity blossomed in areas around the eastern end of the Mediterranean Sea, which included Egypt, the Sinai Peninsula, Palestine, Syria and Cappadocia.

These early experiments took on the features of a more organized movement after Constantine came to power in the early fourth century. Constantine's decision to grant the church legal status and then to offer it special favors had an irreversible impact on the church. Church attendance grew steadily (perhaps as much as fivefold during the first half of the fourth century), the office of bishop emerged as politically influential, and church buildings began to dominate the urban landscape. Standards of church membership, however, were gradually relaxed, and the church began to take on the characteristics of an established institution that wielded a great deal of power, especially after Theodosius I designated Christianity the official religion of the empire near the end of the fourth century. Thus a church that had been persecuted became a church of privilege and power.

Not everyone welcomed these changes. A small trickle of ascetics, often called *monks*, moved to the desert to witness against the perceived decline and compromise of the church. Early experiments of asceticism gradually gave way to standard forms and practices. *Anchorites* or *hermits* spent much of their time alone, living in huts or caves (called *cells*). They practiced such ascetic disciplines as fasting, vigils and poverty, prayed "without ceasing," plied a trade (e.g., plaiting rope or weaving mats), kept a small garden and, when opportunity presented itself, served the poor and needy, and practiced hospitality to visitors who crossed their path. These anchorites had to submit to the guidance of a spiritual master too, known as an *Abba* (or *Amma*, in the case of women), who usually functioned as a mentor to apprentices living nearby (in Palestine and Syria known as a *lavra*). *Cenobites* lived in more organized communities, again mostly in the desert, where they answered to an abbot and lived by a *regula vitae* (rule of life). They practiced a wide variety of trades to support their life together, worshiped according to a set rhythm (later called the *Divine Office*), and ministered to the needs of the surrounding community.

Eventually a tradition emerged that defined the general history and character of the movement. Antony of Egypt became the "first"—and ideal—anchorite, and Pachomius the founder of the "first"—and successful—monastery, though neither of them was really the first. Over time some members of the movement became holy men and women, healers and teachers who wielded special powers. Their stories and examples set a standard of discipleship that lasted for centuries. The movement became so popular, in fact, that Antony himself proclaimed that the desert had become a city.

THEOLOGICAL CONTEXT AND ASSUMPTIONS

Certain features—many quite contrary to modern sensibilities—reflected the world out of which the movement emerged.[4] For example, the desert fathers took the Bible seriously.[5] They knew it well, memorized it, meditated on it and discussed it among themselves, which eventually produced an oral tradition of interpretation. Still, however well informed and well grounded in Scripture, their overall approach to the Bible seems—and, in fact, is—foreign to the modern age. They jumped from text to text, as if by free association, making connections that would appear odd to us, and they interpreted the Bible allegorically, which gives the impression that their interpretation is informed more by fanciful imagination than by careful exegesis. Equally peculiar, they often applied the Bible literally, which explains why someone like Antony could do *exactly* what Jesus told the rich young ruler to do. Still, what kept them on course—and what keeps us on course when reading them—is the central role that Christ played. The desert fathers viewed Christ as the hermeneutical key to the Bible; in their minds he unites and fulfills the entire biblical story.[6]

---

[4]William Harmless, *Desert Christians: An Introduction to the Literature of Early Monasticism* (New York: Oxford University Press, 2004). See also Hubertus R. Drobner, *The Fathers of the Church: A Comprehensive Introduction,* trans. Siegfried S. Schatzmann (Peabody, MA: Hendrickson, 2007); Everett Ferguson, *Backgrounds of Early Christianity,* 3rd ed. (Grand Rapids: Eerdmans, 2003); and Luke Timothy Johnson, *Among the Gentiles: Greco-Roman Religion and Christianity* (New Haven, CT: Yale University Press, 2009).
[5]Douglas Burton-Christie, *The Word in the Desert: Scripture and the Quest for Holiness in Early Christian Monasticism* (New York: Oxford University Press, 1993).
[6]John J. O'Keefe and R. R. Reno, *Sanctified Vision: An Introduction to Early Christian Interpretation of the Bible* (Baltimore: Johns Hopkins University Press, 2005); and Robert Louis Wilken, *The Spirit of Early Christian Thought* (New Haven, CT: Yale University Press, 2003), pp. 50-79.

The landscape of the Eastern Mediterranean played an important role in the development of the literature, for massive deserts dominate the entire region. The "desert" became a kind of code word for a place "outside" the dominant religion and culture of the day, and thus "rural" as opposed to "urban," "backwards" as opposed to "progressive," "simple" and "humble" as opposed to "sophisticated." Some deserts in the region were largely inhospitable to human life and survival, though a few giants of the movement still spent at least some time there, as if to establish their credentials as heroic figures. But most of the desert fathers lived in deserts located nearer to civilization, where they created settlements (sometimes virtual cities) of monks as an alternative to the prevailing social order and worldly climate of the cities. Their purpose was to launch a counter-movement of discipleship in order to protest, resist and challenge the compromised faith of the established church. The desert, therefore, served as both literal place and spiritual symbol. It provided a setting to practice severe forms of discipline, to pursue holiness of life and to submit self to God. It functioned like a gymnasium where they could train themselves to become spiritual athletes.

It was also in the desert that they were exposed to and fought against the demons. Demons appear everywhere in the literature, which, once again, contradicts our modern sensibilities. The desert fathers seemed almost obsessed with demons and speculated about their origins, organization and strategies. It is *how* the demons function in the literature that seems most peculiar. The desert fathers believed that there was a demon for every temptation imaginable, a demon for lust, for gluttony, for avarice and the like, however small and trivial and, for that matter, *human* the temptation seemed to be. Still, the desert fathers did not view humans as helpless victims. What makes us vulnerable, they believed, is the inherent weakness and rebelliousness of the human heart. The demons can suggest and manipulate, even torment, but they cannot gain access to the inner person unless access is granted. The greatest battle we fight, then, is the battle for the heart, which depends ultimately on the free agency of the will. "For no one," taught Abbot Piamun, "is more my enemy than my own heart which is truly the one of my household closest to me." He admitted that he could not be injured by anyone, including demons, "if I do not fight against myself with warlike heart. But if I am injured, the fault is not owing to other's attack but to my own [weakness]."[7]

This battle for the heart involved high stakes, nothing less, in fact, than the very restoration of paradise. The desert fathers believed that how they lived on earth would point the way to the future age of the kingdom. Their stories tell tales of extraordinary feats that show signs of the coming of paradise, like crocuses breaking ground in early spring. One desert father had a pet lion that did his bidding; another crossed the Nile by walking on the backs of crocodiles; still another could fly from place to place. These miraculous powers—clairvoyance, healings, control of nature—hinted at the full restoration of Paradise that was yet to come, just as their ascetic discipline of the body in this life looked to the resurrection of the body in the next. Meanwhile, they turned their attention to the interior world of the soul, which they sought to purify and prepare for heaven.

This introduces us to still another peculiarity in the literature. The desert fathers *worked* hard in the spiritual life. They practiced the ascetic disciplines with a degree of devotion that seems incomprehensible and perhaps unhealthy. Progress in the spiritual life—and the quest for salvation itself—seemed to rest squarely on *their* shoulders, which poses an obvious theological problem. To be sure, there is grace to be found in the literature, but it is subtle and elusive. It is more akin to God's help or assistance, like a boost to get someone over the bar, and thus a far cry from Luther's "grace alone," which accomplishes salvation from start to finish.

A final characteristic of the desert fathers is the regimentation of their daily life. It was highly structured, highly demanding, even highly legalistic. They believed that discipleship requires serious training, and they could and did cite the New Testament for support. "Train yourself for godliness," Paul exhorted Timothy, one of many texts they were fond of quoting (1 Tim 4:7). Such regimentation flies in the face of the religious consumerism that permeates much of Western Christianity today. That church

[7]Cassian, *Conferences*, p. 458.

members feel free to switch churches if they dislike a pastor or find the worship music offensive would shock and sadden the desert fathers, who were less interested in style and more interested in substance. Christianity was not for them a spectator sport; they were training themselves to become spiritual athletes.

HERMENEUTICAL FRAMEWORK

1. Hagiography. The earliest form of literature, at least in chronology, is the spiritual biography or *hagiography*, which tells stories of the heroes of the movement. Most of these biographies consist of short vignettes that focus on one specific feature of the saint's life. At first they were circulated in oral form, spreading from person to person and community to community. Then enterprising bishops, most of whom had spent considerable time in the desert, collected, edited and published the stories. By so doing they hoped to preserve the memory of the desert masters, to promulgate models of true discipleship and to advance their own ecclesiastical interests. For example, Palladius published his *Lausiac History* in the early fifth century, telling the stories of the monks of Egypt. An anonymous author published a similar account titled *History of the Monks of Egypt* during the same period. Over the next two centuries Paphnutius compiled stories about the monks of Upper Egypt, while Theodoret of Cyrrhus sketched portraits of the monks of Syria, and Cyril of Scythopolis of the monks of Palestine. Perhaps the most fascinating collection comes from the pen of John Moschos, who in the early seventh century traveled in an arc from Constantinople, through Asia Minor, Syria, Palestine and Egypt, all the way to Upper Egypt to report on the state of the movement just before the Persians and the Muslims conquered the area.[8]

---

[8]For these collections of stories of the desert fathers and mothers, see Carolinne White, ed., *Early Christian Lives* (New York: Penguin, 1998); Tim Vivian, ed., *Journeying into God: Seven Early Monastic Lives* (Minneapolis: Fortress Press, 1996); *Palladius: The Lausiac History*, trans. Robert T. Meyer (Westminster, MD: Newman Press, 1965); *The Lives of the Saints of the Holy Land and the Sinai Desert* (Buena Vista, CO: Holy Apostles Convent, 1988); *The Lives of the Desert Fathers*, trans. Norman Russell (Kalamazoo, MI: Cistercian Publications, 1980); *Paphnutius: Histories of the Monks of Upper Egypt and The Life of Onnephrius*, trans. Tim Vivian (Kalamazoo, MI: Cistercian Press, 1993); *Theodoret of Cyrrhus: A History of the Monks of Syria*, trans. R. M. Price (Kalamazoo, MI: Cistercian Publications, 1985); *Cyril of Scythopolis: The Lives of the Monks of*

The Life of Antony. Another genre of hagiography consists of much
longer and richer accounts of desert luminaries. Of these the most important by far, in both reputation and influence, is the story of Antony
of Egypt, which was written by his friend and protégé, Athanasius,
bishop of Alexandria (328-373), who met Antony while in exile. Athanasius wrote the *Life of Antony* to portray him as the prototype of the
desert saint. In so doing he created a new genre of literature and shaped
the character of thousands of other hagiographies that would follow. He
turned Antony into a hero for the whole church, however culturally
marginal Antony appeared to be.[9]

As the story goes, Antony (c. 251-356), an uneducated Copt, heard the
story of the rich young ruler one day and responded by doing exactly
what the text commands. He sold the lands inherited from his parents,
distributing most of the assets to the poor, and arranged for his younger
sister to be cared for by a community of virgins. Then he apprenticed
himself to a village holy man. Eventually he withdrew into the desert, far
from civilization, and followed a regimen of ascetic discipline. He performed manual labor, prayed every waking moment, subdued his appetites by eating a Spartan diet, memorized Scripture and "weighed" his
thoughts (a form of self-examination).

In that day the desert was considered the devil's domain. Antony
chose, therefore, to invade the devil's own territory. The devil in turn
used every weapon in his arsenal to tempt and defeat him. The devil
brought into Antony's mind memories of his past life to remind him of
what he had left behind so sacrificially, but Antony refused to let his
mind indulge in self-pity. The devil tried to exploit Antony's appetites—
his desire for food, sex and wealth. Antony resisted. Frustrated by re-
peated failure, the devil finally appeared in the form of beastly appari-
tions to intimidate Antony. But Antony kept faith, seeking Christ and
increasing the severity of his ascetic routine.

Eventually Antony took up residence in an abandoned military for-

Palestine, trans. R. M. Price (Kalamazoo, MI: Cistercian Publications, 1991); Laura Swan, *The Forgotten Desert Mothers* (New York: Paulist Press, 2001); John Eviratus (John Moschos), *The Spiritual Meadow* (Kalamazoo, MI: Cistercian Publications, 1992).
[9]David Brakke, *Athanasius and the Politics of Asceticism* (Oxford: Clarendon Press, 1995).

tress, where he lived in isolation for some twenty years. Meanwhile, word of his story—his ascetic feats, holiness of life and communion with God—spread. People clamored to see the man who embodied a new kind of Christian, the "bloodless martyr" and "athlete of God." So eager were they to have an audience with Antony, in fact, that they broke down the doors of the fortress to catch a glimpse of the man who had fought the devil and won. Athanasius describes that first encounter: "Antony came forth as though from some shrine, having been led into divine mysteries and inspired by God." They were surprised by his vitality and strength, considering the ordeals he had faced. "They were amazed to see that his body had maintained its former condition, neither fat from lack of exercise, nor emaciated from fasting and combat with demons, but was just as they had known him prior to his withdrawal."[10] Over time Antony became a famous teacher, miracle worker, prophet, seer and sage who roundly defeated pagan philosophers in debate. He also emerged as a champion of orthodoxy.

The Life of Saint Macrina. A second example is the story of Macrina the Younger (c. 327-379), written by her brother, the famous bishop and theologian Gregory of Nyssa. Born into a wealthy Cappadocian family, Macrina refused to consider marriage again after her fiancé suddenly died when she was only twelve years old. At that point she chose to devote herself to the pursuit of holiness, turning away many suitors. She became a mentor to her younger siblings (including Gregory and Peter, both of whom became bishops), assistant to her mother and manager of the estate. She eventually founded a monastery, which served as a model for the larger monastic enterprise her brother Basil, bishop of Caesarea, was soon to found. She thus refused to fulfill the traditional role imposed on wealthy women of her day. Instead of indulging herself, she became a master of ascetic discipline; she sacrificed for the sake of her family, cared for those in need and functioned as an abbess to dozens of women. Like Antony, she became a miracle worker too.

These biographies introduce us to people who in their own day fell far outside the circle of what was deemed traditional, conventional and

---

[10] *Athanasius: The Life of Antony and The Letter to Marcellinus,* trans. Robert C. Gregg (New York: Paulist Press, 1980), p. 42.

normal. Neither Antony or Macrina received a classical education, yet both became notably wise; neither amassed great wealth, yet both were generous; neither pursued pleasure, prestige and power, yet both became renown for their influence. What makes this genre of literature accessible and applicable to us, therefore, is to view these figures as *outsiders* and *alternatives* to the status quo. During that period the church was beginning to become comfortable with the state, and religious leaders with the emperor. Athanasius and Gregory wrote biographies to expose contemporaries to the ideal Christian, the "spiritual athlete" who was as serious about spiritual training as an Olympian is about bodily training, and thus to a new model of religious authority, the holy man or woman, who wielded power and exercised influence by staying on the margins of society, just as Jesus did.

Antony was ruled by the Spirit, not by the flesh; his holiness of life and closeness to Christ gave him special powers. He healed the sick, discerned thoughts, cast out demons and taught with wisdom. Though unlettered, he became a mediator, adviser and judge. He had these powers not because he attained a lofty position in society or associated with the rich and powerful or achieved an advanced education or imposed his will on others, but because he was a holy man. Ironically, his feats in the desert accomplished what the best and brightest living in cities had failed to do. Macrina functioned similarly, as Gregory makes very clear. In fact, Gregory issues a warning to readers who were inclined to use their own pitifully low standards of spiritual discipline and achievement to define what a real disciple is. "For most people judge the credibility of what is told them by the yardstick of their own experience, and what goes beyond the power of the hearer, this they have no respect for, suspecting that it is false and outside the truth."[11]

2. *Sayings of the fathers.* A second genre of literature consists of the teachings of the abbas and ammas of the movement, which were collected and edited as the *Sayings of the Fathers* in the fifth century. These short, pithy and often esoteric teachings were at first entirely oral—and thus collected, taught, memorized, discussed and practiced in the communal

---

[11]*Gregory of Nyssa: The Life of Saint Macrina*, trans. Kevin Corrigan (Eugene, OR: Wipf & Stock, 2001), p. 54.

setting of the desert as a master trained apprentices. The *Sayings* functioned as a kind of practical commentary on and illustration of the Bible, the primary text of the movement. Over time the *Sayings* were passed on more systematically in two forms, either according to original source (the abba or amma who taught it) or according to theme (e.g., prayer, compunction, humility). Many of the individual sayings are actually found in both collections.[12] They were put to writing in the fifth century.

The theme of the soul's struggle dominates the literature. Once we grasp this dominant theme, the *Sayings* themselves start to make sense. Human nature is fallen and badly damaged, and the devil is prowling about, conniving to lead people away from God. A battle is being waged between God and the devil. This world is the battlefield; the salvation of humanity is the prize. Followers of Jesus should expect to face temptation and struggle for the rest of their earthly lives. "This is the great task of man," Abba Antony said to his disciples, "that he should hold his sin before the face of God, and count upon temptation until his last breath."[13] A young monk who had been living in the desert for eight years admitted discouragement to his spiritual mentor, Abba Theodore of Pferme, to which Theodore responded, "Believe me, I have been a monk for seventy years, and I have not been able to get a single day's peace. And so you want to have peace after eight years?"[14] One master put it succinctly, "We cannot make temptations vanish, but we can struggle against them."[15]

The literature makes it clear that struggle is both normal and necessary in the Christian life. A novice in the community confessed that he battled constantly against the temptation of lust. An old master asked

---

[12]*The Sayings of the Desert Fathers* have come to us in two forms: sayings arranged according to topic, as we find in Owen Chadwick's book, and sayings arranged according to the original source, namely, the abba to whom the saying is attributed. For examples of the former, see Owen Chadwick, ed., *Western Asceticism* (Philadelphia: Westminster Press, 1958); *The Desert Fathers: Sayings of the Early Christian Monks*, trans. Benedicta Ward (New York: Penguin, 2003); and Thomas Merton, ed., *The Wisdom of the Desert* (New York: New Directions, 1960). For examples of the latter, see *The Sayings of the Desert Fathers: The Alphabetical Collection*, trans. Benedicta Ward (Kalamazoo, MI: Cistercian Press, 1975); and Laura Swan, ed., *The Forgotten Desert Mothers* (New York: Paulist Press, 2001).

[13]Antony, cited in Anselm Greun, *Heaven Begins Within You: Wisdom from the Desert Fathers* (New York: Crossroad, 1999), p. 38.

[14]Chadwick, *Western Asceticism*, p. 83.

[15]Ibid., p. 64.

him, "Do you want me to ask the Lord to release you from your trouble," to which the young man replied, "Abba, I see that although it is a painful struggle, I am profiting from having to carry the burden." Then he added, "But ask God in your prayers, that he will give me long-suffering, to enable me to endure." The master was humbled by his apprentice's wisdom and courage. "Now I know that you are far advanced, my son, and beyond me."[16] Abba Poemen once told Abba John the Short that he had asked God to take away his passions. His prayer had been answered, and his heart had become tranquil. So he said to himself, "I find that I am at rest, with no war of flesh and spirit." But Abba John warned him, "Go, ask the Lord to stir a new war in you. Fighting is good for the soul."[17]

The desert fathers went to extreme measures to win this war. Their major weapon was the practice of the ascetic disciplines. They suppressed the desire for sleep, food and possessions, believing that without vigilance and strict discipline those earthly needs and desires would dominate them.[18] Abba Dioscorus made a resolution each year: "not to meet anyone for a year, or not to speak, or not to taste cooked food, or not to eat any fruit, or not to eat vegetables. This was his system in everything. He made himself master of one thing, and then started on another, and so on each year."[19] It was not unusual for the masters to pray nearly all night long. They fasted constantly, believing that fasting would help them subdue and control the appetites. "When the monk's body is dried up with fasting," said Abba Hyperichius, "it lifts his soul from the depths. Fasting dries up the channels down which worldly pleasures flow."[20] Finally, they pursued the life of poverty. Abba Evagrius told the story of a brother who had no possessions but a Gospel, which he sold to feed the poor, exclaiming, "I have even sold the word which commands me to sell all and give it to the poor."[21]

---

[16]Ibid., p. 65.
[17]Ibid., pp. 84-85.
[18]For the practice of asceticism in the desert fathers and mothers, see Peter Brown, *The Body and Society: Men, Women, and Sexual Renunciation in Early Christianity* (New York: Columbia University Press, 1988); Margaret R. Miles, *Fullness of Life: Historical Foundations for a New Asceticism* (Philadelphia: Westminster Press, 1981); and Elizabeth Clark, *Reading Renunciation: Asceticism and Scripture in Early Christianity* (Princeton: Princeton University Press, 1999).
[19]Chadwick, *Asceticism*, p. 50.
[20]Ibid., p. 56.
[21]Ibid., p. 78.

They did not, however, view ascetic discipline as an end, which adds a cautionary note to a literature that can otherwise seem excessive and extreme. Abba Joseph once asked Abba Poemen, "How should we fast?" Abba Poemen answered, "I would have everyone eat a little less than he wants, every day." Surprised by the answer, Abba Joseph reminded Poemen that he used to fast for days on end, to which Poemen replied, "The great elders have tested these things, and they found that it is good to eat something every day, but on some days a little less. And they have shown that this is the king's highway, for it is easy and light."[22] Masters of the movement even resorted to making fun of fanatical monks who simply tried too hard. Some of the old men were fond of saying, "If you see a young man climbing up to heaven by his own will, catch him by the foot and pull him down to earth: it is not good for him."[23]

Discipline was necessary, to be sure, but without the intervention of God's grace it was vain and useless; they needed help from outside themselves. The famous Abba Apollos once reassured a young man who was tormented by lust. "Not a single person could endure the enemy's clever attack, nor quench, nor control the leaping fire natural to the body, unless God's grace preserved us in our weakness. In all our prayers we should pray for his grace to save us, so that he may turn aside the scourge aimed even at you."[24]

Virtue was the ultimate goal. A young disciple once asked an abba which of two men was more acceptable to God—the man who fasted six days at a time or the man who cared for the sick. The old man replied, "If the brother, who fasts six days, even hung himself up by his nostrils, he could never be the equal of him who ministers to the sick."[25] Hospitality was considered of special value because it provided a concrete way of showing charity. Accused of breaking his fast during Lent, one old man said, "Fasting is ever with me. I cannot keep you here forever. Fasting is useful and necessary, but we can choose to fast or not fast. God's law demands from us perfect charity. In you I receive

[22]Ibid., p. 115.
[23]Ibid., p. 130.
[24]Ibid., pp. 60-62.
[25]Ibid., p. 185.

Christ: and so I must do all I can to show you the offices of charity."[26]

The theme of struggle illuminates what might seem contradictory and confusing in the *Sayings*—severity *and* moderation, discipline *and* grace, rejection of the world *and* influence in the world, the war against vice *and* the quest for virtue. As we saw in the case of Antony and Macrina, the desert fathers wanted to become spiritual athletes, and they submitted themselves to a rigorous training program to achieve that goal. Training by its very nature requires struggle, self-discipline, hard work. If looking for an easy way to reach Christian maturity, this literature will make little sense. But if there is willingness to embrace the same goal, then the *Sayings* will inspire and convict.

3. Monastic Rules. A third literature provides guidelines for monks living in community (cenobites). These became known as monastic *Rules*. As in the case of the *Sayings*, the original Rules were probably oral, produced over time and through trial and error by groups of ascetics living in urban communities. One man, however, is now credited with having written the first monastic Rule.[27] The son of pagans, Pachomius (d. 346) was conscripted into the Roman army and while stationed in Thebes met a group of Christians, whom he described as doing "all manner of good to everyone. . . . They treat us with love for the sake of the God of heaven." He was so impressed by their behavior that he purposed to convert to Christianity after his release from the army and to serve the poor and needy just as they did. When his tour of duty came to an end, he joined a Christian community and submitted to baptism. At first he was content to remain in a local church. But then he withdrew into the desert and practiced asceticism under the supervision of an abba. Eventually Pachomius was told in a vision to "serve mankind" and "to fashion the souls of men so as to present them pure to God." Curiously, Pachomius chose to obey this command by starting the first mon-

---

[26]Ibid., pp. 144-45.

[27]Philip Rousseau, *Pachomius: The Making of a Community in Fourth-Century Egypt* (Berkeley: University of California Press, 1985); C. H. Lawrence, *Medieval Monasticism: Forms of Religious Life in Western Europe in the Middle Ages* (New York: Longman, 2001); Marilyn Dunn, *The Emergence of Monasticism: From the Desert Fathers to the Early Middle Ages* (Oxford: Blackwell, 2000); Mayeul de Dreuille, *Seeking the Absolute Love: The Founders of Christian Monasticism* (New York: Crossroad, 1999).

astery. By the end of the fourth century the communities started under Pachomius's leadership numbered some seven thousand monks.[28] The purpose of these monasteries was not merely to establish a regimen of discipline but to nurture spiritual—and therefore interior—growth, and thus restore the image of God in sinful humans. "When you see a man who is pure and humble, that is a vision great enough. For what is greater than such a vision, to see the invisible God in a visible man, his temple?"[29]

Basil and Augustine. Prominent leaders also began to organize communities outside Egypt.[30] Two founders stand out, and they authored Rules that are still being followed today. Basil the Great (c. 330-379), bishop of Caesarea, grew up in a wealthy, Christian home in Cappadocia, Asia Minor.[31] He received his formal education in Antioch and Athens. He then embarked on a tour of monasteries in Egypt, where he was exposed to the desert fathers and to the mystical writings of Origen. Returning to Cappadocia, he was ordained as presbyter in 364 and bishop of Caesarea in 370. Over the next few years Basil laid the foundation for Eastern Orthodox monasticism, and his Shorter Rule and Longer Rule established guidelines for the monasteries he founded.[32] Basil reasoned that while the solitary life leads to self-discipline, "this is plainly in conflict with the law of love which the apostle fulfilled when he sought not his own advantage, but that of the many which might be saved."[33] He also believed that monasteries had a responsibility to serve the common good of society, arguing that "it is God's will that we should nourish the hungry, give the thirsty to drink, clothe the naked." Consequently, Basil started hostels, soup kitchens, hospitals and other ministries to the poor, and he used his pulpit to preach against exploitation, conspicuous consumption, profiteering and avarice.

Augustine (354-430), bishop of Hippo, played a similar role, only in the West. After his conversion Augustine returned to his native North

[28]Rousseau, *Pachomius*, pp. 75-76.
[29]Ibid., p. 146.
[30]Kathryn Smith Fladenmuller and Douglas J. McMillan, *Regular Life: Monastic, Canonical, and Mendicant Rules* (Kalamazoo, MI: Medieval Institute Publications, 1997).
[31]Hans Von Campenhausen, *The Fathers of the Greek Church* (New York: Pantheon, 1955); Anthony Meredith, *The Cappadocians* (Crestwood, NY: St. Vladimir's Seminary Press, 1995).
[32]McMillan and Fladenmuller, *Regular Life*.
[33]Dunn, *Emergence of Monasticism*, pp. 38-40.

Africa to start a monastic community of study and prayer. He was appointed bishop of Hippo only a few years later. But even as a bishop he organized a quasi-monastic community for pastors of the church. He also sketched a Rule for monasteries. In a letter to a community of women Augustine outlined principles that a community should follow if it hopes to be healthy. Like Basil, he believed that living with others is necessary for the cultivation of spiritual maturity, for life in community provides the best—in fact, the only—setting in which the most important of all virtues can be formed, and that is the virtue of love. Over time this Rule of St. Augustine, as it came to be called, was adapted to a variety of settings, and it became the standard for monks involved in parish ministry, which later became known as the Canons Regular.

Rome's decline and collapse created a vacuum that the monastic movement was poised to fill. In 410 a migrant people invaded Italy and marched toward Rome, eventually sacking the city. Over the next century the western half of the empire fell into ruins—cities declined in population, trade routes were cut off, the economy suffered and agricultural production fell. Thus began the period in the history of Western Europe known as the "Dark Ages." It would last for several hundred years, though not without significant periods of cultural renewal (Charlemagne's accomplishments come to mind here). The fall of Rome catapulted the West into a major crisis. "Suddenly the illusion of stability and solid security that political and economic prosperity had created shimmered and started to dissolve."[34] Monasteries emerged as a force for good in a world that teetered on the edge. Over the next several centuries literally hundreds of monasteries were founded and became the most stable feature of the European landscape.

The Rule of St. Benedict. The stage was finally set for Benedict of Nursia (c. 480-c. 550), the most influential monastic leader in the Western Church.[35] Benedict grew up on an estate in Italy, which was at the time occupied by Ostrogoths. Attending school in Rome, he recoiled

---

[34]Anthony C. Meisel and M. L. del Mastro, eds., *The Rule of St. Benedict* (New York: Doubleday, 1975), p. 14.

[35]"Gregory the Great: Life of Benedict," in *Early Christian Lives*, ed. Carolinne White (New York: Penguin, 1998), pp. 161-204.

from the worldly behavior he observed in his fellow students. He left Rome at the age of twenty to practice severe asceticism in a cave. Eventually a handful of young, zealous believers heard about his ascetic exploits and asked that he organize them into a monastic community. His first attempt failed because the monks under his charge resented his rigorous demands. So Benedict withdrew once more into solitude. Then another group of disciples approached him. Benedict tried again, this time moving to Monte Cassino, where his experiment thrived. Benedict wrote a Rule to lay down guidelines for the community. Now known as the Rule of St. Benedict, it is still used around the world today. The success of the document is due to the balance it strikes between severity and moderation, structure and flexibility, general principles and specific rules, and it uses Scripture throughout to support its guidelines. It has become one of the most influential documents in Western Civilization.[36]

What seems most striking to the modern reader is the severe, almost insufferable regimentation of the monastery, though in that day it was actually viewed as moderate. In his Rule Benedict seems to lay down a rule for everything (e.g., what, when and how much to eat, what to wear). Of course an awareness of the cultural setting helps explain the reasons for the Rule's rigidity and rigor, for the Western world, near chaos, needed order, which Benedictine monasteries provided. That the Rule was written for monks, and not for lay people, also helps in making sense of its severity. It was, after all, not written for people *like us*.

Still, the idea of a Rule—that is, a set of principles by which communities of people try to live—could and does apply to a much broader range of situations. It is not, in fact, altogether unfamiliar to us. Athletic teams follow a "Rule" of sorts, as do families and businesses and schools, for teams, homes and organizations need order, discipline and, well, rules to function properly and productively. I teach a January term course on Christian spirituality at a camp in the Cascade Mountain Range, where students live in community for three weeks. In that iso-

---

[36]Esther De Waal, *Seeking God: The Way of St. Benedict* (Collegeville, MN: Liturgical Press, 2001); Columba Stewart, *Prayer and Community: The Benedictine Tradition* (Maryknoll, NY: Orbis, 1998); Peter-Damian Belisle, *The Language of Silence: The Changing Face of Monastic Solitude* (Maryknoll, NY: Orbis, 2003).

lated setting (students must fast from the use of all media) I introduce students to a modified version of the Rule of St. Benedict. Toward the end of the three weeks I assign them the task of writing their own "Rule of life" (*Regula Vitae*). The setting is different, to be sure, but the principle behind it remains the same.

The genius of Benedict's Rule consists of the rhythm it established. Benedict required monasteries to weave together a way of life that included, broadly speaking, both prayer and work (*ora et labora*). Monks were called to surrender their lives to God, which in Benedict's mind implied that they could own nothing. "The vice of private ownership must be uprooted from the monastery. No one, without the abbot's permission, shall dare give, receive or keep *anything*—not book, tablet or pen—nothing at all."[37] The Rule required monks to perform common labor, including kitchen duty. They developed specialties too, like copying manuscripts or making wine. Further, the Rule encouraged growth in virtue, which was considered another kind of work. Benedict considered three virtues in particular as sine qua non for the spiritual life of the monastery. The work of *silence* forced monks to discipline the most dangerous weapon the monks had—the tongue. Gossip, foul talk, judgment and even idle chatter were strictly forbidden. The work of *obedience* helped monks to become subservient to Christ, to Scripture, to the Rule and to the abbot, in that order. The work of *humility* made them lowly in spirit, broke their pride and set them on a course toward heaven.[38] This commitment to work permeated the life of the monastery.

The Rule obviously mandated that monks pray too. The primary vehicle for prayer was the observance of the Divine Office, which consisted of eight short worship services a day, each of which had an individual name (Matins was the first, which began at 2 a.m., followed by Lauds at dawn, then Prime, Terce, Sext, and None, Vespers at sundown, and finally Compline, which ended the day).[39] Every day the monks gathered in the *oratory* (chapel), where they would chant psalms, listen

---

[37]Ibid., pp. 76-77.
[38]Ibid., pp. 54-61.
[39]Paul F. Bradshaw, *Daily Prayer in the Early Church: A Study of the Origin and Early Development of the Divine Office* (New York: Oxford University Press, 1982).

to readings from Scripture, sit in silence and pray. The Divine Office focused their attention on God.

Study united the two tasks of the monastery—prayer and work— into a seamless whole, for monks did the hard work of study in a spirit of prayer. They learned to read and write in the monastery if they were illiterate when they first joined. They read John Cassian's *Conferences*, the *Lives of the Saints* and patristic theology. Above all, they studied Scripture. The primary method of study was *lectio divina*, which involved a reflective, repetitive and meditative reading of texts, especially the biblical text.[40]

That rhythm of life makes the Rule applicable to our setting, however foreign the Rule itself might appear to be. The rhythm of prayer and work choreographed each Benedictine day. The day was ordered and busy, but never hurried and frantic. Prayer protected them from turning their work into an idol, and work kept their prayers from becoming an empty exercise. They worshiped God, and they served the common good of the community. They studied sacred texts in a meditative, leisurely way, aiming for the transformation of their lives, and they performed manual labor to provide for their needs. Peter Levi, a former professor of poetry, expressed his appreciation of such rhythm after spending time in a Benedictine monastery. "If one spends a week or a month [in a monastery], a different scale and pattern of time imposes itself, which at first one resists as if one were in prison. When this new time-scale is accepted, it soaks into one's bones and penetrates one's mind."[41]

4. Ascetic theology. A fourth genre includes works that are more strictly theological. Informed by the Bible, classical sources and the wisdom of the desert, the writers of this literature presented a more systematic summary of the teachings of the desert and applied its wisdom to the larger church, as if introducing the desert to the city. Origen played such a role early on in the movement,[42] as did Evagrius Ponticus,

---

[40]Jean Leclercq, *The Love of Learning and the Desire for God: A Study of Monastic Culture* (New York: Fordham University Press, 1982), p. 18.

[41]Peter Levi, *The Frontiers of Paradise: A Study of Monks and Monasteries* (New York: Weidenfeld & Nicolson, 1987), pp. 19-20.

[42]Origen, "An Exortation to Martyrdom" and "On Prayer," in *Origen*, trans. Rowan A Greer (New York: Paulist Press, 1979), pp. 41-170.

Origin's disciple, who as an ascetic in Egypt wrote a number of works on such topics as prayer and the "Eight Deadly Thoughts."[43] The Cappadocian Fathers—brothers Basil of Caesarea and Gregory of Nyssa, along with their best friend Gregory Nazianzen—functioned similarly in Asia Minor, thus shaping the theological tradition of Eastern Orthodoxy.[44] Ascetic theology even found its way into the pulpit. The sermons of church leaders like John Chrysostom, who spent six years as a cenobite and anchorite before being drafted into ecclesiastical office, applied the principles of the movement to the life of the laity who would not or could not leave the city for the desert.[45]

John Cassian (c. 360-435), however, became the primary theological interpreter of the desert to the Western church. He is still read today as part of the standard curriculum in Benedictine monasteries around the world. As I have already mentioned, Cassian traveled to Egypt with his friend, Germanus, where he studied under many of the early masters of the movement, including Evagrius Ponticus. He fled for his life in 399 when his Origenist sympathies fell out of favor with Theophilus, the bishop of Alexandria. He made his way to Constantinople with other desert refugees, where he met John Chrysostom and was ordained to church office. He eventually landed in Gaul and helped to found two monasteries. A local bishop asked him to interpret the teachings of the desert for the West.[46] Cassian wrote two books on the subject. The latter

---

[43]John Bamberger, ed., *Evagrius Ponticus: The Praktikos and Chapters on Prayer* (Spencer, MA: Cistercian Publications, 1970).

[44]*Basil of Caesarea: On the Holy Spirit*, trans. D. Anderson (Crestwood, NY: St. Vladimir's Seminary Press, 1980); *Gregory of Nyssa: Ascetical Works*, trans. V. Woods Callahan, Fathers of the Church 58 (Washington, DC: Catholic University of America Press, 1967); and *Life of Moses*, trans. E. Ferguson (New York: Paulist Press, 1978); F. W. Norris, ed., *Faith Gives Fullness to Reasoning: The Five Theological Orations of Gregory Nazianzen*, trans. L. Wickham and F. Williams (New York: Brill, 1991).

[45]*Palladius: Dialogue on the Life of St. John Chrysostom*, trans. Robert T. Meyer (New York: Newman Press, 1985); See J. N. D. Kelly, *Golden Mouth: The Story of John Chrysostom—Ascetic, Preacher, Bishop* (Ithaca, NY: Cornell University Press, 1995); R. A. Krupp, *Shepherding the Flock of God: The Pastoral Theology of John Chrysostom* (New York: Peter Lang, 1991). For examples of his sermons, see *On Wealth and Poverty* (Crestwood, NY: St. Vladimir's Seminary Press, 1988); *On Marriage and Family Life* (Crestwood, NY: St. Vladimir's Seminary Press, 1986); *On Living Simply* (Liguori, MO: Liguori Publications, 1996).

[46]Columba Stewart, *Cassian the Monk* (New York: Oxford University Press, 1998); and Philip Rousseau, *Ascetics, Authority, and the Church in the Age of Jerome and Cassian* (Notre Dame, IN: University of Notre Dame Press, 2010).

and longer, *The Conferences*, presents the wisdom of the desert fathers in the form of a series of interviews with Egyptian masters, covering such topics as discernment, chastity and prayer. Unlike the esoteric and pithy teachings that came out of Egypt, *Conferences* outlines a logical and nuanced system of desert theology, adapting it to the needs and circumstances of monasteries in the Western Empire.[47]

The earlier and shorter work *The Institutes* explains the dress, daily life, disciplines and organization of the monks of Egypt, underscoring their superior—that is, highly rigorous and disciplined—way of life, and then explores the "Eight Deadly Thoughts" first developed by Evagrius. Cassian turned the terse teaching of Evagrius into a profound and insightful exploration of the landscape of the soul, showing how human beings fall into temptation and what they can do to resist it.[48]

Cassian's emphasis on the interiority of the spiritual life opens his works to modern readers, for his writings provide a kind of map of the soul's terrain that shows how to travel safely and securely in a place where divine light shines but darkness seems to lurk around every corner. His view of human nature in particular—its fallenness and fragility, its inclination to vice and its capacity for virtue—makes his writing seem surprisingly relevant, especially if we overlook the monastic idiosyncrasies that run through it. He provides diagnostic tools that invite the reader to look inward to examine the state of the soul and that help the reader to grasp what makes us vulnerable to sin and what gives us a capacity for holiness.

Cassian outlines eight points of vulnerability to sinfulness, which always begin in the mind and imagination (Evagrius called it *logismoi*). In other words, long before we commit any actual sin we think or fantasize about it. His list of eight deadly thoughts includes lust (fornication), gluttony, avarice, anger, sadness (self-pity), *acedia* (listlessness, boredom, impatience with routine), vainglory and pride, the deadliest of all. To combat these deadly thoughts, Cassian prescribed one or more disciplines to practice (fasting to combat lust, for example) and a virtue that should take its place.

47Cassian, *Conferences*.
48*John Cassian: The Institutes*, trans. Boniface Ramsey (New York: Newman Press, 2000).

His comments on anger seem especially relevant, considering how defensive and angry people in our culture get at even the slightest provocation. Cassian allows for no excuses, no matter how severe and unfair the provocation. He thus challenges the assumption, which must have been as widespread in his day as it is in ours, that anger is an understandable, legitimate and excusable response to the wrongdoing of others. Cassian believed that the provocation to anger, which comes from outside the self (in other words, from external circumstances) always leads to some kind of reaction. One is anger; if indulged, it leads to vice. The other is patience; if cultivated, it leads to virtue. The formation of virtue is no more dependent on favorable circumstances than anger is justified by bad circumstances, for virtue is formed in the face of adversity, the very thing that gives rise to anger.

> The sum total of our improvement and tranquility, then, must not be made to depend on someone else's willing, which will never be subject to our sway; it comes, rather, under our own power. And so our not getting angry must derive not from someone else's perfection but from our own virtue, which is achieved not by another person's patience but by our forbearance.[49]

POSSIBLE USE FOR THE CHURCH TODAY

Cassian's writing is a good place to end, and for a personal reason too. I lead a pastors reading group. We decided at our first meeting some five years ago to limit our reading to Christian classics, mostly from the early Christian period, assuming that we were least likely to read those works on our own. We are currently reading Cassian's *Institutes*. Though written some sixteen hundred years ago for a group of monks, it reads as if it were written for us. One pastor told me just yesterday, "This man is dissecting my soul. I feel laid open and exposed." Cassian's intricate map of the soul shows why we yield to sin so quickly and easily, and what we can do about it. He has been challenging us—this small group of pastors (and me, a university professor)—to live as disciples. His

---

[49]Ibid., p. 201.

writing is ancient, yet it still speaks, which is true of much of the writing that comes from this period and movement.

However peculiar, this literature is useful in at least four ways. First, it emphasizes the value of the stories of heroic figures. The Bible, after all, tells the stories of many saints. What would we do without the exploits of Joseph and Ruth, of Job and Esther and David? These stories provide perspective, build faith and inspire imitation. So do the stories of holy heroes who have lived over the past two thousand years. Their circumstances were different from ours, of course, but they still trusted, loved and obeyed the same God Christians know today. That they are different might actually work to our advantage, exposing blind spots in us that need correction (materialism, self-indulgence and laziness, for example).

Second, their method of training was mentoral, relational, oral and experiential, with a master training spiritual apprentices. The desert fathers thus kept alive the ancient catechumenate, that program of training that the church developed and used to prepare people for baptism. There is, of course, a doctrinal dimension to Christianity. Christians cannot believe in something unless they know what it is, as the church fathers made abundantly clear. But discipleship requires more than knowledge. One cannot become a disciple merely by reading a book or sitting in a classroom. It requires training. It is no surprise that the favorite metaphor of the desert fathers was the "spiritual athlete." They knew that athletes do not achieve greatness through study alone, however necessary; they need a coach, a regimen of training, an opportunity to develop skills, a target of measurable goals to reach. If this movement teaches us anything, it is that the church today needs to rediscover the importance—no, the necessity—of spiritual apprenticeship and training.

Third, the literature underscores the importance of the desert, which they defined as that place "outside" the status quo, outside security and power. They viewed the desert as a place of suffering and combat, and they considered struggle a normal and necessary part of the Christian faith. Rather than try to avoid or mitigate it, they confronted it directly and turned it into an opportunity for Christian growth. They refused to assume that happiness and contentment result from favorable circumstances. They aimed for internal transformation—intimacy with God and a life of virtue. Very few of us, of course, will ever withdraw into a literal desert, nor do we have to. The real desert of the Christian faith is the "narrow way" of discipleship, which we have an opportunity to choose every day.

Finally, they learned to live in a tension, as all of us must, between human responsibility and divine initiative. Paul urges us to work out our own salvation with fear and trembling, but then assures us that God is at work in us both to will and work for his good pleasure. Again, he tells us to make maturity *our* own because Christ Jesus has made us *his* own. The desert fathers and mothers practiced spiritual discipline with an unrelenting ferocity. But they recognized the need for grace too. The final word goes to Cassian.

> Who would be sufficient without God's grace to give continual attendance to reading and constant earnestness in work, receiving no advantage of present gain? And all these matters, as we cannot desire them continuously without divine inspiration, so in no respect whatever can we perform them without His help. . . . There is no carrying out of our purpose, unless the power to perform it has been granted by the mercy of the Lord.[50]

OTHER IMPORTANT TEXTS FROM THE DESERT FATHERS

Origen (c. 185-c. 254) played a key theological role in laying a foundation for ascetic theology. His two treatises "Exhortation to Martyrdom" and "On Prayer" were often quoted in the later ascetic literature of the desert.

John Chrysostom (c. 347-407) spent some six years in isolation before being drafted into church office. His sermons reflect his ascetic commitment, as his collections *On Wealth and Poverty* and *On Marriage and Family* illustrate.

John Moschos (c. 550-619) compiled *The Spiritual Meadow*, the last great collection of stories of the desert before the Persians and then the Muslims overran the Eastern Mediterranean.

---

[50]Cassian, *Conferences*, pp. 321-22.

John Cassian's *The Conferences*, a long and illuminating work, includes the wisdom of a dozen of the great Egyptian masters of the movement. Cassian adapted their theology to the Western church.

Evagrius Ponticus (346-399) wrote *Praktikos* and *Chapters on Prayer*. He became the great psychologist and mystic of the desert, and he exercises enormous influence over many who followed, including John Cassian.

SUGGESTED READING

Harmless, William. *Desert Christians: An Introduction to the Literature of Early Monasticism*. Oxford: Oxford University Press, 2004.

Rousseau, Philip. *Ascetics, Authority, and the Church in the Age of Jerome and Cassian*. New York: Oxford University Press, 1978.

Chitty, Derwas J. *The Desert a City: An Introduction to the Study of Egyptian and Palestinian Monasticism Under the Christian Empire*. Crestwood, NY: St. Vladimir's Seminary Press, 1999.

12

The Medieval Traditions

Greg Peters

THE MIDDLE AGES OR MEDIEVAL ERA is perhaps the most neglected historical time period by evangelicals. Though the early, patristic
era has received renewed attention by evangelical scholars in the past
fifteen years or so, the Middle Ages continue to remain neglected and
relegated to the status of a second-class citizen.[1] Yet the Middle Ages
comprise the longest time frame of the historical divisions of Christian
history—longer than the early/patristic, Reformation and modern periods. In fact, the Middle Ages lasted for about a millennium, depending
on how one chooses to date the time period. Within Byzantine studies,
it is generally understood that the Middle Ages began with the Council
of Nicaea in 325 and lasted until the fall of the city of Constantinople to
the Ottoman Turks in 1453.[2] Scholars of the Western European Middle
Ages most frequently date the beginning of the era to 604, with the
death of pope Gregory the Great, and place its terminus at 1517, when
Martin Luther posted his "Ninety-Five Theses" to the door of the Castle
Church in Wittenberg, Germany. In either case the Middle Ages lasted

---

[1]See, for example, D. H. Williams, *Retrieving the Tradition and Renewing Evangelicalism: A Primer
for Suspicious Protestants* (Grand Rapids: Eerdmans, 1999); and Bryan M. Litfin, *Getting to Know
the Church Fathers: An Evangelical Introduction* (Grand Rapids: Brazos, 2007).

[2]"Byzantine" is the name given to Christian history in the eastern portion of the Roman empire,
with the dividing line between the Western, Latin church and the Eastern, Greek church being
roughly equivalent to the Danube River. The word *Byzantine* comes from the city of Byzantion,
later renamed Constantinople.

for approximately one thousand years, accounting for about one half of Christian history thus far. This chapter will focus on the Western, Latin Middle Ages.

HISTORICAL CIRCUMSTANCES

Given its length, the medieval period experienced many dramatic cultural shifts and major historical events, only a few of which can be included here. First is the mass conversion of most European peoples to the Christian faith.[3] In 312 the Roman emperor Constantine defeated his co-emperor of the Roman Empire, Maxentius. At his final battle in this crusade, at the Milvian Bridge near Rome, Constantine had a vision that he would conquer his foe, which he interpreted as a sign from the Christian God. After his victory, and in gratitude to God, Constantine legalized the practice of Christianity and began a process of Christianizing all of his lands. This legalization of Christianity led to widespread evangelization and Christian missionary activity, especially that conducted by monks. Yet what is significant in most medieval conversion narratives is that whole people groups followed their ruler. For example, ancient Rus' (modern Ukraine and Russia) was converted to the Christian faith *en masse* when their ruler, grand prince of Kiev Vladimir I, converted in 988, forcing his subjects to either follow him or die. Though many of these conversions may have been superficial and orthodox Christianity continued to struggle for a secure foothold in Europe, it is striking that by the end of the first millennium *anno Domini* that Europe was Christian in faith and practice.

A second major historical event during the Middle Ages is the rise in the power and prominence of the papacy and the centralization of the church into all areas of medieval society. Though this began as early as the papacy of Gregory I from 590-604, it reached its zenith with Pope Boniface VIII's promulgation of the bull *Unam Sanctam* in 1302.[4] In this bull Boniface decrees that "it is altogether necessary to salvation for

[3]Richard Fletcher, *The Barbarian Conversion: From Paganism to Christianity* (New York: Henry Holt, 1997).
[4]A "bull" is a charter issued by the pope whose contents must be followed by all the faithful.

every human creature to be subject to the Roman Pontiff."[5] Though this belief would not go unchallenged, it was a sign in fourteenth-century Europe of the struggle between the Holy Roman Emperor and the papacy.[6] Martin Luther's consistent attention to political theology and to the need for godly rulers is, at least in part, a reaction to such papal claims. What such papal pronouncements demonstrate, however, is that during the course of the Middle Ages the organized church grew quite strong and exercised enormous power; so much so that whole countries were at times placed under interdicts, being forbidden by the pope to receive the sacraments, which were seen as salvific.[7]

Third, the Middle Ages were a time of vast learning and saw the creation of the first universities in Western Europe. For years, if not centuries, the medieval era was wrongly known as the "Dark Ages."[8] This unfortunate label came to be used of the Middle Ages because some thought of the period as one of ignorance, superstition, narrow-mindedness and cultural backwardness. The Middle Ages were a period of darkness when compared to other historical eras, especially that of the Renaissance. Yet scholars have now shown that there was no such thing as the Dark Ages. In fact, the Middle Ages were a period of learning, ongoing intellectual discovery and cultural enrichment. During the eleventh century a group of scholars teaching at various cathedral schools around Paris formed the basis of what would become the University of Paris, receiving its official papal statutes in 1215. At about the same time the University of Oxford came into existence and, like its Parisian sister, focused on the teaching of theology. Other early and important universities of medieval Europe were Bologna (canon and civil law), Montpellier (medicine) and Cambridge (theology). Important inventions to come out of the Middle Ages are eyeglasses, the mechanical

---

[5]Brian Tierney, *Sources of Medieval History*, vol. 1, *The Middle Ages*, 4th ed. (New York, 1983), p. 316.

[6]The movement against such papal aggrandizement is known as Conciliarism, where the greatest theological power is invested in the church meeting together in a council.

[7]For example, Pope Innocent III placed all of England under interdict between 1208-1213 over a disagreement between the pope and King John regarding who should be appointed as Archbishop of Canterbury.

[8]This term was first used by Caesar Baronius, a Roman Catholic cardinal, in his *Annales Ecclesiastici* of 1602.

clock, the heavy plough and, most importantly, the printing press. The Middle Ages were also a time of great cultural and artistic activity. One only needs to think of such famous illuminated manuscripts as the Lindisfarne Gospels and the *Les Très Riches Heures* of Duke de Berry and such monumental paintings as the *Life of St. Francis* cycle by Giotto in the Upper Church in Assisi to appreciate the visual arts produced during the Middle Ages. Architecturally the medieval period saw the rise and perfecting of the Gothic style, with its associated window tracery. Further, the movement known as the Renaissance was, at least in part, a medieval phenomena, with its recovery of classical literature and art and focus on textual studies.

Last, the Middle Ages were a time of drought, famine, plague and warfare. From the middle of the tenth to the middle of the fourteenth centuries there was approximately one major period of drought every one hundred years. Overall, however, these centuries were a period of warmer temperatures leading to high crop yields. From 1315-1317, though, there was the so-called Great Famine, when millions of people died of starvation as crime and disease increased. Conditions were so bad that it led one contemporary historian to report that "men and women in many places secretly ate their own children." Adding to this was the major outbreaks of bubonic plague in the fourteenth century with perhaps as many as 25 million dying between 1347 and 1352. In addition to drought, famine and plague there was also constant warfare of some kind on the European continent throughout the Middle Ages. The ostensible Barbarian invasions characterized much of the early Middle Ages, only to be replaced with ongoing warfare between the Holy Roman Empire and contenders to the throne. In 1095, pope Urban II called for the first crusade to recover Jerusalem from the Muslims. By the time of the Fourth Crusade in 1204, the Western, papal troops were content to sack the Eastern, Greek Christian city of Constantinople, driving the final nail into the coffin of the Great Schism of 1054. Other notable wars include the English dynastic struggles between the Houses of Lancaster and York that lasted throughout the fifteenth century and known as the War of the Roses, and the long-lasting Hundred Years' War between the English and French from 1337 to 1453.

THEOLOGICAL CONTEXT AND ASSUMPTIONS

Despite its geographical breadth and chronological length, the medieval era was characterized by a fairly consistent set of theological presuppositions. First, the basis of the faith was to be found in the Nicene and Apostolic Creeds. Deviation from either was heresy as was a rejection of the papacy or papal pronouncements. Second, the bishop of Rome (i.e., the pope) was God's appointed head of the church and all power to forgive sins was granted to him by way of the keys of Peter (cf. Mt 16:18-19). Only bishops and priests in communion with the pope were God's true representatives on earth.[9] Third, salvation came by way of the sacraments, especially those of baptism and Eucharist. All parents were expected to have their children baptized, and everyone was expected to attend the Eucharist, having prepared for it appropriately by making confession to their local priest. By 1215, however, the church hierarchy was insisting that everyone needed to go to confession and Eucharist at least once a year.[10] Not only had frequent Communion become rare by the thirteenth century but taking Communion in one kind (the bread only) was commonplace in the high and late Middle Ages. Fourth, it was frequently believed by medieval theologians that society was divided into three discreet orders: worker, fighters and pray-ers.[11] This division was hierarchical, in that those who prayed were thought to be in a superior order to those who worked. This led to the belief that priests, monastics and other church vocations were better than all other possible callings, including marriage and parenthood. This, of course, resulted in a bifurcation in society, resulting in various forms of elitism and a perspective that the church was in control of one's eternal salvation or damnation.

Another important theological assumption and perhaps one of the most important was the medieval era's conception that even among those who prayed, those engaged in the contemplative life were engaging in a far better endeavor than those pursuing the active life.[12] This

---

[9] Walter Ullmann, *A Short History of the Papacy in the Middle Ages* (London: Routledge, 2003).

[10] *Concilii quarti Lateranensis Constitutiones* 21, in Tierney, *Sources of Medieval History*, 1:244-45.

[11] See Greg Peters, "Monastic Orders," in *Encyclopedia of Christian Civilization*, ed. G. T. Kurian (Malden, MA: Wiley-Blackwell, 2011).

[12] M. Elizabeth Mason, *Active Life and Contemplative Life: A Study of the Concepts from Plato to the Present* (Milwaukee: Marquette University Press, 1961).

thinking, which certainly was the majority opinion until at least the thirteenth century, with the arrival of the active, mendicant orders, says that of those who are intently seeking union with God, those more removed from the world will see him sooner than those involved in the active life. In short, the contemplative life was the life of the monk, free of unnecessary distractions and wholly devoted to God. On the other hand, the active life involved frequent contact with others and with the "world" and was the life of priests and bishops. This dualistic thinking had a great impact on the spiritual treatises of the Middle Ages.

The final theological distinction to mention is the role accorded to reason vis-à-vis theological methodology by high and late medieval theologians. Though not without its weaknesses, it is possible to see two primary methods of theological methodology in the Middle Ages: monastic and scholastic.[13] Monastic theology tended focus on the words of the biblical texts and those of the early Christian writers, whereas scholastic theology was more concerned with being logical and achieving clarity, thereby giving a greater role to ancient philosophers, particularly Aristotle. Monastic theology tended to have a great tolerance for and respect of mystery in the theological project, while scholastic theologians strove for comprehensiveness. Last, monastic theology had a great respect for tradition. Scholastic theologians respected the tradition as well but sought to make theological progress and add to the body of theological knowledge. Though reason was employed in both methodologies, it took a leading role in the work of scholastic theologians, such as Thomas Aquinas.[14] It is important to state, nevertheless, that despite this reliance on reason these medieval theologians never forsook tradition or the Scriptures. Quite the opposite. For example, despite his heavy reliance on reason and Aristotelian philosophy, Thomas Aquinas insisted until his last day that he was a *magister de sacra pagina*, a master of the sacred pages of the Bible. Yet what was certain by the end of the Middle Ages was that reason had a role to play in theology, alongside the Bible, experience and tradition.

---

[13]Jean Leclercq, *The Love of Learning and the Desire for God*, trans. Catharine Misrahi (New York: Fordham University Press, 1982), pp. 191-235.

[14]A good introduction to Thomas Aquinas is Rik van Nieuwenhove and Joseph Wawrykow, eds., *The Theology of Thomas Aquinas* (Notre Dame, IN: University of Notre Dame Press, 2005).

HERMENEUTICAL FRAMEWORK

Like all eras of Christian history, the spiritual literature of the Middle Ages encompasses a range of genres, such as biblical commentaries, letters, treatises, records of visionary accounts and lives of the saints. Perhaps two to the greatest challenges to reading medieval literature concern biblical commentaries and saint's lives. By and large medieval biblical commentators adopted the fourfold method of biblical interpretation inherited from the early Christian church. In this methodology the commentator strives to offer four interpretations of the text: the literal/historical, allegorical, tropological/moral and anagogical. According to the Venerable Bede (d. 735), "the table of the tabernacle has four feet because the words of the celestial oracle are customarily taken in either a historical, or an allegorical, or a tropological (that is, moral), or even an anagogical sense."[15] He goes on to say that the historical is concerned with those things that have been done or said according to the letter. For example, the Israelites built a real tabernacle in the desert. The allegorical is concerned with the presence of Christ and the church's sacraments by way of "mystical" words or things. Thus, the shoot from the root of Jesse of Isaiah 11:1 is a reference to Christ whereas the blood of the lamb in Exodus 12 refers to Christ's freeing of the church from the devil at his crucifixion. The tropological interpretation is concerned with the manner of one's morals and the correction of life; therefore, says Bede, Solomon's reference to white garments in Ecclesiastes 9:8 means that one's works need to be pure. Last, the anagogical is "that which discusses, in words either mystical or plain, future rewards and what the future life in heaven consists of."[16] This methodology was so commonplace by the high Middle Ages that Nicholas of Lyra (d. 1340) could put it into poetic form:

> The letter teaches facts,
> Allegory what you should believe,
> The moral teaches what you should do,
> Anagogy what mark you should be aiming for.[17]

---

[15]Bede, cited in *Bede: On the Tabernacle*, trans. Arthur G. Holder (Liverpool: Liverpool University Press, 1994), p. 25.

[16]Ibid., p. 26.

[17]From Nicholas's *Postilla* on the Letter to the Galatians. Henri de Lubac says that this is first

The other medieval genre that is challenging to read well is saint's lives, which are usually written in an overt hagiographical manner.[18] The word *hagiography* is derived from the Greek words *hagios* (holy) and *graphē* (writing) and refers to the body of Christian literature that concerns the saints. Though the concept of sainthood goes back to the New Testament, where, for example, the apostle Paul calls all Christians "saints" (e.g., Eph 1:1), a full theology and practice of sainthood and sanctity did not develop until the early Christian era. By the medieval period "saints" were those who entered the kingdom of heaven immediately upon death. They were in no need of purgation due to their holiness, therefore they were able to enter directly into God's presence and enjoy beatitude. In the thirteenth century the papacy took control of determining who could be considered a saint, in a process called canonization. Hagiography played a fundamental role in this process because the composition and use of a hagiographical life showed that its subject received ecclesial recognition. These hagiographical lives were not meant to only honor the saint but were also written to provide a model or norm for all Christians to emulate. Thus, the saints became exemplars of the Christian life and the hagiographer intended his or her text to serve as an example to others. So, when one reads a hagiographical saint's life one must remember that the author was not intending to write a modern-style biography but was offering a model for others to copy. This often led to reports of extraordinary feats and images of the saint behaving like a biblical personage or another saint. The works are filled with types (*topoi*) that harken to other saints, including Jesus: monastic founders often begin with twelve disciples, and saints often walk on water or bring others back from the dead and can endure extreme ascetical punishments, for example. When reading a hagiographical text, therefore, one must be careful to keep in mind the extraordinary nature of the text, being aware at all times the original author's intention.

---

found in Augustine of Dacia's *Rotulus pugillaris* around 1260. See Henri de Lubac, *Medieval Exegesis*, vol. 1, *The Four Senses of Scripture*, trans. Mark Sebanc (Grand Rapids: Eerdmans, 1998), pp. 1-2.

[18]See Thomas Head, ed., *Medieval Hagiography: An Anthology* (New York: Routledge, 1999).

POSSIBLE USE FOR THE CHURCH TODAY

As mentioned above, two assumptions of the medieval era are its understanding of the active versus the contemplative life and its distinction between the theological methods of monastic and scholastic theology. Both of these assumptions have something to teach the church today. Since the Reformation of the sixteenth century there has been an intense focus, especially among Calvinistic-Reformed authors, on the concept of vocation. Vocation, however, is often understood in Protestantism as an active way of life (pastor/missionary/evangelist), but this was not always so in the Scriptures.[19] The contemplative aspect of religious vocation was an understood reality in the biblical era, in both the Old and New Testaments. Though the theologians of the Middle Ages created a false dichotomy between the active and contemplative life, placing them in opposition to one another, it is important that the Christian life, especially for those in vocational Christian ministry, be made up of both active and contemplative elements. For example, many pastors today view themselves as the CEO of a corporation. Their ministry often involves more management, human resourcing and budget analysis than it does pastoral care, biblical meditation and ongoing theological formation. In short, they are by far more active than contemplative. Since these two aspects of Christian formation are ultimately not in tension with one another, it is imperative that Christians embrace the active-contemplative life that Jesus Christ modeled for the church, balancing times of active ministry with focused attention on God. Action and contemplation are not in conflict; they are complementary. The Middle Ages help us today to see the riches of intentional and sustained contemplation, modeled in the life and writings of such medieval illuminati as Bernard of Clairvaux or Richard of St. Victor, discussed below.

Another negative tendency in the Protestant church is to rely too much on Enlightenment views of epistemology and metaphysics, resulting in our own versions of medieval scholasticism. Medieval monastic theology, on the other hand, provides a model of a different way, a way that is based more on the texts and history of the Christian tradition as well as a fidelity

---

[19]See Douglas J. Schuurman, *Vocation: Discerning Our Callings in Life* (Grand Rapids: Eerdmans, 2004).

to the biblical text, not only in its teachings but also in its language. Within Protestant academia there has already been a move toward a more monastically influenced theology. This is seen in the recovery of a so-called theological interpretation of Scripture,[20] where there's more of an emphasis on the theological import of biblical texts and not only on their meaning in light of the historical and cultural context in which they originated. There is also a renewed interested in meditation, a practice that has its roots in the early and medieval church's approach to Scripture reading and exegesis, usually called *lectio divina*.[21] It was medieval monks and nuns who sat for hours, reading, meditating and ruminating on the biblical texts before offering their interpretations, which were most often concerned more with spiritual growth than they were with proving points of dogma. Medieval scholastic theologians were concerned with the relationship between the ideas of the apostle Paul and Aristotle, whereas medieval monastics were more concerned with the relationship between the Scriptures and the Spirit. Medieval monastic texts and authors should be studied today for their countercultural approach to doing theology. Reason should not be rejected, but it should be moderated by the Christian tradition, and monastics like Bonaventure and Hildegaard of Bingen (discussed below) can show us the way.

IMPORTANT MEDIEVAL AUTHORS AND GENRES

It is impossible in an essay of this length to mention, let alone discuss, all of the classics that originated in the Middle Ages. In order to illustrate, therefore, the breadth and diversity of medieval spiritual texts, I have selected a number of the best known authors, using selected works that also illustrate the genres of medieval literature. I will conclude with a list of other significant texts and authors.

Anselm of Canterbury (c. 1033-1109). Anselm was a Benedictine monk and Archbishop of Canterbury from 1093 until his death.[22] For much of

---

[20]For example, see J. Todd Billings, *The Word of God for the People of God: An Entryway to the Theological Interpretation of Scripture* (Grand Rapids: Eerdmans, 2010).

[21]See John Jefferson Davis, *Meditation and Communion with God: Contemplating Scripture in an Age of Distraction* (Downers Grove, IL: InterVarsity Press, 2012).

[22]Good introductions to his thought include G. R. Evans, *Anselm* (London: Continuum, 2002); and R. W. Southern, *Saint Anselm and His Biographer: A Study of Monastic Life and Thought,*

his early life and education Anselm was taught by a relative, but he left home in 1056 and became a monk four years later. As a monk at the Benedictine monastery of Bec (in modern-day Normandy, France), Anselm was greatly influenced by the Rule of Benedict and Augustine of Hippo (d. 430), not to mention his monastic teacher Lanfranc (d. 1089). His most well-known theological works are the *Cur Deus Homo* (*Why the God-Man*) and *Proslogion* (or *Fides Quaerens Intellectum, Faith Seeking Understanding*), though Anselm was the author of many other theological and philosophical works.[23] His greatest spiritual work, however, is a series of prayers and meditations.[24] All but one of these prayers and meditations were written while Anselm was a monk or abbot of the monastery of Bec. They were composed at the request of his fellow monks and were innovative at the time because they were longer than normal written prayers and did not employ as much biblical quotation as traditionally found in monastic prayers. The prayers were meant to be prayed in private and were expected to lead the monk into deeper prayer and contemplation of God.[25] Anselm's prayers follow a fourfold pattern: (1) the prayers are read in solitude in one's "inner room of the heart"; (2) by reading these prayers the monk's mind is excited, bringing forth in him the image of God that is overlaid with sin; (3) one is then moved "to the love or fear of God, or to self-examination"[26]; and (4) the reader begins to sorrow for his sins, shedding tears of despair or terror at the horror of sin and the judgment it deserves, culminating in tears of love, longing and delight in God.[27]

Though these prayers and meditations were originally written for monks, they are still of interest to the spiritual reader today. However,

---

1059-c. 1130 (Cambridge: Cambridge University Press, 1963). A translation of his life by Eadmer can be found in *The Life of St. Anselm, Archbishop of Canterbury*, trans. R. W. Southern (Oxford: Clarendon Press, 1979). On Benedictine monasticism see Christopher Brooke, *The Age of the Cloister: The Story of Monastic Life in the Middle Ages* (Mahwah, NJ: HiddenSpring, 2003), pp. 44-85.

[23]Many of these works are available in translation in Brian Davies and G. R. Evans, eds., *Anselm of Canterbury: The Major Works* (Oxford: Oxford University Press, 1998).

[24]*The Prayers and Meditations of St. Anselm, with the Proslogion*, trans. Benedicta Ward (London: Penguin, 1973).

[25]See Anselm's letter to Countess Mathilda of Tuscany in *The Prayers and Meditations of St. Anselm*, p. 90.

[26]*The Prayers and Meditations of St. Anselm*, p. 89.

[27]Ibid., pp. 51-58.

the high Marian theology may be off-putting for evangelical readers. Still, good hermeneutical questions to ask while reading these prayers are provided by Anselm himself. The modern reader can even now benefit from Anselm's fourfold understanding of prayer and turn these steps into a paradigm of hermeneutical questions. First, am I reading and meditating on these prayers from a place of solitude, that is, from my inner heart? The point of this question is to discern if the reader is reading the prayers and meditations with a proper disposition. Am I approaching them only intellectually or am I also allowing myself to read them affectively? Second, am I seeing the depths of my own sinfulness as I read and meditate? Is the realization of my sinfulness causing me to desire God's mercy and grace? Third, how am I being moved to love and fear God? How are these prayers moving me to examine myself, and what am I learning about myself in this process? Fourth, am I mindful of the depth of God's judgment, and how am I growing in love and longing for God? What steps will I take to delight in him?

The final edition of the prayers and meditations contains nineteen prayers and three meditations. As already stated, not all of the prayers will resonate with an evangelical readership. Recurring themes, however, that the reader should focus on include Anselm's doctrine of sin, humankind's need for salvific deliverance and God's forgiving, saving nature. There is perhaps no medieval author who theologized as well and as often about sin as Anselm. Not only is sin present throughout the prayers and meditations but several other works from Anselm take it up as their primary focus. In his "Prayer to St. John the Baptist" Anselm writes on the depths of sin, both original and volitional sins:

> In sin I was conceived and born,
>> but you washed me and sanctified me;
>> and I have defiled myself still more.
> Then I was born in sin of necessity,
>> but now I wallow in it of my own free will.
> In sin I was conceived in ignorance,
>> but these sins I commit willingly, readily, and openly.[28]

---

[28]Ibid., p. 128.

This theology of sin is echoed in similar language in his "Prayer to the Holy Cross." Fallen humanity's need of salvation and deliverance is also a recurring theme throughout the prayers and meditations, especially the "Meditation on Human Redemption." Employing the Anselmian atonement theology of sanctification, that humankind needs to atone for its sins by satisfying God's wrath, Anselm says that humans could not be restored to their original state of sinlessness unless God forgives them and humankind makes satisfaction for their sins. Yet, Anselm writes eloquently that God is a God of grace, therefore he avoids creating a scheme of works righteousness. In the "Prayer to Christ" Anselm says that he is awaiting "the inbreathing of [God's] grace."[29] Further, Anselm is mindful of God's passion which has purchased his salvation; therefore Anselm awaits the arrival of Christ's consolation. In great appreciation for Christ's sacrifice, Anselm implies that had he been at the resurrection, he would have kissed the very nail wounds in Christ's hands and feet. Access to this divine offering is by way of the sacrament of the Eucharist, which incorporates all believers into God's church.[30]

Though praying to saints will likely offend some readers of this work, those who use the prayers for their original purpose (i.e., to lead to further prayer) will likely find that Anselm's prayers facilitate a deeper season of prayer. One other element in the prayers and meditations that reflects their medieval context heavily is Anselm's reliance on the concept of a treasury of merit. This theology teaches that some saints have a surplus of sanctity that is then stored up for other's use.[31] Despite such medievalisms, however, the prayers and meditations can certainly benefit those today who read them as they were intended by Anselm to be read.

Bernard of Clairvaux (1090-1153). Bernard was a Cistercian monk, abbot of Clairvaux and preacher of the failed Second Crusade.[32] With

---

[29]Ibid., p. 94.

[30]See the "Prayer Before Receiving the Body and Blood of Christ."

[31]See especially "Prayer to St. John the Evangelist (2)."

[32]The best studies of Bernard include Adriaan H. Bredero, *Bernard of Clairvaux: Between Cult and History* (Grand Rapids: Eerdmans, 1996); and John R. Sommerfeldt, *The Spiritual Teachings of Bernard of Clairvaux* (Kalamazoo, MI: Cistercian Publications, 1991). For a history of the Cistercians see Brooke, *Age of the Cloister*, pp. 166-94; and C. H. Lawrence, *Medieval Monasticism: Forms of Religious Life in Western Europe in the Middle Ages*, 2nd ed. (New York: Longman, 1989), pp. 174-205.

enormous energy and intellectual gifts, Bernard of Clairvaux is one of the leading lights of the Middle Ages. During his lifetime he traversed Europe on business for both the Cistercians and the papacy, fought with leading theologians, including Abelard and Peter the Venerable, and corresponded with Europe's ecclesial "who's who." In spite of this activity he still managed to write nearly a dozen major treatises, countless sermons (the most important being his sermon on the Song of Songs), letters, a saint's life (*The Life of St. Malachy*) and a defense of the new monastic knighthoods arising during his lifetime. In many respects Bernard is the quintessential monastic theologian and had gained such respect and prominence in the years after his death that Dante Alighieri has him guide Dante the pilgrim into God's presence in the *Divine Comedy*. Like other monastic writers Bernard was greatly influenced by the Rule of Benedict, Augustine of Hippo, Gregory the Great and especially the Bible.[33] In 1135 Bernard began a series of sermons on the Song of Songs. This work, begun at the insti- gation of another monk, consists of eighty-six sermons and contains Bernard's most developed ideas on his entire spiritual program: to direct humankind's love to God and to restore with the help of God's grace a twisted power that clings unduly to creatures in order that once freed it may find again the dignity of its origin. In Bernard's own words: "Love is a great reality, and if it returns to its beginning and goes back to its origin, seeking its source again, it will always draw afresh from it, and thereby flow freely."[34] Written over the latter years of his life, these sermons only comment up to Song of Songs 3:4 and were continued by two later Cistercians, Gilbert of Hoyland and John of Ford.

By Bernard's time it was a common practice for a spiritual writer to comment on the Song of Songs, and had been done by such noteworthy commentators as Origen, Gregory the Great and Venerable Bede before

---

[33]On the Bible-centeredness of Bernard's thought see Denis Farkasfalvy, *L'inspiration de l'Écriture sainte dans la theologie de Saint Bernard* (Rome: Herder, 1964). See also Cuthbert Butler, *Western Mysticism: The Teaching of SS. Augustine, Gregory and Abelard on Contemplation and the Contem- plative Life*, 3rd ed. (London: Constable, 1967).

[34]Bernard of Clairvaux, Sermon 83.4, in *Bernard of Clairvaux: On the Song of Songs IV*, trans. Irene Edmonds (Kalamazoo, MI: Cistercian Publications, 1980), p. 184.

Bernard, and by Thomas Aquinas and Denys the Carthusian after Bernard.[35] No longer was the Song viewed as a literal description of a man's love for his wife and a woman's love for her husband, but it was understood to be an allegory for God's love for the church or God's love for the individual Christian. Along these lines Bernard's commentary is a "mystical" rendering of the Song of Songs; that is, it sought to replicate the spiritual, nuptial relationship that exists between God and the believer. The reason for commenting on the Song of Songs, largely done by male monks, is likely due to the fact that the monks saw themselves as living "at a point of intersection between this world and the next, between time and eternity, between light and dark, between anticipation and fulfillment. This meant that the concept of love as a 'yearning' or 'longing' . . . exactly expressed what they wanted by way of a language of love."[36] Though Bernard's nuptial imagery is perhaps foreign to today's mind, it was commonplace in the Middle Ages. Therefore, hermeneutical questions to ask when reading Bernard's commentary on the Song of Songs (and others like it) are, what is the purpose of the commentary and, as a result, what is the primary motive in guiding the author's commentary? There are medieval commentaries that focus on the literal meaning of the text under consideration, but commentaries such as Bernard's have a different purpose. That overall purpose will guide the author's comments. For example, Bernard sees his Songs commentary as only being possible for his monastic audience because they are in a third stage of spiritual development. In the first sermon Bernard explains that he will comment on the Songs in a spiritual manner, by which, of course, he means a nonliteral approach. This is possible because the monks are now ready to move past the milk fit for beginners and to consume the bread that is offered in the Songs. The monks are ready for this bread of the Songs because they have already "eaten" from the books of Ecclesiastes and Proverbs. For Bernard, Ecclesiastes provides an antidote to a misguided love of the world while Proverbs provides an antidote to an excessive love of the self. These books also foster the discipline of self-

---

[35] Denys Turner, *Eros and Allegory: Medieval Exegesis of the Song of Songs* (Kalamazoo, MI: Cistercian Publications, 1995).

[36] Turner, *Eros and Allegory*, p. 20.

control, cultivate a fear of God and zeal to observe his commandments.[37] In light of Bernard's own explanation, the modern reader can ask, what message is Bernard now trying to instill into his audience? Moreover, what behaviors is Bernard trying to cultivate by preaching through the Song of Songs?

With these questions, the reader is now able to engage the texts more appropriately. It will be tempting for the modern evangelical reader to spend much of the time disagreeing with Bernard's exegetical method. Yet, to read medieval biblical commentaries fruitfully one needs to keep in mind that the fourfold method of scriptural interpretation is *the* way in which the Bible was interpreted. Medieval commentators were more concerned with facilitating life change than they were with adhering to a literal exegesis; thus they viewed the allegorical, tropological and ana-gogical meanings of the text as significant as the literal. Modern interpreters will have to accept this and read medieval commentaries differently. Recurring themes in Bernard's sermons on the Songs include love and desire, both of which are technical Bernardine terms. Bernard uses four words for love in his works: *dilectio, caritas, amor* and *cupiditas*. According to Michael Casey, *dilectio* is part of a willed response where a person has adopted a program of goodness and given assent to it. *Amor* is pre-will and is more passionate, involving the whole person. *Amor* is a spontaneous love that invigorates life, whereas *dilectio* is more controlled and willed. *Amor*, therefore, is in need of direction and ordering. When *amor* is ordered to its proper end it becomes *caritas* and when it is turned away from its end it becomes *cupiditas*.[38] For Bernard then, love is an activity of the will. Love is a properly ordered will directed toward God. In Bernard's thought, desire can be either good or bad, depending on its object. So, a desire for good things is good and a desire for evil is itself evil. A final theme to look for in Bernard is his nuptial imagery between Christ and the church or Christ and the individual person. With such imagery it is good to ask, what is the nature of the

---

[37]*Bernard of Clairvaux: Song of Songs I*, trans. Kilian Walsh (Kalamazoo, MI: Cistercian Publications, 1971), pp. 1-2.

[38]Michael Casey, *Athirst for God: Spiritual Desire in Bernard of Clairvaux's Sermons on the Song of Songs* (Kalamazoo, MI: Cistercian Publications, 1987), p. 91.

intimacy that Bernard is trying to depict given his use of the metaphor? It may also be helpful to ask, when does Bernard push the nuptial metaphor too far? Not everything encountered in a medieval text is right or beneficial to the modern reader seeking spiritual formation.

Bonaventure (c. 1217-1274). Bonaventure was a Franciscan friar, university professor, minister general of the Franciscan order and cardinal whose theological and spiritual treatises exercised a profound influence on late medieval thought.[39] A contemporary of the famous Dominican theologian Thomas Aquinas, Bonaventure was no less an intellectual giant than his Dominican peer, though Bonaventure, in addition to heady theological tracts, also left a substantial body of spiritual texts.[40] Bonaventure is representative of the important shift in religious life occurring in the thirteenth century. Though the Fourth Lateran Council of 1215 had disallowed the formation of new religious orders unless the new order adopted the rule and institutes of an already existing order, Francis of Assisi was able to gain final approval from pope Honorius III in 1223 for his group of itinerant poor men, taking the name of "Little Friars" or "Friars Minor." Before long the order grew and was sending friars to the recently established university in Paris to receive the necessary training to engage in extensive preaching missions. Bonaventure was one of these friars, becoming a master in theology in 1253/4 and holding the Franciscan chair in theology from 1253 to 1257. In 1257 he was elected head of the Franciscan order, a position he held until his death. While minister general, Bonaventure wrote two important spiritual works that allow us to look at two other medieval genres, the mystical treatise and the saint's life: *The Soul's Journey into God* and *The Life of St. Francis*. The former work was influenced by the thought of Pseudo-Dionysius the Areopagite, a sixth-century Syrian author writing in Greek who claims to be the convert of Paul in Acts 17, and the latter by the long history of writing saint's lives, but especially the lives of Francis composed by Thomas of Celano.

---

[39]A good, recent study of Bonaventure is Christopher M. Cullen, *Bonaventure* (Oxford: Oxford University Press, 2006). On the rise and influence of the orders of friars see C. H. Lawrence, *The Friars: The Impact of the Early Mendicant Movement on Western Society* (New York: Longman, 1994).

[40]Zachary Hayes, *Bonaventure: Mystical Writings* (New York: Crossroad, 1999).

The Soul's Journey into God provides an itinerary for the soul's journey
to God, beginning with contemplating God's reflection in the material
world and moving on to contemplating God as he is in himself. As one
scholar has noted, "Bonaventure's division of the journey into six stages
is a refinement of a larger division of three stages: . . . meditation on
nature, on the soul and on God."[41] Though this tripartite division can
be traced back to early monastic authors, such as Evagrius of Pontus,
Bonaventure most likely encountered it in his reading the Pseudo-
Dionysius, who had been available in Latin translation since the ninth
century. In this work Bonaventure offers six stages for the soul to pass
through on its way to union with God himself that are based on his
belief that the human mind has "three principal perceptual orienta-
tions": exterior material objects, within itself, and above itself.[42] These
six stages are (1) contemplating God in his vestiges in the universe, (2)
contemplating God in the sense world, (3) contemplating God through
his image stamped on humankind's natural powers, (4) contemplating
God in his graced, reformed image in us, (5) contemplating the divine
unity through its being, and (6) contemplating the Trinity in its name,
which is Good. Having progressed through these stages the mind is
then able to enter into ecstasy when one's affection passes over into God.
Though such language will be unfamiliar to many evangelical readers,
there are several hermeneutical questions that will aid in reading this
mystical treatise: What are the meanings of Bonaventure's terms? Do I
understand them as he understood them as opposed to understanding
them from my own theological perspective? What does Bonaventure
mean by "contemplating"? Though this text lacks many explicit biblical
quotations or allusion, in what ways is Bonaventure employing biblical
categories? The reader should remember that Bonaventure's text is a
mystical treatise; that is, it is attempting to explain how the human
mind/soul comes to union with God—it is not a how-to manual of spirituality. Thus, when reading the text it is good to keep in mind that Bonaventure is theologizing about the mind's journey and that he sees

---

[41]*Bonaventure: The Soul's Journey into God, The Tree of Life, The Life of St. Francis*, trans. Ewert
Cousins (New York: Paulist Press, 1978), p. 20.
[42]Ibid., p. 61.

these steps as paradigmatic. Exactly how one comes to a place of being able to contemplate in this manner is left unstated in the text itself, though being a monk or friar is presupposed.

In 1228, a Franciscan named Thomas of Celano was given the task of writing the first life of Francis of Assisi, which he finished the following year. During the course of his lifetime, however, Thomas would write another life of Francis. Bonaventure was asked, in 1260, by the Franciscan general chapter to write a life of Francis, making use of those already in existence. Bonaventure's goal was to "gather together the accounts of his virtues, his actions and his words."[43] What he accomplished, though, was a biography whose structure is based on the tripartite schema of purgation, illumination and perfection discussed in chapter five, "Spiritual Theology: A Historical Overview," elsewhere in this volume.[44] This tripartite division is based on the virtues that Francis cultivated in his life, which Bonaventure details in nine chapters of the life. In the purgative stage Francis cultivated mortification, humility and poverty. In the illuminative stage he cultivated piety, charity and prayer. The stage of perfection is evidenced by his understanding of the Scriptures and his gift of prophecy, his effective preaching and healing abilities, and his receiving the stigmata, that is, the sacred wounds of Jesus on his hands, feet and side. It is this kind of miraculous occurrence that will likely keep the evangelical reader at bay.

Yet such a miraculous event being reported in a saint's life reminds us that we need to be careful of the contents of this genre. As discussed earlier, saint's lives typically adopt a number of types and images whose purpose is to elevate the sanctity of the person being discussed. Bonaventure's *The Life of St. Francis* is no exception. In addition to the stigmata there are other types to notice. First, Bonaventure asserts that Francis "imitated angelic purity" and was a "fellow citizen of the angels."[45] That saints actually lived a life so holy as to make them more like the unfallen angels than humans is a common hagiographical type going back to earliest mo-

---

[43]Ibid., pp. 182-83.
[44]I am indebted to Ewert Cousins for this observation, who in turn is indebted to Regis Armstrong. See Cousins, trans., *Bonaventure*, pp. 42-44; and Regis J. Armstrong, "The Spiritual Theology of the *Legenda Major* of Saint Bonaventure" (PhD diss., Fordham University, 1978).
[45]Cousins, trans., *Bonaventure*, pp. 181, 272.

nasticism.[46] Second, Francis's conversion comes through hearing Matthew 16:24: "If anyone would come after me, let him deny himself and take up his cross and follow me." This conversion experience bears similarities to conversion narratives in many saint's lives, but especially one of the most popular—Athanasius of Alexandria's *Life of Anthony*. Third, Francis is seized at times with a burning desire to be martyred for his faith. In early Christian saint's lives and hagiographical texts, martyrdom was the surest sign of a person's sanctity. Given that the thirteenth century did not afford many opportunities for true martyrdom, Bonaventure is clear that Francis desired martyrdom, even if he was unable to achieve it. Thus, Francis is as holy as those literally martyred for their faith. A final example, Francis engages regularly in being God's agent of healing others, either directly or by way of his personal items kept by others. In one example Bonaventure says that upon coming into a town, a man in possession of a cord worn by Francis was able to heal many who were ill simply by having the sick drink water that had come into contact with the cord (cf. Acts 19:11-12). That saints heal in a manner similar to Jesus and the earliest disciples is a typical hagiographical device. Consequently, when reading a saint's life like that of Bonaventure's Francis, one must bear in mind the nature of hagiographical literature (discussed earlier), asking the following questions: Where has the author taken hagiographical license? What is the purpose of these hagiographical types? What is the author's intent; that is, what am I to learn from this text about virtue, holiness and the like?

Julian of Norwich (c. 1342-c. 1416). Julian is one of the most well-known medieval spiritual writers and one of the few women from the period whose works continue to be read and studied copiously.[47] Julian was an anchoress who lived in solitude in Norwich, England.[48] While

---

[46]See Karl Suso Frank, *Angelikos Bios: Begriffsanalytische und begriffsgeschichtliche Untersuchung zum 'engelgleichen Leben' im frühen Mönchtum* (Münster: Aschendorff, 1964).

[47]See John Julian, *The Complete Julian of Norwich* (Orleans, MA: Paraclete Press, 2009).

[48]Greg Peters, "Monasteries," in *Encyclopedia of Christian Civilization*, ed. George T. Kurian, (Malden, MA: Wiley-Blackwell, 2011): Anchorholds "were constructed in either a churchyard or another part of the village. Frequently, these structures were adjoined directly to the church itself, often on the church's north wall. After entering the space, the monk or nun would be locked (commonly from the outside) into the enclosure. Oftentimes an anchorhold contained a window into the chancel of the church so that the anchorite could join with the congregation in the celebration of the liturgy. Another window on the outer wall of the anchorhold was used to receive food and to communicate with others" (pp. 1546-47).

living as an anchoress she received a series of revelations or "showings" on May 8, 1373, when she was thirty years old. These revelations have come down to us in two versions: the "long text" and the "short text." From these revelations we learn that Julian was influenced especially by the Bible, Augustine of Hippo and the writings of medieval spiritual writers such as William of St. Thierry. By examining the revelations of Julian we meet our final important medieval genre: visionary literature. Though Julian's *Showings* are quite tame compared with the revelations of other medieval visionaries, such as Mechthild of Magdeburg or Elisabeth of Schönau, they are well-known and somewhat paradigmatic of late medieval visionary literature. Receiving visions has been common throughout Christian history and it is most often associated with women.[49] As an ecstatic occurrence or spiritual phenomena, visions allowed women, whose voices often went unheard, to gain a hearing, for who would dare reject a so-called direct teaching from God, even if it came from the mouth and pen of a woman? And it is this very aspect that makes medieval visionary texts one of the most difficult genres of medieval literature to read and appropriate. Using the long text of Julian's *Showings* as a guide, let's investigate the nature of medieval visionary literature.

Julian tells us that she received her sixteen revelations in the course of one night while she was extremely sick, so much so in fact she received the last rites from her priest since she was not expected to live through the night. This sickness, however, did not take her life. In fact, her pain was taken suddenly from her and she began to regain health. This caused Julian to meditate on the passion of Jesus Christ. While doing so she was given a vivid vision of the crucifixion: "suddenly I saw the red blood running down from under the crown, hot and flowing freely and copiously, a living stream."[50] This vision helped Julian to understand that Jesus was both God and man and that he suffered for her. Importantly, Julian notes that this awareness came "without any intermediary"; that is, God spoke directly to her. Thus, the first aspect to notice about vi-

---

[49]See Elizabeth Avilda Petroff, *Medieval Women's Visionary Literature* (Oxford: Oxford University Press, 1986).

[50]*Julian of Norwich: Showings*, trans. Edmund Colledge and James Walsh (New York: Paulist Press, 1978), p. 181.

sionary literature is that it most often comes as a direct encounter between the visionary and God, without any other human or institutional
mediation. For the modern reader, instead of adopting a skeptical attitude to such a claim, it is better to ask, Despite this direct encounter
between the person and God, does the vision maintain and is it consistent with orthodox Christian theology? Is the visionary claiming to
receive new knowledge of God, or is the vision simply reinforcing accepted theology? If the visionary is claiming to receive a kind of revelation that would supplement the Bible, then such literature is likely not
worth the investment of the modern spiritual reader. If the vision is
making received theology more explicit, then the modern reader can
likely benefit from reading the text. In Julian of Norwich's case, she remains orthodox throughout.[51]

Julian's vision not only makes orthodox theology explicit, it also provides a developed spiritual theology. This makes Julian's revelations a
grammar of ascent given by God (i.e., they are visions purported to be
from God) as opposed to other kinds of visionary literature that serves
other purposes. For example, Catherine of Siena (1347-1380), we are told,
had a visionary experience where she was "mystically" married to Jesus,
who told her to leave her monastic enclosure and become involved in
public life, including a call for a new crusade. Primarily, however, this
public service involved Catherine's role in helping to restore the papacy
in Rome after its "captivity" in Avignon, France. Given Catherine's unusual visionary experiences and overt political agenda, the modern
evangelical reader would benefit less from her texts than from a visionary like Julian. Consequently, other questions to ask are, What is the
author/visionary trying to accomplish by receiving these visions and
recording them for others to read? Is there an overt agenda to the visions that would make them too historically cultured? In short, visionary texts are a mixed bag and should be read with caution. Many,
nevertheless, are deep spiritual texts that deserve to be read.

---

[51]Though Julian is well known for referring to God as "Mother," she saw this as a property of God.
That is, not only was he fatherly and lordly but he was also motherly. This emphasis on God as
also father and lord keeps Julian's theology orthodox.

OTHER IMPORTANT MEDIEVAL TEXTS

Given the breadth, depth and quantity of medieval spiritual texts it is impossible to provide an exhaustive list. The following, therefore, along with those already discussed, are the most important and frequently studied.

Dante Alighieri (c. 1265-1321). Dante has been referred to as the greatest Italian poet and is the author of the hugely influential *Divine Comedy*.[52] Dante was greatly influenced by the theological writings of Thomas Aquinas and Bonaventure, as well as by the spiritualities of Pseudo-Dionysius and Augustine of Hippo. Divided into three books (*Inferno*, *Purgatory* and *Paradise*), the *Divine Comedy* recounts the journey of Dante from hell to heaven, all the while laying out a theology of spiritual ascent that highlights the role of the church and God's grace.

Hildegaard of Bingen (1098-1179). Hildegaard was the abbess of the Benedictine monastery at Disibodenberg, Germany, a visionary and one of the leading intellectual lights of the Middle Ages. Hildegaard is the author of many theological and spiritual texts as well as musical compositions and medical texts. A correspondent of many leading medieval personages, including Bernard of Clairvaux, Hildegaard's treatises show that she was influenced by contemporary nuptial imagery like that found in Bernard and by her monastic tutor Jutta von Sponheim (1091-1136), as well as having a strong mystical bent. Hildegaard's most important theological and spiritual text, *Scivias*, was endorsed by pope Eugenius III in 1147.

Walter Hilton (c. 1343-1396). Walter Hilton was an English Augustinian canon educated in law at Cambridge who wrote the well-known and influential *Scale of Perfection*. Consisting of two books, the *Scale* was written during two different periods. Book 1 envisions the contemplative life as the domain, in principle, of those vowed to the contemplative religious state whereas book 2 sees contemplation as something to which every Christian should aspire, whatever his or her state in life. Oftentimes book 2 takes up a point made in book 1, developing the topic in greater detail.

---

[52]*Dante Alighieri: The Inferno*, trans. Anthony Esolen (New York: Modern Library, 2002); *Dante Alighieri: Purgatory*, trans. Anthony Esolen (New York: Modern Library, 2003); and *Dante Alighieri: Paradise*, trans. Anthony Esolen (New York: Modern Library, 2004).

READING THE CHRISTIAN SPIRITUAL CLASSICS

Meditation on the Life of Christ *(c. 1300). Meditation on the Life of Christ* is a Pseudo-Bonaventuran text, likely written by an Italian Franciscan, extant in hundreds of manuscripts of different medieval languages.[53] Consisting in three parts, the first and third are narratives of the life of Christ while the second is a treatise on the active and contemplative lives. One of the main sources for the *Meditation* was Bernard of Clairvaux.

Meister Eckhart *(c. 1260-1327).* Meister Eckhart was a Dominican philosopher and spiritual theologian whose works were commonly misunderstood and sometimes condemned in the Middle Ages. Writing and preaching in both German and Latin, Eckhart's spirituality is characterized by his love of paradox and apophatic approach (e.g., "God's going out is his going-in"). At the center of his spirituality is the theology that God is the "ground" and "consciousness of the ground, a form of awareness different from all other forms of experience and knowing, is the foundation of Meister Eckhart's mysticism."[54]

Pseudo-Dionysius *(c. 500).* Pseudo-Dionysius was likely a Syrian monk writing in Greek whose works were translated into Latin beginning in the ninth century. His primary methodology is one of negative theology, which is speaking of God and his creation by what it is not (e.g., "we assert what is beyond every assertion"). Three of his most important works are *The Divine Names, The Mystical Theology* and *The Celestial Hierarchy.*

Richard of St. Victor *(d. 1173).* Richard of St. Victor was a canon at the abbey of St. Victor in Paris and was greatly influenced by Pseudo-Dionysius and Augustine of Hippo. His major spiritual works, *The Twelve Patriarchs* and *The Mystical Ark*, are concerned with assisting the reader in attaining contemplation, which he defines as "the free, more penetrating gaze of a mind, suspended with wonder concerning manifestations of wisdom."[55] This is accomplished by contemplating the various "manifestations" provided by God by way of the imagination, reason, understanding or any combination thereof.

---

[53]Sarah McNamer, "The Origins of the *Meditationes Vitae Christi*," *Speculum* 84 (2009): 905-55.

[54]Bernard McGinn, *The Mystical Thought of Meister Eckhart: The Man from Whom God Hid Nothing* (New York: Herder & Herder, 2001), p. 38.

[55]*Richard of St. Victor: The Twelve Patriarchs, The Mystical Ark, Book Three of the Trinity*, trans. Grover A. Zinn (New York: Paulist Press, 1979), p. 157.

Thomas à Kempis (c. 1380-1471). Thomas à Kempis was associated early in his life with the Brethren of the Common Life, but became an Augustinian canon in 1399. The author of many books, Thomas is known primarily for his *The Imitation of Christ*. Influenced greatly by the Bible, the *Imitation* consists of four books concerning both the inner and outer spiritual lives. This book is one of the greatest of all spiritual classics, influencing many later spiritual leaders, focusing on the need for not only a robust theology but also an affective disposition.

SUGGESTED READINGS

McGinn, Bernard. *The Growth of Mysticism: Gregory the Great through the Twelfth Century*. New York: Crossroad, 1994.

_____. *The Flowering of Mysticism: Men and Women in the New Mysticism–1200-1350*. New York: Crossroad, 1998.

_____. *The Harvest of Mysticism in Medieval Germany*. New York: Crossroad, 2005.

McGinn, Bernard, John Meyendorff and Jean Leclercq, eds. *Christian Spirituality I: Origins to the Twelfth Century*. New York: Crossroad, 1985.

Raitt, Jill, ed. *Christian Spirituality II: High Middle Ages and Reformation*. New York: Crossroad, 1987.

13

The Reformation Traditions

Timothy George

THE REFORMATION OF THE SIXTEENTH CENTURY was an era of transition that witnessed the death throes of the Middle Ages on one hand and the birth pangs of modern times on the other.[1] Between the discovery of America by Columbus in 1492 and the coming of the Pilgrims to Plymouth in 1620, Christianity in the West experienced a fundamental reorientation and reinterpretation in Christian belief and practice. So significant was this transformation for both Catholics and Protestants that we might well consider it a spiritual revolution, a revolution that resulted in the reordering of Christianity first in Europe, then in the New World and subsequently throughout the global Christian movement. Like a great earthquake, the Reformation and the energies it released continues to resonate five centuries later.

The Reformation was a revolution in the original scientific sense of

---

[1] *The Oxford Encyclopedia of the Reformation*, ed. Hans J. Hillerbrand, 4 vols. (New York: Oxford University Press, 1996) is the standard reference work in Reformation studies. Other recent studies include Timothy George, *Reading Scripture with the Reformers* (Downers Grove, IL: InterVarsity Press, 2011); Diarmaid MacCulloch, *The Reformation* (New York: Viking, 2004); Andrew Pettegree, ed., *The Reformation World* (London: Routledge, 2002); G. W. Bernard, *The King's Reformation: Henry VIII and the Remaking of the English Church* (New Haven, CT: Yale University Press, 2005); Euan Cameron, *The European Reformation* (New York: Oxford University Press, 1991); Alister E. McGrath, *Christianity's Dangerous Idea: The Protestant Revolution: A History from the Sixteenth Century to the Twenty-first* (New York: HarperOne, 2007); Carter Lindberg, *The European Reformations* (Oxford: Blackwell, 1996); Steven E. Ozment, *Protestants: The Birth of a Revolution* (New York: Doubleday, 1992); and Bruce Gordon, *The Swiss Reformation* (Manchester, UK: Manchester University Press, 2002).

the term: the return of a body in orbit to its original position. The Reformation was a "back to the future" movement. With few exceptions, the Reformers of the sixteenth century understood themselves as renovators, not innovators. Their aim was to re-form the church, to restore the pattern of discipleship found in the Scriptures and the early church fathers, and to renew the spiritual vitalities that had been lost or diminished in the intervening centuries. The result of the Reformation was a reordering of societal structures and ecclesial polities, with new confessions of faith, catechisms and liturgies published in prolific profusion. At the heart of this activism, however, was a spiritual quest: to know, to love and to serve the living God of the inspired Scriptures. Reformation spirituality was not a separate track or preoccupation for the godly elite. The Reformation was a movement of spiritual and ecclesial renewal with profound implications for every believer and follower of Jesus Christ.

HISTORICAL CIRCUMSTANCES

The drama of the Reformation was shaped by major currents in the political, social, intellectual and spiritual traditions of the later Middle Ages. We can summarize these developments by reference to four "universalizing" structures of medieval Europe: the Holy Roman Empire, the papacy, the university and monasticism.

First, the Reformation witnessed the decline of the Holy Roman Empire and the rise of the modern nation-state. Since the time of Charlemagne, the Holy Roman Empire had enjoyed a close, if often contentious, relationship with the church. Medieval society presupposed "two swords" (Lk 22:38), one temporal, the other spiritual. In principle, empire and church were bound together in a nexus of mutual support symbolized by the fact that every new emperor was crowned by the pope in a ceremony of liturgical solemnity. By the time of the Reformation, however, this relationship was sorely frayed as a result of tensions not fully resolved by the twelfth-century Investiture Controversy. There was also a struggle between the pope and emperor over the appointment of bishops and the rise of competing centers of political power—the modern nation-states. The medieval balance of power was completely shattered in 1527 when the troops of the Holy Roman emperor, Charles V, sacked the city of Rome and took as a prisoner the pope himself. Both papacy and the empire were also threatened by the rise of Islam in the East. The diminution of imperial authority contributed to a crisis of order in the Reformation era. This political vacuum was filled in part by new political forces, including powerful city-states such as Bern and Geneva in Switzerland, and Protestant territorial princes, such as Frederick the Wise of electoral Saxony in Germany.

Second, the authority of the pope to serve as a unifying force was increasingly challenged not only by competing political powers but also by developments within the church itself. The exalted papal claims made by Pope Innocent III (1198-1216) and Boniface VIII (1294-1303) were undermined by the so-called Babylonian Captivity when the papacy was forced into exile in Avignon (1309-1377). This was followed by the scandal of the Great Schism (1378-1417), when there were two and then three popes at the same time, each claiming to be the sole vicar of Christ on earth. The specter of the body of Christ divided into three papal obediences was finally resolved by the Council of Constance (1414-1417), the gathering at which the Bohemian reformer John Hus was burned alive at the stake. The Reformation did not begin as a frontal assault against the papacy, but it did occur at a time when the papal monarchy of the high Middle Ages was already under assault. It was a time ripe for reform. The demand for *reformatio in capite et in membris*—reformation in head and members—resounded throughout Europe.

Third, many of the theological debates of the sixteenth century grew out of the system of disputation and university-based learning known as Scholasticism, a sophisticated effort to apply the tools of reason to the data of revelation. Within this broad system of thought, there were different schools based on various philosophical and theological commitments. Luther himself was a kind of radical Augustinian, while one of his principal Catholic opponents, Thomas de Vio (Cajetan), revived the theology of the great Dominican teacher Thomas Aquinas. But Reformation theology was also shaped in a decisive way by the New Learning, a term that refers to the revival of letters and the recovery of ancient texts stemming from the Renaissance. A key figure in this movement was Desiderius Erasmus, a Dutch scholar who may be considered the

first public intellectual of early modern Europe. Erasmus was an inde-
fatigable scholar and editor of classical texts, including the writings of
the early church fathers. In 1516 he published the first critical edition of
the Greek New Testament, a work used by Luther and William Tyndale
in their respective translations of the New Testament into German and
English. It is hard to exaggerate the importance of the advent of printing
in the spread of the New Learning, including the proliferation of the
Bible translations and other texts of spiritual theology. Protestantism
was the first religious movement to take full advantage of the new
powers of the press, and Luther's German New Testament (1523) was the
world's first bestseller.[2]

Fourth, although it is well known that Luther renounced his monastic vows and married a runaway nun, his own spiritual theology was
nonetheless decisively shaped by the monastic culture in which he was
formed. Nowhere is this more evident than in the pattern of Bible study
known as *lectio divina*, a prayerful and contemplative engagement with
the text of Scripture. The Reformers were well versed in the writings of
the great medieval spiritual masters, including Bonaventura and
Bernard of Clairvaux. In addition, the mystical traditions of the late medieval period remained a vital source of spiritual life and theological
reflection throughout the Reformation. Luther's first published book
was an edition of the sermons of Johannes Tauler, which he called the
Theologia Deutsch (German Theology). The eve of the Reformation was
an age of spiritual vitality that witnessed renewed interest in relics, pilgrimages and saints. Many popular religious movements—the Lollards
in England, the Hussites in Bohemia, the Waldensians and Spiritual
Franciscans in Italy and France—responded to the thirst for God
throughout Europe. There were also the Brothers and Sisters of the
Common Life, lay Christians who practiced a life of piety and prayer

---

[2]Elizabeth L. Eisenstein, "The Advent of Printing and the Protestant Revolt: A New Approach to
the Disruption of Western Christendom," in *Transition and Revolution: Problems and Issues of
European Renaissance and Reformation History*, ed. Robert M. Kingdon (Minneapolis: Burgess,
1974), pp. 235-36. See also Mark U. Edwards Jr.'s comment: "The printed word played a crucial
role in the early Reformation and when multiplied by the effects of preaching and conversation,
can be said to be a major factor in spreading a relatively coherent message throughout the
German-speaking lands" (Mark U. Edwards, *Printing, Propaganda, and Martin Luther*
[Minneapolis: Fortress Press, 1994], p. 172).

and the daily reading of the Scriptures. The most famous book to come out of this movement was the *Imitation of Christ* by Thomas à Kempis, a manual of devotion that has remained in print for more than five centuries. The Brothers and Sisters of the Common Life became the great scribes and copyists of pre-Reformation Europe, and also the major schoolteachers of the time, counting among their pupils both Luther and Erasmus.

In recent decades much attention has been given to what is called "reforming from below," that is, the shaping of religious beliefs and devotional practices that marked the popular culture of the majority of the population in the age of the Reformation. Social historians have taught us to examine the diverse pieties of townspeople and city folk, of rural religion and village life, as well as the emergence of lay theologies and the experiences of women in the religious tumults of Reformation Europe.[3] New methods of studying the Bible along with the invention and rapid development of printing resulted not only in learned commentaries, catechisms and manuals of devotion, but also in numerous citations from the Bible and expositions of its meaning in everyday correspondence, court depositions, records of public disputations, hymns and popular songs, even last wills and testaments. All of this points to the fact that the century of the Reformation, like the one that preceded it, was an age marked by "an immense appetite for the divine."[4]

THEOLOGICAL CONTEXT AND ASSUMPTIONS

Looking back on the age of the Reformation we are prone to see the stark division that resulted from the conflict between Protestants and Catholics. This division was indeed real and still continues to separate the two major families within Western Christianity, despite increasing goodwill and ecumenical efforts to mend the breach. However, when we consider the Reformation within the overarching storyline of Christian faith through the ages, what is remarkable is the continuity between

[3]See Peter Matheson, ed., *Reformation Christianity* (Minneapolis: Fortress Press, 2007). See also Susan C. Karant-Nunn, *The Reformation of Ritual: An Interpretation of Early Modern Germany, Christianity, and Society in the Modern World* (London: Routledge, 1997).
[4]Lucien Febvre, "The Origins of the French Reformation: A Badly-put Question?" *A New Kind of History*, ed. Peter Burke (New York: Harper & Row, 1973), p. 43.

Protestants and Catholics. The trinitarian and christological consensus of the early church was embraced by Protestants and Catholics alike. That is to say, they both worshiped and adored the one and only, true and living God, the Father, the Son and the Holy Spirit. They further believed that this triune God of holiness and love had become incarnate in Jesus of Nazareth, the Son of Man of the four canonical Gospels. They confessed Jesus Christ to be the only Lord of heaven and earth, the only begotten Son of God, Light from Light, true God from true God. Both Catholics and Protestants understood themselves to stand in fundamental continuity with the 318 fathers of Nicaea, the 150 fathers of the first Council of Constantinople, as well as the canons of Ephesus, including the affirmation of the *Theotokos* and the condemnation of Pelagianism. They also embraced the classic christological definition put forth at the Council of Chalcedon. They argued over exactly how faithful they each were to this received consensus—for example, did the semi-Pelagianism of medieval soteriology undermine the Augustinian emphasis on the priority of grace?—but this was an argument within a shared framework of discourse.

Many of the church-dividing disputes at the time of the Reformation centered on what later historians called the formal and material principles of the Protestant movement. The formal principle is sometimes referred to by the slogan *sola scriptura*. The Protestant Reformers understood this principle not in terms of "the Bible only" but rather "the Bible supremely." *Sola scriptura* did not mean *nuda scriptura!* The Protestants, no less than the Catholics, read the Bible in dialogue with the exegetical tradition of the church and often cited the writings of the church fathers and schoolmen who came before them. But, as important as such writings were, they could never be regarded as equal with, much less superior to, the inspired text of the Bible itself. Debates over the inspiration and inerrancy of Scripture were post-Reformation developments. During the Reformation, the key question about the Bible was its relative authority vis-à-vis the teaching office of the church, a still unresolved issue in Catholic-Protestant dialogue today.[5]

---

[5]See Timothy George, "An Evangelical Reflection on Scripture and Tradition," *Pro Ecclesia* 9, no. 2 (2000): 184-207.

The material principle of the Reformation refers to the doctrine of justification by faith alone. The Protestant Reformers claimed to find the doctrine of justification in the liturgy of the church and the prayers of the saints, including the favored Bernard of Clairvaux. The Protestants insisted that salvation was by grace alone, through faith alone, in Jesus Christ alone. This Christocentrism shaped their patterns of piety and prayer, as well as their ethics and eschatology—what Jeremy Taylor in the seventeenth century would call "holy living and holy dying." The doctrine of justification by faith alone came to be seen as "the article by which the church stands or falls." Jaroslav Pelikan has summarized well the Protestant understanding of this key teaching:

> If the Holy Trinity was as holy as the trinitarian dogma taught; if original sin was as virulent as the Augustinian tradition said it was; and if Christ was as necessary as the Christological dogma implied—then the only way to treat justification in a manner faithful to the best of Catholic tradition was to teach justification by faith.[6]

A final assumption, shared by Protestants and Catholics alike, was the *embodiment* of spirituality. For example, the Bible was meant to be not only read, studied, translated, memorized and meditated upon, it was also to be enacted in preaching, baptism, the Lord's Supper, singing, praying and service in the world. As good Augustinians, Protestant theologians could extol the reality of the invisible church, the company of elect saints known only to God, but they also called their congregations to worship at the church in the town square next to the marketplace where the people of God gathered week by week around pulpit and table.

HERMENEUTICAL FRAMEWORK

When one reads the spiritual classics of the Reformation, it is important to keep several questions in mind. What is the context of the document? Was it produced in response to a particular controversy or pastoral crisis in the life of the church? Are distinctive Reformational emphases, such as the doctrine of predestination or justification by faith alone, inter-

---

[6]Jaroslav Pelikan, *Obedient Rebels* (New York: Harper & Row, 1964), pp. 50-51.

woven in this text? What gave this document its staying power? The fact that it became a classic indicates that it must have resonated with many people over some period of time. What does this document tell us about the Christian life and what it means to follow Jesus Christ today?

Given the diversity of religious impulses and traditions during the sixteenth century, some scholars prefer to speak of "Reformations," in the plural. Whether or not we adopt this convention, it is certainly necessary to recognize the diverse streams and tributaries that flow into this fertile historical reservoir. Here are some of the ways historians define the various Reformation groupings:

Biblical humanists. The key figure here is Erasmus, but this group includes many others, both Catholics and Protestants, who sought to renew the church by the recovery of classical learning and the close study of the Scriptures.

Lutherans. To ask whether there would have been a Reformation without Martin Luther is like asking whether there would have been an early church without St. Paul. But Luther was not a lone ranger, and he gathered around him a cadre of able theologians and leaders, including Philip Melanchthon, Justus Jonas, Johannes Bugenhagen, Nikolaus von Amsdorf and Johannes Brenz.

Reformed. The key figures here are Huldrych Zwingli and Heinrich Bullinger in Zurich, and John Calvin and Theodore Beza in Geneva. John Knox and Peter Martyr Vermigli also belong here, as does Martin Bucer, who is a more mediating figure.

Anglicans. Thomas Cranmer shaped the piety and theology of the reformed Church of England through his Book of Common Prayer. William Tyndale is a key figure through his translation of the Bible, as are Hugh Latimer, John Hooper and Nicholas Ridley, all bishops martyred under Mary Tudor. And later in the sixteenth century John Jewel, Richard Hooker and William Perkins were great apologists and pastoral theologians of the Anglican way.

Radical Reformers. These Reformers represented diverse spiritual impulses including Anabaptism (Balthasar Hubmaier and Menno Simons), spiritualism (Kaspar Schwenckfeld) and evangelical rationalism (Faustus Socinus).

Catholic reformers. Many streams of Catholic reform flourished in the early sixteenth century, including the work of great scholars such as John Colet in England and Jacques Lèfevere d'Etaples of France. Also important were powerful preachers such as Savanarola of Italy. The creation of new religious orders—the Capuchins, the Theatines, the Oratory of Divine Love and, most important, the Society of Jesus—shaped the spiritual traditions of post-Reformation Catholicism. Among the leading exponents of Catholic Reformation spirituality were Ignatius Loyola and two shapers of the reformed Carmelite movement—Teresa of Ávila (later recognized as a doctor of the church) and the Spanish mystic John of the Cross.

A concluding word should be said about the way in which the Reformers read the Bible. Beginning with Thomas Aquinas and Nicholas of Lyra in the Middle Ages and continuing into the Reformation, the literal sense of Scripture became more prominent, even if more complex, as it absorbed more and more of the content of the spiritual meanings. The Bible opened up a field of possible meanings that allowed for considerable exegetical creativity, but that also imposed limits on the interpreter. The Reformers knew that both allegory and typology were biblical terms (Gal 4:24; 1 Cor 10:11) and they allowed for a chastened use of both while emphasizing the grammatical and historical meaning of the text.[7] In looking at spiritual classics of the Reformation era, it is important to emphasize both the personal and corporate character of devotion, prayer and Bible reading. In the sixteenth century, translations of the Bible were accompanied by the translations of the liturgy. Luther's *German Mass and Order of Service* was published in 1526; Calvin's *Form of Prayers* came out in 1542. As part of their protest against clerical domination of the church, the Protestant Reformers aimed at full participation in worship. Their reintroduction of the vernacular was jarring to some since it required that divine worship be offered to Almighty God in the language used by businessmen in the marketplace and by husbands and wives in the privacy of their bedchambers. The intent of the

---

[7]Richard A. Muller and John L. Thompson, eds., *Biblical Interpretation in the Era of the Reformation: Essays Presented to David C. Steinmetz in Honor of His Sixtieth Birthday* (Grand Rapids: Eerdmans, 1996).

Reformers was not so much to secularize worship as to sanctify common life. For them the Bible was not merely an object for academic scrutiny in the study or the library; it was meant to be enacted as the people of God gathered for prayer and praise and proclamation.

IMPORTANT REFORMATION AUTHORS

Out of numerous Reformation classics that deserve attention, I have chosen to focus on seven well-known figures and some of their most popular and accessible writings. A brief mention of other important Reformation spiritual classics will follow this review.

Desiderius Erasmus (c. 1469-1536). Erasmus pioneered an approach to educational reform and moral life that he called *philosophia Christi,* "the philosophy of Christ." His *Enchiridion militis Christiani* (Handbook of the Christian Knight), published in 1503, was a succinct summary of Erasmian piety.[8] This volume became a classic during Erasmus's own lifetime with over fifty Latin editions and translations into many vernaculars. According to John Foxe, William Tyndale made the first English translation in the 1520s. The word *enchiridion* has a double meaning: it is both a sword or dagger carried by a soldier in battle and a little book of instruction kept close at hand. In his *Enchiridion,* Erasmus wants to equip the soldier of Christ with the right weapons to withstand evil and pursue a godly life in the world. Among the chief weapons the Christian knight will need are prayer and the reading of Scripture, especially the New Testament. Erasmus presents twenty-one rules by which the Christian knight can overcome evil and resist the power of the seven deadly sins. Two things should be noted about the spiritual approach set forth in the *Enchiridion.* First, it called for a religion of inwardness with personal devotion to Christ overshadowing, if not replacing, external rites and sacraments of the institutional church. Erasmus's disdain for externals in faith and his call for an interior devotion presuppose a Platonic understanding of reality. Second, Erasmus promotes a distinctively lay piety, a spirituality for everyone. This emphasis anticipated the Protestant doctrine of the priesthood of

---

[8]Desiderius Erasmus, *Enchiridion militis Christiani: An English Version,* ed. Anne M. O'Donnell (New York: Oxford University Press, 1981).

all believers and the importance of making the Scriptures available to all. As Erasmus would later write,

> Christ wishes his mysteries to be published as widely as possible. I would wish even all women to read the Gospel and the epistles of St. Paul, and I wish they were translated into all the languages of the Christian people, that they might be read and known. . . . I wish that the husbandman may sing parts of them at his plow, that the weaver may warble them at his shuttle, and that the traveler with their narratives beguile the weariness of the way.[9]

Martin Luther (1483-1546). Luther is a titanic figure in the history of Christian spirituality, and one can easily drown in the plethora of his writings, which comes to 118 folio volumes in the modern critical edition.[10] To the end of his life Luther saw himself as a faithful and obedient member of the one, holy, catholic and apostolic church. It was never his intention to start a brand new church from scratch. As a young monk he sought to find a gracious God in the spiritual disciplines of his monastic order and followed its rules so strictly that, as he later said, "If ever a monk got to heaven by his monkery, it was I!" His pathway to a new life in Christ was slow and torturous, though he did have a decisive breakthrough in his understanding of the doctrine of justification by faith. This came about as he studied the Bible and pondered the meaning of "the righteousness of God," as used by Paul in Romans 1:17.

Luther eventually came up with three rules that he recommended to everyone for reading and studying the Scriptures: prayer, meditation and temptation. (1) *Oratio:* In studying the Bible, Luther said, the first place to begin is with prayer for no one can penetrate the meaning of Scripture by study and talent alone. "Kneel down in your little room (Matt. 6:6) and pray to God with real humility and earnestness, that he

---

[9]Erasmus, cited in J. F. Mozley, *William Tyndale* (New York: Macmillian, 1937), p. 34.

[10]Roland Bainton's *Here I Stand: A Life of Martin Luther* (Nashville: Abingdon, 1950) is still unsurpassed in its vivid portrayal of the German Reformer. Among many other books on Luther, the following are worthy of note: Eric W. Gritsch, *Martin: God's Court Jester* (Philadelphia: Fortress, 1983); Heiko A. Oberman, *Luther: Man Between God and the Devil* (New Haven, CT: Yale University Press, 1983); Philip D. W. Krey and Peter D. S. Krey, eds., *Luther's Spirituality* (New York: Paulist Press, 2007); and David C. Steinmetz, *Luther in Context* (Bloomington: Indiana University Press, 1986).

through his dear Son may give you his Holy Spirit, who will enlighten you, lead you, and give you understanding."[11] (2) *Meditatio:* If Luther's first rule relates to the inner disposition of the heart in seeking divine help in understanding the Scriptural text, his second rule, meditation, focuses on something external—the performance of Scripture in repeating and pondering it out loud. Such meditation is a lifelong vocation. In his first lecture series on the Psalms, Luther distinguished meditating and thinking by defining the former as "to think carefully, deeply, and diligently . . . to muse in the heart, to stir up in the inside, or to be moved in the innermost self." This is a rule of life that involves meditating on God's law "day and night." By "day and night," Luther commented, the psalmist refers not only to matins and vespers but to every season of human existence, good times and bad times, times of prosperity and times of adversity, of contemplation and activism, of life and death. (3) *Tentatio:* Temptation is a weak translation of what Luther meant by *tentatio* or *Anfechtung* in German. The word *Anfechtung* derives from the world of fencing: a *Fechter* is a fencer or gladiator. A *Fechtboden* is a fencing room. Thus *Anfechtungen* refers to spiritual attacks, bouts of dread, despair, anxiety, assault, conflicts that rage both within the soul of every believer and also in the great apocalyptic struggle between God and Satan. There is no genuine spirituality without such conflicts for, as Luther declared, "Experience alone makes one a theologian."[12]

These rules inform all of Luther's writings on the spiritual life, including his three famous treatises of 1520. In *To the Christian Nobility of the German Nation,* Luther set forth his teaching on the priesthood of all believers as he called on the lay leaders of his country to take the lead in reforming church and society. *The Babylonian Captivity of the Church* was a frontal assault on the penitential-sacramental system of medieval Catholicism. *The Freedom of a Christian* was the shortest of these three treatises, but perhaps the most radical and consequential of Luther's early writings. Here we see Luther's distinction between law and gospel,

[11]*Luther's Works,* vol. 34, *Career of the Reformer* 4, ed. Helmut T. Lehmann and Lewis W. Spitz (Philadelphia: Muhlenberg, 1960), pp. 285-86.
[12]*Luther's Works,* vol. 54, *Table Talk* (Philadelphia: Fortress Press, 1967), p. 7 (Weimarer Ausgabe 25, p. 106). For an insightful exposition of Luther's three rules, see Oswald Bayer, *Martin Luther's Theology: A Contemporary Interpretation* (Grand Rapids: Eerdmans, 2008).

and his teaching that there is absolutely nothing one can do to merit the favor and grace of God. The gratuity of divine grace is the only basis for a right relationship with God. However, justification by faith does not lead to a life of detachment and isolation from others. By releasing the sinner from futile attempts at self-justification, this teaching allows the believer in Christ truly to serve his or her neighbor, indeed to become "a little Christ" unto them. Through the grace of Christ, Luther says, a Christian person is a free sovereign, above all things, and subject to no one. But this same Christian person is at the same time a beautiful servant in all things and subject to everyone. This is the paradox of Christian existence.

Next to his translation of the Bible into German, Luther's Small Catechism of 1529 is his most enduring and significant work. It was incorporated, along with his Large Catechism from the same year, into the Book of Concord (1580), the definitive collection of Lutheran confessional documents.[13] The Small Catechism was originally printed as a booklet with illustrations aimed for use with children. Luther lamented the deplorable conditions of both family and church life in Germany, a situation that required careful catechetical instruction. While pastors and teachers are responsible for teaching the Christian faith to those in their charge, this is primarily the work of parents in the home. The Small Catechism begins with a series of questions on the Ten Commandments, followed by the Apostles' Creed, the Lord's Prayer and sections on baptism, confession and the Lord's Supper, then morning and evening prayers, grace at table, and a concluding table of duties. This table consists of well-chosen passages of Scripture selected for "various estates and conditions of people" from bishops and pastors to husbands and wives, parents and children, and Christians in general. Once the Small Catechism had been carefully taught, it was necessary, Luther said, to move on to the Large Catechism with its fuller, more theologically explicit formulations. Here, in his explanation of the first commandment, Luther described the heart of true theology as a matter of trust, not merely abstract thinking.

---

[13]Robert Kolb and Timothy J. Wengert, eds., *The Book of Concord: The Confessions of the Evangelical Lutheran Church* (Minneapolis: Fortress Press, 2000).

What is it to have a god? What is God? Answer: A god is that to which we look for all good and in which we find refuge in every time of need. To have a god is nothing less than to trust and believe him with our whole heart. As I have often said, the trust and faith of the heart alone make both God and an idol. If your faith and trust are right, then your god is the true God. On the other hand, if your trust is false and wrong, then you have not the true God. For these two belong together: faith and God. That which to your heart clings and entrusts itself is, I say, really your god.[14]

Nowhere is Luther's spiritual theology better glimpsed than in his personal letters and correspondence. Many of these have been brought together in a fascinating collection edited by Theodore G. Tappert, *Luther: Letters of Spiritual Counsel.*[15] These letters show Luther the pastor up close and personal as he offers comfort for the sick and dying, consolation for the bereaved, and admonitions of cheer for those engulfed by doubt and depression. A woman named Barbara Lisskirchen was deeply troubled by the doctrine of predestination and questioned whether she had been chosen as one of God's elect. To her, Luther offered this pastoral advice:

> The highest of all God's commands is this, that we hold up before our eyes the image of his dear Son, our Lord Jesus Christ. Everyday he should be our excellent mirror wherein we behold how much God loves us and how well, in his infinite goodness, he has cared for us in that he gave his dear Son for us. In this way, I say, and in no other does one learn how to deal properly with the question of predestination. It will be manifest that you believe in Christ. If you believe, then you are called. And if you are called, then you are most certainly predestinated. Do not let this mirror and throne of grace be torn away from before your eyes. If such thoughts still come and bite like fiery serpents, pay no attention to the thoughts or serpents. Turn away from these notions and contemplate the brazen serpent, that is, Christ given for us. Then, God willing, you will feel better.[16]

---

[14]Weimarer Ausgabe 31/1, p. 132, cited in Heinrich Bornkamm, *Luther in Mid-Career, 1521-1530* (Philadelphia: Fortress Press, 1983), pp. 597-98.

[15]*Luther: Letters of Spiritual Counsel*, ed. and trans. Theodore G. Tappert (Philadelphia: Westminster Press, 1955). Originally published as part of the Library of Christian Classics, this volume was reprinted in 2003 by Regent College Publications.

[16]Ibid., p. 116.

Huldrych Zwingli (1484-1531). A powerful preacher at the Great Minster of Zurich, Zwingli was the major Reformer of German-speaking Switzerland.[17] A follower of Erasmus, his break with the medieval tradition was more radical than that of Luther. Among his many contributions to the Reformed tradition was his practice of preaching chapter by chapter through various books of the Bible, a method of proclamation taken up by Calvin and other Reformers. In 1522 he addressed an assembly of Dominican nuns in Zurich on "the clarity and certainty of the Word of God." This sermon was published in expanded form and reprinted many times. It is a classic expression of the essential role of the Bible in the Christian life and in the reform of the church. Zwingli knew that the living Word of God was Jesus Christ himself, but he also referred to the gospel as the Word of God and defined it as "not only what Matthew, Mark, Luke, and John had written, but all that God has ever revealed to men."[18] Zwingli emphasized the role of the Holy Spirit in our recognizing and understanding the Word of God in Holy Scripture. The Scripture is self-authenticating in the sense that the Holy Spirit enlightens the text of the Bible in such a way that the reader confesses it to be the Word of God. The "prevenient clarity" of the Bible, as Zwingli called it, results from an inviolable linkage between the Spirit's inspiration of the biblical text and his illumination of those who read and study the Bible today. Zwingli concludes "On the Clarity and Certainty of the Word of God" with twelve practical admonitions and a brief *epiclesis*, a prayer of supplication for the Holy Spirit. Here is Zwingli's conclusion:

> Ninth, when you find that the Word of God renews you, and begins to be more precious to you than formerly when you heard the doctrines of men, then you may be sure that this is the work of God within you.
>
> Tenth, when you find that it gives you assurance of the grace of God and eternal salvation, it is of God.

---

[17]On Zwingli, see the recent studies *Huldrych Zwingli: Writings*, eds. E. J. Furcha and H. W. Pipkin (Allison Park, PA: Pickwick, 1984); Gottfried W. Locher, *Zwingli's Thought: New Perspectives* (Leiden: E. J. Brill, 1981); Peter Stephens, *The Theology of Huldrych Zwingli* (Oxford: Oxford University Press, 1986); and Ulrich Gäbler, *Huldrych Zwingli: His Life and Work* (Philadelphia: Fortress Press, 1986).

[18]Huldrych Zwingli, cited in *Zwingli and Bullinger*, ed. G. W. Bromiley (Philadelphia: Westminster Press, 1953), p. 86.

Eleventh, when you find that it crushes and destroys you but magnifies God himself within you, it is a work of God.

Twelfth, when you find that the fear of God begins to give you joy rather than sorrow, it is a sure working of the Word and Spirit of God.

May God grant us that Spirit. Amen.[19]

John Calvin (1509-1564). John Calvin's *Institutes of the Christian Religion*, first published at Basel in 1536, went through successive editions until it became a massive tome in its definitive form in 1559.[20] Calvin is often depicted as a single-issue theologian preoccupied mainly with the doctrine of predestination, but a survey of his many writings will reveal a thinker of great range and enormous spiritual power. His letters are filled with spiritual wisdom as well as keen pastoral advice. His biblical commentaries, which cover nearly the entire canon of Scripture, reveal a master exegete at work. Calvin's spiritual theology was marked by a strong emphasis on the believer's union with Christ. Calvin was also a theologian of prayer, which he called "the chief exercise of faith, and the means by which we daily receive God's benefits." The longest chapter in the 1559 *Institutes* is devoted to prayer, and it is one of the great spiritual classics on this theme. Calvin began this chapter by setting forth four rules of prayer to guide the Christian in his or her "conversation with God." The first rule is that we approach God reverently, that we frame our prayers "duly and properly." This requires that we not arrogantly demand of God any more than he allows but, as Scripture teaches, ask everything in accordance with his will. The second rule of prayer is that it must come from the heart, "out of the depths," as the psalmist said (Ps 130:1). Prayer should be earnest and urgent: in prayer we yearn, desire, hunger, thirst, seek, request, beseech, cry out. The third rule requires us to yield all confidence in ourselves and humbly plead for pardon. It is appropriate to begin our prayer by confessing our sins and claiming the

[19]Ibid.

[20]On Calvin see the recent studies *The Cambridge Companion to John Calvin*, ed. Donald K. McKim (New York: Cambridge University Press, 2004); William J. Bouwsma. *John Calvin: A Sixteenth-Century Portrait* (New York: Oxford University Press, 1988); Randall C. Zachman. *Image and Word in the Theology of John Calvin* (Notre Dame, IN: University of Notre Dame Press, 2007); Herman J. Selderhuis; *John Calvin: A Pilgrim's Life* (Downers Grove, IL: IVP Academic, 2009); Alister E. McGrath, *A Life of John Calvin: A Study of the Shaping of Western Culture* (Oxford: Basil Blackwell, 1990).

promise of forgiveness. The final rule of prayer is that we pray with con-
fident hope: "Cast down and overcome by true humility, we should be
nonetheless encouraged to pray by a sure hope that our prayer will be
answered" (*Institutes* 3.20.11). Calvin reminds us that we pray through
the Holy Spirit, who is our teacher in prayer and who "arouses in us assurance, desires and size, to conceive which our natural powers would
scarcely suffice" (*Institutes* 3.20.5). In public worship, Calvin emphasized the importance of singing as a form of public prayer. The singing
of metrical psalms after the pattern of Geneva became a mainstay of
Reformed and Puritan worship.

Menno Simons (1496-1561). A former priest in the Netherlands,
Menno Simons came to question both the doctrine of transubstantiation
and the practice of infant baptism.[21] In the 1530s a newly baptized and
reordained Menno Simons became the most outstanding leader of the
Anabaptist branch of the Radical Reformation. In 1540 he published what
was to become his most influential writing, *The Foundation of Christian
Doctrine*, an apology for evangelical Anabaptism and a summary of its
primary teachings. These included the practice of adult baptism based
on an experience of the new birth, the correlation of faith and discipleship, an emphasis on free will rather than divine predestination, and a
view of the church that stressed its purity and separation from the world
reinforced by the strict practice of congregational discipline (the ban).

Sixteenth-century Anabaptists were harried and persecuted by Catholics and Protestants alike, which left them little time to write. However,
they did publish several works of devotion that have become spiritual
classics. Three of these are Menno Simons's *The Cross of the Saints* (c.
1554), a martyrology known as *The Martyrs' Mirror*, and a collection of
Anabaptist hymns called the *Ausbund*. In *The Cross of the Saints*, Menno
takes as his theme the beatitude, "Blessed are they which are persecuted
for righteousness's sake." He reminded his readers that they were not the
first to undergo "the angry, wolfish tearing and rending, the wicked

---

[21]On Simons see Timothy George, *Theology of the Reformers* (Nashville: Broadman, 1988); Myron
S. Augsburger, *The Fugitive: Menno Simons, Spiritual Leader in the Free Church Movement* (Scottdale, PA: Herald Press, 2008); *The Complete Writings of Menno Simons*, trans. Leonard Verduin,
ed. J. C. Wenger (Scottdale, PA: Herald Press, 1978).

animal-like torturing and bloodsheding of this godless world against
the righteous."[22] Menno recalled the biblical examples of martyrdom,
beginning with Abel, and he appealed to Eusebius of Caesarea's *Ecclesiastical History* in order to establish the continuity between the martyrs
of the early church and those of his own church and generation. He
summoned his fellow Anabaptists to enroll in the *militia Christi*, the
army of Christ that sheds no blood: "Therefore, O ye people of God,
gird yourselves and make ready for battle; not with external weapon and
armor as the bloody, mad world is wont to do, but only with firm confidence, a quiet patience, and a fervent prayer."[23]

*The Bloody Theatre or Martyrs' Mirror of the Defenseless Christians
Who Baptized Only Upon Confession of Faith, and Who Suffered and Died
for the Testimony of Jesus Their Savior* was first published in Dutch in
1660 as a folio volume of 1,290 pages.[24] It is the Anabaptist counterpart to
John Foxe's *Acts and Monuments of the Christian Martyrs*. The first part
of the *Martyrs' Mirror* recounts the stories of heroic Christian martyrs up
to the sixteenth century, followed by gripping accounts of those "who
gave their lives for the truth since the great Reformation." The names of
803 recently executed Anabaptist martyrs are listed, and the circumstances of their deaths are described in gripping detail—drownings,
burnings, beheadings, hangings, torturings. These stories circulated
among the Anabaptist faithful and served to encourage those who might
be faced with similar trials. One of the most remarkable documents included in the *Martyrs' Mirror* is a letter of Janneken Muntsdorp to her
infant daughter, also named Janneken, who had been born in prison
while her mother and father awaited execution for their faith: "I bid you
adieu, my dear Janneken Muntsdorp, and kiss you heartily, my dear lamb,
with a perpetual kiss of peace. Follow me and your father, and be not
ashamed to confess us before the world, for we were not ashamed to
confess our faith before the world, and this adulterous generation."[25]

---

[22]Simons, *Complete Writings*, p. 595.
[23]Ibid., p. 621.
[24]Thieleman J. Van Braght, *The Bloody Theater or Martyrs' Mirror* (Scottdale, PA: Mennonite Publishing House, 1951).
[25]This letter is reprinted in Hans Hillerbrand, *The Protestant Reformation* (New York: Harper &
Row, 1968), pp. 146, 152. See the discussion in George, *Theology of the Reformers*, pp. 297-302.

Like so many of the Christian martyrs in the early church, the Anabaptists went to their deaths quoting the Bible and singing hymns of the faith. Many of the distinctive Anabaptist hymns were collected in the *Ausbund*, a hymnbook first gathered by the Swiss Brethren and still in use by the Amish in North America today. Some of the *Ausbund* songs are catechetical in nature and present Anabaptist views on baptism, the Lord's Supper and a vivid hope in the second coming of Christ. Most, however, depict the sturdy faith of those Anabaptists who were called to lay down their lives because of their religious commitment. One of the martyr ballads, "*Wer Christo jetzt will folgen nach*," commemorates the martyrdom of George Wagner, who was accused of denying priestly mediation of forgiveness and the salvific character of water baptism. Following are four of the eighteen stanzas:

> Who Christ will follow now, new born,
> Dare not be moved by this world's scorn,
> The cross must bear sincerely;
> No other way to heaven leads,
> From childhood we're taught clearly.
>
> This did George Wagner, too, aspire,
> He went to heav'n 'mid smoke and fire,
> The cross his test and proving,
> As gold is in the furnace tried,
> His hearts' desire approving.
>
> Two barefoot monks in grey array,
> George Wagner's sorrows would allay,
> They would him be converting;
> He waved them to their cloister home,
> Their speech he'd be averting.
>
> Men fastened him to ladder firm
> The wood and straw was made to burn,
> Now was the laughter dire;
> Jesus! Jesus! did he four times
> Call loudly from the fire.[26]

---

[26]This appears as hymn no. 11 in the *Ausbund*. The complete hymn with German text is found in

Ignatius Loyola (1491-1556). Ignatius Loyola was a Spanish soldier who experienced a profound conversion while recovering from a wound received in battle.[27] With several companions, he founded a new religious order, the Society of Jesus, approved by Pope Paul III in 1540. His *Spiritual Exercises* became a standard manual of devotion not only for Jesuits but for many other Catholic believers in the age of the Counter Reformation. The *Exercises* deal with five major themes—creation, humankind, the kingdom of God, Jesus Christ, and the Trinity. These basic doctrines are covered in four separate "weeks" of prescribed meditations, though the term *week* was used flexibly to mean more or less than seven days. Specific exercises were designed to lead to repentance and purification (the first week), focus the mind on the life of Christ, his deeds and sufferings on the cross (second and third weeks), and celebrate the glory of his risen life (the fourth week). The *Exercises* were intended to prepare the followers of Jesus to engage in spiritual warfare against the power of Satan. In other words, the goal of Ignatian contemplation is the active service of Christ in the world. The imitation of Christ and devotion to his cause is the purpose of the *Exercises*. Ignatian spirituality is both personal and ecclesial. It includes specific "rules for thinking with the church" as well as a pattern of "discerning the Spirit" in one's own vocation and service to Christ. Since the time of the Reformation, the *Spiritual Exercises* have become a devotional model for many pilgrimages and retreats. Their basic biblical content and Christocentric focus have made them appealing to Protestants as well as Catholics.

Thomas Cranmer (1489-1556). Thomas Cranmer was the Archbishop of Canterbury under King Henry VIII and the principal reformer of the Church of England during the reign of King Edward VI.[28]

The Christian Hymnary (Uniontown, OH: Christian Hymnary, 1972), p. 418.

[27]On Loyola see the recent studies by John Patrick Donnelly, *Ignatius of Loyola: Founder of the Jesuits* (New York: Pearson Longman, 2004); Mary Purcell, *The First Jesuit, St. Ignatius Loyola* (Chicago: Loyola University Press, 1981); André Ravier, *Ignatius of Loyola and the Founding of the Society of Jesus* (San Francisco: Ignatius Press, 1987); *Exercitia Spiritualia: The Spiritual Exercises of St. Ignatius*, trans. Anthony Mottola (New York: Image Books, 1989).

[28]On Cranmer see Diarmaid MacCulloch, *Thomas Cranmer: A Life* (New Haven, CT: Yale University Press, 1996); Paul Ayris and David Selwyn, eds., *Thomas Cranmer: Churchman and Scholar* (New York: Boydell, 1993); Geoffrey W. Bromiley, *Thomas Cranmer, Theologian* (New York: Oxford University Press, 1956).

His great and most enduring masterpiece was the Book of Common Prayer, which he compiled and published in two editions during his lifetime (1549, 1552). It was revised once more when Elizabeth came to the throne in 1559 and again in 1662. Cranmer was also involved in the production of the Great Bible (1539), the first "authorized" translation of the Scriptures into English. He also compiled the *Book of Homilies* (1547), a collection of model sermons intended to elevate the role of preaching in the Church of England and to instruct the common people in the true Protestant faith.

The Book of Common Prayer included tables for the daily reading of Scripture, services of morning and evening prayer, an order for baptism and Holy Communion, as well as services for weddings, funerals and confirmations. There was also an ordinal for the consecration of bishops and the ordination of deacons and priests—the three orders of ministry recognized in the Anglican tradition. John E. Booty has said of the Book of Common Prayer: "It provided worship for every day of the year as well as Sunday by Sunday through the church year, and for all of life from birth to death. And it did so in one comparatively modest volume, printed in English."[29] The Book of Common Prayer continues to be used by Anglican churches today in various editions. Despite these changes, much of Cranmer's masterful English prose still remains, and the impact of this great classic extends far beyond the Anglican world. Two of the rubrics from the Service of Holy Communion reveal the heart of Cranmer's Protestant piety. The first is his description of the death of Christ as "a full perfect oblation and satisfaction for the sins of the whole world." The other is the "Prayer of Humble Access" offered by the communicants prior to their receiving the bread and wine of communion.

> We do not presume to come to this thy table, O merciful Lord, trusting in our own righteousness, but in thy manifold and great mercies. We are not worthy so much as to gather up the crumbs under thy table. But thou art the same Lord, whose property is always to have mercy: Grant us therefore, gracious Lord, so to eat the flesh of thy dear Son Jesus Christ, and to drink his blood, that our sinful bodies may be made clean by his

---

[29]John E. Booty, "Book of Common Prayer," *The Oxford Encyclopedia of the Reformation*, ed. Hans Hillerbrand (New York: Oxford University Press, 1996), 1:191.

body, and our souls washed through his most precious blood, and that we may evermore dwell in him, and he in us. Amen.

POSSIBLE USES FOR THE CHURCH TODAY

What can we learn about the Christian life from reading the spiritual classics of the Reformation today? As a historical movement the Reformation of the sixteenth century is now behind us. We live in a different age with different challenges, and we cannot simply deracinate the Reformers from their time and bring them into our own without remainder. At the same time, many of our own spiritual questions recall the struggles of the Reformation era. How do we deal with personal and corporate guilt? How can we find meaning and purpose in a world marked by violence, war and death? What can we as a society do when the institutions we have trusted have let us down? What is our only hope in life and death?

Like the Reformers of the sixteenth century, we too live in an age of transition—from modernism to postmodernism, from an age of certainty to one of ambiguity and anxiety. Compared to many transcendence-starved spiritualities, the spiritual theology of the Reformers is filled with good news about God's grace and God's purpose, the good news of justification by faith in a crucified Savior.

The spiritual classics of the Reformation also help us to find our place within the wider body of Christ. Jesus prayed for his disciples that they would be one, as he and the Father are one, so that the world might believe. In the perspective of the Reformation, the church of Jesus Christ is that communion of saints and congregation of the faithful which has heard the Word of God in Holy Scripture and bears witness to that Word in the world. We can celebrate and participate in the quest for Christian unity precisely because we take seriously the Reformation concept of the church, not merely a church once and for all reformed, but rather a church always to be reformed, a church ever in need of further reformation on the basis of the Word of God. In the body of Christ we come closer to one another as we come together closer to Christ. The spiritual classics of the Reformation point us to the priority of the gospel and prompt us to pray, with John Calvin, "My heart I offer to you, Lord, eagerly and earnestly."

Suggested Readings

Argula von Grumbach (1492-c. 1554). Argula Von Grumbach was a Bavarian noblewoman who defended the Protestant cause by challenging theologians at the University of Ingolstadt. Her "open letter" of 1523 is an early example of vernacular theology as she wrote in her native German tongue appealing to the Catholic theologians on the basis of her reading of the Bible.[30]

William Tyndale (c. 1494-1536). William Tyndale was the catalyst in translating the Bible into English in the early sixteenth century. He worked from the original Hebrew and Greek texts, and though influenced by Luther's German New Testament, Tyndale gave his own distinctive cast to the English Bible. *A Pathway into Holy Scripture,* published in 1530, offered an apology for the translation project and a brief exposition of key biblical terms including the Old Testament, the New Testament, law, Gospel, Moses, Christ, nature, grace, works and faith. Tyndale was executed in 1536 and is rightly remembered as one of the great martyrs of the English Reformation.

Katharina Schütz Zell (1498-1562). Katharina Schütz Zell was, to use her own term, a "church mother" of the Reformation in Strasbourg. Married to the Protestant preacher Mathias Zell, Katharina was a reformer, author and pastor in her own right. Elsie McKee has collected and translated a number of Schütz Zell's writings.[31] These include letters of consolation, devotional treatises, biblical meditations, catechetical instructions, sermons and a set of four hymn booklets.

Heinrich Bullinger (1504-1575). Heinrich Bullinger was Zwingli's successor as the chief pastor and reformer of Zurich.[32] A prolific author and

---

[30]Peter Matheson, ed., *Argula von Grumbach: A Woman's Voice in the Reformation* (Edinburgh: T & T Clark, 1995).

[31]See Katharina Zell, *Church Mother: The Writings of a Protestant Reformer in Sixteenth-Century Germany* (Chicago: University of Chicago Press, 2006); Elsie Anne McKee, *Katharina Schütz Zell* (Leiden: Brill, 1999); Elsie Anne McKee, *Reforming Popular Piety in Sixteenth-Century Strasbourg: Katharina Schütz Zell and her Hymnbook* (Princeton: Princeton Theological Seminary, 1994).

[32]See Thomas Harding, ed., *The Decades of Henry Bullinger,* 4 vols. (Cambridge: Cambridge University Press, 1849-1852); Bruce Gordon and Emidio Campi, *Architect of Reformation: An Intro-*

commentator on nearly every book in the Bible, he also produced a collection of fifty sermons called the *Hausbuch* or, in English translation, the *Decades.* Bullinger's sermons became a staple of spiritual reading for Protestants in Germany, the Netherlands and especially England. The *Decades* brought together the central ideas of the Protestant message with a distinctively Reformed approach to preaching, prayer and biblical exposition.

The Heidelberg Catechism (1562). Published in the Palatinate, the Heidelberg Catechism was the major confessional document of the Reformed movement in Germany and was later recognized as a major standard in the Dutch Reformed tradition.[33] This document consists of 129 questions and answers. Its pastoral tone, emphasis on humility and encouragement to gratitude make it one of the most enduring spiritual classics of the Reformation era. "Lord's Day One" reveals the tone and spiritual depth of the entire document:

> *Question:* What is your only comfort in life and death?
> *Answer:* That I am not my own, but belong with body and soul, both in life and in death, to my faithful Savior Jesus Christ. He has fully paid for all my sins with his precious blood, and has set me free from all the power of the devil. He also preserves me in such a way that without the will of my heavenly Father, not a hair can fall from my head; indeed, all things must work together for my salvation. Therefore, by his Holy Spirit, he also assures me of eternal life and makes me heartily willing and ready from now on to live for him.

Teresa of Ávila (1515-1582). Teresa of Ávila was a major reformer of the Carmelite Order and a leading example of Catholic Reformation spirituality.[34] In addition to writing a compelling autobiography, *The Life of Teresa of Jesus,* her greatest work was the *Interior Castle.* In this treatise she described a vision of the Christian life as a journey through seven stages or "mansions" leading finally to union with God. Teresa

---

duction to *Heinrich Bullinger, 1504-1575* (Grand Rapids: Baker Academic, 2004).

[33]See Lyle D. Bierman et al., *An Introduction to the Heidelberg Catechism: Sources, History, and Theology* (Grand Rapids: Baker Academic, 2005); Caspar Olevianus, *A Firm Foundation: An Aid to Interpreting the Heidelberg Catechism,* trans. and ed. Lyle D. Bierma (Grand Rapids: Baker, 1995).

[34]See Teresa of Ávila, *The Interior Castle,* trans. Kieran Kavanaugh and Otiloio Rodriquez (New York: Paulist Press, 1979); and Dwight H. Judy, *Embracing God: Praying with Teresa of Avila* (Nashville: Abingdon, 1996).

explores many dimensions of the spiritual life in this work, including the fear of God, prayer, love and the mystical marriage of the soul and God. In 1970, Teresa of Ávila was declared a Doctor of the Church for her writings and teaching on prayer.

John of the Cross (1542-1591). John of the Cross, a Christian mystic, was born Juan de Yepes y Álvarez in central Castile.[35] He longed for a life of solitude and contemplation and in 1563 entered a Carmelite monastery. In 1567 he met nun Teresa of Ávila, an encounter that dramatically altered his life. Finding his order disappointingly lax, John was drawn to the charismatic Teresa and her vision of Carmelite rule. Following her model of a reformed Carmelite house for women, he became the first of the Discalced (or reformed) Carmelite friars.

The remaining twenty-four years of his life were dedicated to this reform movement, despite the opposition of his Carmelite superiors, who had him imprisoned and beaten. While a prisoner in Toledo in 1577-1578 he began an extraordinary corpus of poetry. His masterpieces include "The Spiritual Canticle," "The Living Flame of Love," "The Ascent of Mount Carmel" and "The Dark Night of the Soul." John had a great influence on the development of monastic life but is best remembered as a spiritual writer and director of souls. He was beatified by the Catholic Church in 1675 and made a saint in 1726.

Johann Gerhard (1582-1637). Johann Gerhard was a leading Lutheran theologian in the early seventeenth century, best known for his magisterial *Theological Commonplaces* (1610-1622).[36] But his work also reflects a deep pastoral and spiritual approach. His *Handbook of Consolations,* published in 1611, stands in the tradition of Christian literature referred to by scholars as *ars moriendi,* the art of dying. Gerhard's *Handbook* provided practical encouragements for those facing death and those caring for the sick and dying.

---

[35]Jodi Bilinkoff, "John of the Cross," in *The Oxford Encyclopedia of the Reformation,* ed. Hans Hillerbrand (New York: Oxford University Press, 1996), 2:351-52. For further reading see *The Collected Works of St. John of the Cross,* 2nd ed. and trans. Kieran Kavanaugh and Otilio Rodriquez (Washington, DC: Institute of Carmelite Studies, 1991).

[36]See Johann Gerhard, *Handbook of Consolations for the Fears and Trials That Oppress Us in the Struggle with Death,* trans. Carl L. Beckwith (Eugene, OR: Wipf & Stock, 2009). For a good introduction to the literature on consolation, see Austra Reinis, *Reforming the Art of Dying: The Ars Moriendi in the German Reformation (1519-1528)* (Burlington, VT: Ashgate, 2007).

14

The Puritan and Pietistic Traditions

Tom Schwanda

SOME READERS OF THIS BOOK MIGHT BE surprised to discover a chapter devoted to spiritual classics of Puritanism and Pietism. Both terms were initially used pejoratively, yet amid the slander and abuse heaped upon the early leaders and followers there arose a rich and vital expression of Christian spirituality.[1] In fact, Puritanism has often been understood as a "devotional movement, rooted in religious experience" that sought to complete what was begun in the Protestant Reformation and that dealt primarily with theology and ecclesiology.[2] The same claim can be made regarding Reformed and German Pietism as well. However, it is crucial to recognize that the desire for greater spiritual experience and focus on the heart was also present in Roman Catholicism in Jansenism and Quietism.[3]

---

[1]On Puritanism and its definition see John Coffey and Paul C. H. Lim, eds., *The Cambridge Companion to Puritanism* (Cambridge: Cambridge University Press, 2008), pp. 1-7; and Tom Schwanda, "'Hearts Sweetly Refreshed': Puritan Spiritual Practices Then and Now," *Journal of Spiritual Formation and Soul Care* 3, no. 1 (2010): 21-23. On Pietism and its definition see Dale W. Brown, *Understanding Pietism*, rev. ed. (Grantham, PA: Evangel Publishing, 1996), pp. 11-14; and Jonathan Strom, "Problems and Promises of Pietism Research," *Church History* 71, no. 3 (2002): 536-54.

[2]Charles Hambrick-Stowe, *The Practice of Piety* (Chapel Hill: University of North Carolina Press, 1982), p. vii, cf. pp. 23, 38, 53, 113. Cf. J. I. Packer, *A Quest for Godliness* (Wheaton, IL: Crossway, 1990), p. 28.

[3]See, for example, Ted A. Campbell, *The Religion of the Heart* (Eugene, OR: Wipf & Stock, 1991), pp. 18-41.

Historical Circumstances

The seventeenth and eighteenth centuries, often known as the early modern period, were dynamic and turbulent times within Protestantism. Theologically, the aftereffect of the Protestant and Roman Catholic Reformations of the sixteenth century continued to shape spirituality and stir controversy. The Enlightenment, with its strong penchant for reason, challenged both the faith and practice of believers, creating the context for doubt, but also increased the growing emphasis upon the individual and the importance of experience.

Seventeenth-century England was a caldron of political, social and religious turmoil. This escalated into the fissiparous nature between the king and Parliament that lead to the Civil Wars in the 1640s and the eventual execution of King Charles I in 1649. In 1662 the Act of Uniformity evicted two thousand Puritan-minded pastors and church leaders from their pulpits. A close theological affinity developed between English Puritanism and the *Nadere Reformatie* of the Netherlands. This movement within Reformed Pietism is best translated as the "Second" or "Further" Reformation.[4] Further, many English Puritans fled to the Netherlands due to their increased religious toleration. However, a more nuanced distinction must be articulated between the Reformed and German expressions of Pietism. While there were many similarities, the Dutch expression organically arose from within the orthodox wing of the Reformed Church rather than in growing opposition to it as in German Pietism.

The Thirty Years' War (1618-1648) was the most violent manifestation of the theological and political battles that raged across the continent. The devastating effects of this protracted fighting destroyed approximately one-third of Europe's population, burdened the struggling peasants and working class with increasing taxation, and continued to destroy an already weakened economy. Hostility and renewed warfare resumed in varying degrees with greater intensity following the 1670s. Within this context the established Lutheran Church developed a strong form of confessionalism and orthodoxy that sought to create and pre-

---

[4]Joel R. Beeke, "The Dutch Second Reformation (*Nadere Reformatie*)," *Calvin Theological Journal* 28, no. 2 (1993): 300-307.

serve a proper theological system that emphasized right theology but often, at least in the minds of the Pietist critics, at the expense of a vital personal experience of God.

THEOLOGICAL CONTEXT AND ASSUMPTIONS

While there are fine points of distinctions between the three different geographical and historical traditions there is sufficient commonality to broadly sketch the theological assumptions of Protestantism during this period. Due to the concerted efforts toward orthodoxy that were evident in both Protestantism and Roman Catholicism, there was an increasing emphasis on right doctrine and belief. Regrettably this approach diminished the biblical legitimacy of the heart and experience. Therefore, a theology of experience, often expressed as experimental piety, sought to integrate the mind with the heart. Since German Pietism experienced greater pressure from confessional orthodoxy than both the English Puritans and the *Nadere Reformatie*, the German stream reveals a greater emphasis on the heart than the other two streams.

Conversion or justification by faith through grace marked the beginning of a person's union with Christ. While there were variations within the three traditions, all agreed on the importance of spiritual birth. Unlike large portions of the Roman Catholic tradition that had predominantly followed the Neoplatonic threefold pathway of purgation, illumination and union, Protestants understood union as the beginning of one's journey, not the end. Further, most Protestants employed the biblical metaphor of spiritual marriage (e.g., Song of Songs; Is 54:5; 62:4-5; Jer 3:14; Hos 2:19; Mt 22:2; 25:1-13; Rev 19:7) to remind themselves that union was something that needed to be intentionally cultivated throughout one's life to encourage greater growth and intimacy with Jesus Christ.

A critical distinction between Roman Catholics and Protestants, and indeed one of the causes of the Protestant Reformation, was the importance of translating Scripture into the vernacular and making it available for the laity to read and study on their own. Every writer included in this chapter shared a common passion for preaching, teaching and encouraging personal study of the Bible. While some discontinuities have been elucidated in relation to Roman Catholicism, there were also significant areas of continuity. Unlike Luther and Calvin, who were more reticent to read Scripture allegorically,[5] most of the authors of this chapter practiced a spiritual reading of the Song of Songs that was more consistent with Bernard of Clairvaux than Luther or Calvin.[6]

Growing in grace and godliness represented the importance of sanctification. It combined the interaction of the Holy Spirit with various ascetical spiritual practices that typically were borrowed from Roman Catholicism. Protestants eagerly performed these individually, within the family or small groups, and publically in worship. Two central spiritual disciplines that guided these Christians were meditation and sabbath keeping. Protestants also followed the Augustinian emphasis on desire and enjoyment of God. This relates to spiritual marriage and often included the cultivation of a contemplative awareness and response to God and inspired a deepening union and communion with God. While godliness emphasized the vertical relationship of loving God, it equally stressed the importance of loving one's neighbor.

Eschatology shaped by a millenarian piety was also evident during this period. While this varied greatly from person to person and was always stronger in the radical wing of Puritanism and Pietism, these writers possessed a greater awareness of the imminent return of Jesus Christ than the church today. This eschatological sensitivity affected piety, including greater emphasis upon desire and longing for heaven so the person could be fully united with Jesus and increase social compassion for those less fortunate.

HERMENEUTICAL FRAMEWORK

Spiritual classics have been produced in many genres. During the early modern period sermons were the primary form of spiritual writing.

---

[5]Contemporary understandings of allegorical reading, which may favor wildly divergent interpretations of Scripture, are quite different from those practiced in the early modern period. For a helpful summary of the primary issues related to this see *Dictionary for Theological Interpretation of the Bible*, ed. Kevin Vanhoozer (Grand Rapids: Baker Academic, 2005), pp. 34-36, 823-27.

[6]Both Philipp Jacob Spener and August Hermann Francke eschewed the allegorical reading of Song of Songs. However, Count Zinzendorf greatly embraced this method for reading Canticles.

Many treatises and devotional manuals were initially collections of sermons preached to a local congregation. Spiritual classics took many other forms, including diaries, especially among the Puritans, letters of spiritual counsel and encouragement, and hymns written for worship. Further, theological works often included polemical arguments that sought to justify their position over an opposing group.

Since the primary focus of spiritual reading is to enter into the text with one's mind and heart it is helpful to seek the Holy Spirit's guidance. As you slowly read through a text ask yourself, what do you notice? What is the author's context and who is his or her audience? What is the origin and motivation for writing the specific classic? It is critical that contemporary readers respect the historical distance between the text and our world. We must also recognize that our questions, as important as they are to us, might not have been the questions of an earlier time. Further, how do you respond to the spiritual classic you are reading? What attracts you and invites you into the text? What creates confusion or resistance as you read the passage? For example, in observing the principle of repetition, what key words, phrases or metaphors are used? What themes receive the greatest attention? What seems missing or unusual, or would you have expected to be included? Conversely, what surprised you that was included? What are the sources, both biblical and nonbiblical, employed by the author? What is the structure of the work and how does the author develop the main points? Further, realize that not everything from earlier centuries translates into our own time period. Therefore, what themes are no longer relevant for retrieval, and conversely what insights could instruct the contemporary church? Additionally, recognize that polemical writings present a one-sided treatment of a topic.

ENGLISH PURITANS

John Bunyan's perennial classic *The Pilgrim's Progress* is the most popular spiritual classic of Puritanism.[7] However, because of its great reputation

---

[7]For a good overview to Puritanism see Frances J. Bremer, *Puritanism: A Very Short Introduction* (Oxford: Oxford University Press, 2009); John Spurr, *English Puritanism, 1603-1689* (New York: St. Martin's Press, 1998); and Leland Ryken, *Worldly Saints* (Grand Rapids: Zondervan, 1986).

that continues even today, other less well-known sources to contemporary readers will be examined.[8]

Lewis Bayly (d. 1631). Lewis Bayly, ordained as a Church of England minister, served in a variety of positions and in 1616 became the bishop of Bangor, Wales.[9] *The Practice of Piety*, with its subtitle *Directing a Christian How to Walk, that He May Please God*, was based on a series of sermons probably preached early in his ministry that soon became a bestselling classic. The initial publication is uncertain, but the second edition appeared in 1612, quickly followed by a third in 1613. This popular work appeared in Dutch, French, German, Swedish, Hungarian, Polish, Czech and even in the Native American language in Massachusetts. In fact, next to Bunyan's *Pilgrim's Progress*, *The Practice of Piety* was the most significant book in England. Bunyan acknowledges that *The Practice of Piety*, one of two books his wife brought into their marriage, was instrumental in his own conversion. Additionally, *The Practice of Piety* strongly influenced both the *Nadere Reformatie* and German Pietists.

This classic work, written in the genre of a devotional manual, was intended specifically for the laity. A helpful question to guide reading such a work is, what is the nature and purpose of a devotional manual and how should one seek to read it? Clearly the primary purpose is to promote godly living with God and one's neighbor. Further, it is essential to recognize that a devotional manual is not read as other books are. Rather, one must approach it prayerfully, reading slowly, pausing to ponder and practicing the spiritual exercises. This reflects the self-implicating nature of spiritual writings,[10] that is, how are you as the reader challenged, encouraged and refreshed by your reading of a given text? Additionally, since this manual seeks to teach a method of meditation,

---

[8]For a good introduction to Bunyan and *Pilgrim's Progress* see Richard L. Greaves, *John Bunyan* (Grand Rapids: Eerdmans, 1969); and Gordon Wakefield, *John Bunyan the Christian* (London: Fount, 1992).

[9]Surprisingly, despite Bayly's great importance in shaping Puritan and later Pietistic devotional writing, little has been written on him. The best sources are J. E. Bailey, "Bishop Lewis Bayly and His 'Practice of Piety,'" *Manchester Quarterly* 2 (1883): 201-19; and C. J. Stranks, *Anglican Devotion* (London: SCM Press, 1961), pp. 36-63. Bayly was the subject of a 2009 conference in the Netherlands. However, this work is in Dutch. W. J. Op't Hof, A. A. den Hollander and F. W. Huisman, eds., *De Praktijk der Godzaligheid: Studies over De Praktijk ofte Oeffeninghe der Godzaligheyd (1620) van Lewis Bayly* (Amsterdam: Free University of Amsterdam, 2009).

[10]Schwanda, "Hearts Sweetly Refreshed," p. 30.

one must linger over the passages seeking to experience them more fully. Some scholars detect indebtedness to Ignatius of Loyola's method of meditation.[11] While Bayly was cognizant of these early methods, he brought them into harmony with his own Calvinistic theology. Therefore, while his meditations are likely derivative and reflect a sensory awareness and form reminiscent of Ignatius, they are also strongly distinctive in both his content and motivation for meditation. Regardless of the extent of Ignatian influence, the Roman Catholic Church placed *The Practice of Piety* on its lists of banned books.[12]

Bayly begins *The Practice of Piety* by examining God's nature. He reminds readers of the great importance of God's majesty that is beyond human reason and understanding. In reality, Bayly warns about being overly curious and neglecting to recognize the mystery that surrounds God.[13] Once he establishes God's nature, he categorizes the two possible paths of humanity: one of misery and rebellion from God, and the other of obedience and seeking after God. The bishop often provided specific models of prayer for guiding his readers. This alerts readers that seventeenth-century Puritans, who were the forerunners to evangelicalism, were not averse to using form prayers. They recognized that Christians often needed models to teach them how to pray. Additionally Bayly devotes two rather lengthy sections to sabbath keeping and the Lord's Supper, and also explores in great detail sickness and preparing for death.

Hermeneutically, readers will need to be attentive to a number of key metaphors in *The Practice of Piety*. Significantly, Bayly employs the language of "ravishment," which will be noticed in other classics in this chapter as a term of spiritual delight.[14] This language from the Song of Songs 4:9 (see NRSV) reflects the great intensity of love that was common

---

[11]Gordon Wakefield, *Puritan Devotion* (London: Epworth Press, 1957), p. 87; and Carl Trueman, "Lewis Bayly and Richard Baxter," in *The Pietist Theologians*, ed. Carter Lindberg (Malden, MA: Blackwell, 2005), p. 54.

[12]Bailey, "Bishop Lewis Bayly," p. 204. For a more nuanced treatment of the distinctions between Ignatian and Puritan mediation see Tom Schwanda, *Soul Recreation: The Contemplative-Mystical Piety of Puritanism* (Eugene, OR: Pickwick, 2012), pp. 140-42.

[13]Lewis Bayly, *The Practice of Piety* (Morgan, PA: Soli Deo Gloria, n.d.), p. 10. This book is based on the 1842 edition that unfortunately reduced many of Bayly's patristic and medieval marginal references. For the complete references see the 1616 edition available at the Early English Books Online database. All citations are from Soli Deo Gloria edition.

[14]Bayly, *Practice of Piety*, pp. 51, 66, 70, 188, 339.

in spiritual writing. It also relates to Bayly's usage of bridal language that pictures Jesus as the bridegroom and the Christian as the bride. This is dependent on union with Christ, or as the Puritans often called it, spiritual marriage. Bayly writes, "[O] Saviour, put my soul in a readiness, that like a wise virgin, having the wedding-garment of thy righteousness and holiness, she may be ready to meet thee at thy coming with oil in her lamp. Marry her unto thyself, that she may be one with thee in everlasting love and fellowship."[15] Bayly follows the long tradition within the church that in spiritual marriage Jesus Christ marries the soul of the believer, and not the actual person. The Puritans recognized that the human soul was feminine, and therefore Jesus Christ as husband would be marrying the feminine soul of both women and men.[16] This language has a long and rich history that began before the medieval period, and most Puritan and Pietist authors greatly admired Bernard of Clairvaux (1090-1153) who frequently employed this metaphor.

Those who engage in Bayly meditatively will discover some sections that do not resonate with them. For example, some are likely to disagree with his exegesis that sickness is a result of human sin.[17] Further his polemic against Roman Catholicism for their "false worship of Popery" and "abuse of popish auricular confessions" are reflective of his seventeenth-century context.[18] This reminds us that not every topic from spiritual classics is accurate or relevant for today. Nonetheless, the insights and wisdom of this work can still challenge and refresh any person who reads it slowly and devotionally.

Richard Baxter (1615-1691). Richard Baxter, pastor and theologian, was the most prolific of any seventeenth-century Puritan writer.[19] Amazingly, he accomplished this through an education that was largely self-taught. During his early formative years William Perkins (1558-1602) and Richard Sibbes (1577-1635) strongly influenced him. Baxter was extremely well read and knew the best of patristic and medieval sources as

---

[15]Ibid., p. 290.
[16]Ibid., pp. 33, 242.
[17]Ibid., p. 263.
[18]Ibid., pp. 137, 320-21.
[19]For background see Geoffrey F. Nuttall, *Richard Baxter* (London: Nelson, 1965); and Neil Keeble, *Richard Baxter: Puritan Man of Letters* (Oxford: Clarendon Press, 1982).

well as those of the Protestant Reformation. Augustine, Cyprian and Jean Gerson are frequently quoted in his ever-popular *Saints' Everlasting Rest* (1650).[20] Baxter grounds this classic in more historical sources than any of the works examined in this chapter.[21] Baxter's numerous writings were instrumental in converting many fellow Puritans and greatly influenced the next generations of evangelicals, including John Wesley, Philip Doddridge, Isaac Watts, George Whitefield, William Wilberforce and Charles Spurgeon in the next century. Baxter served as a chaplain in the Parliamentary Army until a serious illness forced his retirement in 1647. His struggle with fragile health that began in childhood would plague him throughout his long life. This sickness lasted five months, and the uncertainty of recovering motivated his meditation on Hebrews 4:9 and the Christian's eternal rest and future hope of heaven's glory. The initial publication of the *Saints' Everlasting Rest* contained only part one, which defined the nature of this heavenly rest, and part four, which offered a directory of how to attain this rest. Later Baxter added part two, which includes a lengthy biblical proof of the believer's rest, and part three, which examines why people might neglect this rest, including the many hindrances that one might face and the critical necessity of not ignoring this greatly needed discipline.

Baxter is a popular but not necessarily easy writer to comprehend. His tendency toward verbosity and lengthy paragraphs that can run for a number of pages challenge the contemporary reader. However, once you recognize that Baxter is a man of method, and ask the proper questions of interpretation, the potential for confusion radically decreases. Two very helpful hermeneutical questions to ask when reading Baxter relate to his method of writing and his method for meditation. First, while Baxter employs various ways of writing, there are two relevant themes in particular to recognize at this point. On the one hand he is fond of making comparisons, moving from the concrete to the abstract. Repeatedly he seeks to convince his readers that the earthly life is insig-

---

[20]A valuable analysis of this classic remains John Knott, *The Sword of the Spirit* (Chicago: University of Chicago Press, 1980), pp. 62-82.

[21]Unfortunately the Christian Focus Publication edition used for this article includes only a few of Baxter's extensive references. See Baxter, *Saints' Everlasting Rest*, Christian Directory 3 (Morgan, PA: Soli Deo Gloria, n.d.), for the complete citations.

nificant in comparison to the heavenly life. On the other hand Baxter frequently utilizes the Puritan technique of "spiritualizing" the creature. He invites his readers to

> make an advantage of every object thou seest, and of every passage of Divine providence, and of everything that befalls in thy labour and calling, to mind thy soul of its approaching rest. . . . Every creature hath the name of God, and of our final rest, written upon it, which a considerate believer may as truly discern, as he can read upon a post or hand, in a cross-way, the name of the town or city which it points to.[22]

Second, it is even more critical to identify the method of meditation employed by Baxter. *Saints' Everlasting Rest* is primarily a manual on heavenly meditation. Readers who grasp his method of meditation are helped with the deepening awareness of the insight and wisdom that is still highly germane for the contemporary church. For Baxter, meditation is essentially the same as heavenly contemplation. He relies heavily on the rational nature of the human person. This principle relates to "consideration," which was a method of moving rational thoughts from the head to the heart so that they could be better experienced. Soliloquy is another aspect of Baxter's method, which he defines as "preaching to one's self."[23] He illustrates this by his "O my soul" formulas sprinkled throughout the text. The purpose of a soliloquy is to stir up the affections to encourage greater experience of the biblical truth. Equally important for Baxter is the sanctified use of imagination when meditating on Scripture. For Baxter the fruit of this heavenly meditation is a contemplative enjoyment of God that is available to anyone who follows this form of meditation. Clearly, this spiritual practice should be engaged regularly because of the possible benefits that a person might experience,

> habituate thyself to such contemplations, and let not those thoughts be seldom and cursory, but settle upon them; dwell here: bathe thy soul in heaven's delights; drench thine affections in these rivers of pleasure, or rather, in this sea of consolation. . . . Thou wilt then find thyself in the suburbs of heaven, and as it were, in a new world.[24]

---

[22]Baxter, *Saints' Everlasting Rest*, p. 541.
[23]Ibid., p. 594.
[24]Ibid., p. 484.

The *Saints' Everlasting Rest* is a massive work that runs 672 pages in the edition used for this chapter. This vast size can be daunting to many readers. Therefore, it might be helpful to first read the introductory section of part one, which defines the heavenly rest, and then to read part four. [25] This section, "A Directory for the Getting and Keeping of the Heart in Heaven," provides the richest devotional treatment of this valuable classic. Baxter concludes this section with a thirty-one-page sample meditation to demonstrate both his method as well as the potential fruit of this spiritual discipline. This meditation integrates all of his previous principles and lavishly illustrates the language of ravishment and contemplative enjoyment of God. Western readers who have attained even a very modest means of success by worldly standards and can easily be tempted to the deception of the abundance of this present earthly life would greatly benefit from the reorientation that Baxter's *Saints' Everlasting Life* offers.

Samuel Rutherford (c. 1600-1661). Samuel Rutherford, Scottish theologian and devotional and political writer, often found himself in the middle of controversy.[26] His Presbyterianism and strong desire for a covenantal form of church government frequently clashed with the episcopacy of the Scottish Church. Twice he appeared before the high commission for his nonconformist resistance. In 1636 he was deposed from his ministry at Anwoth and exiled for two years to Aberdeen, a bastion of episcopacy. The emotional and spiritual anguish of separation from his much beloved congregation became the inspiration for 220 of his 365 letters. The devotional genre of *Letters* is personal and Rutherford never intended them for publication. While letters by their very nature are highly contextual and specific, their content often transcends time with wisdom that speaks across the centuries. The enduring legacy of these letters of spiritual guidance is traced to the recurring themes of God's comfort, hope and deepening intimacy with Jesus Christ even

---

[25]Ibid., pp. 4-33, 454-658.
[26]For background see John Coffey, "Letters by Samuel Rutherford (1600-1661)," in *The Devoted Life: An Invitation to the Puritan Classics*, ed. Kelly M. Kapic and Randall C. Gleason (Downers Grove, IL: InterVarsity Press, 2004), pp. 92-107. For a more detailed study see John Coffey, *Politics, Religion and the British Revolutions: The Mind of Samuel Rutherford* (Cambridge: Cambridge University Press, 1997).

amid the numerous afflictions of life. Rutherford's *Letters* became a spiritual classic, influencing many. John Wesley edited some for his *Christian Library* (1750). Additionally Charles Spurgeon, Alexander Whyte and Hudson Taylor all attested to their value. In popularity and importance they surpass Martin Luther's *Letters of Spiritual Counsel*. Rutherford also served as a delegate to the Westminster Assembly (1643-1649), during which time he composed *Lex Rex* (1644), which defended the peoples' right to armed resistance against Charles I.

Reading Rutherford's *Letters* for the first time may create strong reactions of shock and confusion. Indeed it is not uncommon for contemporary readers to be repulsed by the strong erotic language of this writing. Therefore, a valuable hermeneutical principle would be to first read through the book of Song of Songs allegorically or spiritually in one sitting, recognizing that Jesus is the bridegroom and that we are his bride. John Coffey helpfully provides another interpretative principle for reading Rutherford, asserting that his "favorite theme was the beauty of Christ."[27] Once we understand the deep personal relationship between Rutherford and Jesus, the themes and metaphors take on greater significance. This further highlights the great importance of union with Christ or the spiritual marriage metaphor of intimacy. Moreover, Rutherford is continually referring to Jesus as the bridegroom and husband, and Rutherford and his readers as the spouse or bride of Jesus.

The author frequently speaks of violence and comments, "Your Master, Christ, won heaven with strokes: it is a besieged castle; it must be taken with violence."[28] This reference to Matthew 11:12 was frequently used in Puritan literature. They recognized the seriousness and pervasiveness of sin. Violence was often combined with vehemence and the intensity of God's love was stressed as a necessity to overcome the power of sin. From this flows an almost continuous fountain of love language to capture Rutherford's desire and deep longing for Jesus Christ as well as his prayers for his readers to experience the same. A sampling of the semantic range of this bridal language includes "love-beams," "love-

---

[27]Coffey, "Letters by Samuel Rutherford," p. 103.
[28]Samuel Rutherford, cited in *The Letters of Samuel Rutherford*, ed. Andrew Bonar (Edinburgh: Banner of Truth, 1984), p. 271.

smiles," "love-sick" and "sick of love," "love-letters," "love-fever," "love-banquets" and "love-songs." Additionally the references to the kisses of Jesus are voluminous. Rutherford declares,

> Oh, who knoweth how sweet Christ's kisses are! Who hath been more kindly embraced and kissed than I, His banished prisoner? If the comparison could stand, I would not exchange Christ with heaven itself. He hath left a dart and arrow of love in my soul, and it paineth me till He come and take it out.[29]

Clearly there is a reciprocal relationship in this love language, as Rutherford confesses; "Christ hath given me the marriage kiss, and He hath my marriage-love: we have made up a full bargain, that shall not go back on either side."[30] Significantly gender appears to have no effect on the style of these letters since half of them were written to men.

One must further recognize the effect of Rutherford's exile from his friends and his ability to provide them with pastoral care. His separation from his beloved congregation echoes the repetitive cycle of withdrawal and return of the bridegroom in the Song of Songs, which reminded the Puritans that there would be periods of isolation in which they did not sense the "felt presence" of God. But just as the bridegroom returned, so would there be new periods of communion. Therefore, while God never withdraws from the union between believers, there are times in which the joyful sense of communion fades. Clearly the combination of exile and affliction are powerful motivators for deepening desire and intimacy for both human friends and spiritual marriage with Jesus.

These well-loved letters are still read today by those in the Reformed and evangelical traditions, and they help to orient readers to the importance of not only enjoying life on earth but looking forward with greater delight to heaven. One longs for heaven, not to escape from the turmoil and tension of this life but rather since one has already tasted the love of Jesus Christ, the divine Bridegroom and Husband, one longs for the consummation and fulfillment of that union with Christ. Rutherford

---

[29]Rutherford, *Letters of Samuel Rutherford*, pp. 226-67.
[30]Ibid., p. 251.

further reminds contemporary readers of the providential care and sustaining support of God amid temptations and struggles of life.

NADERE REFORMATIE

Willem Teellinck (1579-1629). Willem Teellinck, known as the Father of the *Nadere Reformatie*, had originally studied law.[31] However, during his first visit to England in 1604 he experienced a radical conversion at a Puritan day of prayer. Living with a Puritan family further shaped his faith, encouraging him to study theology and become a pastor. Teellinck's spectrum of reading was broadly ecumenical. He drew his greatest inspiration through reading Puritan writings, especially those of William Perkins and William Ames (1576-1633). He was also shaped by Bernard of Clairvaux, Johann Tauler (c. 1300-1361), and in particular, Thomas à Kempis (c. 1380-1471) and his well-known *Initiation of Christ*. In fact, Teellinck has been called the second Thomas à Kempis.[32] Not surprisingly, these works formed a vital contemplative theme within his piety. However, Teellinck's usage of à Kempis and other Western Catholic devotional writers were refined through his own Calvinistic theology. Teellinck's oeuvre totals 127 works, but unfortunately the only major book translated into English is *The Path of True Godliness*. Some of his other significant spiritual classics include *The New Jerusalem*, *The Key to True Devotion* and "his most mystic work," *Soliloquy*.[33] Teellinck's writings influenced many readers both within the *Nadere Reformatie* and Reformed circles in Germany.

A critical hermeneutical principle that contemporary readers must face in reading ancient texts is sensitivity to the historical context so as

---

[31]For a good introduction to *Nadere Reformatie* see Fred van Lieburg, "From Pure Church to Pious Culture: The Further Reformation in the Seventeenth-Century Dutch Republic," in *Later Calvinism: International Perspectives*, ed. W. Fred Graham (Kirksville: Northeast Missouri State University, 1995), pp. 408-29. For more information, see the Nadere Reformatie website: www .ssnr.nl. For background on Willem Teellinck see Arie de Reuver, *Sweet Communion: Trajectories of Spirituality from the Middle Ages Through the Further Reformation*, trans. James A. DeJong (Grand Rapids: Baker Academic, 2007), pp. 105-60; and Willem Teellinck, *The Path of True Godliness*, trans. Annemie Godbehere, ed. Joel R. Beeke (Grand Rapids: Baker, 2003), pp. 11-29.

[32]De Reuver, *Sweet Communion*, p. 105.

[33]Willem op't Hof, "Protestant Pietism and Medieval Monasticism," in *Confessionalism and Pietism: Religious Reform in Early Modern Europe*, ed. Fred van Lieburg (Mainz: Verlag Philipp von Zabern, 2006), p. 48.

not to project their own expectations on earlier generations. Likewise, some individuals avoid reading introductions to a work. That would be a serious mistake, especially with Teellinck, since his background information is essential for understanding the seventeenth-century Dutch culture and church life. He was deeply frustrated by the anemic faith and lack of a more consistent and godly lifestyle of people. Further, the footnotes throughout this book provide valuable insights for recognizing themes that would otherwise likely elude readers.

One of the primary goals of the *Nadere Reformatie* was the recovery of a practical godliness that both informed the mind and inspired the heart. *The Path of True Godliness* reflects this critical integration revealing the necessity for all Christians to deepen their spiritual maturity with God. Teellinck begins this work of sanctification by exploring the character of true godliness. He then examines both the kingdom of darkness, which opposes God, and the kingdom of grace, which inspires faithful living for God. The remainder of this work considers the various means for motivating and attaining the practice of godliness.

There are two hermeneutical questions that provide helpful guidance for reading Teellinck. The first is related to structure and the second to the nature of his theology. There is no denying that Teellinck's writing style tends toward verbosity. Ultimately this is a structural issue related to the influence of Perkins, often called the "Father of Puritanism." Perkins developed his preaching style, in part, based on the Aristotelian method that had been refined by Peter Ramus (1515-1572). This method employed a series of divisions and subdivisions that can become quite exhausting and difficult for contemporary readers to follow. However, this is a good reminder that classics are often best read five to ten pages at a time to encourage greater reflection and meditation on the wisdom of the given classic.

Second, an awareness of Teellinck's theology provides a helpful guidance for reading this work. Most authors of this period shared his perception of God's transcendence without compromising God's immanence. This created a strong awareness of God's holiness, and like Bayly, Teellinck took sin seriously and recognized the manifold ways it could destroy relationships between God and other persons. Unfortunately, our contemporary age tends to treat sin and holiness more casually and therefore may question Teellinck's almost relentless concern for recognizing the effects of sin in the believer's life. Central to understanding Teellinck is his passionate desire for intimate union and communion with God. Clearly the Holy Spirit orchestrates this process of sanctification and cultivates the passionate longing and love for Jesus. This explains the meticulous concern for behavior, both internal and external, that at times earned the *Nadere Reformatie* the name of precisionists.[34] Further, a central key to grasping the significance of Teellinck's agenda for sanctification is the importance of a "teachable heart." Moreover, he challenges his readers "to open [their] heart to God's promises."[35] This reinforces the importance of watching over one's heart. Readers aware of the Russian Orthodox classic of Theophan the Recluse (1815-1894), *The Unseen Warfare*, will recognize a number of interesting parallels with Teellinck's treatment of self-examination. Additionally, Teellinck's theology of suffering and affliction is more nuanced than that of Bayly. Once again one detects the consistent concern for living a faithful life unto God and one's neighbors, which is still critical in our day.

THE GERMAN PIETISTS

Philipp Jacob Spener (1635-1705). Philipp Jacob Spener, often known as the father of German Pietism, was greatly disturbed by the lack of spiritual vitality in his native Lutheran church.[36] At an early age he read the Puritan writings of Bayly, Baxter and others who introduced him to the importance of experimental piety. Later he was deeply inspired by Johann Arndt's (1555-1621) *True Christianity* and the former Jesuit turned Reformed mystic Jean de Labadie (1610-1674). Additionally, in *Pia Desideria* (i.e., heartfelt desires) Spener declares the importance of many patristic writers, the medieval mystics Tauler and à Kempis, but most importantly Luther. He, in turn, profoundly influenced Francke, Zinzendorf, and

---

[34]See, for example, Teellinck, *Path of True Godliness*, pp. 176-236.

[35]Ibid., pp. 154-55, 223; cf. Beeke, "Dutch Second Reformation," p. 301.

[36]For a good introduction to German Pietism see Brown, *Understanding Pietism*; and F. Ernest Stoeffler, *The Rise of Evangelical Pietism* (Leiden: Brill, 1971), pp. 180-246. For background on Spener see K. James Stein, *Philipp Jakob Spener: Pietistic Patriarch* (Chicago: Covenant Press, 1986); and Brown, *Understanding Pietism*, pp. 25-89.

many future church leaders. Spener became frustrated with the excessively rigid orthodoxy of his Lutheran Church. At the request of others in 1670 he created a small group for the purpose of cultivating spiritual edification. This group, which met twice weekly in his home, became known as *collegia pietatis* (i.e., pious groups) and included a commentary on the most recent sermon or other devotional reading, an opportunity to discuss that message or writing, and concluded by signing a hymn. While these small groups, often called conventicles, were more common in Puritanism and the *Nadere Reformatie* that had previously made provision for reading Scripture and prayer outside of worship, they created controversy within Lutheranism. Many Lutheran church leaders feared the potential for separatism, which unfortunately became reality. In response to this increasing controversy, Spener distanced himself from these groups and concentrated his efforts on catechizing children.

Pia Desideria first appeared as Spener's introduction to Arndt's *True Christianity* in 1675. The positive response to his introduction prompted its publication as a stand-alone work later that same year. A critical hermeneutical principle for reading spiritual classics is recognizing the nature and dynamics of the specific genre being studied. This further entails a realization of the context of the author. While this awareness is essential for reading any work, it is perhaps more crucial in reading Spener than other authors in this chapter. This work belongs to the genre of devotional and edification literature. While that is clearly true, the first section has a polemical edge as Spener critiques the overly academic and sterile use of Scripture within the Lutheran Church. There are three parts to this book: a diagnosis of the ineffectiveness of the Lutheran Church in properly using Scripture, the possibility for restoring the church and a sixfold suggestion toward that renewal.

While some readers launch immediately into a book before reading the introduction, given Spener's context it is essential to first comprehend his setting.[37] His primary goal for writing is recovering the proper reading and formative power of Scripture. That awareness provides an entry to his double critique of his context. His first concern was that, in Luther-

---

[37]Philip Jacob Spener, *Pia Desideria*, trans. Theodore G. Tappert (Philadelphia: Fortress Press, 1964), pp. 1-28.

anism, while Scripture was readily available to the common person, it was treated overly academically and objectively in Lutheran sermons. Therefore, rather than serving its proper intention of transforming readers for practical Christian living, it became a tool for disputation and display of the preacher's erudite knowledge of the original biblical languages. Further, the previous efforts of Luther and Arndt of integrating the head and heart in reading Scripture had vanished.

Spener's second critique against the Roman Catholic Church becomes evident once one enters the text. He refers to them as the "anti-Christian Babel."[38] This reflects the residual consequences of the Thirty Years' War, but even more it is a reaction to the systematic suppression of any use of Scripture by the laity. Spener's frequent attacks on Roman Catholicism can be difficult for modern readers who live in a greater ecumenical age. Clearly, the distance between Protestants and Roman Catholics has diminished in many areas. But readers must recognize that Spener's concerns against Rome actually existed until Vatican II (1962-1965), when the Bible was finally returned to the people and parishes organized small groups for Bible study and education.

Unquestionably the third section of *Pia Desideria* gives this classic its vital influence. Here Spener outlines his sixfold proposal for the renewal of the church. First, the use of Scripture needs to be expanded and read more frequently in homes and small groups. Second, the laity needs to be given greater opportunities for serving and participating in the church's ministry. Third, one must not only hear the Word but also actually demonstrate it in love to others. Fourth, one should be guided by love and unity of the church when drawn into controversy. Fifth, the education of ministers should emphasize piety by transforming seminaries into "nurseries of the church." Sixth, preaching should edify believers and produce the fruits of faith. However, it would be a mistake to ignore the first two parts of this book that prepares the reader for both the need and importance of his proposals. Readers will soon recognize Spener's priority for the biblical principle of cultivation of the inner life of the heart.[39] One should remember that this was Jesus' primary

---

[38]Ibid., p. 40; cf. pp. 69-75.
[39]Ibid., pp. 116-17.

concern with the Pharisees, who tended to focus on the externals of religion in a similar highly orthodox manner (see Mk 7:1-23). Another possible difficulty in reading *Pia Desideria* occurs in his fourth proposal.[40] Spener's description for the proper handling of theological controversy could appear to modern readers to be rather arrogant in his intention to correct and convince others that he knows the truth. Controversy and debate were common, however, and it is important to realize that Spener expected a wholehearted embrace of Scripture as the sole basis for truth. Further, Spener is quick to acknowledge his own lack of perfection and need for continual self-examination. He invites others to reveal his own weaknesses and shortcomings of the truth.[41] A similar pattern of humility that desires to read and apply Scripture to one's life would strengthen and renew today's church.

August Hermann Francke (1663-1727). August Hermann Francke was the second-generation leader of German Pietism. Before he met Spener, Francke faced a lengthy spiritual struggle for repentance (*Busskampf*).[42] This wrestling reached a climax in 1687 when he was invited to preach his first sermon. During his study of John 20:31 he finally experienced his long-desired spiritual rebirth. Following his conversion Francke met Spener, who in turn became his mentor. Francke's intense spiritual struggle and radical shift of rebirth highlight a significant distinction between them.[43] Spener never faced the same uncertainty regarding his faith, nor could he date the time of his conversion, and therefore it possessed a different meaning for him. This is a good reminder: throughout this chapter, whether we consider the Puritans or Pietists, there were distinctions not only between these similar devotional movements but equally within them. As an outgrowth of Francke's more belabored conversion there also arose a growing sense of legalism that was not present in Spener.

Due to Francke's passion for heart experience and his increasing

---

[40]Ibid., pp. 97-102.

[41]Ibid., p. 45; cf. pp. 85-86.

[42]For background on Francke see Gary R. Sattler, *God's Glory, Neighbor's Good* (Chicago: Covenant Press, 1982); and Richard L. Gawthrop, *Pietism and the Making of Eighteenth-Century Prussia* (Cambridge: Cambridge University Press, 1993), pp. 121-222.

[43]Gawthrop, *Pietism and Eighteenth-Century Prussia*, pp. 139-44.

criticism of the orthodox Lutheran clergy, his early years were filled with controversy and short-term pastorates. His life took a sharp turn when he was appointed professor of Hebrew and Greek languages at the newly formed Halle University, as well as pastor of Glaucha, a suburb of Halle known for its immorality. Francke later received the additional position of professor of theology. His concern for the poor and various needs of the town intersected with his creative and organizational genius as he began developing multiple institutions (*stiftungen*) that covered the spectrum from education for poor children, an orphanage, a medical dispensary, publishing house for printing Bibles and various mission efforts. Clearly there was a strong activist strain in Francke's life as he sought to reform both church and society; however, he did not neglect the cultivation of his spiritual life as demonstrated in his spiritual classics.

Francke was deeply indebted to Johann Arndt's *True Christianity* and also the French Quietist Miguel de Molinos (1628-1697), when he translated Molinos's *Spiritual Guide* into Latin. Additionally he drew wisdom from Chrysostom, Bernard, the *Devotio Moderna* and Puritan devotional writings. Francke and Cotton Mather, the New England Puritan pastor, engaged in a lengthy transatlantic correspondence. Surprisingly, considering Francke's fame, there is no complete edition of his works, and the few that have been translated into English have been rarely republished with any degree of frequency. Nonetheless there are a few samples that provide a helpful perspective into the spirituality of this great leader of German Pietism.

Perhaps the most significant work of Francke's personal piety and the best public expression of that is his "Scriptural Rules for Life" (1695).[44] This work reflects the devotional genre of resolutions. Unlike the genre of a diary that records and reflects on past events, resolutions look to the future and express the desire for reforming one's belief and behavior more fully around some Christian ideal. Francke originally wrote this for himself in 1689 but later published it at the urging of his friends. One potential stumbling block for a first-time reader is the realization that in

---

[44]Sattler, *God's Glory, Neighbor's Good*, pp. 199-237.

the early modern period even conservative Christians quoted the Apocrypha. While they did not grant it the same authority as the sixty-six canonical books of Scripture, they did appreciate its value when it supported Scripture. Therefore, Francke's frequent references to Sirach were normal for his day, as it was also for the Puritans.

Since this was a personal account it represents the desires and vision of Francke's life. He sought to live a balanced Christian life, including the importance of fellowship with God through solitude and cultivating healthy company with other Christians. This is clearly depicted in his phrase "God's glory and neighbor's best," which accurately summarizes his life and ministry.[45] There are times when it appears Francke privileges solitude, and he was known for his practice of spending a half a day in solitude with God. But this must be read in conjunction with his concern that unhealthy company is highly injurious to your faith. Further, one recognizes his concern of spiritual dryness of the Lutheran clergy and his reticence to use written prayers.[46] But just as it is critical to sustain a proper balance between fellowship with God and humanity, it is equally essential to maintain the proper balance between the mind and heart. Since Francke emphasizes the omnipresence of God, he realizes that he is always in God's presence. Therefore, he asserts the importance of the fear of God, or as we would say today, reverence, so that the person might preserve an inner tranquility and awareness of God.

Francke preached a sermon in 1697, based on the parable of the rich man and Lazarus (Lk 16:19-31), titled "The Duty to the Poor."[47] The occasion was the dedication of his fund for alleviating poverty. It is crucial to grasp the historical context before reading this sermon. It was addressed to the nobility and scholars of Glaucha. This suburb not only had an immoral reputation, but it was equally demoralized by poverty, and the children often were uneducated. Francke accurately exegetes this text leaving no confusion that his listeners all qualified as wealthy and had a responsibility to help anyone less fortunate than themselves. Once again readers will notice his consistent practice of quoting Scripture and

---

[45]Ibid., pp. 211, 230; cf. p. 226.
[46]Ibid., p. 220; cf. p. 218.
[47]Ibid., pp. 155-85.

the Wisdom of Sirach and the Wisdom of Solomon. This moving sermon still has the potential to convict readers of their responsibility to not only love God but equally to love anyone who is in need today.

Nicholas Ludwig von Zinzendorf (1700-1760). Nicholas Ludwig von Zinzendorf was a Lutheran Pietist and leader of the *Unitas Fratrum* or Moravian Church.[48] While trained as a lawyer, Zinzendorf also pursued theological studies. He was educated in Francke's Halle Pietism, which inspired his missionary zeal. However, Zinzendorf later distanced himself from this strong conversion-centered approach. His theology of the heart was strongly Christocentric and emphasized resting in the wound of Christ's side, which figured prominently in both his sermons and hymns. This was linked to his teaching on spiritual marriage to the crucified Christ that envisioned Jesus as the husband of each Christian soul. Like Rutherford, Zinzendorf enthusiastically embraced the erotic language of the Song of Songs. This deeply inward, experiential spirituality was combined with a fervent zeal for witnessing and missionary efforts.

While grounding himself in Bernard, Luther, Arndt, Spener and Francke, Zinzendorf was also appreciative of Reformed and Roman Catholic theology. His ecumenical spirit, renewed by a strong sense of grace, created a relentless desire to encourage Christian unity through love of Jesus Christ. Over time he became more controversial, especially with the pietistic Lutheran leaders. This tension centered on Zinzendorf's ecumenical spirit, the greater receptivity to enthusiasm and fears that his emphasis on spiritual marriage with Jesus created a distorted understanding of sexuality and gender order. More positively Zinzendorf influenced later evangelicals, in particular John Wesley, as well as Friedrich Schleiermacher and Karl Barth.

Zinzendorf was prolific in producing sermons, letters and liturgical resources. However, his hymns, which number more than two thousand, are the best source for understanding him.[49] Zinzendorf confessed that

---

[48]For background on Zinzendorf see Peter Vogt, "Nicholas Ludwig von Zinzendorf," in *Pietist Theologians*, ed. Carter Lindberg (Malden, MA: Blackwell, 2005), pp. 207-23; and John R. Weinlick, *Count Zinzendorf* (Bethlehem: Moravian Church in America, 1984).

[49]Two helpful studies on Zinzendorf's hymns are Paul Peucker, "The Songs of Sifting: Understanding the Role of Bridal Mysticism in Moravian Piety During the Late 1740s," *Journal of*

"the hymnal is a kind of response to the Bible, an echo and an extension thereof. In the Bible one perceives how the Lord communicates with mankind; and in the hymnal, how mankind communicates with the Lord."[50] Further, "for Zinzendorf, hymns were not ordinary texts but rather a better expression of divine truths; they were theology on a higher level."[51] The devotional genre of hymns reinforces the importance of poetic imagery and reading more slowly and reflectively than the prose of a sermon or a letter of spiritual counsel. In addition to attentiveness to the metaphors and biblical imagery employed, specific hermeneutical guidelines for reading hymns include both the directionality of hymns and how they focus on God. The words of hymns can be directed from God's perspective to humanity or upward from humanity to God or horizontally as the community addresses each other for edification. Further, hymns may be trinitarian in focus or emphasize one member of the Godhead to the exclusion of the others. The most common themes recognized in Zinzendorf's hymns revolve around the passion of Jesus Christ, enjoying union and communion with Christ and other Christians, and witnessing or spreading the gospel.

His best-known hymns, "The Saviour's Blood and Righteousness" and "Christian Hearts, in Love United," regularly appear in contemporary evangelical hymnals.[52] Examining "The Saviour's Blood and Righteousness" reveals many of the classic themes of Zinzendorf. The first nine stanzas of this Christocentric hymn are addressed horizontally to remind the singers of the passion of Jesus, "the spotless Lamb of God." These stanzas are replete with the common Moravian theme of Jesus' blood that paid the ransom for sinful humanity. The final three stanzas transition to the praise of God. Another theme reflecting the strong missionary impetus of the early Moravians is the reminder to witness for the "Lord with zeal and love" (stanza 5, cf. stanza 9). One can readily

Moravian History 3 (2007): 51-71; and C. Daniel Crews, *Zinsendorf: The Theology of Song* (Winston-Salem, NC: Moravian Archives and Moravian Music Foundation, 1999).

[50]*Hymnal and Liturgies of the Moravian Church* (Bethlehem, PA: Moravian Church in America, 1969), p. ii.

[51]Peucker, "Songs of Sifting," p. 54.

[52]The most complete collection of Zinzendorf's hymns in English is *The Liturgy and the Offices of Worship and Hymns of the American Province of the Unitas Fratrum, or Moravian Church* (Winston-Salem, NC: n.p., 1908).

recognize the formative power of this hymn in shaping a theology of gratitude for "my Saviour's blood and death."

"Christian Hearts, in Love United" is another compact summary of Zinzendorf's theology. Like the previous hymn, this also begins horizontally with the congregation affirming the transformative example of Jesus' love. In the first stanza the question is raised, "Has He not your love excited?" followed by the appropriate response, "Then let love inspire each breast." Since Christians share in union with Christ, his love inspires and guides us to grow in unity with others. Clearly this reflects the strong ecumenical character of Zinzendorf. Midway through the fourth stanza the directionality changes in what is the fulcrum of this wonderful hymn, "As Thou art with Him united, Lord may we be one in Thee." The remainder of the hymn continues the same vertical emphasis drawing on the imagery of John 15:1-11, celebrating the union and communion that is available to those who abide in Christ.

One hymn that actually unites both the passion themes of Jesus as the Lamb of God and the potential for union and communion with Christ is "Happy Race of Witnesses." This robust trinitarian hymn blends the imagery of the Passover (Ex 12:7, 13) with the fulfillment that is found in Jesus, the Lamb of God, and follows the same pattern of the previous two hymns. It begins with a horizontal voice to one another, employing rich bridal language waiting until the last two lines of the final stanza before transitioning to a reminder that "this communion love-feast keep" (stanza 3) is "only by Thy blood, O Lamb." What was later said about the early Methodists learning more of their theology from Charles Wesley's hymns than John Wesley's sermons was clearly prefigured for the Moravians in Zinzendorf's hymns.

POSSIBLE USE FOR THE CHURCH TODAY

It would not be surprising if some themes of these spiritual classics created varying levels of discomfort for contemporary readers. Even though our initial tendency might be to reject these emphases because they challenge us, perhaps that is the very reason why they deserve greater attention and possible retrieval for today. First, while there may be opposition to the allegorical reading of the Song of Songs, it was one possible way of reading this text for much of church history. The church frequently argued that since other Scripture communicated the same message (see earlier "Theological Assumptions") it was not inappropriate to extend those themes to Song of Songs. Careful spiritual reading guided by the Holy Spirit could grant the church today a more robust language of desire and delight for intimacy with Jesus Christ. Clearly an intentional reading of this Scripture with a balanced integration of head and heart is likely to cultivate a deepening experience of the triune God.

Second, and directly related, is the importance of reclaiming the biblical metaphor of spiritual marriage. No doubt many readers eagerly embrace the principle of union with Christ. However, this is typically built on the forensic nature of justification, with little awareness of the relational dimension of communion that was so richly present in many of our writers.

Third, within our Western world a preoccupation with externals frequently dominates Christianity. Much time and energy are often devoted to creating a polished image of our relationships with God and others that exaggerate the reality of our lives. Our classics stress the importance of interiority and Jesus' warning not to neglect one's heart (Mt 6:19-21; Lk 6:45). A prayerful reading of these classics will motivate us to chisel off the veneers that often block the deeper penetration of the gospel.

Fourth, a practical means toward integrating these three prophetic guidelines for today is a recovery of the discipline of heavenly meditation. Unfortunately, many Western Christians act as if they have already attained the Promised Land. There is little awareness that our accumulated material possessions are fleeting and lack eternal value. Instead, the intentional practice of heavenly contemplation will transform our gaze from its frozen earth-bound nature and look on Christ who is seated in the heavens (Col 3:1-2). This does not suggest an abandonment of those in need, but rather by spending more time in "the suburbs of heaven" it will transform us to live more fully and compassionately to those around us now.

OTHER IMPORTANT PURITAN AND PIETIST TEXTS

In addition to the broad spectrum of spiritual classics already presented, the following summaries provide an expanded list of other significant spiritual writings.

George Herbert (1593-1633). George Herbert was an English Anglican priest and poet, and while his spirituality was not representative of either Puritanism or Pietism, his contribution to this time period cannot be neglected. He is best known for his work on pastoral care, *The Country Parson*, which vividly describes the themes of holiness and spiritual guidance, as well as his longer work *The Temple*.[53] This far-ranging collection of poems is divided into three sections: "The Church Porch," "The Church" and "The Church Militant."

Paul Gerhardt (1607-1676). Paul Gerhardt, German Lutheran pastor and hymn writer, is best known today for his translation of the meditative Good Friday hymn "O Sacred Head Now Wounded," which has frequently been attributed to Bernard of Clairvaux and his stirring Advent hymn, "O Lord, How Shall I Greet Thee." The largest categories within Gerhardt's hymnal are "Songs of the Cross and Consolation" and "Prayer and the Christian Life."[54]

John Owen (1616-1683). John Owen has frequently been described as the greatest of all Puritan theologians and one of the most articulate writers of Reformed orthodoxy. His corpus includes significant treatises on the nature of sin, justification, Christology, the Holy Spirit and a massive commentary on the book of Hebrews. But he also wrote for the layperson, and his *On Communion with God* provides a refreshing invitation for a person to enjoy fellowship with the Father, the Son and the Holy Spirit.[55]

Henry Scougal (1650-1678). Henry Scougal served briefly as a pastor in his native Scotland before becoming professor of divinity at the University of Aberdeen. His classic *The Life of God in the Soul of Man* was written to encourage virtue and holiness.[56] This work is an extended

---

[53]George Herbert, *The Country Parson, The Temple*, ed. John N. Wall Jr. (Mahwah, NJ: Paulist Press, 1981).

[54]Paul Gerhardt, *Spiritual Songs*, trans. John Kelly (London: Alexander Straham, 1867).

[55]Kelly M. Kapic and Justin Taylor, eds., *Communion with the Triune God* (Wheaton, IL: Crossway Books, 2007). There are numerous editions of this popular work; this contemporary version provides an excellent introductory chapter that explores Owen's trinitarian spirituality.

[56]Henry Scougal, *The Life of God in the Soul of Man* (Ross-shire, UK: Christian Focus Publications, 1996).

meditation on Galatians 4:19 on how a person might experience union with God. Charles Wesley sent it as a gift to George Whitefield, who acknowledged its role in his own conversion.

Elizabeth Singer Rowe (1674-1737). Elizabeth Singer Rowe was an English poet and devotional writer who began writing at the age of twelve. Alexander Pope and Samuel Johnson were two among many who praised her works. Her best known spiritual classic is *Devout Exercises of the Heart*, which explores the themes of assurance of salvation, love of Jesus, enjoyment of God, longing for Christ's return and daily experiences of God's gracious providence.[57]

Philip Doddridge (1702-1751). Philip Doddridge was an English Nonconformist minister and devotional writer who played an active role in the evangelical revival of the eighteenth century and encouraged efforts in evangelism, mission and assorted works of charity. He is best known for *The Rise and Progress of Religion in the Soul* (1745), which was instrumental in the conversion of William Wilberforce.[58] This work represents the best of experimental piety of earlier Puritans and offers practical guidance to deepen a person's life in Christ.

Jonathan Edwards (1703-1758). Jonathan Edwards has often been considered America's most outstanding theologian. His preaching made a significant contribution to the Great Awakening. Edwards is known for many outstanding works, but two spiritual classics are his *Religious Affections*, which guides readers in discerning whether spiritual experiences are genuine from God or counterfeit, and his brief *Personal Narrative*, which offers a rare and surprising glimpse into the spiritual practices and contemplative experiences from an early period of Edwards's life.[59]

---

[57]Elizabeth Rowe, *The Works of Mrs. Elizabeth Rowe*, vol. 2, *Devout Exercises of the Heart* (London: John & Arthur Arch, 1796).

[58]Philip Doddridge, *The Rise and Progress of Religion in the Soul* (Grand Rapids: Baker, 1977).

[59]Jonathan Edwards, *The Religious Affections* (Carlisle, PA: Banner of Truth, 1961); and Jonathan Edwards, *Personal Narrative*, in *Letters and Personal Writings*, ed. George Claghorn (New Haven and London: Yale University Press, 1998), 16:790-804.

Suggested Reading

PRIMARY READINGS OF SPIRITUAL CLASSICS

Aelred of Rievaulx, *Spiritual Friendship*. Kalamazoo, MI: Cistercian Publications, 2005.

Alighieri, Dante. *The Inferno*. Translated by Anthony Esolen. New York: Modern Library, 2002.

———. *Paradise*. Translated by Anthony Esolen. New York: Modern Library, 2004.

———. *Purgatory*. Translated by Anthony Esolen. New York: Modern Library, 2003.

Anonymous. *The Way of the Pilgrim*. Translated by R. M. French. San Francisco: HarperCollins, 1965.

Anselm of Canterbury. *The Major Works*. Edited by Brian Davies and G. R. Evans. Oxford: Oxford University Press, 1998.

———. *The Prayers and Meditations of St. Anselm, with the Proslogion*. Translated by Benedicta Ward. London: Penguin, 1973.

Aquinas, Thomas. *Summa Theologiae*. London: Eyre & Spottiswoode, 1964.

Arndt, Johann. *Johann Arndt: True Christianity*. Translated by Peter C. Erb. New York: Paulist Press, 1979.

Athanasius, *The Life of Antony and the Letter to Marcellinus*. Classics of Western Spirituality. New York: Paulist Press, 1980.

Augustine. *Augustine of Hippo, Selected Writings*. Classics of Western Spirituality. New York: Paulist Press, 1984.

———. *The Confessions*. Edited by John E. Rotelle. Translated by Maria Boulding. Hyde Park, NY: New City Press, 1997.

———. *Expositions of the Psalms*, 5 vols. The Works of Augustine: A translation for the 21st century. Edited by John E. Rotelle. Hyde Park, NY: New City Press, 2000.

———. *Homilies on 1 John 7.5*. In *Nicene and Post-Nicene Fathers*, First Series. Vol. 7. Translated by H. Browne. Edited by Philip Schaff. Buffalo, NY: Christian Literature Publishing, 1888, www.newadvent.org/fathers/170207.htm.

Bamberger, John, ed. *Evagrius Ponticus: The Praktikos and Chapters on Prayer.* Spencer, MA: Cistercian Publications, 1970.

Basil of Caesarea. *Basil of Caesarea: On the Holy Spirit.* Translated by D. Anderson. Crestwood, NY: St. Vladimir's Seminary Press, 1980.

Baxter, Richard. *The Practical Works of Richard Baxter.* Vol. 1, *A Christian Directory.* Morgan, PA: Soli Deo Gloria, 2000.

———. *The Practical Works of Richard Baxter.* Vol. 3, *The Saint's Everlasting Rest.* Morgan, PA: Soli Deo Gloria, 2000.

Bayly, Lewis. *The Practice of Piety.* Morgan, PA: Soli Deo Gloria, 1994.

Bede. *Bede: On the Tabernacle.* Translated by Arthur G. Holder. Liverpool: Liverpool University Press, 1994.

Benedict of Nursia. *RB 1980: The Rule of St. Benedict in Latin and English with Notes.* Edited by Timothy Fry. Collegeville, MN: Liturgical Press, 1981.

———. *The Rule of St. Benedict.* Edited by Anthony C. Meisel and M. L. del Mastro. New York: Doubleday, 1975.

Bernard of Clairvaux. *Bernard of Clairvaux: On Loving God.* Translated by Robert Walton. Kalamazoo, MI: Cistercian Publications, 1995.

———. *Bernard of Clairvaux: On the Song of Songs I.* Translated by Kilian Walsh. Kalamazoo, MI: Cistercian Publications, 1971.

———. *Bernard of Clairvaux: On the Song of Songs IV.* Translated by Irene Edmonds. Kalamazoo, MI: Cistercian Publications, 1980.

———. *Bernard of Clairvaux, Treatises II: The Steps of Humility and Pride and On Loving God.* Kalamazoo, MI: Cistercian Publications, 1980.

———. *On Loving God,* 1.1. In *Bernard of Clairvaux: Selected Works.* Translated by G. R. Evans. Classics of Western Spirituality. New York: Paulist Press, 1987.

———. *Talks on the Song of Songs.* Edited by Bernard Bangley. Brewster, MA: Paraclete Press, 1980.

Bonar, Andrew, ed. *The Letters of Samuel Rutherford.* Edinburgh: Banner of Truth, 1984.

Bonaventure. *Bonaventure: The Soul's Journey into God, The Tree of Life, The Life of St. Francis.* New York: Paulist Press, 1978.

———. *The Soul's Journey into God.* Translated by Ewert Cousins. Classics of Western Spirituality. New York: Paulist Press, 1978.

Brother Lawrence. *Practicing the Presence of God.* Brewster, MA: Paraclete Press, 2007.

Bullinger, Heinrich. *The Decades of Henry Bullinger.* Translated by Thomas Harding. Charleston, SC: Nabu Press, 2010.

Bunyan, John. *The Pilgrim's Progress.* Edited by N. H. Keeble. Oxford: Oxford University Press, 1966.

Calvin, John. *The Soul of Life: The Piety of John Calvin*. Profiles in Reformed Spirituality. Grand Rapids: Reformation Heritage, 2009.

Cassian, John. *The Conferences*. Translated by Boniface Ramsey. New York: Paulist Press, 1997.

———. *John Cassian: The Conferences*. Ancient Christian Writers. New York: Paulist Press, 1997.

———. *John Cassian: The Conferences*. Bloomington, IN: Xlibris., 2000.

———. *The Institutes*. Translated by Boniface Ramsey. New York: Newman Press, 2000.

———. *The Monastic Institutes*. London: The Saint Austin Press, 1999.

Catherine of Siena. *The Dialogue*. Translated by Suzanne Noffke. Classics of Western Spirituality. New York: Paulist Press, 1980.

Chrysostom, John. *On Living Simply*. Liguori, MO: Liguori Publications, 1996.

———. *On Marriage and Family Life*. Crestwood, NY: St. Vladimir's Seminary Press, 1986.

———. *On Wealth and Poverty*. Crestwood, NY: St. Vladimir's Seminary Press, 1988.

Cyril of Scythopolis. *The Lives of the Monks of Palestine*. Translated by R. M. Price. Kalamazoo, MI: Cistercian Publications, 1991.

Eckhart, Meister. *Meister Eckhart: The Essential Sermons, Commentaries, Treaties and Defense*. Edited by Bernard McGinn. Translated by Edmund Colledge. Classics of Western Spirituality. New York: Paulist Press, 1981.

Edwards, Jonathan. *Personal Narrative* in *Letters and Personal Writings*. Edited by George Claghorn. The Works of Jonathan Edwards. New Haven, CT: Yale University Press, 1998.

———. *The Religious Affections*. Carlisle, PA: Banner of Truth, 1961.

Egeria. *Egeria's Travels*. Translated by John Wilkinson. Oxford: Aris & Phillips, 1999.

Ephrem the Syrian. *Hymns on Paradise*. Translated by Sebastian Brock. Crestwood, NY: St. Vladimir's Seminary Press, 1990.

Erasmus, Desiderius. *Enchiridion militis Christiani: An English Version*. Edited by Anne M. O'Donnell. Oxford: Oxford University Press, 1981.

Erb, Peter C., ed. *Pietists, Selected Writings*. Classics of Western Spirituality. New York: Paulist Press, 1983.

Evagrius Ponticus. *The Praktikos. Chapters on Prayer*. Translated by John Eudes Bamberger. Kalamazoo, MI: Cistercian Publications, 2006.

Francis of Assisi. *Francis and Claire: The Complete Works*. New York: Paulist Press, 1982.

Gerhard, Johann. *Handbook of Consolations*. Translated by Carl L. Beckwith. Eugene, OR: Wipf & Stock, 2009.

Gerhardt, Paul. *Spiritual Songs*. Translated by John Kelly. London: Alexander Straham, 1867.

Gregory of Nyssa. *From Glory to Glory: Texts from Gregory of Nyssa's Mystical Writings*. Edited by Jean Danielou. Translated by Herbert Musurillo. Crestwood, NY: St. Vladimir's Seminary Press, 1979.

——. *Gregory of Nyssa: Ascetical Works*. Translated by V. Woods Callahan. Fathers of the Church 58. Washington, DC: Catholic University of America Press, 1967.

——. *Gregory of Nyssa: The Life of Saint Macrina*. Translated by Kevin Corrigan. Eugene, OR: Wipf & Stock, 2001.

——. *The Life of Moses*. HarperCollins Spiritual Classics. New York: HarperOne, 2006.

——. *Life of Moses*. Translated by E. Ferguson. New York: Paulist Press, 1978.

Gregory the Great. "Life of Benedict by Gregory the Great." In *Early Christian Lives*. Edited by Carolinne White, pp. 161-204. New York: Penguin, 1998.

——. *Morals on the Book of Job, by S. Gregory the Great, Volume II*. Oxford: John Henry Parker, 1845.

Grumbach, Argula von. *Argula von Grumbach: A Woman's Voice in the Reformation*. Edited by Peter Matheson. Edinburgh: T & T Clark, 1995.

Head, Thomas, ed. *Medieval Hagiography: An Anthology*. New York: Routledge, 1999.

Herbert, George. *George Herbert: The Complete English Poems*. Edited by John Tobin. London: New York: Penguin Classics, 2005.

——. *George Herbert: The Country Parson and the Temple*. New York: Paulist Press, 1981.

Hildegard von Bingen. *Hildegard of Bingen: Scivias*. Translated by Mother Columba Hart and Jane Bishop. Classics of Western Spirituality. New York: Paulist Press, 1990.

——. *Mystical Visions: Translated from Scivias*. Translated by Bruce Hozeski. Rochester, VT: Bear & Company, 1985.

Hilton, Walter. *Walter Hilton: The Scale of Perfection*. Translated by John P. H. Clark and Rosemary Dorward. Classics of Western Spirituality. New York: Paulist Press, 1990.

Holy Apostles Convent. *The Lives of the Saints of the Holy Land and the Sinai Desert*. Buena Vista, CO: Holy Apostles Convent, 1988.

Ignatius of Loyola. *Ignatius of Loyola: The Spiritual Exercises and Selected Works*. Edited by George E. Ganss. Classics of Western Spirituality. New York: Paulist Press, 1991.

——. *The Spiritual Exercises*. New York: Random House, 2000.

——. *Spiritualia: The Spiritual Exercises of St. Ignatius*. Translated by Anthony Mottola. New York: Image Books, 1989.

Jacob of Sarug. *A Metrical Homily on Holy Mar Ephrem.* Translated by Joseph P. Amar. Patrologia Orientalis 47.1. Belgium: Brepols, 1995.

John of the Cross. *The Collected Works of St. John of the Cross.* Translated by Kiernan Kavanaugh and Otilio Rodriguez. Washington, DC: Institute of Carmelite Studies, 1991.

———. *The Dark Night of the Soul.* New York: Image Books Doubleday, 1959.

Julian of Norwich. *Julian of Norwich: Showings.* Translated by Ewert Cousins and James Walsh. New York: Paulist Press, 1978.

———. *The Revelation of Divine Love.* Ligouri, MO: Triumph Books, 1994.

———. *Showings.* Translated by Edmund Colledge and James Walsh. Classics of Western Spirituality. New York: Paulist Press, 1977.

Kapic, Kelly M., and Justin Taylor, eds. *Communion with the Triune God.* Wheaton, IL: Crossway Books, 2007.

Law, William. *An Humble, Earnest, and Affectionate Address, to the Clergy.* Edinburgh: Guthrie & Tait, 1817.

Luther, Martin. *Luther: Letters of Spiritual Counsel.* Translated and edited by Theodore G. Tappert. Philadelphia: Westminster Press, 1955.

———. *Luther's Spirituality.* Edited by Philip D. Krey and Peter D. S. Krey. Classics of Western Spirituality. Mahwah, NJ: Paulist Press, 2007.

Maximus the Confessor. *Maximus Confessor: Selected Writings.* Translated by George C. Berthold. Mahwah, NJ: Paulist Press, 1985.

Merton, Thomas, ed. *The Wisdom of the Desert.* New York: New Directions, 1960.

Moschos, John. *The Spiritual Meadow.* Translated by John Wortley. Kalamazoo, MI: Cistercian Publications, 1992.

Newman, John Henry. *The Dream of Gerontius.* London: Longmans, Green, 1888.

Origen. *Exhortation to Martyrdom, Prayer, and Selected Works.* Classics of Western Spirituality. Translated by Rowan A. Greer. New York: Paulist Press, 1979.

———. *Origen: The Song of Songs, Commentary and* Homilies. Edited by R. P. Lawson. Ancient Christian Writers. Mahwah, NJ: Paulist Press, 1957.

Orthodox Eastern Church. *The Festal Menaion.* Translated by Mother Mary and Kallistos Ware. South Canaan, PA: St. Tikhon's Seminary, 1998.

———. *The Lenten Triodion.* Translated by Mother Mary and Kallistos Ware. South Canaan, PA: St. Tikhon's Seminary, 2002.

Overholt, John J., ed. "Hymn 11 in the Ausbund." In *The Christian Hymnary.* Uniontown, OH: Christian Hymnary Publishers, 1972.

Palladius. *Palladius: Dialogue on the Life of St. John Chrysostom.* Translated by Robert T. Meyer. New York: Newman Press, 1985.

————. *Palladius: The Lausiac History*. Translated by Robert T. Meyer. Westminster, MD: Newman Press, 1965.

Paphnutius. *Histories of the Monks of Upper Egypt and The Life of Onnephrius*. Translated by Tim Vivian. Kalamazoo, MI: Cistercian Press, 1993.

The Philokalia. Vols.1-4. London: Faber & Faber, 1979, 1982, 1986, 1999.

Pseudo-Bonaventure. *Meditation on the Life of Christ: An Illustrated Manuscript of the Fourteenth Century*. Edited by Rosalie B. Green. Translated by Isa Raqusa. Princeton Monographs in Art and Archaeology. Princeton, NJ: Princeton University Press, 1961.

Pseudo-Dionysius. *Pseudo-Dionysius: The Complete Works*. Translated by Colm Luibheid. Mahwah, NJ: Paulist Press, 1987.

Richard of St. Victor. *Richard of St. Victor: The Books of the Patriarchs, The Mystical Ark, Book Three of the Trinity*. Translated by Grover A. Zinn. Classics of Western Spirituality. New York: Paulist Press, 1979.

Rowe, Elizabeth. *Devout Exercises of the Heart* in *The Works of Mrs. Elizabeth Rowe*. Vol. 2. London: John & Arthur Arch, 1796.

Russell, Norman, trans. *The Lives of the Desert Fathers: Historia Monachorum in Aegypto*. Cistercian Studies 34. Kalamazoo, MI: Cistercian Publications, 1980.

Sayings of the Desert Fathers: The Alphabetical Collection. Translated by Benedicta Ward. London: Cistercian Publications, 1975.

Scougal, Henry. *The Life of God in the Soul of Man*. Ross-shire, Scotland: Christian Focus, 1996.

Simons, Menno. *The Complete Writings of Menno Simons*. Edited by J. C. Wenger. Translated by Leonard Verduin. Scottdale, PA: Herald Press, 1978.

Spener, Philip Jacob. *Pia Desideria*. Translated by Theodore G. Tappert. Philadelphia: Fortress Press, 1964.

Symeon the New Theologian. *The Discourses*. Classics of Western Spirituality. New York: Paulist Press, 1980.

————. *Hymns of Divine Love*. Translated by Norman Russell. Denville, NJ: Dimension Books, 1976.

Teellinck, Willem. *The Path of True Godliness*. Edited by Joel R. Beeke. Translated by Annemie Godbehere. Grand Rapids: Baker, 2003.

Teresa of Ávila. *The Collected Works of Teresa of Avila*. 3 Vols. Washington, DC: Institute of Carmelite Studies, 1976.

————. *The Interior Castle*. Translated by Kiernan Kavanaugh and Otilio Rodriguez. Classics of Western Spirituality. New York: Paulist Press, 1979.

Theodoret of Cyrrhus. *Commentary on the Song of Songs*. Translated by Robert C. Hill. Strathfield, Australia: St. Paul's Publications, 2001.

———. *A History of the Monks of Syria.* Translated by R. M. Price. Kalamazoo, MI: Cistercian Publications, 1985.

Thompson, William M. ed., *Bérulle and the French School: Selected Writings.* Translated by Lowell M. Glendon. Classics of Western Spirituality. Mahwah, NJ: Paulist Press, 1989.

Thomas à Kempis. *The Imitation of Christ.* Hendrickson Christian Classics. Peabody, MA: Hendrickson, 2004.

Van Braght, Thieleman J. *The Bloody Theater or Martyrs' Mirror.* Scottdale, PA: Mennonite Publishing House, 1951.

Ursinus, Zacharius. *The Heidelberg Catechism.* Christian Reformed Church. Kalamazoo, MI: Faith Alive, 1990.

Ward, Benedicta, trans. *The Desert Fathers: Sayings of the Early Christian Monks.* New York: Penguin, 2003.

Wesley, John, and Charles Wesley. *John and Charles Wesley: Selected Prayers, Hymns, Journal Notes, Sermons, Letters, and Treatises.* Edited by F. Whaling. New York: Paulist Press, 1981.

Wesley, Susanna. *Susanna Wesley: The Complete Writings.* Oxford: Oxford University Press, 1997.

Zell, Katharina. *Church Mother: the Writings of a Protestant Reformer in Sixteenth-Century Germany.* Chicago: University of Chicago Press, 2006.

Zinzendorf, Nicholas Ludwig von. *The Liturgy and the Offices of Worship and Hymns of the American Province of the Unitas Fratrum, or Moravian Church.* Winston Salem, np., 1908.

Zwingli, Ulrich. *Huldrych Zwingli: Writings.* Edited by E. J. Furcha and H. W. Pipkin. Allison Park, PA: Pickwick, 1984.

SECONDARY READINGS

"About the Book Business," *The King's Business* 3, no. 5 (1912): 131, www2.biola.edu/kingsbusiness/view/3/5/36.

Andrews, Frances. *The Other Friars: The Carmelite, Augustinian, Sack and Pied Friars in the Middle Ages.* Woodbridge, UK: Boydell, 2006.

Armstrong, Regis J. "The Spiritual Theology of the *Legenda Major* of Saint Bonaventure." PhD diss., Fordham University, 1978.

Armstrong, Regis J., and Ingrid J. Peterson. *The Franciscan Tradition.* Spirituality in History Series. Collegeville, MN: Liturgical Press, 2010.

Arnold, Clinton E. "Early Church Catechesis and New Christians' Classes in Contemporary Evangelicalism." *Journal of the Evangelical Theological Society* 47, no. 1 (2004): 39-54.

Ashbrook, R. Thomas. *Mansions of the Heart: Exploring the Seven Stages of Spiritual Growth.* San Francisco: Jossey-Bass, 2009.

Augsburger, Myron S. *The Fugitive: Menno Simons, Spiritual Leader in the Free Church Movement.* Scottdale, PA: Herald Press, 2008.

Aumann, Jordon. *Spiritual Theology.* London: Sheed & Ward, 1980.

Averbeck, Richard E. "God, People, and the Bible: The Relationship Between Illumination and Biblical Scholarship" In *Who's Afraid of the Holy Spirit? An Investigation into the Ministry of the Spirit of God Today.* Edited by Daniel B. Wallace and M. James Sawyer, pp. 137-66. Dallas: Biblical Studies Press, 2005.

Ayres, Lewis. "Augustine, Christology, and God as Love: An Introduction to the Homilies on 1 John." In *Nothing Greater, Nothing Better: Theological Essays on the Love of God.* Edited by Kevin Vanhoozer, pp. 67-93. Grand Rapids: Eerdmans, 2001.

Ayris, Paul and David Selwyn, eds. *Thomas Cranmer: Churchman and Scholar.* New York: Boydell, 1993.

Bailey, J. E. "Bishop Lewis Bayly and His 'Practice of Piety.'" *Manchester Quarterly* 2 (1883): 201-19.

Bainton, Roland. *Here I Stand: A Life of Marin Luther.* Nashville: Abingdon, 1950.

Bayer, Oswald. *Martin Luther's Theology: A Contemporary Interpretation.* Grand Rapids: Eerdmans, 2008.

Beeke, Joel R. "The Dutch Second Reformation (*Nadere Reformatie*)." *Calvin Theological Journal* 28, no. 2 (1993): 300-307.

Beeke, Joel R., and Randall Pedersen. *Meet the Puritans.* Grand Rapids: Reformation Heritage Books, 2006.

Belisle, Peter-Damian. *The Language of Silence: The Changing Face of Monastic Solitude.* Maryknoll, NY: Orbis, 2003.

Berding, Kenneth. *What Are Spiritual Gifts? Rethinking the Conventional View.* Grand Rapids: Kregel, 2006.

Berkhof, Louis. *Systematic Theology.* Grand Rapids: Eerdmans, 1996.

Bernard, G. W. *The King's Reformation: Henry VIII and the Remaking of the English Church.* New Haven, CT: Yale University Press, 2005.

Bierman, Lyle D., et al. *An Introduction to the Heidelberg Catechism: Sources, History, and Theology.* Grand Rapids: Baker Academic, 2005.

Bilinkoff, Jodi. "John of the Cross." In *Oxford Encyclopedia of the Reformation.* Edited by Hans J. Hillerbrand, 2:351-52. New York: Oxford University Press, 1996.

Bloesch, Donald G. *Holy Scripture: Revelation, Inspiration & Interpretation.* Downers Grove, IL: InterVarsity Press, 1994.

Boersma, Hans. *Nouvelle Theologie and Sacramental Ontology: A Return to Mystery*. Oxford: Oxford University Press, 2010.

Booty, John E. "Book of Common Prayer." In *Oxford Encyclopedia of the Reformation*. Edited by Hans J. Hillerbrand, 1:191. New York: Oxford University Press, 1996.

Bornkamm, Heinrich. *Luther in Mid-Career, 1521-1530*. Philadelphia: Fortress Press, 1983.

Bouwsma, William J. *John Calvin: A Sixteenth-Century Portrait*. New York: Oxford University Press, 1988.

Bouyer, Louis. *The Christian Mystery: From Pagan Myth to Christian Mysticism*. Petersham, MA: Saint Bede's, 1990.

Bradshaw, Paul F. *The Apostolic Tradition: Hermeneia, A Critical and Historical Commentary on the Bible*. Minneapolis: Augsburg Press, 2002.

——. *Daily Prayer in the Early Church: A Study of the Origin and Early Development of the Divine Office*. New York: Oxford University Press, 1982.

Brakke, David. *Athanasius and Asceticism*. Baltimore: Johns Hopkins University Press, 1998.

——. *Athanasius and the Politics of Asceticism*. Oxford: Clarendon Press, 1995.

Bredero, Adriaan H. *Bernard of Clairvaux: Between Cult and History*. Grand Rapids: Eerdmans, 1996.

Bremer, Frances J. *Puritanism: A Very Short Introduction*. Oxford: Oxford University Press, 2009.

Bright, Pamela, ed. *Augustine and the Bible*. Notre Dame, IN: Notre Dame University Press, 1999.

Brock, Sebastian. *The Luminous Eye: The Spiritual Vision of Ephrem the Syrian*. Cistercian Studies 124. Kalamazoo, MI: Cistercian Publications, 1992.

Bromiley, Geoffrey W. *Thomas Cranmer, Theologian*. New York: Oxford University Press, 1956.

——, ed. *Zwingli and Bullinger*. Philadelphia: Westminster Press, 1953.

Brooke, Christopher. *The Age of the Cloister: The Story of Monastic Life in the Middle Ages*. Mahwah, NJ: HiddenSpring, 2003.

Brower, Kent E., and Andy Johnson, eds. *Holiness and Ecclesiology in the New Testament*. Grand Rapids: Eerdmans, 2007.

Brown, Dale W. *Understanding Pietism*. Rev. ed. Grantham, PA: Evangel Publishing House, 1996.

Brown, Peter. *Body and Society: Men, Women, and Sexual Renunciation in Early Christianity*. New York: Columbia University Press, 1988.

Bruce, F. F. *The Epistles to the Colossians, to Philemon, and to the Ephesians*. Grand Rapids: Eerdmans, 1984.

————. *Paul: Apostle of the Heart Set Free*. Grand Rapids: Eerdmans, 2000.

Burke, Kevin F., and Eileen Burke-Sullivan. *The Ignatian Tradition*. Spirituality in History. Collegeville, MN: Liturgical Press, 2009.

Burton-Christie, Douglas. *The Word in the Desert: Scripture and the Quest for Holiness in Early Christian Monasticism*. New York: Oxford University Press, 1993.

Butler, Cuthbert. *Western Mysticism: The Teaching of SS. Augustine, Gregory and Bernard on Contemplation and the Contemplative Life*. 3rd ed. London: Constable, 1967.

Byassee, Jason. *Praise Seeking Understanding: Reading the Psalms with Augustine*. Grand Rapids: Eerdmans, 2007.

Cairns, Scott. *Short Trip to the Edge: Where Earth Meets Heaven—A Pilgrimage*. San Francisco: HarperOne, 2007.

Callen, Barry L. *Authentic Spirituality*. Grand Rapids: Baker Academic, 2001.

Cameron, Euan. *The European Reformation*. New York: Oxford University Press, 1991.

Cameron, Michael. *"Inerrationes in Psalmos."* In *Augustine Through the Ages*. Edited by Allan D. Fitzgerald. Grand Rapids: Eerdmans, 1999.

Campbell, Ted A. *The Religion of the Heart*. Eugene, OR: Wipf & Stock, 1991.

Campenhausen, Hans von. *The Fathers of the Greek Church*. New York: Pantheon, 1955.

Carey, Philip. *Inner Grace: Augustine in the Traditions of Plato and Paul*. New York: Oxford University Press, 2008.

————. *Outward Signs: The Powerlessness of External Things in Augustine's Thought*. New York: Oxford University Press, 2008

Carmichael, Liz. "Catholic Saints and Reformers." In *The Story of Christian Spirituality: Two Thousand Years, from East to West*. Edited by Gordon Mursell, pp. 224-44. Oxford: Lion, 2001.

Casey, Michael. *Athirst for God: Spiritual Desire in Bernard of Clairvaux's Sermons on the Song of Songs*. Kalamazoo, MI: Cistercian Publications, 1987.

Castelli, Elizabeth A. *Imitating Paul: A Discourse of Power*. Louisville: KY: Westminster/John Knox, 1991.

Certeau, Michel de. *The Mystic Fable*. Translation by Michael B. Smith. Chicago: University of Chicago Press, 1995.

Chadwick, Owen. *Western Asceticism*. Philadelphia: Westminster Press, 1958.

Charry, Ellen T. *By the Renewing of Your Minds*. New York: Oxford University Press, 1997.

Chitty, Derwas J. *The Desert A City: An Introduction to the Study of Egyptian and Palestinian Monasticism under the Christian Empire*. Crestwood, NY: St. Vladimir's Seminary Press, 1999.

Chryssavgis, John. *Light Through Darkness: The Orthodox Tradition*. Maryknoll, NY: Orbis, 2004.

Clanchy, M. T. *Abelard, A Medieval Life*. Oxford: Blackwell, 1999.

Clark, Elizabeth. *Reading Renunciation: Asceticism and Scripture in Early Christianity*. Princeton, NJ: Princeton University Press, 1999.

Clement, Oliver. *The Roots of Christian Mysticism*. New York: New City Press, 1995.

Clowney, Edmund P. *The Church*. Downers Grove, IL: InterVarsity Press, 1995.

Cocque, Andre La, and Paul Ricoeur. *Thinking Biblically: Exegetical and Hermeneutical Studies*. Translated by David Pellauer. Chicago: University of Chicago Press, 1998.

Coe, John H. "Spiritual Theology: A Theological-Experiential Methodology for Bridging the Sanctification Gap." *Journal of Spiritual Formation and Soul Care* 2, no. 1 (2009): 4-43.

Coe, John H., and Todd Hall. *Psychology in the Spirit: Contours of a Transformational Psychology*. Downers Grove, IL: IVP Academic, 2010.

Coffey, John. "Letters by Samuel Rutherford (1600-1661)." In *The Devoted Life: An Invitation to the Puritan Classics*. Edited by Kelly M. Kapic and Randall C. Gleason, pp. 92-107. Downers Grove, IL: InterVarsity Press, 2004.

———. *Politics, Religion and the British Revolutions: The Mind of Samuel Rutherford*. Cambridge: Cambridge University Press, 1997.

Coffey, John, and Paul C. H. Lim, eds. *The Cambridge Companion to Puritanism*. Cambridge: Cambridge University Press, 2008.

Cole, Graham A. *He Who Gives Life*. Wheaton, IL: Crossway, 2004.

Crews, C. Daniel. *Zinzendorf: The Theology of Song*. Winston-Salem, NC: Moravian Archives and Moravian Music Foundation, 1999.

Cullen, Christopher M. *Bonaventure*. Oxford: Oxford University Press, 2006.

Cunningham, Lawrence S. "The Way and the Ways: Reflections on Catholic Spirituality." In Greenman and Kalantzis, *Life in the Spirit*, pp. 82-96.

Dalrymple, William. *From the Holy Mountain: A Journey in the Shadow of Byzantium*. London: Flamingo, 1998.

Daly, Lowrie J. *Benedictine Monasticism, Its Formation and Development through the 12th Century*. New York: Sheed & Ward, 1965.

Danielou, Jean. *From Shadows to Realities: Studies in the Biblical Typology of the Fathers*. Translated by W. Hibberd. London: Burns & Oats, 1960.

Davies, Oliver, and Thomas O'Loughlin. *Celtic Spirituality*. Classics of Western Spirituality. New York: Paulist Press, 1999.

De Boer, Willis Peter. *The Imitation of Paul: An Exegetical Study*. Kampen, Germany: J. H. Kok, 1962.

De Saint Joseph, Lucian Marie. "École de Spiritualité." In *Dictionnaire De Spiritualité: Ascétique Et Mystique, Doctrine Et Histoire*. Edited by Marcel Viller, Charles Baumgartner, and André Rayez, pp. 116-28. Paris: G. Beauchesne et ses fils, 1932-1995.

De Waal, Esther. *Seeking God: The Way of St. Benedict*. Collegeville, MN: Liturgical Press, 1984.

Demacopoulos, George E. *Five Models of Spiritual Direction in the Early Church*. Notre Dame, IN: University of Notre Dame Press, 2007.

Demarest, Bruce. *Satisfy Your Soul: Restoring the Heart of Christian Spirituality*. Colorado Springs: NavPress, 1999.

Dodd, Brian. *Paul's Paradigmatic "I": Personal Example as Literary Strategy*. Sheffield, UK: Sheffield Academic Press, 1999.

Doddridge, Philip. *The Rise and Progress of Religion in the Soul*. Grand Rapids: Baker, 1977.

Donnelly, John Patrick. *Ignatius of Loyola: Founder of the Jesuits*. New York: Pearson Longman, 2004.

Dreuille, Mayeul de. *Seeking the Absolute Love: The Founders of Christian Monasticism*. New York: Crossroad, 1999.

Drobner, Hubertus R. *The Fathers of the Church: A Comprehensive Introduction*. Translated by Siegfried S. Schatzmann. Peabody, MA: Hendrickson, 2007.

Dubay, Thomas. *Fire Within: St. Teresa of Ávila, St. John of the Cross, and the Gospel—on Prayer*. San Francisco: Ignatius Press, 1989.

Dunn, Marilyn. *The Emergence of Monasticism: From the Desert Fathers to the Early Middle Ages*. Oxford: Blackwell, 2000.

Dupré, Louis, and Don E. Saliers, eds. *Christian Spirituality: Post-Reformation and Modern*. New York: Crossroad, 1989.

Eadmer. *The Life of St. Anselm, Archbishop of Canterbury*. Translated by R. W. Southern. Oxford: Clarendon Press, 1979.

Edwards, Mark U., Jr. *Printing, Propaganda, and Martin Luther*. Minneapolis: Fortress Press, 1994.

Egan, Keith J. "Carmelite Spirituality." In *The New Dictionary of Catholic Spirituality*. Edited by Michael Downey, pp. 117-124. Collegeville, MN: Liturgical Press, 1993.

Eisenstein, Elizabeth L. "The Advent of Printing and the Protestant Revolt: A New Approach to the Disruption of Western Christendom." In *Transition and Revolution: Problems and Issues of European Renaissance and Reformation History*. Edited by Robert M. Kingdon Minneapolis: Burgess, 1974.

Elm, Susanna. *"Virgins of God": The Making of Asceticism in Late Antiquity*. Oxford: Clarendon Press, 1994.

Erickson, Millard. *Christian Theology*. 2nd edition. Grand Rapids: Baker, 1998.

Erickson, R. J. "Flesh." In *Dictionary of Paul and His Letters*. Edited by Gerald F. Hawthorne, Ralph P. Martin and Daniel G. Reid, pp. 303-6. Downers Grove, IL: InterVarsity Press, 1993.

Evans, G. R. *Anselm*. London: Continuum, 2002.

Fairbairn, Donald. *Eastern Orthodoxy Through Western Eyes*. Louisville, KY: Westminster John Knox Press, 2002.

Farkasfalvy, Denis. *L'inspiration de l'Écriture sainte dans la theologie de Saint Bernard*. Rome: Herder, 1964.

Febvre, Lucien. "The Origins of the French Reformation: A Badly-put Question?" In *A New Kind of History*. Edited Peter Burke, pp. 44-107. New York: Harper & Row, 1973.

Fee, Gordon, D. *The First Epistle to the Corinthians*. Grand Rapids: Eerdmans, 1987.

———. *Paul's Letter to the Philippians*. Grand Rapids: Eerdmans, 1995.

Ferguson, Everett. *Backgrounds of Early Christianity*, 3rd ed. Grand Rapids: Eerdmans, 2003.

Fladenmuller, Kathryn Smith, and Douglas J. McMillan. *Regular Life: Monastic, Canonical, and Mendicant Rules*. Kalamazoo, MI: Medieval Institute Publications, 1997.

Fletcher, Richard. *The Barbarian Conversion: From Paganism to Christianity*. New York: Henry Holt, 1997.

Foster, Richard J. *Celebration of Disciple: The Path to Spiritual Growth*. San Francisco: HarperCollins, 1978.

Foster, Richard J., and Gayle D. Beebe. *Longing for God*. Downers Grove, IL: InterVarsity Press, 2009.

Foster, Richard J., and James Bryan Smith, eds. *Devotional Classics: Selected Readings For Individuals and Groups*. San Francisco: HarperCollins, 1990.

Fowl, S. E. "Imitation of Paul/of Christ." In *Dictionary of Paul and His Letters*. Edited by Gerald F. Hawthorne, Ralph P. Martin and Daniel G. Reid, pp. 428-31. Downers Grove, IL: InterVarsity Press, 1993.

Fredette, Paul A., and Karen Karper Fredette. *Consider the Ravens: On Contemporary Hermit Life*. New York: iUniverse, 2008.

Gäbler, Ulrich. *Huldrych Zwingli: His Life and Work*. Philadelphia: Fortress Press, 1986.

Gadamer, Hans-Georg. *Truth and Method*. Translated by Joel Weinsheimer and Donald G. Marshall. Rev. ed. New York: Continuum, 1989.

Gawthrop, Richard L. *Pietism and the Making of Eighteenth-Century Prussia*. Cambridge: Cambridge University Press, 1993.

George, Timothy. "An Evangelical Reflection on Scripture and Tradition." *Pro Ecclesia* 9, no. 2 (2000): 184-207.

———. *Reading Scripture with the Reformers*. Downers Grove, IL: InterVarsity Press, 2011.

———. *Theology of the Reformers*. Nashville: Broadman, 1988.

Gerhard, Johann. *Handbook of Consolations for the Fears and Trials That Oppress Us in the Struggle with Death*. Translated by Carl L. Beckwith. Eugene, OR: Wipf & Stock, 2009.

Gillet, Archimandrite Lev. *The Jesus Prayer*. Rev. ed. Crestwood, NY: St. Vladimir's Seminary Press, 1997.

Goehring, James E. *Ascetics, Society, and the Desert: Studies in Early Egyptian Monasticism*. Harrisburg, PA: Trinity Press International, 1999.

Gordon, Bruce, and Emidio Campi. *Architect of Reformation: An Introduction to Heinrich Bullinger, 1504-1575*. Grand Rapids: Baker Academic, 2004.

Gordon, Bruce. *The Swiss Reformation*. Manchester, UK: Manchester University Press, 2002.

Greaves, Richard L. *John Bunyan*. Grand Rapids: Eerdmans, 1969.

Green, Julien. *God's Fool: The Life and Times of Francis of Assisi*. San Francisco: Harper & Row, 1985.

Greenman, Jeffrey P., and George Kalantzis. *Life in the Spirit: Spiritual Formation in Theological Perspective*. Downers Grove, IL: IVP Academic, 2010.

Greun, Anselm. *Heaven Begins Within You: Wisdom from the Desert Fathers*. New York: Crossroad, 1999.

Griffiths, Paul. *The Vice of Curiosity: An Essay on Intellectual Appetite*. Winnipeg, MB: Canadian Mennonite Press, 2006.

Gritsch, Eric W. *Martin—God's Court Jester*. Philadelphia: Fortress Press, 1983.

Groeschel, Benedict J. *Spiritual Passages: The Psychology of Spiritual Development*. New York: Crossroads, 2002.

Grudem, Wayne. *Systematic Theology*. Grand Rapids: Zondervan, 1994.

Gutiérrez, Gustavo. *A Theology of Liberation: History, Politics, and Salvation*. Maryknoll, NY: Orbis, 1988.

Hageman, Howard G. "Reformed Spirituality." In *Protestant Spiritual Traditions*. Edited by Frank C. Seen, pp. 55-79. New York: Paulist Press, 1986.

Hambrick-Stowe, Charles. *The Practice of Piety*. Chapel Hill: University of North Carolina Press, 1982.

Hanson, R. P. C. *Allegory and Event: A Study in the Sources and Significance of Origen's Interpretation of Scripture*. Richmond: Westminster John Knox, 2002.

Harding, Thomas, ed. *The Decades of Henry Bullinger*, 4 vols. Cambridge: University Press, 1849-1852.

Harmless, William. *Desert Christians: An Introduction to the Literature of Early Monasticism.* Oxford: Oxford University Press, 2004.

Harvey, Paul. *The Oxford Companion to Classical Literature.* Oxford: Oxford University Press, 1989.

Hayes, Zachary. *Bonaventure: Mystical Writings.* New York: Crossroad, 1999.

Herbert, George. *The Country Parson, The Temple.* Edited by John N. Wall Jr. Mahwah, NJ: Paulist Press, 1981.

Herbert, Thomas Walter. *John Wesley as Editor and Author.* Princeton: Princeton University Press, 1940.

Hillerbrand, Hans. *The Protestant Reformation.* New York: Harper & Row, 1968.

Hindmarsh, Bruce D. "Contours of Evangelical Spirituality." In *The Zondervan Dictionary of Christian Spirituality.* Edited by Glen G. Scorgie, pp. 146-52. Grand Rapids: Zondervan, 2011.

———. "Seeking True Religion: Early Evangelical Devotion and Catholic Spirituality." In Greenman and Kalantzis, *Life in the Spirit*, pp. 115-37.

Hinson, E. Glenn. "Puritan Spirituality." In *Protestant Spiritual Traditions.* Edited by Frank C. Senn, pp. 165-82. New York: Paulist Press, 1986.

Hodge, Charles. *Systematic Theology*, 3:692-709. London: James Clarke, 1960.

Holder, Arthur. "The Problem with 'Spiritual Classics'." *Spiritus* 10, no. 1 (2010): 22-37.

Houston, James M. "A Guide to Devotional Reading." In *Classics of Faith and Devotion.* Vancouver: Regent Publishing, 1984.

———, ed. *Juan de Valdes, The Benefit of Christ.* Portland: Multnomah Press, 1984.

———. *Letters of Faith Through the Seasons.* Vol. 1. Colorado Springs: Cook Communications, 2006.

———. *Letters of Faith Through the Seasons.* Vol. 2. Colorado Springs: Cook Communication, 2007.

———. "Reflections on Mysticism: How Valid Is Evangelical Anti-Mysticism?" In *Loving God and Keeping His Commandments.* Edited by Markus Bockmuehl and Helmut Burkhardt. Giessen, Basel: BrunnenVerlag, 1991.

Howard, Evan B. "Evangelical Spirituality." In *Four Views of Christian Spirituality.* Edited by Bruce Demarest. Grand Rapids: Zondervan, 2012.

———. "What Did the Protestants Protest? Reflections on the Context of Reformation Spirituality as a 'Break' with Roman Catholicism." Evangelical Scholars in Christian Spirituality, 1993, www.evangelicalspirituality.org/papers/other papers/protprot.

Hymnal and Liturgies of the Moravian Church. Bethlehem, PA: Moravian Church in America, 1969.

Jacob, Christoph. "The Reception of the Origenist Tradition in Latin Exegesis." In *Hebrew Bible/Old Testament*. Edited by Magne Saebo, pp. 682-700. Göttingen: Vandenhoeck & Ruprecht, 1996.

Jaeger, Werner. *Early Christianity and Greek Paideia*. Cambridge, MA: Belknap Press, 1961.

Jantzen, Grace M. *Julian of Norwich: Mystic and Theologian*. New York: Paulist Press, 1988.

Jeanrond, Werner. "Love." In *The New Westminster Dictionary of Christian Spirituality*. Edited by Philip Sheldrake, pp. 414-15. Louisville: Westminster John Knox Press, 2005.

Johnson, Luke Timothy. *Among the Gentiles: Greco-Roman Religion and Christianity*. New Haven, CT: Yale University Press, 2009.

Judy, Dwight H. *Embracing God: Praying with Teresa of Ávila*. Nashville: Abingdon Press, 1996.

Julian, John. *The Complete Julian of Norwich*. Orleans, MA: Paraclete Press, 2009.

Kavanaugh, Kieran, and Otilio Rodriguez, trans. *The Collected Works of St. John of the Cross*. Washington, DC: Institute of Carmelite Studies, 1973.

Karant-Nunn, Susan C. *The Reformation of Ritual: An Interpretation of Early Modern Germany, Christianity, and Society in the Modern World*. London: Routledge, 1997.

Keeble, Neil. *Richard Baxter: Puritan Man of Letters*. Oxford: Clarendon Press, 1982.

Keller, David G. R. *Oasis of Wisdom*. Collegeville, MN: Liturgical Press, 2005.

Kelly, J. N. D. *Golden Mouth: The Story of John Chrysostom—Ascetic, Preacher, Bishop*. Ithaca, NY: Cornell University Press, 1995.

Kenney, John Peter. *The Mysticism of Saint Augustine: Rereading the Confessions*. New York: Routledge, 2005.

King, Preston, and Heather Devere, eds. *The Challenge to Friendship in Modernity*. Portland: Frank Cass, 2000.

Knott, John. *The Sword of the Spirit*. Chicago: University of Chicago Press, 1980.

Kolb, Robert, and Timothy J. Wengert, eds. *The Book of Concord: The Confessions of the Evangelical Lutheran Church*. Minneapolis: Fortress Press, 2000.

Krey, Philip D. W., and Peter D. S. Krey, eds., *Luther Spirituality*. New York: Paulist Press, 2007.

Krupp, R. A. *Shepherding the Flock of God: The Pastoral Theology of John Chrysostom*. New York: Peter Lang, 1991.

Kugel, James L. *The Bible as It Was*. Cambridge, MA: Belknap Press, 1997.

Lawrence, C. H. *The Friars: The Impact of the Early Mendicant Movement on Western Society*. New York: Longman, 1994.

———. *Medieval Monasticism: Forms of Religious Life in Western Europe in the Middle Ages*. New York: Longman, 2001.

Leclerc, Jean. *The Love of Learning and the Desire for God*. New York: Fordham University Press, 1974.

———. "Monastic and Scholastic Theology in the Reformers of the Fourteenth to Sixteenth Centuries." In *From Cloister to Classroom, Monastic and Scholastic Approaches to Truth*. Edited by E. Rozanne Elder. Kalamazoo, MI: Cistercian Publications, 1986.

Leith, John H., ed. *Creeds of the Churches*. 3rd ed. Louisville: John Knox Press, 1982.

Levi, Peter. *The Frontiers of Paradise: A Study of Monks and Monasteries*. New York: Weidenfeld & Nicolson, 1987.

Lewis, C. S. *God in the Dock: Essays on Theology and Ethics*. Grand Rapids: Eerdmans, 1970.

———. *Letters of C. S. Lewis*. Edited by W. H. Lewis. London: Geoffrey Bles, 1966.

———. *Letters to an American Lady*. Grand Rapids: Eerdmans, 1967.

Lieburg, Fred van. "From Pure Church to Pious Culture: The Further Reformation in the Seventeenth-Century Dutch Republic." In *Later Calvinism: International Perspectives*. Edited by W. Fred Graham. Kirksville: Northeast Missouri State University, 1995.

Lindberg, Carter. *The European Reformations*. Oxford: Blackwell, 1996.

Litfin, Bryan M. *Getting to Know the Church Fathers: An Evangelical Introduction*. Grand Rapids: Brazos, 2007.

Locher, Gottfried W. *Zwingli's Thought: New Perspectives*. Leiden: E. J. Brill, 1981.

Louth, Andrew. *The Origins of the Christian Mystical Tradition: From Plato to Denys*. 2nd ed. Oxford: Oxford University Press, 2007.

Lovelace, Richard F. "Evangelical Spirituality: A Church Historian's Perspective." *Journal of the Evangelical Theological Society* 31, no. 1 (1988): 25-35.

———. "The Sanctification Gap." *Theology Today* 29, no. 4 (1973): 363-69.

Lubac, Henri de. *Medieval Exegesis*. Translated by Mark Selbanc. Grand Rapids: Eerdmans, 1998.

MacCulloch, Diarmaid. *The Reformation*. New York: Viking, 2004.

———. *Thomas Cranmer: A Life*. New Haven, CT: Yale University Press, 1996.

Maddox, Randy L., and Jason E. Vickers. eds. *The Cambridge Companion to John Wesley*. Cambridge Companions to Religion. Cambridge: Cambridge University Press, 2010.

Marakides, Kyriacos C. *The Mountain of Silence: A Search for Orthodox Spirituality*. New York: Image Books, 2001.

Marshall, Paul V. "Anglican Spirituality." In *Protestant Spiritual Traditions*. Edited by Frank C. Senn, pp. 125-64. New York: Paulist Press, 1986.

Mason, M. Elizabeth. *Active Life and Contemplative Life: A Study of the Concepts from Plato to the Present*. Milwaukee: Marquette University Press, 1961.

Matheson, Peter, ed. *Reformation Christianity*. Minneapolis: Fortress Press, 2007.

Mathewes-Green, Frederica. *The Jesus Prayer: The Ancient Desert Prayer that Tunes the Heart to God*. Brewster, MA: Paraclete Press, 2009.

Matter, E. Ann. *The Voice of my Beloved: The Song of Songs in Western Medieval Christianity*. Philadelphia: University of Pennsylvania Press, 1990.

McBrien, Richard P. *Catholicism*. Minneapolis: Winston Press, 1980.

McGinn, Bernard. *The Flowering of Mysticism: Men and Women in the New Mysticism–1200-1350*. New York: Crossroad, 1998.

———. *The Growth of Mysticism: Gregory the Great through the Twelfth Century*. New York: Crossroad, 1994.

———. *The Harvest of Mysticism in Medieval Germany*. New York: Crossroad, 2005.

———. *The Mystical Thought of Meister Eckhart: The Man from Whom God Hid Nothing*. New York: Herder & Herder, 2001.

McGinn, Bernard, John Meyendorff and Jean Leclercq, eds. *Christian Spirituality I: Origins to the Twelfth Century*. New York: Crossroad, 1985.

McGrath, Alister E. *Christianity's Dangerous Idea: The Protestant Revolution: a History from the Sixteenth Century to the Twenty-first*. New York: HarperOne, 2007.

———. *A Life of John Calvin: A Study of the Shaping of Western Culture*. Oxford: Basil Blackwell, 1990.

McGuckin, John Anthony. *Standing in God's Holy Fire: The Byzantine Tradition*. Maryknoll, NY: Orbis, 2001.

McKee, Elsie Anne. *Katharina Schütz Zell*. Leiden: Brill, 1999.

———. *Reforming Popular Piety in Sixteenth-Century Strasbourg: Katharina Schütz Zell and Her Hymnbook*. Princeton: Princeton Theological Seminary, 1994.

McKim, Donald K. *The Cambridge Companion to John Calvin*. New York: Cambridge University Press, 2004.

McMahon, Robert. *Understanding the Medieval Meditative Ascent: Augustine, Anselm, Boethius and Dante*. Washington, DC: Catholic University of America Press, 2006.

McNamer, Sarah. "The Origins of the *Meditationes Vitae Christi*," *Speculum* 84 (2009): 905-55.

Meredith, Anthony. *The Cappadocians*. Crestwood, NY: St. Vladimir's Seminary Press, 1995

———. *Gregory of Nyssa*. New York: Routledge, 1999.

Merrick, Teri. "Teaching Philosophy: Instilling Pious Wonder or Vicious Curiosity?" *Christian Scholar's Review* 34, no. 4 (2010): 401-20.

Merton, Thomas. *Mystics and Zen Masters*. New York: Farrar, Straus & Giroux, 1967.

———. *Zen and the Birds of Appetite*. New York: New Directions, 1968.

Meyendorff, John. *St. Gregory Palamas and Orthodox Spirituality*. New York: St. Vladimir's Seminary Press, 1974.

Milavec, Aaron. *The Didache: Text, Analysis, and Commentary*. Collegeville, MN: Liturgical Press, 2003.

Miles, Margaret R. *Fullness of Life: Historical Foundations for a New Asceticism*. Philadelphia: Westminster Press, 1981.

Mohrmann, Christine. *Etudes sur le latin des Chretiens*. Rome: Storiae Letteratura, 1958.

Moorman, John R. H. *A History of the Franciscan Order from Its Origins to the Year 1517*. Oxford: Clarendon Press, 1968.

Mozley, J. F. *William Tyndale*. New York: Macmillan, 1937.

Muller, Richard A., and John L. Thompson, eds. *Biblical Interpretation in the Era of the Reformation: Essays Presented to David C. Steinmetz in Honor of his Sixtieth Birthday*. Grand Rapids: Eerdmans, 1996.

Muto, Susan Annette. *A Practical Guide to Spiritual Reading*. Denville, NJ: Dimension, 1976.

Nieuwenhove, Rik van, and Joseph Wawrykow, eds. *The Theology of Thomas Aquinas*. Notre Dame, IN: University of Notre Dame Press, 2005.

Norris, Frederick W., ed. *Faith Gives Fullness to Reasoning: The Five Theological Orations of Gregory Nazianzen*. Translated by L. Wickham and F. Williams. New York: Brill, 1991.

Nouwen, Henri. *The Life of the Beloved: Spiritual Living in a Secular World*. New York: Crossroad, 1992.

Nuttall, Geoffrey F. *Richard Baxter*. London: Nelson, 1965.

Oberman, Heiko A. *Luther: Man Between God and the Devil*. New Haven, CT: Yale University Press, 1983.

O'Keefe, John J., and R. R. Reno. *Sanctified Vision: An Introduction to Early Christian Interpretation of the Bible*. Baltimore: Johns Hopkins University Press, 2005.

Olevianus, Caspar. *A Firm Foundation: An Aid to Interpreting the Heidelberg Catechism*. Translated and edited by Lyle D. Bierma. Grand Rapids: Baker, 1995.

Olson, Ryan S. *Tragedy, Authority, and Trickery: The Poetics of Embedded Letters in Josephus*. Cambridge, MA: Harvard University Press, 2010.

O'Malley, John W. *The First Jesuits*. Cambridge, MA: Harvard University Press, 1993.

Op't Hof, Willem. *De Praktijk der Godzaligheid: Studies over De Praktijk ofte Oef-feninghe der Godzaligheyd (1620) van Lewis Bayly*. Edited by A. A. den Hollander and F. W. Huisman. Amsterdam: Free University of Amsterdam, 2009.

———. "Protestant Pietism and Medieval Monasticism." In *Confessionalism and Pietism: Religious Reform in Early Modern Europe*. Edited by Fred van Lieburg, pp. 31-50. Mainz: Verlag Philipp von Zabern, 2006.

The Oxford Encyclopedia of the Reformation. Edited by Hans Hillerbrand. 4 vols. New York: Oxford University Press, 1996.

Ozment, Steven E. *Protestants: The Birth of a Revolution*. New York: Doubleday, 1992.

Packer, J. I. *Keep in Step with the Spirit*. Grand Rapids: Baker, 2004.

———. *A Quest for Godliness: The Puritan Vision of the Christian Life*. Wheaton, IL: Crossway, 1990.

Palladius. *The Lausaic History of Palladius*. Willits, CA: Eastern Orthodox Books, n.d.

Payton, James R., Jr. *Getting the Reformation Wrong: Correcting Some Misunderstandings*. Downers Grove, IL: IVP Academic, 2010.

———. *Light from the Christian East: An Introduction to the Orthodox Tradition*. Downers Grove, IL: IVP Academic, 2007.

Pelikan, Jaroslav. *Obedient Rebels*. New York: Harper & Row, 1964.

Pennington, M. Basil. *Engaging the World with Merton*. Brewster, MA: Paraclete Press, 2005.

Peters, Greg. "Evagrius of Pontus (c. 346-399)." In *The Zondervan Dictionary of Christian Spirituality*. Edited by Glen G. Scorgie, pp. 434-35. Grand Rapids: Zondervan Academic, 2010.

———. "Monasteries." In *Encyclopedia of Christian Civilization*. Edited by George T. Kurian. Oxford: Wiley-Blackwell, 2011.

———. "Monastic Orders." In *Encyclopedia of Christian Civilization*. Edited by George T. Kurian. Oxford: Wiley-Blackwell, 2011.

Peterson, Eugene. *Eat This Book*. Grand Rapids: Eerdmans, 2006.

Petroff, Elizabeth Avilda. *Medieval Women's Visionary Literature*. Oxford: Oxford University Press, 1986.

Pettegree, Andrew, ed. *The Reformation World*. London: Routledge, 2002.

Peucker, Paul. "The Songs of Sifting: Understanding the Role of Bridal Mysticism in Moravian Piety During the Late 1740s." *Journal of Moravian History* 3 (2007): 51-71.

Pieper, Josef. *The Four Cardinal Virtues*. Notre Dame, IN: University of Notre Dame Press, 1966.

Porter, Steve. "Theology as Queen and Psychology as Handmaid: The Authority of Theology in Integrative Endeavors." *Journal of Psychology and Christianity* 29, no. 1 (2010): 3-14.

———. "Sanctification in a New Key: Relieving Evangelical Anxieties Over Spiritual Formation." *Journal of Spiritual Formation and Soul Care* 1, no.2 (2008): 129-48.

Pourrat, Pierre. *Christian Spirituality.* 4 vols. London: Burns, Oates & Washbourne, 1922.

Purcell, Mary. *The First Jesuit, St. Ignatius Loyola.* Chicago: Loyola University Press, 1981.

Rahner, Karl. "Reflections on the Problem of the Gradual Ascent to Christian Perfection." *Revue d'Ascétique et de Mystique* 19 (1944): 65-78.

Raitt, Jill, ed. *Christian Spirituality II: High Middle Ages and Reformation.* New York: Crossroad, 1987.

Ravier, André. *A Do-It-At-Home Retreat: The Spiritual Exercises of St. Ignatius of Loyal According to the "Nineteenth Annotation."* San Francisco: Ignatius Press, 1991.

———. *Ignatius of Loyola and the Founding of the Society of Jesus.* San Francisco: Ignatius Press, 1987.

Reinis, Austra. *Reforming the Art of Dying: The* Ars Moriendi *in the German Reformation (1519-1528).* Burlington, VT: Ashgate, 2007.

Reuver, Arie de. *Sweet Communion: Trajectories of Spirituality from the Middle Ages through the Further Reformation.* Translated by James A. DeJong. Grand Rapids: Baker Academic, 2007.

Rousseau, Philip. *Ascetics, Authority and the Church in the Age of Jerome and Cassian.* New York: Oxford University Press, 1978.

———. *Pachomius: The Making of a Community in Fourth-Century Egypt.* Berkeley: University of California Press, 1985.

Rupp, Gordon. *Religion in England 1688-1791.* Oxford: Clarendon Press, 1986.

Ryken, Leland. *Worldly Saints.* Grand Rapids: Zondervan, 1986.

Ryle, J. C. "Evangelical Religion." In *Knots Untied: Being Plain Statements on Disputed Points in Religion from the Standpoint of an Evangelical Churchman.* London: National Protestant Church Union, 1898.

Sattler, Gary R. *God's Glory Neighbor's Good.* Chicago: Covenant Press, 1982.

Saucy, Robert L. *Scripture: Its Power, Authority, and Relevance.* Nashville: Word, 2001.

Schwanda, Tom. "'Hearts Sweetly Refreshed': Puritan Spiritual Practices Then and Now." *Journal of Spiritual Formation and Soul Care* 3, no. 1 (2010): 21-41.

———. "Soul Recreation: Spiritual Marriage and Ravishment in the Contemplative-Mystical Piety of Isaac Ambrose." PhD diss., Durham University, 2009.

Selderhuis, Herman J. *John Calvin: A Pilgrim's Life*. Downers Grove, IL: IVP Academic, 2009.

Seventer, Jan N. *Paul and Seneca*. Leiden: E. J. Brill, 1961.

Shedd, William G. T. *Dogmatic Theology*. Edited by Alan W. Gomes. Phillipsburg, NJ: P & R, 2003.

Sheldrake, Philip. "Interpretation." In *New Westminster Dictionary of Spirituality*. Edited by Philip Sheldrake, pp. 13-18. Louisville: Westminster John Knox, 2005.

———. *Spirituality and History*. Maryknoll, NY: Orbis, 1995.

———. *Spirituality and Theology*. Maryknoll, NY: Orbis, 1998.

Sittser, Gerald. *Water from a Deep Well: Christian Spirituality from Early Martyrs to Modern Missionaries*. Downers Grove, IL: InterVarsity Press, 2007.

Sommerfeldt, John R. *The Spiritual Teachings of Bernard of Clairvaux*. Kalamazoo, MI: Cistercian Publications, 1991.

Southern, R. W. *Saint Anselm and His Biographer: A Study of Monastic Life and Thought, 1059-c. 1130*. Cambridge: Cambridge University Press, 1963.

Spurr, John. *English Puritanism, 1603-1689*. New York: St. Martin's Press, 1998.

Stalker, James. *Imago Christi: The Example of Jesus Christ*. New York: A. C. Armstrong, 1889.

Stein, K. James. *Philipp Jakob Spener: Pietistic Patriarch*. Chicago: Covenant Press, 1986.

Steinmetz, David C. *Luther in Context*. Bloomington: Indiana University Press, 1986.

Stephens, Peter. *The Theology of Huldrych Zwingli*. Oxford: Oxford University Press, 1986.

Stewart, Columba. *Cassian the Monk*. New York: Oxford University Press, 1998.

———. *Prayer and Community: The Benedictine Tradition*. Maryknoll, NY: Orbis, 1998.

Stoeffler, F. Ernest. *The Rise of Evangelical Pietism*. Leiden: Brill, 1971.

Stranks, C. J. *Anglican Devotion*. London: SCM, 1961.

Strom, Jonathan. "Problems and Promises of Pietism Research." In *Church History* 71, no. 3, (2002): 536-54.

Suso, Karl. *Angelikos Bios: Begriffsanalytische und begriffsgeschichtliche Untersuchung zum 'engelgleichen Leben' im frühen Mönchtum*. Münster: Aschendorff, 1964.

Swan, Laura. *The Benedictine Tradition*. Spirituality in History. Collegeville, MN: Liturgical Press, 2007.

———. *The Forgotten Desert Mothers*. New York: Paulist Press, 2001.

Talbot, John Michael. *The Way of the Mystics*. San Francisco: Jossey-Bass, 2005.

Tanquerey, Adolphe. *The Spiritual Life; A Treatise on Ascetical and Mystical Theology*. 2nd ed. Tournai, Belgium: Desclée, 1938.

Tierney, Brian. *The Middle Ages*. Vol. 1. *Sources of Medieval History*. 4th ed. New York: McGraw-Hill, 1983.

Tomkins, Stephen. *John Wesley: A Biography*. Grand Rapids: Eerdmans, 2003.

Toon, Peter. *Spiritual Companions: An Introduction to Christian Classics*. Grand Rapids: Baker, 1990.

Torrey, R. A. "Light on Puzzling Passages and Problems." *The King's Business* 7, no. 1 (1916): 23-24.

Towner, Philip H. *1–2 Timothy & Titus*. Downers Grove, IL: InterVarsity Press, 1994.

Tracy, David. *The Analogical Imagination: Christian Theology and the Culture of Pluralism*. New York: Crossroad, 1981.

Trigg, Joseph W. *Origen*. The Early Church Fathers. New York: Routledge, 1998.

Trueman, Carl. "Lewis Bayly and Richard Baxter." In *The Pietist Theologians*. Edited by Carter Lindberg, pp. 52-67. Malden, MA: Blackwell, 2005.

———. "Why Should Thoughtful Evangelicals Read the Medieval Mystics?" *Themelios* 33, no. 1 (2008): 2-4.

Tugwell, Simon. *Early Dominicans: Selected Writings*. Classics of Western Spirituality. New York: Paulist Press, 1982.

Turner, Denys. *Eros and Allegory: Medieval Exegesis of the Song of Songs*. Kalamazoo, MI: Cistercian Publications, 1995.

Tyerman, Luke. *The Life and Times of the Rev. John Wesley, Founder of the Methodists*. London: Hodder & Stoughton, 1876.

Tyler, Peter. "Triple Way." In *The New Westminster Dictionary of Christian Spirituality*. Edited by Philip Sheldrake, pp. 626-27. Louisville: Westminster John Knox Press, 2005.

Ullmann, Walter. *A Short History of the Papacy in the Middle Ages*. London: Routledge, 2003.

Vanhoozer, Kevin, ed. *Dictionary for Theological Interpretation of the Bible*. Grand Rapids: Baker Academic, 2005.

———. *Is There a Meaning in This Text?* Grand Rapids: Zondervan, 1998.

Vivian, Tim, ed. *Journeying into God: Seven Early Monastic Lives*. Minneapolis: Fortress Press, 1996.

Vogt, Peter. "Nicholas Ludwig von Zinzendorf." In *The Pietist Theologians: An Introduction to Theology in the Seventeenth and Eighteenth Centuries*. Edited by Carter Lindberg, pp. 207-23. Oxford: Blackwell, 2011.

Waaijman, Kees. *Spirituality: Forms, Foundations, Methods*. Leuven: Peeters, 2002.

Wakefield, Gordon. *John Bunyan the Christian*. London: Fount, 1992.

———. *Puritan Devotion*. London: Epworth, 1957.

Waltke, Bruce, and James M. Houston. *The Psalms as the Church's Worship*. Grand Rapids: Eerdmans, 2010.

Ward, W. R. *Early Evangelicalism: A Global Intellectual; History, 1670-1789*. Cambridge: Cambridge University Press, 2006.

Ware, Kallistos. *The Orthodox Church*. Rev. Ed. New York: Penguin, 1993.

————. *The Orthodox Way*. Rev. ed. Crestwood, NY: St. Vladimir's Seminary Press, 1995.

Warner, Larry. *Journey with Jesus: Discovering the Spiritual Exercises of Saint Ignatius*. Downers Grove, IL: InterVarsity Press, 2010.

Watson, David Lowes. "Methodist Spirituality." In *Protestant Spiritual Traditions*. Edited by Frank Senn, pp. 217-73. New York: Paulist Press, 1986.

Weinlick, John R. *Count Zinzendorf*. Bethlehem, PA: Moravian Church in America, 1984.

Welch, John. *The Carmelite Way: An Ancient Path for Today's Pilgrim*. New York: Paulist Press, 1996.

Wesley, John. "Advice on Spiritual Reading." In *John and Charles Wesley*. Classics of Western Spirituality. Edited by Frank Whaling, pp. 88-89. New York: Paulist Press, 1981.

White, Carolinne, ed. *Early Christian Lives*. New York: Penguin, 1998.

Wilhoit, James C. *Spiritual Formation As If the Church Mattered: Growing in Christ Through Community*. Grand Rapids: Baker, 2008.

Wilken, Robert Louis. *The Spirit of Early Christian Thought*. New Haven, CT: Yale University Press, 2003.

Willard, Dallas. *Hearing God: Developing a Conversational Relationship with God*. Downers Grove, IL: InterVarsity Press, 1984.

————. *The Spirit of the Disciplines: Understanding How God Changes Lives*. San Francisco: HarperCollins, 1988.

————. "When God Moves In." In *Indelible Ink*. Edited by Scott Larsen, pp. 49-56. Colorado Springs: WaterBrook, 2003.

Williams, D. H. *Retrieving the Tradition and Renewing Evangelicalism: A Primer for Suspicious Protestants*. Grand Rapids: Eerdmans, 1999.

Wilson-Hartgrove, Jonathan. "Review of *Julian of Norwich: A Contemplative Biography* by Amy Frykholm." *Christianity Today*, August 2010, p. 51.

Witherington, Ben, III. *Friendship and Finances in Philippi*. Valley Forge, PA: Trinity Press International, 1994.

Wolters, Clifton. "The English Mystics." In *The Study of Spirituality*. Edited by Cheslyn Jones, Geoffrey Wainwright, and Edward Yarnold, pp. 328-37. New York: Oxford University Press, 1986.

Young, Robin Darling. *To Train His Soul in Books: Syriac Asceticism in Early Chris-*

tianity. Cua Studies in Early Christianity. Washington, DC: Catholic University of America Press, 2011.

Zachman, Randall C. *Image and Word in the Theology of John Calvin*. Notre Dame, IN: University of Notre Dame Press, 2007.

Zagano, Phyllis, and Thomas C. McGonigle. *The Dominican Tradition*. Spirituality in History Series. Collegeville, MN: Liturgical Press, 2006.

List of Contributors

Betsy A. Barber, PsyD, teaches psychology and spirituality at Talbot School of Theology's Institute for Spiritual Formation, Biola University. Dr. Barber is the associate director of the Institute for Spiritual Formation and the director of the Center for Spiritual Renewal at Biola University. One of her professional joys is to train spiritual directors. She comes to teaching from a career in missions with Wycliffe Bible Translators and SIL. Dr. Barber serves on the editorial board of the *Journal of Spiritual Formation and Soulcare* and is a practicing psychologist.

Dr. John Coe is the director of the Institute for Spiritual Formation at Talbot School of Theology and Biola University and has been associate professor of spiritual theology and philosophy at Rosemead Graduate School of Psychology, Biola University, since 1987. Dr. Coe primarily teaches and writes in the areas of spirituality, theology, psychological maturity and gender issues, as well as the integration between theology, psychology, philosophy and ethics. Dr. Coe received an MA and PhD in philosophy from the University of California, Irvine, MA in theology from Talbot School of Theology, MA in humanities from Western Kentucky University, and BA in Bible and theology from Biola University.

Bruce Demarest has taught theology and spiritual formation at Denver Seminary for more than thirty years. He is the author of fifteen books and many articles.

Timothy George has been the dean of Beeson Divinity School at Samford University since its inception in 1988. A prolific author, he has written more than twenty books and regularly contributes to scholarly journals. His *Theology of the Reformers* is the standard textbook on Reformation theology in many schools and seminaries and has been translated into multiple languages.

Michael Glerup is the executive director of the Center for Early African Christianity at Eastern University in St. Davids, Pennsylvania. He was a volume editor for *Ezekiel, Daniel* in the Ancient Christian Commentary on Scripture and *Commentaries on Genesis 1–3* by Severian of Gabala and Bede the Venerable in the Ancient Christian Texts series, and writes the feature "Ancient Christian Wisdom" for *Conversations Journal*.

Jamin Goggin (PhD candidate, University of Wales Trinity Saint David) is a pastor at Saddleback Church. He holds an MA in spiritual formation and soul care and an MA in New Testament from Talbot School of Theology. His areas of interest include systematic theology and spiritual formation.

James Houston was founding principal of Regent College, Vancouver, Canada, and is now emeritus professor of spiritual theology. Dr. Houston was formerly University Lecturer in Geography and Fellow of Hertford College at Oxford University in England. His speciality has always been in the history of ideas. He has edited eight classics and most recently collaborated with Bruce Waltke on two volumes on the Psalms: *The Psalms as Christian Worship* and *The Psalms as Christian Lament*. With the psychiatrist Michael Parker, he has coauthored *A Vision for the Aging Church*. Other of his books include *The Transforming Friendship*, *The Heart's Desire*, *The Mentored Life* and *Joyful Exiles*.

Evan B. Howard, PhD, is the founder and director of Spirituality Shoppe, an Evangelical Center for the Study of Christian Spirituality. He lectures in philosophy, spirituality and religion at Colorado Mesa University and other institutions. He is the author of *The Brazos Introduction to*

Christian Spirituality and leads workshops and seminars on Christian spirituality worldwide.

James R. Payton Jr. is professor of history at Redeemer University College in Ancaster, Ontario. He has published *Light from the Christian East: An Introduction to the Orthodox Tradition* (IVP Academic, 2007), *Getting the Reformation Wrong: Correcting Some Misunderstandings* (IVP Academic, 2010), and *Irenaeus on the Christian Faith: A Condensation of "Against Heresies"* (Pickwick Publications, 2011).

Greg Peters is associate professor of medieval and spiritual theology in the Torrey Honors Institute of Biola University. He is the author of *Peter of Damascus: Byzantine Monk and Spiritual Theologian* and the forthcoming *Reforming the Monastery: Protestant Theologies of the Religious Life.* He is also a visiting professor of monastic studies at St. John's School of Theology in Collegeville, Minnesota, and priest-in-charge at Anglican Church of the Epiphany in La Mirada, California.

Steve L. Porter is associate professor of theology and philosophy at Talbot School of Theology and Rosemead School of Psychology (Biola University). His areas of interest include spiritual formation, theological methodology and philosophical theology. Steve has contributed articles to the *Journal of the Evangelical Theological Society, Faith and Philosophy, Philosophia Christi, Journal for Psychology and Theology* and *Journal of Psychology and Christianity,* and authored *Restoring the Foundations of Epistemic Justification* (Lexington, 2005). He also serves as the managing editor of the *Journal of Spiritual Formation and Soul Care.*

Fred Sanders is associate professor of theology in the Torrey Honors Institute at Biola University, where he has served since 1999. His PhD is from the Graduate Theological Union in Berkeley, California, and he holds an MDiv from Asbury Theological Seminary. He is the author of *The Deep Things of God: How the Trinity Changes Everything* (Crossway, 2010) and numerous articles.

Tom Schwanda (PhD, Durham University) is associate professor of Christian formation and ministry at Wheaton College. His publications include *Soul Recreation: The Contemplative-Mystical Piety of Puritanism* (Pickwick, 2012). He is currently preparing a volume in the Classics of Western Spirituality series for Paulist Press on eighteenth-century evangelical spirituality.

Gerald L. Sittser is professor of theology at Whitworth University in Spokane, WA. He also serves as chair of the department and chair of the MA in Theology program. He is the author of *Water from a Deep Well, A Cautious Patriotism: The American Churches and the Second World War* and *The Will of God as a Way of Life*, in addition to the bestselling *A Grace Disguised* and the recently released sequel, *A Grace Revealed*. He has written several articles on the desert fathers and mothers as well. His current research interest is the history of the catechumenate.

Kyle Strobel is assistant professor of theology at Grand Canyon University. He has written *Jonathan Edwards's Theology: A Reinterpretation* (T & T Clark, 2013), *Formed for the Glory of God: Learning from the Practices of Jonathan Edwards* (IVP Academic, 2013), and has edited *Charity and Its Fruits: Living in the Light of God's Love* (Crossway, 2012).

Subject and Author Index

METAmorpha.com

Metamorpha Ministries is a spiritual formation ministry with a particular focus on articulating a distinctively *evangelical* understanding of the Christian life. Reaching back through our tradition to mine robustly Protestant and spiritual resources, Metamorpha seeks to proclaim the depths of the gospel for a lived existence before the face of God. Our resources seek to be biblically, theologically and spiritually informed, such that Christ never ceases to be the center.

In addition, Metamorpha.com is a ministry resource for pastors, to help them live and lead in a healthy way in dependence upon Christ; for churches, to help them create communities of people growing in grace; and for individuals who are on a journey with Christ, to encourage, guide and nurture an openness to the call of Christ on their lives.